Edited by

Kent Masterson Brown

THE CIVIL WAR IN KENTUCKY

Battle for the Bluegrass State

Savas Publishing Company

Manufactured in the United States of America

The Civil War in Kentucky
Battle for the Bluegrass State
Edited by Kent Masterson Brown

Includes bibliographic references and index

Printing Number
10 9 8 7 6 5 4 3 2
First Edition

ISBN 1-882810-47-3
LCCN 99-63648

Savas Publishing Company
202 First Street SE, Suite 103A
Mason City, IA 50401

(515) 421-7135 (editorial offices)
(800) 732-3669 (distribution)

This book is printed on 50-lb. acid-free paper. It meets or exceeds the guidelines for permanence and durability of the Committee on Production Guidelines for Book Longevity of the Council on Library Resources

To the memory of three distinguished Kentucky historians,

Holman Hamilton
Hambleton Tapp
J. Winston Coleman, Jr.

true gentlemen who freely gave me as a youth
their time and wonderful counsel.
I will never forget them.

Table of Contents

Introduction i

Lincoln, Grant, and Kentucky in 1861
John Y. Simon 1

The Confederate Defense of Kentucky
Charles P. Roland 23

Mill Springs: The First Battle for Kentucky
Ron Nicholas 47

The Government of Confederate Kentucky
Lowell H. Harrison 79

The Decisive Battle of Richmond, Kentucky
D. Warren Lambert 103

Munfordville: The Campaign and Battle
Along Kentucky's Strategic Axis
Kent Masterson Brown 137

"Grand Havoc": The Climactic Battle of Perryville
Kenneth W. Noe 175

General Patrick R. Cleburne: Earning His Spurs
as a Field Commander in Kentucky, 1862
Wiley Sword 221

continued. . .

Table of Contents (continued)

General John Hunt Morgan and His Great Raids into Kentucky
James A. Ramage 243

A Tribute to the Orphan Brigade of Kentucky
Kent Masterson Brown 271

The Contributors 307

Index 309

List of Maps

The Upper Heartland, Sept. 4-6, 1861 15
The Upper Heartland, Jan. 1-19, 1862 35
The Upper Heartland, Feb. 1-March 31, 1862 42
The Battle of Mill Springs, Jan. 19, 1862 67
The Upper Heartland, Aug. 1-30, 1862 107
The Battle of Richmond (12:30 p.m.) 123
The Battle of Richmond (Late Afternoon) 127
The Upper Heartland, Sept. 1-17, 1862 144
The Battle of Munfordville (Dawn to 10:00 a.m.) 156
The Upper Heartland, Sept. 20-Oct. 8, 1862 178
Battle of Perryville (2-5:00 p.m.) 195
Battle of Perryville (Night) 201
Morgan's Great Raids 248
Campaigns of the Orphan Brigade 295

List of Photos and Illustrations

General Albert Sidney Johnston iii
Mass Confederate graves on Perryville Battlefield v
The White House, Jessamine County, Kentucky vi
President Abraham Lincoln 2
General Robert Anderson 7
General Ulysses S. Grant 11
General Henry W. Halleck 17
Company H, 44th Indiana Infantry 18
President Jefferson Davis 24
Albert Sidney Johnston 26
General Leonidas Polk 29
General Pierre G. T. Beauregard 38
Nashville and the Tennessee State Capitol 39
General Felix Kirk Zollicoffer 49
General George Henry Thomas 50
General George Bibb Crittenden 55
Speed Smith Fry 61
Attack of the 2nd Minnesota Infantry 65
Governor George W. Johnson 81
Graves of Governor George W. Johnson and his wife 91
Governor Richard Hawes 92
Old State Capitol Building, Frankfort, Kentucky 96
General Edmund Kirby Smith 104
General Horatio G. Wright 109
General William "Bull" Nelson 110
Mt. Zion Church 118
Richmond, Kentucky Cemetery 125
Main Street, Lexington, Kentucky, 1860 129
General Braxton Bragg 141
Colonel John T. Wilder 145
General James R. Chalmers 148
Company B, 9th Mississippi Infantry 150

List of Photos and Illustrations (continued)

The Battle of Munfordville 158
General Simon Bolivar Buckner 162
Army of the Ohio crossing the Barren River 167
General Don Carlos Buell 177
General Thomas L. Crittenden 182
General Lovell Harrison Rousseau 184
General Benjamin Franklin Cheatham 186
General James S. Jackson 188
The Battle of Perryville 190
Perryville Battlefield 191
The Squire Henry P. Bottom House, Perryville, 1885 193
A company of the 21st Michigan Infantry 199
General Patrick Ronayne Cleburne 222
General Bushrod R. Johnson 224
Perryville Battlefield from Loomis's Heights 226
Perryville Battlefield from Loomis's Heights 228
Hardee-pattern battle flag 232
General John Hunt Morgan 244
General John Hunt Morgan as he looked in the field 246
Morgan's men in Allegheny Prison, Pittsburgh, Pennsylvania 253
General Basil Wilson Duke 260
Private John Hampton Short, Co. E, 3rd KY(Confederate) Inf. 272
General John Cabell Breckinridge 278
Colonel Robert Trabue 281
Monroe brothers' graves in the Frankfort, Kentucky, Cemetery 284
General William Preston 286
General Roger Weightman Hanson 288
General Benjamin Hardin Helm 291
General Joseph H. Lewis 293
Orphan Brigade Ribbons 297
Monument to General Roger Weightman Hanson and his wife 298

Introduction

Kentucky is a land of contrasts. From the Appalachian plateau to the Bluegrass to the "Barrens" and the Mississippi River bluffs, Kentucky's geography is notable for its remarkable variations. With mountains as well as sprawling flatlands, the Bluegrass State is drained by the largest number of navigable streams of any state in the Union. Occupying these varied lands in 1861 were different peoples sustained by widely varying regional economies. Although the Ohio River forms its northern boundary and its economy was in many respects tied to Ohio, Indiana and Illinois, Kentucky, nevertheless, considered itself a Southern state. Despite its close economic ties to Northern states, Kentucky remained a land of slaves, slaveowners and, for many years, a vigorous slave trade. Tobacco, hemp, grain and livestock were its staple crops.

This varied land produced both Abraham Lincoln and Jefferson Davis. Both men, as presidents of the contending sections during the Civil War, vied for Kentucky's loyalty. Many families in the state were bitterly divided. Brother fought against brother. The Bluegrass State's tragedy even reached the White House. Lincoln's wife, a Kentuckian, hailed from a slaveowning family whose sons fought and died for the Confederacy. One fell in battle at Shiloh, another fell near Baton Rouge, Louisiana. Confederate Gen. Benjamin Hardin Helm, commander of the Orphan Brigade who fell at Chickamauga, was married to Mary Todd Lincoln's half-sister, Emily. Lincoln, it was recorded, wept upon hearing of Helm's death.

Notable Confederate generals such as Albert Sidney Johnston, John Cabell Breckinridge, Simon Bolivar Buckner, William Preston, John Bell Hood, George Bibb Crittenden, Charles W. Field, John Hunt Morgan and Basil W. Duke were Kentuckians. Noted Union generals such as Thomas Leonidas Crittenden (George Bibb Crittenden's brother), Lovell H. Rousseau, Thomas John Wood, William "Bull" Nelson, John Buford and Speed S. Fry, to name a few, as well as Maj. Robert Anderson, whose occupation of Fort Sumter touched off the war, were Kentuckians.

The Orphan Brigade and John Hunt Morgan's cavalry were noted Kentucky Confederate commands. The Union raised vast numbers of infantry, artillery and cavalry regiments in the Bluegrass State, most of which saw action at Shiloh, Stone's River, Vicksburg, Chickamauga, Chattanooga, Atlanta, Franklin, Nashville and elsewhere. Nearly 80,000 Kentuckians fought in the Union armies—more than three times the number of Kentuckians who took up arms for the Confederacy.

To successfully prosecute the war, Lincoln had to secure Kentucky for the Union. His designs on Kentucky became evident at the very outbreak of hostilities. When Confederate Gen. Leonidas Polk seized Columbus, Kentucky on the Mississippi River, Union forces under Gen. Ulysses S. Grant took the mouths of the Tennessee and Cumberland Rivers at Paducah and Smithland, respectively, in the fall of 1861. Lincoln's armies were then in a position to penetrate Kentucky and Tennessee by ascending the northward-flowing Tennessee and Cumberland Rivers.

General Albert Sidney Johnston, from his Department No. 2 headquarters at Bowling Green, struggled to hold the Bluegrass State for the Confederacy. Kentucky's geography, coupled with the size and power of Johnston's enemy—including its freshwater navy with troop transports and ironclad and timberclad gunboats—combined to cripple his efforts. After the disastrous battle at Mill Springs in southeastern Kentucky on January 19, 1862, the forces of Gen. George Bibb Crittenden, which held the right wing of Johnston's Confederate defensive line, withdrew through rain and sleet into Tennessee. Grant seized the opportunity to move upstream, putting his Army of the Tennessee in motion. General Johnston's thin Confederate line was shattered in bitter cold and wet weather with the fall of Fort Henry on the Tennessee River on February 6, and the fall of nearby Fort Donelson on the Cumberland River on February 16 just below Kentucky's southern border. Johnston withdrew the remainder of his army from Bowling

Introduction

General Albert Sidney Johnston

Library of Congress

Green to Nashville, Tennessee. General Polk's forces withdrew from Columbus down the Mobile & Ohio Railroad into Tennessee. The Bluegrass State was abandoned by Confederate forces.

Ultimately, Johnston collected his widely-scattered forces below the great southern bend of the Tennessee River at Corinth, Mississippi, the site of the crossing of the Mobile & Ohio and Memphis & Charleston railroads. Union General Don Carlos Buell's Army of the Ohio marched into Nashville while Grant's army ascended the Tennessee River. Moving out from Corinth, Johnston struck Grant's forces on April 6, 1862 near a site along the Tennessee River called Shiloh Church. Significant Confederate battlefield advances on the first day stalled with Johnston's fatal wounding. Grant, reinforced by Buell's Army of the Ohio, counterattacked the following morning, retaking lost ground and sealing a Union victory. More than 20,000 men fell at Shiloh, the bloodiest two days of the war to date.

After the Battle of Shiloh the Confederate army withdrew back to Corinth and then to Tupelo, Mississippi. General Braxton Bragg (who took over command of the newly named Army of the Mississippi at Tupelo) and Gen. Edmund Kirby Smith (who commanded a Confederate army at Knoxville, Tennessee) launched in the summer and fall of 1862 the war's longest and most strategically complex operation to retake the Bluegrass State for the Confederacy. In the midst of a devastating three-month drought, Bragg's and Kirby Smith's armies entered Kentucky without any significant opposition, Bragg following the Louisville & Nashville Railroad into central Kentucky and Kirby Smith following the old Wilderness Road into eastern and central Kentucky. But Union General Don Carlos Buell and his Army of the Ohio raced from Nashville to Louisville, Kentucky to meet the threat, and new levies poured into the Bluegrass State from Illinois, Indiana, Ohio and other Union states.

Confederate prospects looked promising. Kirby Smith's stunning and decisive victory at Richmond, Kentucky on August 29 and 30 was followed by Bragg's acceptance of the surrender of Union forces at Munfordville, Kentucky on September 17. Southern hopes, however, were ultimately dashed by a bloody stalemate fought on October 8, 1862 alongside a few stagnant pools of precious water between Buell's Union

Squire Henry P. Bottom at the mass Confederate graves on the Perryville Battlefield in 1885. Bottom was responsible for burying nearly five hundred Confederate dead after the battle. *U.S. Army Military History Institute*

---

forces and Bragg's army near Perryville, Kentucky. Nearly 8,000 men fell at Perryville in less than five hours of fighting. Bragg's withdrawal out of drought-stricken Kentucky followed, and the Bluegrass State was abandoned by the Confederate armies. Never again would Confederates attempt to "retake" Kentucky. In the place of vast troop movements into the state came electrifying cavalry raids by Gen. John Hunt Morgan's command, among others, and grim guerrilla warfare.

The sons of the Bluegrass State who survived the war, having fought heroically on both sides, returned home at war's end. Kentucky then took its place in the "Lost Cause" tradition while, at the same time, celebrating the Union "victory." Bloody family feuds and bitter political battles extended the war's impact on the Bluegrass State across the generations to our own times.

The full scope and breadth of Kentucky's Civil War experience cannot be addressed in a single volume. The wonderful chapters found in this collection are written by some of the nation's leading scholars on the most notable personalities, events and military operations in the

Bluegrass State during those tumultuous years. These readings are rich in drama and irony. It is hoped that they may be the genesis of a greater and broader interest in scholarship on Kentucky's notable and unique role in the nation's most climactic and tragic era.

Any journey to Kentucky's Civil War battlefields is an eye-opening experience. Through vigorous local efforts, virtually all of the battlefields of Mill Springs, Munfordville and Perryville remain today as they did in 1862. Significant portions of the Richmond battlefield are also intact, although they are seriously threatened with development. Fort Craig and the Green River bridge at Munfordville and the Confederate earthworks at Beech Grove near Mill Springs are still extant. Historic structures, some fully restored, still stand along those once-bloody fields.

Haunting sights abound as well. The Confederate mass graves at Perryville, Col. Robert A. Smith's memorial erected by his brother at Munfordville, the Union and Confederate cemeteries at Mill Springs, and Mount Zion Church and the city cemetery at Richmond stand as

The White House, Jessamine County, Kentucky. Gen. Speed S. Fry used the White House as his headquarters at Camp Nelson, the great Union training facility established in 1863. *Malick Studio*

mute testaments to the suffering endured by men of both sides. Even the sites where the contentious Camp Dick Robinson and the vast Camp Nelson were located remain much as they did during the war. Happily, Camp Nelson is even undergoing significant restoration. One can visit all the Civil War sites in Kentucky and, with these readings, gain a better understanding of those stirring times and tragic but strategically important engagements.

* * *

There are those to whom a special note of thanks is in order. To my dear friends John Y. Simon, Charles P. Roland, Lowell H. Harrison, D. Warren Lambert, Kenneth W. Noe, Wiley Sword, James A. Ramage, and Ron Nicholas, I am most grateful for their participation, suggestions and encouragement.

I also want to thank my friend and publisher Theodore P. "Ted" Savas for all his interest and assistance. His efforts, in the end, made this book a reality.

Additionally, I want to thank Mary Winter at the Kentucky Historical Society, Helga Borck at the New York Public Library, William Marshall and Lisa Carter at the University of Kentucky Special Collections, Kurt Holman at the Perryville Battlefield State Historic Site, John Malick and Malick's Studio, Lexington, Kentucky and William Straus, Lexington, Kentucky and the staffs at the Library of Congress, the National Archives, College Park, Maryland, and the United States Army Military History Institute, Carlisle, Pennsylvania for their assistance and patience in locating and reproducing many of the illustrations and allowing their reproduction herein.

To my friend and excellent map maker, Larry Brence, I owe thanks for all of his time and expertise. I also want to thank my friend Robert J. Cull of Louisville, Kentucky for providing his artwork for this book and its dust jacket. Cull is a most accomplished artist and Civil War historian. As well, I want to thank Jeremy Music for his expertise and patience in the production of this manuscript.

A special acknowledgment is due Campbellsville University and its fine President, Kenneth Winters. President Winters first saw the value of conducting a symposium on the Civil War in Kentucky on the campus of the university in 1997. Many of these readings evolved from that memorable event.

Finally, I am deeply indebted to my dear, dear wife, Genevieve, for all her support and help. I love her more than I can say.

Kent Masterson Brown
Lexington, Kentucky

John Y. Simon

Lincoln, Grant, and Kentucky in 1861

At the close of 1861, President Jefferson Davis of the Confederate States of America had reason for satisfaction. He had established a new nation with apparently secure frontiers. In the East, Confederate arms had triumphed in the first major encounter at Bull Run. Concerned about his capital's safety, President Abraham Lincoln had brought Gen. George B. McClellan to command the Union forces. McClellan insisted upon training and disciplining his raw troops and demanded reinforcements to ensure any move southward. An impetuous attempt at quick victory by Gen. Edward D. Baker in October led to a disastrous Union repulse at Ball's Bluff in Virginia. Baker, killed in battle, was a special favorite of Lincoln, who had named a son in his honor. McClellan placed blame elsewhere and became even more cautious about advancing.

In Missouri, at the other end of the theater of war, secessionists were frustrated by Gen. Nathaniel Lyon in schemes to capture the United States Arsenal in St. Louis. But secessionist Gov. Claiborne Fox Jackson had rallied an army in Missouri that proved successful enough at Wilson's Creek, where Lyon was killed, and even more successful at Lexington, where a Union army was captured.

In Kentucky, Gen. Albert Sidney Johnston, appraised by many as the ablest Confederate officer, commanded a western army defending a strategic line from Columbus on the Mississippi River, through Forts Henry and Donelson on the Tennessee and Cumberland rivers, to an anchor at Bowling Green, Kentucky. Union forces held Paducah, at the mouth of the Tennessee River, and Smithland, at the mouth of the Cumberland River, but little of Kentucky's interior.

Abraham Lincoln. Born in Hardin (present-day LaRue) County, Kentucky, Lincoln, as President of the United States, oversaw a relentless political and military effort to seize and hold Kentucky for the Union. *Library of Congress*

3
Lincoln, Grant, and Kentucky

From his capital at Richmond, President Davis surveyed a nation virtually unoccupied by Union forces. His government had "checked the wicked invasion which greed of gain and the unhallowed lust of power brought upon our soil, and has proved that numbers cease to avail when directed against a people fighting for the sacred right of self-government and the privileges of freemen."[1] Neither Missouri nor Kentucky, still contested by the Lincoln government, had formally joined the Confederacy. At the close of 1861, the Union warship *San Jacinto* had stopped the British vessel *Trent* and Capt. Charles Wilkes removed two Confederate emissaries to Europe, James Murray Mason and John Slidell. British protests provoked an international crisis that Davis hoped would end with British support of Southern independence, an outcome that he had tried to encourage with an embargo on shipments of Southern cotton to English mills. Diplomatic triumph for the Confederacy would appropriately follow a year of military success.

Dark clouds were less easily discerned. Confederate hopes rested upon Southern unity, defined as solidarity among people who lived in states in which law upheld the institution of slavery. Believing that Lincoln's election as president had posed an immediate danger to that institution, South Carolina rushed into secession, followed by six more states that had then organized a new federal government even before Lincoln had been inaugurated. Despite enthusiasm for this new nation in the black belt, eight more slaveholding states, including crucial Virginia, remained unaffiliated. Throughout the border slaveholding states, attention turned to Washington to determine if Lincoln's government would launch an assault on slavery that would unite the entire South.

Fully aware of the situation, Lincoln gave earnest assurances in his Inaugural Address that he would not attack slavery in any state. Instead, he pledged to maintain the property of the United States, a point which brought him into collision with Southern determination to seize Fort Sumter in Charleston Harbor, an inadequate fortification where the United States flag flew over a handful of men unprepared for battle or even the consequences of a blockade. When Lincoln resolved the tangled diplomacy of the incident by sending a fleet with food and supplies, assuring the South that no additional troops would land unless the fort were attacked, Davis and his cabinet rashly ordered a bombardment with tragic consequences for the attackers. Davis had begun a war by firing the first shot. He had initiated hostilities at the wrong place, at the wrong time, and for the wrong reasons. He had acted the part of bully, had fired on the flag, and had begun a war not tied directly to the institution of slavery. Throughout the border states, decisions quickly followed Lincoln's call for volunteers to suppress the rebellion; four states joined the Confederacy, four did not.

Of slaveholding states that did not secede, Kentucky was the most vital; Lincoln and Davis saw that from the outset. Both Lincoln and Davis had been born in Kentucky, not many miles apart. One had gone North, the other South. Lincoln had made Kentuckian Henry Clay his political idol. Like other Kentuckians, Lincoln had not forgotten Clay since his death in 1852 and retained Kentucky ties through his marriage into the Todd family of Lexington. Kentucky Senator John Jordan Crittenden had inherited a portion of Clay's political power, which he used to further the principle of compromise. Both Democratic Vice President John Cabell Breckinridge (president of the Senate) and Democratic Governor Beriah Magoffin of Kentucky supported the Crittenden Compromise. Both Lincoln and Jefferson Davis, who rejected that compromise, accelerated the coming of war.

Clay's continuing power in Kentucky maintained his Whig party long after its extinction elsewhere. Not until 1851 did Kentucky elect a Democratic governor. Elected in 1859, Magoffin proved to be one of the most enthusiastic secessionists in the state. In 1856, Breckinridge had been elected James Buchanan's vice president in the only antebellum presidential election carried by Democrats. In 1860, he represented the southern wing of the Democratic party in the presidential election. Despite having a native son on the ballot, Kentuckians gave their electoral votes to John Bell of Tennessee, representing the last gasp of the Whigs, now disguised as the Constitutional Union party. Although only a handful of Kentuckians (1,362) cast votes for Lincoln, this fact was far less significant than the failure of Southern Democrats to carry the state.

For all his nationalism, Clay had represented a southern state, as did Crittenden. Neither recognized a contradiction between support of the Union and support of slavery. Clay had championed the American

Colonization Society, with its fantasy of returning emancipated American blacks to Africa. Clay's opposition to secession in 1850 was no less fervent than Lincoln's in 1861. Slaveholding, however, made Kentucky so Southern that Northerners feared that when war came, Kentucky would join the Confederacy.

Following Crittenden's lead, however, Kentuckians chose neutrality. After the firing on Fort Sumter, Lincoln called upon states for troops to put down the insurrection. Governor Magoffin, a rebel sympathizer, angrily refused to furnish "troops for the wicked purpose of subduing her sister Southern States."[2] Kentucky Unionists, however, sympathized with Magoffin, hoping that some path to restoration might yet be discerned and bloodshed averted. At a large and enthusiastic public meeting in Louisville, former Senator Archibald Dixon urged Kentuckians to "stand firm with her sister Border States in the centre of the Republic, to calm the distracted sections." By doing this, "she saves the Union and frowns down Secession."[3] The meeting resolved that the "duty of Kentucky is to maintain her present independent position, taking sides not with the Administration, nor with the seceding States, but with the Union against them both."[4]

Ardent support for a policy of neutrality did not mean that Kentuckians were truly neutral. Instead, issues of the war divided families like those of the Breckinridges, Crittendens, and Todds. Neutrality represented an ideal or, in retrospect, a way-station between peace and war.

In the years closest to the Civil War, Kentucky had changed from a Southern to a border state. Twelve railroads connected Kentucky to the North, two to the South, altering older patterns of river trade. Patterns of immigration had changed Kentucky from a largely homogeneous Southern state to one of mixed population. As Kentucky grew, the proportion of slaves steadily diminished. Nor were such slaves evenly distributed across a domain that shared some seven hundred miles of border with Northern states. Circumstances of war forced Americans to regard states as more homogeneous than reality dictated. Stretching from Appalachia to the Mississippi River, Kentucky's wide economic and cultural diversity mirrored divisions between North and South.

Neutrality favored a lucrative trade policy involving both Union and Confederacy. Advocates of "free city" status in both New York City and Cairo, Illinois, foresaw promising economic windfalls. Businessmen recognized the advantages of an American Switzerland. When secession interrupted trade on the Mississippi River, the Louisville and Nashville Railroad became a major artery of commerce between North and South. Confederate policy forbidding trade in the great staples of the South eventually closed this avenue of prosperity. Characterizing the Confederacy as "too impatient to be tolerant and too impetuous to be tactful," one historian blamed trade policy for the loss of Kentucky to the Union.[5]

The role of Kentucky in the inevitable conflict depended on statesmanship North and South. Both Lincoln and Davis knew that whatever the futility of neutrality, disrespect for that preposterous policy would cost them potential Kentucky allies. Lincoln had an added burden of continuing to dramatize the war as a struggle for the Union and not against slavery. In a meeting with Kentucky Unionist Garrett Davis, Lincoln again emphasized his intention to "make no attack, direct or indirect, upon the institutions or property of any State," but rather to defend them. Further, that although he possessed the right to send troops wherever needed, "if Kentucky made no demonstration of force against the United States, he would not molest her."[6]

Both sides began to recruit in Kentucky, the South with the support of Governor Magoffin, the North with less official sanction. Simon Bolivar Buckner, who headed the state guard, was generally understood to favor the South, but the legislature, Unionist in sentiment, authorized a rival home guard friendlier to the North. Working through naval officer Gen. William Nelson and old friends James and Joshua Speed, Lincoln secretly sent guns to Kentucky. Lincoln also sent to Kentucky a native Kentuckian, Robert Anderson, the honored hero of Fort Sumter. Originally sent to accept Union troops, Anderson remained across the Ohio to avoid provocation.

Elections for Congress held on June 20 sent a covey of Unionists to Washington. Unionists carried nine of ten districts with a total of 92,460 votes against 37,700 for State Rights candidates. Supporters of neutrality joined supporters of the North in opposition to Confederate

7

Lincoln, Grant, and Kentucky

Robert Anderson, the "Hero of Ft. Sumter." Born at "Soldier's Retreat" near Louisville, Kentucky, Anderson returned to Kentucky after his surrender at Ft. Sumter as a newly-appointed brigadier general and briefly took over command of the Department of Kentucky. *Library of Congress*

sympathizers. Legislative elections in August gave Unionists a majority of 76 to 24 in the Kentucky House and 27 to 11 in the Senate.

In his July 4 message to Congress, Lincoln reviewed the Fort Sumter crisis and steps taken since. Although denouncing secession, he avoided discussing slavery. Without mentioning Kentucky, Lincoln attacked armed neutrality as "disunion completed." This would benefit rebels by enabling them to trade freely with the North through intermediaries to avoid the blockade's consequences. As such, armed neutrality "recognizes no fidelity to the Constitution, no obligation to maintain the Union; and while very many who have favored it are, doubtless, loyal citizens, it is, nevertheless, treason in effect."[7]

Magoffin had sent Buckner to negotiate with General McClellan in Ohio for a guarantee of Kentucky neutrality and later sent Buckner on a similar mission to Gov. Isham Harris of Tennessee. Dissatisfied with the McClellan arrangement, Magoffin sent Buckner to Washington to confer with Lincoln. Buckner returned with a statement that Lincoln, determined to "suppress an insurrection," had "not sent an armed force into Kentucky; nor have I any present purpose to do so." Nonetheless "I mean to say nothing which shall hereafter embarrass me in the performance of what may seem to be my duty."[8] Buckner also returned with an offer of a commission as brigadier general, something he would eventually accept only when it came from the Confederate government.

In August, Lincoln authorized the establishment of recruiting camps in Kentucky. General Nelson claimed that he was organizing Kentuckians to preserve neutrality, a thin excuse further weakened by his simultaneous recruiting and arming of East Tennessee loyalists. Within weeks, Union forces at Cairo, Illinois, had captured a rebel steamboat at Paducah, an action that produced a retaliatory local seizure of a steamboat from Evansville. After negotiating with Kentuckians, Lincoln concluded that "professed Unionists gave him more trouble than rebels." He believed that Magoffin hoped to maneuver the North into firing the first shot in Kentucky.[9] By the end of August, the Confederate government had also initiated recruiting within the borders of Kentucky and had passed a secret resolution appropriating funds for arms. Kentucky neutrality was doomed.

On August 24, Lincoln answered Magoffin's protest against camps established in Kentucky without his consent:

> I believe it is true that there is a military force in camp within Kentucky, acting by authority of the United States, which force is not very large, and is not now being augmented. I also believe that some arms have been furnished to this force by the United States. I also believe this force consists exclusively of Kentuckians, having their camp in the immediate vicinity of their own homes, and not assailing, or menacing, any of the good people of Kentucky. In all I have done in the premises, I have acted upon the urgent solicitation of many Kentuckians, and in accordance with what I believed, and still believe, to be the wish of a majority of all the Union-loving people of Kentucky. While I have conversed on this subject with many eminent men of Kentucky, including a large majority of her Members of Congress, I do not remember that any one of them, or any other person, except your Excellency and the bearers of your Excellency's letter, has urged me to remove the military force from Kentucky, or to disband it. One other very worthy citizen of Kentucky did solicit me to have the augmenting of the force suspended for a time. Taking all the means within my reach to form a judgment, I do not believe it is the popular wish of Kentucky that this force shall be removed beyond her limits; and, with this impression, I must respectfully decline to so remove it. I most cordially sympathize with your Excellency, in the wish to preserve the peace of my own native State, Kentucky; but it is with regret I search, and can not find, in your not very short letter, any declaration, or intimation, that you entertain any desire for the preservation of the Federal Union.[10]

A few days later, Jefferson Davis replied to a similar request for reassurance from Magoffin with flat assurance that the Confederacy "neither intends nor desires to disturb the neutrality of Kentucky." He pledged to respect neutrality "so long as her people will maintain it themselves."[11]

How Kentucky was dragged into the war, by whom and under what circumstances, mattered much to fervent neutralists. Confederate General Gideon J. Pillow had insisted in May that the occupation of Columbus was essential to the defense of his native Tennessee.[12] Wiser heads prevailed—almost any head was wiser than Pillow's—but Pillow persisted in his determination to invade.

In what became Kentucky's decisive month of September, the chief commanders in the western theater were Confederate General Leonidas Polk and Union General John C. Frémont. Neither, in retrospect, appeared suited for such weighty responsibilities. Polk proved arrogant, headstrong, and injudicious, behavior especially surprising in a former bishop. Trained at West Point, he had resigned a few months after graduation to pursue the ministry and had abandoned interest in military affairs before the Civil War. His ambitious subordinate, Gideon J. Pillow, untrained but unafraid, resented his secondary status in the western armies and considered himself better qualified to lead. On August 28 he informed Polk that the Confederate position at New Madrid, Missouri, was inferior, that Columbus was the place to defend Tennessee. Kentucky neutrality, wrote Pillow, existed no longer. Once the federals took Columbus they could not be dislodged. Arguing that the time had come for decision, Pillow pushed the weaker Polk into action.[13]

Frémont was imperious, impetuous, and impatient. Frémont had dallied before going to headquarters in St. Louis to await fittings on his new uniform as major general, then rarely emerged from a St. Louis mansion rented from one of his wife's relatives. Inside, he played the role of "grand Monarque,"[14] surrounded by courtiers exiled from the armies of Europe. As military affairs in Missouri deteriorated, Frémont hoped to recoup with boldness elsewhere.

On August 28, Frémont ordered Gen. Ulysses S. Grant to take command at Cape Girardeau, to cooperate with forces moving eastward from Ironton, and to be aware that Frémont had ordered forces at Cairo to prepare for a move southward. Col. Gustav Waagner had been sent to Belmont, Missouri, opposite Columbus, Kentucky, to destroy Confederate works and to build his own. Frémont intended to occupy Columbus "as soon as possible."[15] Waagner's occupation of Belmont on September 2 triggered the end of Kentucky's neutrality.

Polk had already written to Magoffin that he considered it of "the greatest consequence" to the Confederacy that "I should be ahead of the enemy in occupying Columbus and Paducah."[16] Two days later a spy reported Union forces at Belmont. Under Polk's orders, Pillow embarked for Kentucky, occupying both Hickman and Columbus.

11
Lincoln, Grant, and Kentucky

Ulysses S. Grant as a newly-commissioned brigadier general in 1861. Grant's seizing of the mouths of the Tennessee and Cumberland Rivers in response to Gen. Leonidas Polk occupying Columbus and Hickman, Kentucky, on the Mississippi River set the stage for the collapse of the Confederate defense of the state in early 1862. *Library of Congress*

Governor Harris of Tennessee immediately declared the incursion "unfortunate, as the President and myself are pledged to respect the neutrality of Kentucky."[17] Polk replied that Pillow had moved "under the plenary powers delegated to me by the President" and had occupied Hickman to avoid the cannon at Belmont.[18] Davis outlined a response on Harris's telegram: " Secty of War—Telegraph promptly to Genl. Polk to withdraw troops from Ky—& explain movement Ans—Gov. Harris inform him of action & that movement was unauthorized."[19] Secretary of War Leroy Walker immediately sent Polk orders for a "prompt withdrawal."[20] Polk then explained to Davis that the threat to Columbus justified the movement, vital also to the safety of western Tennessee. Davis replied fatuously but succinctly: "The necessity must justify the action."[21] Polk responded that his invasion was justified by information that a Union expedition to Paducah was already underway before he issued orders to seize Columbus.[22] Walker nonetheless again asked Polk the "reason for General Pillow's movement."[23] In response to yet another message from Harris, Walker responded that Polk had been "ordered to direct the prompt withdrawal of the forces under General Pillow from Kentucky. The movement was wholly unauthorized, and you will so inform Governor Magoffin."[24]

Confusion in Richmond originated through lack of communication between Walker and Davis, the former believing that he was secretary of war, an understandable mistake soon rectified by Walker's dismissal. Walker's instincts were correct, although he did not immediately recognize that the invasion of Kentucky could not be undone, repealed, or erased. Polk's argument that federal occupation of Belmont, across the river from Columbus, represented a threat to Kentucky was militarily correct, politically disastrous. Of course Frémont intended this move as a prelude to an occupation of Columbus but had not yet informed Washington, where Lincoln might well have intervened. Columbus occupied bluffs overlooking the river, Belmont sat on a floodplain. Once Polk and Pillow occupied Columbus, Waagner immediately evacuated Belmont. The issue remained one of respect for Kentucky's neutrality, not that of Missouri. Both Polk and Frémont represented an accident ready to happen; Polk proved the first to blunder. Justifying his action to a committee of the Kentucky legislature, Polk explained that he had infringed Kentucky's neutrality only by seizing Columbus "and so much of the territory between it and the Tennessee line as was necessary for me to pass over to reach it."[25]

On September 2, Col. Richard J. Oglesby, commander at Cairo, was surprised when an unprepossessing stranger, dressed as a civilian because his uniform had not yet arrived, handed him an order assuming command.[26] At Cape Girardeau, Missouri, Brig. Gen. Benjamin M. Prentiss had been similarly surprised a few days earlier when Grant arrived to assume command of the District of Southeast Missouri. Prentiss insisted that he was the senior officer, having held command while Grant vainly sought an opportunity to get into the war. Both had been nominated on the same day, but Grant held higher rank in the old army, and Grant preceded Prentiss on the army list. Prentiss, who eventually placed himself in arrest, may have accelerated Grant's move to Cairo, where he arrived the day before the Confederate advance into Kentucky. Without yet knowing that Polk had taken Columbus, Grant wrote that he wanted to occupy it the next day. "New Madrid will fall within five days after," he added.[27]

The next day word arrived of the Confederate incursion that Grant immediately telegraphed to the speaker of the Kentucky House of Representatives. "I regret to inform you," Grant began, but perhaps was more relieved than regretful. In reality Polk had spared Frémont and Grant the opprobrium of violating Kentucky neutrality.[28] By that afternoon, Grant was ready to start for Paducah, awaiting a telegram from Frémont either sanctioning or forbidding the expedition. Grant based his decision on information received from Charles de Arnaud, one of the more bizarre characters churned up by the war. Despite the name, de Arnaud was a Russian who had arrived in the United States in late 1860 and whom Frémont had commissioned as a spy. On September 5 de Arnaud arrived at Cairo to report that Confederate forces were advancing on Paducah.[29] Grant immediately began to prepare his expedition, which arrived in Paducah on the following morning. He found rebel flags flying and citizens abuzz with news that a Confederate force of 3,800 was sixteen miles away. He thought then and for the rest of his life that only his timely arrival had prevented the enemy from seizing the mouth of the Tennessee River.[30]

On Grant's approach, Lloyd Tilghman of Paducah, organizer of a local pro-Confederate force, fled the city and was later reported with his men at Columbus. As for Pillow's force, believed to be so close, there is no evidence that any troops had ever left Columbus. Initial confusion about nearby rebels and which direction they were heading, to which local sympathizers may have contributed, exaggerated the timeliness and boldness of Grant's expedition.[31] The Confederate occupation of Columbus benefited Grant by providing justification for occupying an even more vital site in Kentucky. Belief that Pillow was headed for Paducah rested upon a logical assumption that Confederates would make the most of their Kentucky invasion. Polk and Pillow did not, however, behave logically.

Grant landed at Paducah at 8:30 a.m. and left at noon. During the morning he ran up the United States flag, deployed his troops, occupied the post and telegraph offices, seized the railroad, disposed of rations and leather, and issued a proclamation remarkable for its measured tone of reassurance:

> I have come among you, not as an enemy, but as your friend and fellow-citizen, not to injure or annoy you, but to respect the rights, and to defend and enforce the rights of all loyal citizens. An enemy, in rebellion against our common Government, has taken possession of, and planted its guns upon the soil of Kentucky and fired upon our flag. Hickman and Columbus are in his hands. He is moving upon your city. I am here to defend you against this enemy and to assert and maintain the authority and sovereignty of your Government and mine. I have nothing to do with opinions. I shall deal only with armed rebellion and its aiders and abetors. You can pursue your usual avocations without fear or hindrance. The strong arm of the Government is here to protect its friends, and to punish only its enemies. Whenever it is manifest that you are able to defend yourselves, to maintain the authority of your Government and protect the rights of all its loyal citizens, I shall withdraw the forces under my command from your city.[32]

Grant discovered Frémont's permission for the expedition to Paducah waiting back at Cairo. Actually, permission had arrived before Grant left Cairo—but in Hungarian![33] Frémont had surrounded himself in St. Louis with officers from many countries, including refugees of the Hungarian revolt of 1848. Their unusually impenetrable language was

15

Lincoln, Grant, and Kentucky

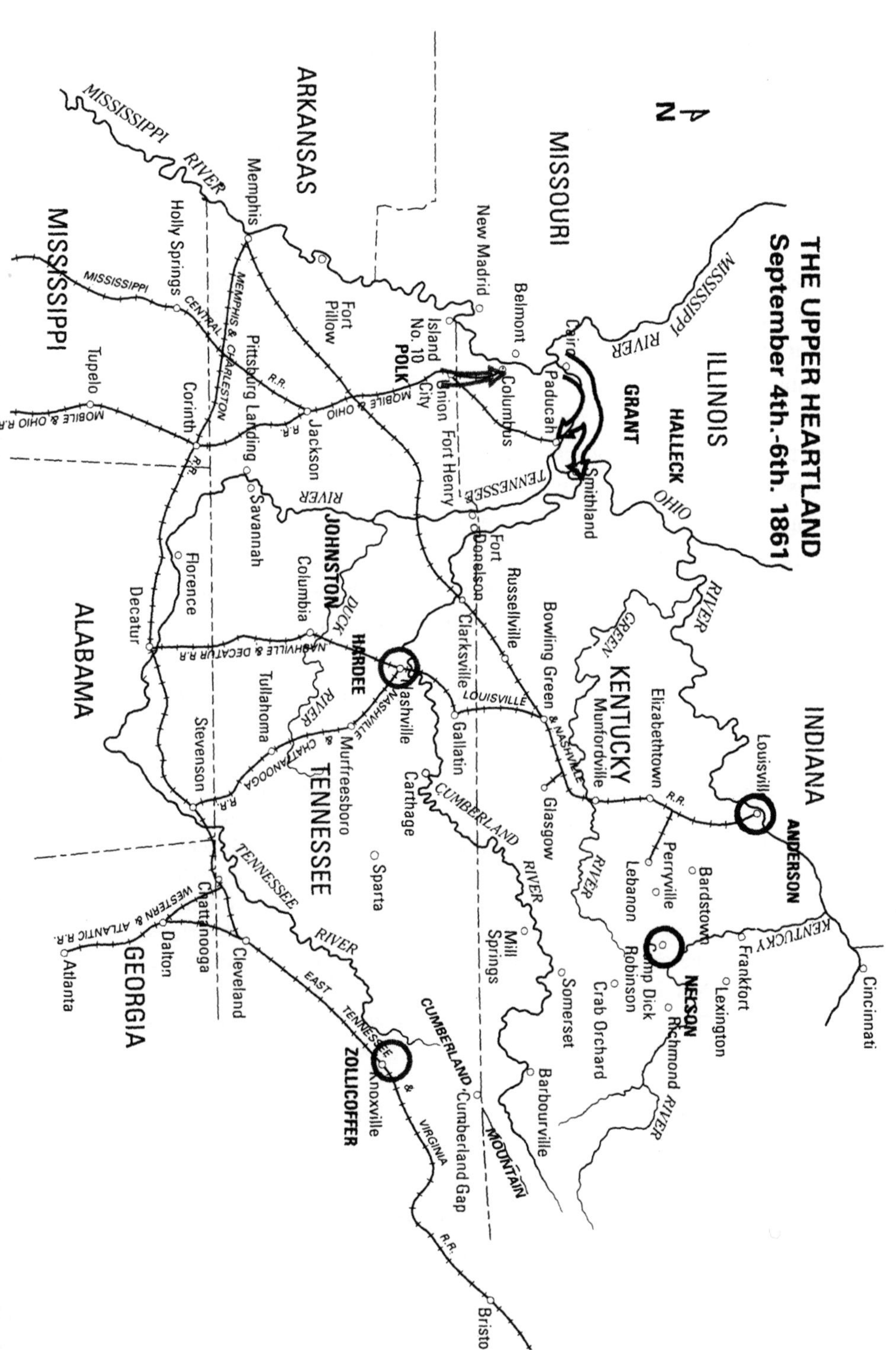

considered especially suitable for confidential messages. Apparently, nobody in Cairo could cope with Hungarian. Grant left for Paducah anyway. Rebuked for communicating with the Kentucky legislature, Grant received no censure for the Paducah expedition, since it had received advance official authorization from headquarters.

Grant continued to believe, however, that he had left for Paducah before receiving approval from his superior and he had gotten away with it. His belief that he could operate aggressively with impunity influenced his impetuous attack at Belmont in November. There he furnished a scare to the garrison at Columbus. Throughout the rest of 1861, Grant wanted to move South.

Frémont's plan to occupy Columbus imperiled the Union cause in Kentucky, as did his proclamation of August 30 declaring martial law in Missouri and threatening to enforce the Confiscation Act passed by Congress against slave property of Missouri rebels. Frémont's popularity in the Republican party led Lincoln to caution in opposing the proclamation. He immediately pointed out, however, that the threat to liberate the slaves of traitors might "perhaps ruin our rather fair prospect for Kentucky."[34]

In privately explaining his policy, Lincoln expanded on his concern for Kentucky:

> The Kentucky Legislature would not budge till that proclamation was modified; and Gen. Anderson telegraphed me that on the news of Gen. Fremont having actually issued deeds of manumission, a whole company of our Volunteers threw down their arms and disbanded. I was so assured, as to think it probable, that the very arms we had furnished Kentucky would be turned against us. I think to lose Kentucky is nearly the same as to lose the whole game. Kentucky gone, we can not hold Missouri, nor, as I think, Maryland. . . . You must not understand I took my course on the proclamation *because* of Kentucky. I took this same ground in a private letter to General Fremont before I heard from Kentucky."[35]

Indeed, the day after Lincoln wrote to Frémont he heard from James Speed of Louisville that Frémont's "foolish proclamation" would "crush out" Kentucky Unionism.[36]

Lincoln's final response to Frémont was to remove him from command and ultimately replace him with Maj. Gen. Henry W. Halleck,

Lincoln, Grant, and Kentucky

Maj. Gen. Henry W. Halleck

Known as "Old Brains," Halleck replaced Gen. John C. Frémont as Commander of Union forces in the West. His headquarters were in St. Louis, Missouri.

Library of Congress

---

the epitome of military correctness and respect for procedure. During the interval between Frémont's removal and Halleck's arrival, Grant seized the opportunity for an adventitious expedition to Belmont, possibly a prelude to an assault on Columbus. Grant's inconclusive tangle with Pillow left both prepared to claim a victory that neither won.

In November, Davis explained his Kentucky policy:

> Finding that the Confederate States were about to be invaded through Kentucky, and that her people after being deceived into a mistaken security, were unarmed, and in danger of being subjugated by the Federal forces, our armies were marched into that State to repel the enemy and prevent their occupation of certain strategic points which would have given them great advantages in the contest—a step which was justified, not only by the necessities of self-defense on the part of the Confederate States, but, also, by a desire to aid the people of Kentucky. It was never intended by the Confederate Government to conquer or co-erce the people of that State; but, on the contrary, it was declared by our Generals that they would withdraw their troops if the Federal Government would do likewise. Proclamation was also made of the desire to respect the neutrality of Kentucky, and the intention to abide by the wishes of her people as soon as they were free to express their opinions. These declarations were approved by me, and I should regard it as one of the best

Company H, 44th Indiana Infantry. These hardened veterans served along the Green River in Kentucky as part of Grant's army before participating in the attack on Ft. Donelson and the Battle of Shiloh. As part of Gen. Don Carlos Buell's Army of the Ohio, they returned to Kentucky and fought at Perryville. Note the broad-brimmed hats which were preferred by Union soldiers in the western theatre of war. *National Archives*

> effects of the march of our troops into Kentucky if it should end in giving to her people liberty of choice and a free opportunity to decide their own destiny according to their own will.[37]

In his annual message of December 3, 1861, Lincoln declared that Kentucky, "for some time in doubt, is now decidedly, and, I think, unchangeably, ranged on the side of the Union." Maryland, Kentucky, and Missouri, "neither of which would promise a single soldier at first, have now an aggregate of not less than forty thousand in the field for the Union; while, of their citizens, certainly not more than a third of that number, and they of doubtful whereabouts, and doubtful existence, are in arms against it."[38]

Lincoln spoke accurately in December, and his remarks about Kentucky Unionism and about enlistment ratios North and South forecast the future. During the war, Kentucky furnished troops to North and South in a ratio of three to one. At the close of the year, despite a record that brought satisfaction in Richmond, the battle for Kentucky had turned into Confederate disaster. In January, rebel defeat at Mill Springs was followed by Halleck's reluctant permission to Grant to advance on Fort Henry. After the fall of Henry led Grant to attack and capture Fort Donelson, the entire Confederate line in Kentucky cracked. Confederate Generals Albert Sidney Johnston and P. G. T. Beauregard united their forces at Corinth, Mississippi.

Lincoln had immediately recognized that the key to maintaining loyalty in Kentucky rested upon emphasis upon the Union, tolerance for slavery, and observation of neutrality. Kentucky's evasion of Civil War reality could not long endure. Confederates blundered by impetuously accepting the burden of invading Kentucky and then failing to make their occupation effective. Operating on false information and without proper authorization, Grant nevertheless made precisely the right move in occupying Paducah. Grant secured bases from which a superior United States Navy could operate on rivers that dominated western Kentucky. Fortification of Columbus confirmed an existing Confederate stranglehold on the Mississippi River without broader military advantages. At the end of 1861, the North harvested the fruits of Lincoln's patient policy of moderation.

Late in August 1861, commanders North and South had recognized that Kentucky neutrality was shattering. Both Frémont and Polk decided to risk the consequences of invading the state in exchange for the occupation of strategic positions. Polk won the race for Columbus with dire consequences. On the day that Polk crossed the border, Frémont wrote to Lincoln that the enemy was "creeping covertly forward into Kentucky lately, and I have been very anxious to anticipate him, but not quite able yet."[39] Had the North seized Columbus, as both Frémont and Grant intended, the outcome of the Civil War might have been different.

NOTES

1. Message to Congress, Nov. 18, 1861, Haskell M. Monroe *et al.*, eds., *The Papers of Jefferson Davis* (Baton Rouge, La., 1971-) (hereinafter cited as *Davis Papers*), 7:413.

2. Beriah Magoffin to Simon Cameron, April 15, 1861, *The War of the Rebellion: A Compilation of the Official Records of the Union and Confederate Armies*, 128 vols. (Washington, D.C., 1880-1901) (hereinafter cited as *O.R.*), III, 1:70.

3. Frank Moore, ed., *The Rebellion Record: A Diary of American Events* (New York, 1864-1868), 1 (documents):76.

4. *Ibid.*, 1:74.

5. E. Merton Coulter, *The Civil War and Readjustment in Kentucky* (Chapel Hill, N.C., 1926; reprinted Gloucester, Mass., 1966), 80.

6. Garrett Davis to George D. Prentice, April 28, 1861, *Congressional Globe*, 37th Congress, Second Session, Appendix, 82-83.

7. Roy P. Basler *et al.*, eds., *The Collected Works of Abraham Lincoln*, 9 vols. (New Brunswick, N.J., 1953-55) (hereinafter cited as *Collected Works*), 4:428.

8. Lincoln to Simon B. Buckner, July 10, 1861, *ibid.*, 444.

9. Aug. 22, 1861, *Lincoln and the Civil War in the Diaries and Letters of John Hay*, Tyler Dennett, ed. (New York, N.Y., 1939), 25.

10. Lincoln to Beriah Magoffin, Aug. 24, 1861, *Collected Works*, 4:497.

11. Jefferson Davis to Beriah Magoffin, Aug. 28, 1861, *O.R.*, I, 4:396-97.

12. Gideon J. Pillow to Jefferson Davis, May 16, 1861, *O.R.*, I, 52 (2):101.

13. Gideon J. Pillow to Leonidas Polk, Aug. 29, 1861, *ibid.*, I, 3:685-87.

14. Andrew Rolle, *John Charles Frémont: Character as Destiny* (Norman, Okla., 1991), 198.

15. John C. Frémont to Ulysses S. Grant, Aug. 28, 1861, John Y. Simon, ed., *The Papers of Ulysses S. Grant* (Carbondale and Edwardsville, Ill., 1967-) (hereinafter cited as *Grant Papers*), 2:151.

16. Leonidas Polk to Beriah Magoffin, Sept. 1, 1861, *O.R.*, I, 4:179.

17. Isham Harris to Leonidas Polk, Sept. 4, 1861, *ibid.*, 180.

18. Leonidas Polk to Isham Harris, Sept. 4, 1861, *ibid.*

19. *Davis Papers,* 7:325; Steven E. Woodworth, *Jefferson Davis and his Generals; The Failure of Confederate Command in the West* (Lawrence, Kan., 1990), 34-45; Steven E. Woodworth, "'The Indeterminate Quantities': Jefferson Davis, Leonidas Polk, and the End of Kentucky Neutrality, September 1861," *Civil War History*, 38 (1992), 289-97.

20. Leroy P. Walker to Leonidas Polk, Sept. 4, 1861, *O.R.*, I, 4:180.

21. Jefferson Davis to Leonidas Polk, Sept. 5, 1861, *Davis Papers*, 7:327. Printed as "The necessity justifies the action" in *O.R.*, I, 4:181.

22. Leonidas Polk to Jefferson Davis, Sept. 6, 1861, *Davis Papers*, 7:328.

23. Leroy P. Walker to Leonidas Polk, Sept. 5, 1861, *O.R.*, I, 4:181.

24. Leroy P. Walker to Isham Harris, Sept. 5, 1861, *ibid.*, 189.

25. Leonidas Polk to John M. Johnston, Sept. 9, 1861, *ibid.*, 186.

26. *Personal Memoirs of U. S. Grant,* 2 vols. (New York, N.Y., 1885-86) (hereinafter cited as *Grant Memoirs*), 1:264.

27. U. S. Grant to John C. Frémont, Sept. 4, 1861, *Grant Papers*, 2:186.

28. U. S. Grant to Speaker, Ky. House of Representatives, Sept. 5, 1861, *ibid.*, 2:189.

29. U. S. Grant to John C. Frémont, Sept. 5, 1861, *ibid.*, 2:193.

30. U. S. Grant to John C. Frémont, Sept. 6, 1861, *ibid.*, 2:196-97; U.S. Grant to Julia Dent Grant, Sept. 8, 1861, *ibid.*, 2:214; *Grant Memoirs*, 1:265-66.

31. On Sept. 7 the general commanding at Cairo in Grant's absence heard that Pillow with 4,000 men would march on Paducah "in two days." John A. McClernand to John C. Frémont, Sept. 7, 1861. *O.R.*, I, 3:475.

32. Proclamation, Sept. 6, 1861, *Grant Papers*, 2:194-95.

33. *Ibid.*, 2:191-92.

34. Lincoln to John C. Frémont, Sept. 2, 1861. *Collected Works*, 4:506.

35. Lincoln to Orville H. Browning, Sept. 22, 1861, *ibid.*, 532.

36. James Speed to Lincoln, Sept. 3, 1861, *ibid.*, 506-7.

37. Message to Congress, Nov. 18, 1861, *Davis Papers*, 7:414.

38. *Collected Works*, 5:50.

39. John C. Frémont to Abraham Lincoln, Sept. 3, 1861, quoted in Allan Nevins, *The War for the Union: The Improvised War, 1861-1862* (New York, N.Y., 1959), 1:333.

Charles P. Roland

The Confederate Defense of Kentucky

Kentucky played an unusual if not unique role in the Civil War. As a slave state which was originally a part of Virginia it held strong ties of kinship and sympathy with the South. As a border state on the Ohio River it held strong economic ties with the states of the Midwest. Also, it harbored powerful sentiments of American nationalism. Its foremost statesman, the late Senator Henry Clay, had represented all of these emotions and interests. A native of Virginia, he was a southerner and a slaveowner, but he was also a dedicated nationalist. He had devoted a great portion of his time and energies to the formulation of compromises designed to avert southern secession and at the same time protect the institutions of the South. He saw with crystal clarity that any effort to sever the Union would result in civil war.

When in 1860 and 1861 secession occurred by eleven of the southern states, Kentucky made a futile attempt to remain neutral. But strong secessionist elements quickly organized a Confederate government in the state, ultimately establishing its capital at Bowling Green. Stretching as the state did from the Appalachians on the east to the Mississippi River on the west, it formed a geographic belt of immense strategic importance between the states of the Union and those of the Confederacy. President Abraham Lincoln has been quoted as having said he hoped God was on the side of the Union, but that it must have Kentucky.

In the fall of 1861, President Jefferson Davis of the Confederacy was urgently in need of a general to command the hastily assembled Confederate military forces in the west. According to family tradition, he was ill in the Confederate White House in early September when he

Jefferson Davis. Born in present-day Todd County, Kentucky, Davis, as President of the Confederate States, tried desperately to hold Kentucky for the Confederacy. *Library of Congress*

heard footsteps on the floor below his room. He is alleged to have said, "That is [Albert] Sidney Johnston's step. Bring him up." Whether this little episode actually took place is indeterminable. What is known is that Johnston journeyed at that time from California to Richmond, Virginia, and tendered his services to the Confederacy.

There can be no doubt that Davis was delighted over this turn of events. He had been a friend and admirer of Johnston since their days together as cadets at West Point; his admiration had grown immensely in their service together in the battle of Monterrey of the Mexican War. Davis said later that Johnston came to the Confederacy without herald or pretension of claim to any position, that "he simply offered himself to the cause."[1]

Johnston was a native of Kentucky; most of his career had been spent in the American west. To Davis, he seemed the ideal candidate for the command of the western theater of the Confederacy. On September 10 the order was issued making Johnston the commander of Confederate Department Number Two, a vast area spreading from the Appalachians on the east, across the Mississippi, and including Indian Territory (later the state of Oklahoma) on the west.[2]

Johnston immediately went by rail to Nashville, the key strategic and industrial city of the upper part of his theater. Greeted warmly by the citizens of the place, he addressed them briefly, calling them "Fellow Soldiers" of the Reserve Corps, to which a local editor responded, "This was a well-timed remark, and showed that, as a military man, he knew what was coming. The South will need all of her force. Every able-bodied man may as well make up his mind to it, and that soon."[3]

Johnston faced a momentous strategic decision: the neutrality of Kentucky had been shattered. General Leonidas Polk, the ranking Confederate officer in the West prior to Johnston's arrival had already seized Columbus, Kentucky, on the east bank of the Mississippi, and Union General Ulysses S. Grant had seized Paducah at the confluence of the Tennessee and Ohio rivers and Smithland at the confluence of the Cumberland and Ohio. While en route to Nashville Johnston had ordered a small contingent of troops from Knoxville to Cumberland Ford in eastern Kentucky for the purpose of guarding the way through the Cumberland Gap. The Kentucky legislature had issued a demand for

General Albert Sidney Johnston. Born in Mason County, Kentucky, Johnston commanded the vast Confederate Department No. 2, which included Kentucky. He had few troops and fewer arms and was expected to hold a line that was nearly six hundred miles long and was broken by three great navigable rivers. *National Archives*

the withdrawal of the Confederates. Ought Johnston comply? Or ought he move forward in an effort to secure this vital state for the Confederacy?

After consulting with Governor Isham Harris of Tennessee and reflecting briefly on his alternatives, Johnston decided to establish his line in Kentucky. On September 17 he sent Gen. Simon Bolivar Buckner and his command of about 5,000 troops by train from Nashville to Bowling Green. His decision was prompted as much by political and economic exigencies as by military requirements. Explaining his actions to the Richmond authorities, he wrote: "The Government of the United States fully appreciating the vast resources to be obtained by the subjugation of Kentucky will make its greatest efforts here for this purpose. If we could wrest this rich fringe from his grasp the war could be carried across the border and the contest speedily decided upon our own terms."[4]

Upon entering Kentucky Johnston sought to soothe the feelings of the people by issuing a proclamation of his motives and intentions. His troops were there, he said, in response to the entrance of Federal troops there; he would withdraw the Confederates if the Federals would withdraw. The presence of his troops, he said, would allow the citizens to choose freely the path they preferred in the war. If they preferred neutrality, they could remain neutral. Or they might choose to join the Confederacy or the Union. "But," he concluded, "if it be true . . . that a majority . . . desire to adhere to the United States and become parties to the war, then none can doubt the right of the other belligerent to meet that war whenever and wherever it may be waged."[5]

The occupation of Bowling Green, along with other military positions already in being, established a Confederate line across the southern portion of Kentucky. The area west of the Mississippi was held by a small force under the command of Brig. Gen. Earl Van Dorn. Johnston described his arrangements as follows: "Bowling Green was fortified for the reasons that in my judgment . . . it was the most defensible point that could be selected to cover Nashville and our Southern line of defence extending from Cumberland Gap to the Mississippi River. It [Bowling Green] is naturally strong, a salient point on the railroads and turnpike roads passing through Kentucky, and the most difficult point to turn by an aggressive enemy that could have been selected."[6] Johnston pointed out also that Bowling Green was protected by the Barren River a few miles north of the city.

Johnston was painfully aware of the weakness of his line. He commanded somewhat over 20,000 troops east of the Mississippi and about 10,000 west of the river. His opponents outnumbered him almost two to one. In the strict sense, Johnston held no line. What he held was a series of points divided by wide stretches of unoccupied territory. He divided his Kentucky front into three sectors: Gen. William J. Hardee commanded the Bowling Green force guarding the Louisville-Nashville line; General Polk, with headquarters at Columbus, was responsible for the Mississippi, Tennessee, and Cumberland river lines; and Gen. Felix Zollicoffer, with headquarters at Cumberland Ford, was responsible for the defense of Cumberland Gap and the roads leading from eastern Kentucky to Nashville.

The geographic configuration of Johnston's department was extremely advantageous to his enemies. It presented no significant natural obstacles to a Union penetration. Instead, the major terrain features, the rivers, seem almost to have been arranged by nature for the purpose of assisting an invader of the South. The Mississippi split Johnston's theater in half; the Tennessee and Cumberland ran north through the upper portion of the theater and emptied into the Ohio behind his opponent's front; the Ohio formed the northern boundary of Kentucky and protected the northwestern states from the threat of Confederate invasion. The Ohio also linked the Mississippi with the Tennessee and Cumberland at points behind the Union front. The town of Cairo, Illinois, situated at the junction of the Ohio and the Mississippi, was a pivot point from which the Union authorities could, by means of their gunboats and transports, quickly move troops against selected positions within the Confederate line.[7]

Columbus on the Mississippi soon became a formidable fortress bristling with guns, and Bowling Green was heavily defended. But Johnston was aware of vulnerable points where the Tennessee and Cumberland rivers ran through his front in an area in which the two streams were only twelve miles apart. The rivers were guarded by hastily constructed forts: Fort Henry on the Tennessee and Fort Donelson on the

General Leonidas Polk. Polk's movement to take Columbus and Hickman, Kentucky, on the Mississippi River (which Unionists claimed breached Kentucky's neutrality) led Gen. Ulysses S. Grant to seize the mouths of the Tennessee and Cumberland Rivers a few days later. *Library of Congress*

Cumberland. Because these forts were begun by the state of Tennessee while Kentucky was still declaring itself neutral, both were located in Tennessee immediately below the Kentucky border. Although Johnston's engineer advised him that they would be better located farther down stream in Kentucky, a lack of time caused Johnston to leave them where he found them. Besides the intrinsic weakness of Fort Henry, the location of the forts fifty miles south of Bowling Green and thirty miles south of Columbus created a dangerous salient protruding into the Confederate line.[8]

Johnston quickly formed a staff to assist him in his duties. He organized it into a Department of Orders, with Lt. Col. W. W. Mackall as the assistant adjutant general; a Quartermaster Department under Maj. Albert J. Smith; a Commissary Department under Capt. Thomas K. Jackson; and an Engineer Corps under Lt. Joseph Dixon, who would soon be superseded by Col. Jeremy Gilmer. Though lacking such modern staff departments as Operations, Intelligence, and Personnel, as well as a chief of staff, Johnston's staff was logically organized, and Colonel Mackall played something of a dual role as personnel officer and chief of staff.

Johnston also set up what he called his personal staff. The makeup of this group gives a significant insight into his thinking at the top strategic level. In addition to an aide-de-camp, the personal staff included two Confederate governors (or pretending governors): George W. Johnson of Kentucky and Thomas C. Reynolds of Missouri. Later he would add Gov. Isham Harris of Tennessee. Reynolds commented perceptively on this arrangement: "This [appointment of political figures by Johnston] was one of the incidents which showed me that he was a complete general, for, while no true soldier will permit any merely political influences around him, yet an able commander should always take into consideration, and be minutely and accurately informed of, the condition, resources, etc., of the country in which he operates."

In addition to its political members, the personal staff included Samuel Tate, an executive of the Memphis and Charleston Railroad. His presence indicated Johnston's keen awareness of the strategic role of the railroads in the war.[9]

In order to purchase time in which to attempt to enlarge his force, Johnston affected what has been called an "arrogant display of power," a bluff to deceive his opponents into believing his army was much stronger than it actually was. He moved his little force at Bowling Green with an appearance of great confidence, instructing reconnaissance and raiding parties to create the impression they were the vanguard of an army that was about to advance.[10]

For a while this ruse worked remarkably well. Union General Robert H. Anderson, whose main defense line was at Muldraugh's Hill some thirty miles south of Louisville, was so upset by the Confederate menace that on October 5 he turned his command over to a subordinate, Brig. Gen. William Tecumseh Sherman, explaining that he could no longer stand the mental pressure and must leave or it would kill him. Sherman did no better. Living in fear of an attack by Johnston, he suffered something of a nervous breakdown, and five weeks later was relieved of command by Brig. Gen. Don Carlos Buell. A northern editor later wrote: "[Johnston] perpetually threatened our army with assault and annihilation, kept Louisville, and even Cincinnati, for a time in a state of perturbation, and delayed the progress of our arms until it seemed his end was on the eve of accomplishment."[11] Johnston thus held the opposing armies at bay for about six months.

During this time he worked diligently to train and equip his own army. His initial concern was that of a lack of sufficient weapons for his troops. "I feel assured that I can command the requisite number of men," he wrote to Davis shortly after arriving in Kentucky, "but we are deficient in arms."[12] He sent letters to the various state governors and staff officers to Gen. Braxton Bragg at Pensacola requesting arms, but all of these overtures met with failure. Bragg had no weapons to spare; the state governors replied that all of their available weapons had been sent to the defense of Virginia or the Gulf Coast. Upon hearing that a shipload of arms purchased in Europe had landed at Savannah, Johnston telegraphed Davis to request 30,000 stand for his army. Davis replied that the vessel at Savannah brought only a fraction of the 30,000 mentioned by Johnston and that he could spare only 1,000 for the western army. He also offered Johnston the unwelcome admonition, "Rely not on rumors."[13]

Johnston soon became convinced that he could not, in fact, "command the requisite number of men," as he put it. Authorized to call upon the states within his theater for recruits, he did so energetically and repeatedly. Aiming for an additional 50,000 recruits, he wrote the various governors such letters as the following [to Gov. John J. Pettus of Mississippi]:

> If troops are given to me, if the people [of your state] can be made to feel how much suffering and calamity would be avoided by the presence now in my camp of 10,000 or 15,000 more brave men, so that I could attack the enemy, and not, from a disparity of force, be compelled to await it—it seems to me that the same generous ardor that induced them to embark in the great struggle for our independence would give me such succors that victory would be certain. . . . A decisive battle will probably be fought on this line; and a company on that day will be worth more than a regiment next year. If the enemy does not attack, the North embarrassed at home, menaced with war by England, will shrink foiled from the conflict, and the freedom of the South will be forever established."[14]

In his dire need for men Johnston violated Confederate policy by accepting twelve-month volunteers who were without arms. To his chagrin, the secretary of war ordered them disbanded. Johnston obeyed the order, then worked around it by accepting the men temporarily until impressed private guns could be altered for military service. He reported to the secretary of war what he was doing and explained it as follows: "The Government thus secured their services. Otherwise they could not have been procured; and the time between mustering in and arming was profitably employed in giving the men all practicable instruction in their duties as soldiers. This, it will be readily perceived, was quite as necessary to their efficiency in the field as placing arms in their hands."[15] Johnston thus anticipated the "wooden guns" training of unarmed American soldiers early in World War II.

To a discouraging extent these calls for additional men failed. "I am disappointed in the state of public sentiment in the South," Johnston commented to a staff officer. "Our people seem to have suffered from a violent political fever, which has left them exhausted. They are not up to the revolutionary point."[16]

Especially bitter to him was the meager response of the Kentuckians, not only because he was a native of the state, but because his advance into Kentucky had been made largely in the hope that it would bring the state's men and other resources flocking to the support of the Confederacy. He wrote the Richmond authorities, saying: "We have received but little accession to our ranks since the Confederate forces crossed the line; in fact, no such demonstration of enthusiasm as to justify any movements not warranted by our ability to maintain our own communications. . . . [The people] appear to me passive, if not apathetic. . . . I shall, however, still hope that the love and spirit of liberty are not yet extinct in Kentucky."[17]

In January 1862, Johnston rendered his final judgment on the Confederate policy of relying on state volunteers. He wrote the secretary of war, "I have hoped to be able to raise an adequate force by the aid of the Governors of the several States of this department; but notwithstanding zealous efforts on their part, thus far I have been able to draw to this place only a force which, when compared in number to the enemy, must be regarded as insufficient."[18]

Meanwhile, he sought repeatedly to convince Richmond of the importance and vulnerability of his theater, and persuade the Confederate leaders to reinforce his army from other, less-threatened areas of the South. He warned that a powerful Union force was preparing to move against him, and said, "They have justly comprehended that the seat of vitality of the Confederacy, if to be reached at all is by this route. It is now palpable that all the resources of [the Federal government] will, if necessary, be employed to assure success on this line. . . . If the public service would permit, I beg leave to suggest that a few regiments might be detached from the several armies in the field and ordered here, to be replaced by new levies."[19]

Two weeks later, Johnston sent the adjutant general a similar message, offered a more specific analysis of what he feared was about to occur, and strongly suggested what ought to be done to meet the threat:

> The enemy will probably undertake no active operations in Missouri and may be content to hold our forces fast in their position on the Potomac for the remainder of the winter, but to suppose with the facilities of movement by water which the well filled rivers of the Ohio, Cumberland, and

> Tennessee give for active operations, that they will suspend them in Tennessee and Kentucky during the winter months is a delusion. All the resources of the confederacy are now needed for the defence of Tennessee."[20]

So urgent was the state of affairs in his department that Johnston violated the normal chain of command in order to bring the situation to the attention of the president. In mid-January, Johnston dispatched an aide, Col. St. John R. Liddell, directly to Jefferson Davis urging that troops be sent to him from Virginia, the lower Atlantic coast, and New Orleans. Liddell said he found Davis careworn and irritable, and that he snapped, "My God! Why did General Johnston send you to me for arms and reinforcements, when he must know that I have neither. He has plenty of men in Tennessee, and they must have arms of some kind—shotguns, rifles, even pikes could be used." According to Liddell, Davis was less irascible the following day, but still refused Johnston's request, saying, "Tell my friend, General Johnston, that I can do nothing for him; that he must rely on his own resources."[21] Thus all of Johnston's efforts to persuade the Confederate authorities to concentrate adequate forces for the defense of their vulnerable western theater came to naught.

A new team of Union commanders in the West was now moving against Johnston's front. The initial thrust had come on November 7, 1861, launched by Gen. Ulysses S. Grant, a then obscure officer, upon the village of Belmont, Missouri, on the opposite bank of the Mississippi from Columbus. By ferrying reinforcements across the river General Polk drove off the attackers; Grant himself only narrowly escaped capture.[22]

On January 19, 1862, Johnston's eastern Kentucky force, now under command of Maj. Gen. George B. Crittenden, suffered a sharp defeat in the battle of Mill Springs (or Logan's Crossroads). General Zollicoffer, second in command, had unwisely moved his troops across the Cumberland. Fearing an attempt to recross the stream in the presence of the enemy, Crittenden attacked the Federals under the command of Brig. Gen. George H. Thomas and was repulsed. Zollicoffer himself was killed in the fray. Crittenden barely managed to get the remainder of his command back across the Cumberland. Mills Springs was a small battle but a serious reverse for the Confederates. By weakening the defense of

The Confederate Defense of Kentucky

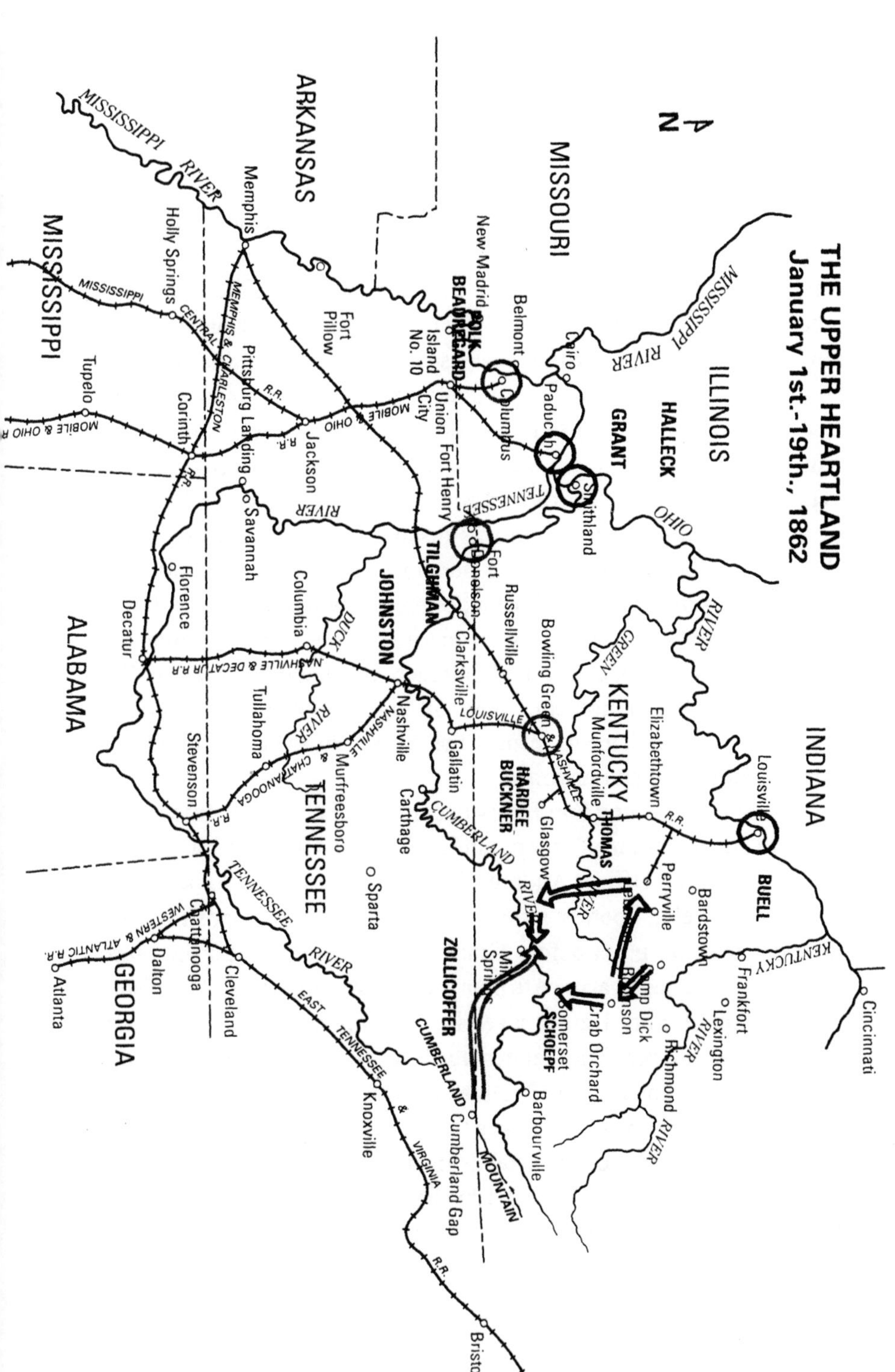

the Cumberland Gap and the roads leading from eastern Kentucky it made Johnston's position vulnerable to a turning movement from that direction.[23]

Although Johnston had anticipated a move against the critical Tennessee and Cumberland river forts, Fort Henry was ill prepared when the assault came. It stood on low ground on the east side of the Tennessee, partially inundated by flood water. Johnston had ordered General Polk to occupy and fortify the high ground on the other bank (where a stronghold to be named Fort Heiman was now planned), which previously had been unfortified because it was located in what was then the neutral state Kentucky. Everything possible to go amiss seems to have done so in the efforts to build Fort Heiman. The local commander, Brig. Gen. Lloyd Tilghman, was unable to get enough nearby slaves to do the labor; Governor Harris of Tennessee failed in his call for slaves for the same purpose; Johnston was disappointed in his search for an adequate number of guns for the position. Tilghman apparently was dilatory in his affairs, and Johnston, burdened with other cares, let the matter slip until too late. On January 17, he wired Tilghman a peremptory order: "Occupy and intrench the heights opposite Fort Henry. Do not lose a moment. Work all night." When Colonel Gilmer arrived a few days later to inspect the work, however, he found Fort Heiman unfinished and unarmed.[24]

The Union attack on Fort Henry occurred on February 6. Intended as a combined operation of troops under General Grant and a gunboat flotilla under Flag Officer Andrew H. Foote, it turned out to be a naval affair exclusively. Foote's seven gunboats blasted the position into surrender by 2:00 p.m., before Grant's troops could invest the place. Grant and Foote began at once to plan their move against Fort Donelson.

The fall of Fort Henry severely compromised the Confederate defense of Kentucky. The Tennessee River was now open to Federal operations; Johnston had no effective defense on the stream. It was open to Union gunboats and transports as far as the Muscle Shoals in northern Alabama. This prevented the establishment of a Confederate defense in depth in Tennessee; the Federals by use of the river could trap any Confederate forces inside its great arc. Two days after the fall of Fort

Henry Union gunboats made a reconnaissance of the Tennessee all the way to Florence, Alabama.[25]

The day after Fort Henry fell Johnston met in the Covington House in Bowling Green with his two immediate subordinates, Gen. P. G. T. Beauregard, his second in command, and General Hardee, to determine a strategy for meeting the emergency. The generals reached the momentous decision that Fort Donelson could not be successfully defended and that the loss of the two forts made the entire present line untenable. Confederate forces were to be withdrawn to locations below the curve of the Tennessee River. The separate forces in western Kentucky (primarily those of General Polk) and at Bowling Green and eastern Kentucky were to operate independently until they could be united at some point in their new location. Until this occurred, Beauregard was to command the western wing, Johnston the eastern wing.[26]

This decision meant the temporary abandonment of Kentucky and the western two-thirds of Tennessee, including Nashville. The "provisional" (that is, Confederate) governor of Kentucky begged Johnston not to withdraw. Such a move, he said, would place the Federals upon the vitals of the South; it would "spread dismay over the whole Confederacy."[27]

Years after the war General Beauregard claimed that he had opposed the decision to abandon the Kentucky line, and had urged Johnston in the Covington House conference to rush to Fort Donelson with his Bowling Green force and confront Grant there. Beauregard argued that by so doing Johnston would have been able to defeat the outnumbered Federals.[28] There is no convincing evidence supporting Beauregard's claim of having opposed the abandonment of the Kentucky line. His own contemporary memorandum of the conference makes no mention of his having done so; and Johnston's description of the conference, written the day afterward, says the group unanimously agreed on a Confederate withdrawal. Hardee wrote the same thing to a lady friend a few days later. Beauregard's postwar assertion seems to have been a typical instance of revisionist history.[29]

If, however, such a plan gave promise of success, Johnston should be held accountable for failing to conceive and execute it. He believed it

General Pierre G. T. Beauregard, the "Hero of Manassas." Second-in-command to Gen. Albert Sidney Johnston in Kentucky, Beauregard quickly proved incapable of meeting the demands of command in the vast Confederate Department No. 2. *Library of Congress*

imperative that he give up what he considered an untenable position in order to preserve his army for action under more auspicious circumstances. He said the risk of engaging in battle against the forces of both Grant and Buell was too great. His Bowling Green troops began the evacuation of that place on February 11 and reached the town of Edgefield, Tennessee, on the north bank of the Cumberland opposite Nashville the night of the 15th.

Meanwhile, Fort Donelson remained in Confederate hands. In considering what action was to be taken there, Johnston committed the most serious mistake of his career. After deciding the fort was indefensible, he nevertheless ordered several thousand additional troops into it. They were commanded by Gen. John B. Floyd, Gen. Gideon Pillow, and Gen. Simon Bolivar Buckner. Johnston instructed the senior

Nashville and the Tennessee State Capitol. When Fort Donelson on the Cumberland River was surrendered on February 16, 1862, the fall of the Tennessee capital city upstream was foreshadowed. *Library of Congress*

officer there, Floyd, to bring the Fort Donelson troops to Nashville to join the Bowling Green column if Fort Donelson could not be held.

On February 14 Foote's gunboats attacked Fort Donelson but were decisively repulsed. Grant's army then invested the fort and its outlying positions. The following day the Confederates launched a massed attack against a selected point in Grant's line and temporarily opened the road to Nashville. Then, incredibly, they returned to their former positions only to have Grant close them in again. During the night Floyd and Pillow fatuously wired Johnston in Nashville that the Confederates at Fort Donelson had won victory "complete and glorious."

As the night progressed, the Confederate officers realized the hopelessness of their situation; the fort could not be held nor could its troops now escape to Nashville. In one of the most shameful episodes of the Civil War Floyd and Pillow passed the command by turns to Buckner, then slipped ignominiously away across the river, leaving the hapless Buckner to accede to Grant's demand for unconditional surrender.[30] Johnston lay down to sleep at midnight on February the 15th, aglow from the victory message, only to be aroused before daybreak with the shattering news that the fort and its defenders would be surrendered at dawn. Exclaiming, "I must save this army," he immediately began moving his troops across the Cumberland and into Nashville to prevent their being trapped north of the river.[31]

Thus Johnston lost Kentucky, and shortly a large part of Tennessee, for the Confederacy. The loss of this important territory probably was unavoidable; Johnston simply did not have enough resources to give him a reasonable chance of holding it. Beauregard estimated with only slight exaggeration that the Federals could bring almost a three-to-one numerical superiority against the Confederate line in Kentucky. But if this line could not have been held, then Johnston ought to have escaped with virtually all of his army. Instead, by sending the additional troops into Fort Donelson after he considered it doomed, he lost more than enough strength there to have assured him of victory later. Some historians argue that he failed to demonstrate the judgment and decisiveness demanded by the situation that confronted him.

In the strictly operational sense, the sequel to the Confederate loss of the Tennessee forts lies outside the story of the Confederate efforts to hold Kentucky. But in the strategic sense, it is very much a part of this story. In the following campaign Johnston demonstrated that, despite his mistakes in the contest for the forts, he had the strategic vision and operational skill to concentrate his forces and the will and courage to employ them aggressively.

Two days before the surrender of Fort Donelson General Beauregard left to take temporary command of the western wing of Johnston's forces in conformity with Johnston's Covington House decision. From his headquarters in Jackson, Tennessee, and later Corinth, Mississippi, Beauregard brought General Polk's troops down the Mobile and Ohio Railroad from Columbus, Kentucky, and located them at Corinth. He also coordinated there the arrival of some 15,000 reinforcements ordered by the Confederate war department from New Orleans, Mobile, and Pensacola.[32]

Corinth was one of the most strategically important places in the western theater of the war. It lay at the intersection of the Mobile and Ohio Railroad, which ran north-south, and the Memphis and Charleston Railroad, which ran east-west. Corinth and its railroads was to Confederate logistical operations what Cairo with its rivers had been to Union logistical operations. Johnston marched the eastern wing of his forces from Nashville to Decatur, Alabama, where he crossed them over the Tennessee River on the Memphis and Charleston bridge. From Decatur he shuttled them by rail to Corinth. By late March he had at his command there some 40,000 effective troops. General Grant with approximately 35,000 troops was now encamped at Pittsburg Landing on the Tennessee River. Another 5,000 Union soldiers were located four miles down river from Pittsburg Landing. The landing was only a day's march from Corinth.

On April 6, 1862, Johnston attacked Grant's unsuspecting army at Pittsburg Landing. The resulting Battle of Shiloh (or Pittsburg Landing) was the first major western battle of the Civil War and one of the fiercest encounters of the entire conflict. The Confederates very nearly won a decisive victory there. But Johnston was killed at the peak of the battle on the first day. Beauregard succeeded to the command and halted the fighting at dusk in order to rest his troops. Grant, heavily reinforced by

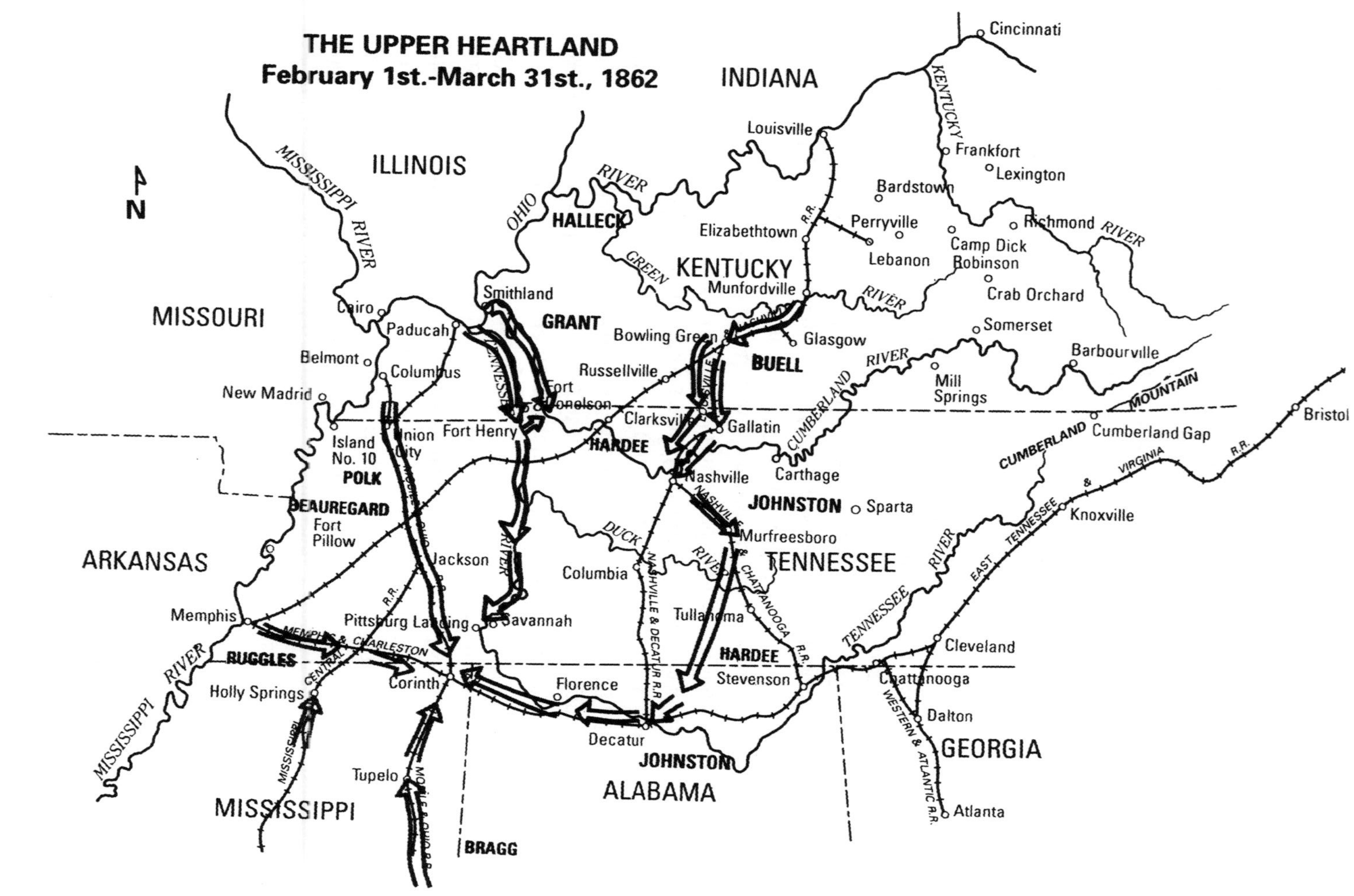
THE UPPER HEARTLAND
February 1st.-March 31st., 1862
N
ILLINOIS
INDIANA
MISSOURI
KENTUCKY
ARKANSAS
TENNESSEE
MISSISSIPPI
ALABAMA
GEORGIA
MISSISSIPPI RIVER
OHIO RIVER
TENNESSEE RIVER
CUMBERLAND RIVER
KENTUCKY RIVER
GREEN RIVER
DUCK RIVER
CUMBERLAND MOUNTAIN
Cincinnati
Louisville
Frankfort
Lexington
Bardstown
Perryville
Lebanon
Elizabethtown
Richmond
Camp Dick Robinson
Crab Orchard
Munfordville
Somerset
Barbourville
Mill Springs
Glasgow
Bowling Green
Russellville
Smithland
Cairo
Paducah
Belmont
Columbus
New Madrid
Island No. 10
Union City
Fort Henry
Fort Donelson
Clarksville
Gallatin
Nashville
Carthage
Sparta
Murfreesboro
Columbia
Tullahoma
Stevenson
Jackson
Fort Pillow
Memphis
Pittsburg Landing
Savannah
Holly Springs
Corinth
Florence
Decatur
Tupelo
Chattanooga
Cleveland
Dalton
Atlanta
Knoxville
Cumberland Gap
Bristol
GRANT
HALLECK
BUELL
HARDEE
JOHNSTON
POLK
BEAUREGARD
RUGGLES
BRAGG
MEMPHIS & CHARLESTON R.R.
MISSISSIPPI CENTRAL R.R.
MOBILE & OHIO R.R.
NASHVILLE & DECATUR R.R.
NASHVILLE & CHATTANOOGA R.R.
WESTERN & ATLANTIC R.R.
EAST TENNESSEE & VIRGINIA R.R.

Buell during the night, counterattacked and drove the Confederates from the field the following day.

Shiloh was a severe Confederate defeat both tactically and strategically. It left a powerful Union army planted deep in the western theater of the Confederacy and poised for the conquest of the remainder of the Mississippi Valley. It also doomed Confederate efforts to hold Kentucky and the western two-thirds of Tennessee. But the Confederates did reap some strategic benefits from Shiloh. The ferocity of the battle stunned the minds of the Union commanders and temporarily halted the Union advance, thus enabling the Confederates to mount a serious counteroffensive later.[33]

Beauregard withdrew his army to Corinth, and when the heavily reinforced Union army approached this town he withdrew to Tupelo, Mississippi, located on the Mobile and Ohio Railroad some forty miles south of Corinth. From this place Gen. Braxton Bragg, Beauregard's successor in command, would launch his effort to regain Kentucky the following fall.

NOTES

1. Jefferson Davis, "Address" 1878, in Dunbar Rowland, ed., *Jefferson Davis, Constitutionalist: His Letters, Papers, and Speeches*, 10 vols. (Jackson, Miss., 1923), 8:232. For an elaboration of the material in this paper, see Charles P. Roland, *Albert Sidney Johnston: Solider of Three Republics* (Austin, Tx., 1964), 258-297. See also, William Preston Johnston, *The Life of General Albert Sidney Johnston* (New York, N.Y., 1878), 423-498.

2. *The War of the Rebellion: A Compilation of the Official Records of the Union and Confederate Armies*, 128 vols. (Washington, D.C., 1880-1901) (hereinafter cited as *O.R.*) (all citations are to Series I), 3:687-688; 4:405.

3. Stanley F. Horn, *The Army of Tennessee* (New York, N.Y., 1941), 56.

4. Albert Sidney Johnston to Samuel Cooper, Oct. 17, 1861, "Headquarters Book of Albert Sidney Johnston" (copy), Louisiana Historical Association Papers, Manuscripts Division, Howard-Tilton Memorial Library, Tulane University, New Orleans.

5. *O.R.*, 4:420-421.

6. "Questions Propounded to Genl. A. S. Johnston by the Special Committee of the House of Representatives and Answers"; and Johnston to "Sir," March 17, 1862, both in War Department Collection of Confederate Records, the National Archives, Washington.

7. Roland, *Albert Sidney Johnston*, 265-267.

8. *Ibid.*, 267-268.

9. *Ibid.*, 268-269.

10. Johnston to William J. Hardee, Nov. 9, 1861, quoted in *O.R.*, 4:531.

11. Quoted in Johnston, *Life of General Johnston*, 726.

12. *O.R.*, 4:416, 430.

13. *Ibid.*, 417.

14. Johnston to J. J. Pettus, Dec. 24, 1861, in "Headquarters Book of Albert Sidney Johnston."

15. Johnston to Judah P. Benjamin, Jan. 12, 1862, in "Headquarters Book of Albert Sidney Johnston."

16. Edward W. Munford, "Albert Sidney Johnston," n. d., Mrs. Mason Barret Collection of Albert Sidney and William Preston Johnston Papers, Manuscripts Division, Howard-Tilton Memorial Library, Tulane University. These papers are cited hereinafter as Johnston Papers, Barret Collection. Munford was one of Johnston's aides.

17. Quoted in Eliza Calvert Hall, "Bowling Green and the Civil War," *The Filson Club History Quarterly* (October, 1937), 11:251.

18. *O.R.*, 7:825.

19. Johnston to Benjamin, Jan. 8, 1862, in "Headquarters Book of Albert Sidney Johnston."

20. Johnston to Cooper, Jan. 22, 1862 in *ibid.*

21. St. John R. Liddell, "Liddell's Record of the Civil War," *Southern Bivouac* (December, 1885), 1:417-419.

22. *O.R.*, 3:304-310, 317. Nathaniel C. Hughes, *The Battle of Belmont: Grant Strikes South* (Chapel Hill, N.C., 1991) provides a complete coverage of this encounter. See also Joseph H. Parks, *General Leonidas Polk, C. S. A.* (Baton Rouge, La., 1962), 190-193.

23. *O.R.*, 3:79-82, 102-110. For descriptions of this encounter, see Lowell H. Harrison, "Mill Springs, the Brilliant Victory," *Civil War Times Illustrated,* 10 (January, 1972), 4-9, 44-49; and C. David Dalton, "Zollicoffer, Crittenden, and the Mill Springs Campaign: Some Persistent Questions," *Filson Club History Quarterly*, 60 (October, 1986), 463-471.

24. James L. Nichols, *Confederate Engineers* (Tuscaloosa, Ala., 1957), 42-45; Isham G. Harris to Johnston, Dec. 31, 1861, in Isham G. Harris Letter Book, Tennessee State Library and Archives, Nashville; Johnston, *Life of General Johnston*, 407-428; Roland, *Albert Sidney Johnston*, 285.

25. *O.R.*, 7:131-152, 153-156. See also Bruce Catton, *Grant Moves South* (Boston, Mass., 1960), 138-144.

26. *O.R.*, 7:861-862.

27. George W. Johnson to Johnston, n. d. (copy), Johnston Papers, Barret Collection.

28. Alfred Roman, *The Military Operations of General Beauregard in the War between the States, 1861-1865*, 2 vols. (New York, N.Y., 1884), 1:217-219, 227-228.

29. Johnston to Benjamin, Feb. 8, 1862, in "Headquarters Book of Albert Sidney Johnston"; William J. Hardee to My Dear Mrs. Shover, Feb. 25, 1862, in William J. Hardee Papers, Manuscript Division, Library of Congress, Washington. See also Roland, *Albert Sidney Johnston*, 294.

30. Roland, *Albert Sidney Johnston*, 292. For a complete account of the campaign for the Tennessee forts, see Benjamin Franklin Cooling, *Forts Henry and Donelson: The Key to the Confederate Heartland* (Knoxville, Tenn., 1987). For the story of the capture of Fort Donelson, see 166-223. 31. Roland, *Albert Sidney Johnston*, 298.

32. *O.R.*, 7:899-901; Roman, *Military Operations of General Beauregard*, 1:221-223.

33. Roland, *Albert Sidney Johnston*, 298-351, presents an analysis of Johnston's role in the Shiloh campaign. See also James L. McDonough, *Shiloh: In Hell Before Night* (Knoxville, Tenn., 1977), and Larry J. Daniel, *Shiloh: The Battle that Changed the Civil War* (New York, N.Y., 1997). These studies offer views on Johnston's conduct that disagree sharply with Roland's views. Wiley Sword, *Shiloh: Bloody April* (New York, N.Y., 1974), gives a lively and informed account of the entire battle. He credits Johnston with having opened at the time of his death a corridor to Pittsburg Landing and a possible Confederate victory. See 276, 280.

Ron Nicholas

Mill Springs: The First Battle for Kentucky

As the storm of the American Civil War broke across the nation in the Spring of 1861, Kentucky faced a difficult choice: would she remain loyal to the Union she had joined in 1792, or join her sister Southern states in setting up a new Confederate government? Kentucky's manpower—the third-largest white population of the slave states—production of wheat and livestock, and strategic location on the Ohio and Mississippi rivers made it a prize both sides wanted to win. Both Presidents Abraham Lincoln and Jefferson Davis recognized the critical importance of their native state to their respective causes.[1]

Unable to choose at first, Kentucky decided that she would not answer Lincoln's call for troops to subdue the Southern states nor would she join the Southern states in their new government; Kentucky, rather, would be "neutral." Neither side violated this neutrality throughout the summer of 1861 in hopes of wooing the state.

In September 1861 Confederate General Leonidas Polk, fearing that Union forces were about to invade the state, ordered his troops to seize Columbus, Kentucky, on the Mississippi River. This invasion of Kentucky's neutrality opened the floodgates and Union and Confederate forces poured into the state. Confederate forces quickly set up a defensive line stretching from the Cumberland Gap in the east to the Mississippi River, six hundred miles to the west. With only 30,000 men, Gen. Albert Sidney Johnston (a native Kentuckian) was given the daunting task of holding this line for the Confederacy and advancing farther into Kentucky whenever possible. To counter the Confederate threat, Union troops in Kentucky, aggregated into the Department of the

Ohio, numbered around 90,000. These troops had a succession of commanders during the first months of the war. First was Gen. Robert H. Anderson, the hero of Fort Sumter, whose health could not stand the strain of command. He was soon replaced by Gen. William Tecumseh Sherman who, in turn, was succeeded by Gen. Don Carlos Buell after Sherman stated that he would need 200,000 more men, thus convincing the Secretary of War Simon Cameron that Sherman had lost his mind. General Buell took over the Department of the Ohio on November 15, 1861. The confusion created by the succession of Union commanders made any offensive operation against the Confederates impossible until the beginning of 1862, and had given the Confederate forces time to seize the initiative from the idle Union Army.

General Johnston decided on a bold strategy for his out-numbered forces. He would hold the important Mississippi River and cover the approaches to Nashville with the majority of his force, while detaching a small command to pro-Union East Tennessee to secure Knoxville and its important rail link with Chattanooga and Virginia. This force would also seize the Cumberland Gap, at this time still a mainland route in and out of Kentucky. By stretching his resources to their limits, Johnston hoped to hold his defensive line in Kentucky until he could receive reinforcements and advance farther into the state.

With his experienced officers already assigned to other important tasks, General Johnston relied upon Brig. Gen. Felix Kirk Zollicoffer as the commander of the small force that would secure East Tennessee and the important railroad at Knoxville. Before the war, Zollicoffer had been a prominent newspaper editor in Nashville as well as a three-term Congressman. His only military experience was as a captain of a company of eighty-four men in 1836 during the Seminole War. What General Zollicoffer lacked in experience, he made up for in zeal and daring. He marched his ill-armed—almost all of his men were using outdated flintlock muskets—and ill-clad army of 6,000 men east and seized Knoxville, secured the railroad and forced many East Tennessee Unionists to flee north into pro-Union eastern Kentucky. Continuing with his bold campaign, Zollicoffer seized the Cumberland Gap. Not content to just hold the line, Zollicoffer pushed his forces deeper into Kentucky along the Old Wilderness Road and established a base at

General Felix Kirk Zollicoffer. His troop dispositions north of the Cumberland River just before the Battle of Mill Springs were made in the face of Gen. Albert Sidney Johnston's strong suggestions to the contrary. *Library of Congress*

Cumberland Ford (present day Pineville, Kentucky). After destroying Camp Andrew Johnson, a Union recruiting camp at Barbourville (and the site of the first battle of the Civil War in Kentucky), Zollicoffer's

General George Henry Thomas. A Virginian who remained loyal to the Union, Thomas commanded the Union forces that marched from Camp Dick Robinson to the Cumberland River, where they defeated Gen. George B. Crittenden's Confederate command at the Battle of Mill Springs. *Library of Congress*

forces raided the Goose Creek salt works in Clay County. Following these two small victories, the Confederate forces continued their advance.

Union Brigadier General George H. Thomas, commander of the First Division of the Department of the Ohio, was assigned the task of defeating Zollicoffer's forces and securing pro-Union Eastern Kentucky and East Tennessee for the Union. From his headquarters at Camp Dick Robinson near Danville, Kentucky, Thomas sent a force under Brig. Gen. Albin Schoepf to intercept his opponent. Schoepf's men moved south along the Wilderness Road, stopping at Wildcat Mountain near London, Kentucky, to entrench and await Zollicoffer's advancing rebels. They did not wait long.

On October 21, 1861, Zollicoffer's force attacked the entrenched Unionists in the Battle of Wildcat Mountain. Because of impassable terrain, the Confederates were only able to engage a small portion of their strength during the engagement. After several hours of fighting, General Zollicoffer concluded that he could not take the Federal position without exposing his command to ruin. He called off the attacks and began retreating toward his base at Cumberland Ford.

Wildcat Mountain was not a serious setback for the Confederates. The fight, however, coupled with the difficulties of keeping the army supplied in the rugged terrain of Eastern Kentucky and the hostility of the local citizens, caused Zollicoffer to abandon his plan to invade the Bluegrass using the Wilderness Road.

Formulating a new strategy, Zollicoffer strengthened the fortification at Cumberland Gap and left a small garrison there to guard that strategic site. Explaining his new strategy to General Johnston, Zollicoffer wrote: "I propose to take and strengthen a position between Monticello and Somerset, Kentucky, giving us facilities for commanding the Cumberland River and the Coal region suppling Nashville and etc."[2] Toward this goal, Zollicoffer moved his army toward Jamestown, Tennessee. Arriving at Jamestown on November 22, Zollicoffer immediately sent his engineers out to find a suitable location for defending the river and establishing a winter camp. The Confederate commander also sent out a detachment of troops in an attempt to seize all of the ferry boats in the area so that they could be used by the army to cross the river. Unfortunately, all of the ferry boats in the area had been destroyed by local Union units to prevent their use by the Confederates. Zollicoffer's engineers, however, had better luck. They reported that they had found a good defensible location at Mill Springs, Kentucky. Arriving with his army on November 29, Zollicoffer found Mill Springs the ideal place for his army. Located on the high bluffs of the south bank of the Cumberland River, Mill Springs boasted a grist and saw mill, which would be of great use to Zollicoffer's forces, as well as command of the river. The strategically located village also gave Zollicoffer control of the approaches to Cumberland Gap, Knoxville, and Nashville, as well as the ability to receive supplies by water from Nashville rather than by wagon from Knoxville. Always thinking in terms of the offensive, Zollicoffer wrote to his superiors: "From this camp as a base of operations, I hope in mild weather to penetrate the country towards London or Danville."[3] It was his proclivity toward aggression that would eventually land General Zollicoffer in trouble with his superiors.

Upon arriving at Mill Springs, Zollicoffer set up his headquarters one mile south of the town in the home of Capt. A. R. West. Captain West was a veteran of the Revolutionary War and well into his nineties when the Confederate army arrived. Although he was pro-Union, West opened his house to the Confederates. General Zollicoffer soon moved his headquarters to the Lanier House, overlooking the river, and later to a cabin across the river at Beech Grove. The West house eventually became a hospital and was used as such both before and after the Battle of Mill Springs. The West family helped care for the sick and buried several of the dead in the family cemetery.

After setting his men to the tasks of making camp and fortifying the area around the town, General Zollicoffer, using his talents as a journalist and politician, issued a proclamation to the "people of Southeastern Kentucky." He assured the Kentuckians that "The brigade I have the honor to command is here for no purpose of war upon Kentuckians, but to repel those Northern hordes who, with arms in their hands, are attempting the subjugation of a sister Southern state."[4] Seeking to rally Kentucky recruits to his army, he closed the proclamation by inviting Kentuckians to "Strike with us for independence and the preservation of your property, and those Northern invaders of your soil will soon be driven across the Ohio."[5] While the proclamation may have eased the fears of some Kentuckians about the intention of the Confederate army in their midst, it failed to rally many recruits to the cause.

Lacking decisive overall leadership, the Union army in Kentucky watched warily as the Confederates moved to Mill Springs. Finally, on November 15, Gen. Don Carlos Buell began to stir. Under heavy pressure from Lincoln to launch a campaign into East Tennessee, Buell ordered General Thomas to transfer his base from Crab Orchard to Lebanon, Kentucky. The move would allow Thomas to be supplied by the Louisville & Nashville Railroad from Louisville, and place him in a position to launch a campaign against Zollicoffer. Arriving in Lebanon on November 29, 1861, with the 17th and 38th Ohio infantry regiments, Thomas waited as the other units that would make up the second and third brigades of his first division arrived.

General Buell, meanwhile, ordered Gen. Albin Schoepf with the first brigade to move west from London to Somerset, Kentucky. Schoepf was to keep an eye on Zollicoffer's camp at Mill Springs and prevent the Confederates from crossing the river. Schoepf and his men arrived in Somerset on December 2 and immediately began fortifying the town. That same day a detachment of Confederate artillery with infantry support shelled Camp Goggins, one of the main Union infantry camps around Somerset. The bombardment caused the Union troops to relocate their camp, and set the tone for the next few weeks as detachments from the Union and Confederate armies sparred in the area. On December 4, at the command of one of General Schoepf's regimental commanders, Col. J. M. Connell, a group of artillery officers rode from Somerset to the north bank of the Cumberland river across from Mill Springs, a site known locally as Beech Grove. They were looking for a location to place artillery in order to prevent the Confederates from crossing. What they found was a detachment of the 2nd Tennessee Cavalry and, as Colonel Connell wrote in his report, he and his entourage "[n]arrowly escaped capture."[6] During the retreat from that tight spot, Colonel Connell's girth broke, leaving him standing in an open field with the pursuing Confederates closing fast. In an act of tremendous gallantry, another Union officer dismounted, gave his horse to Connell, and then made his own escape on foot into the woods. The Confederates those Union officers had encountered formed the advance of Zollicoffer's command. The next day, Zollicoffer's soldiers began crossing the Cumberland River and building a fortified camp in Beech Grove on the north bank. General Schoepf had failed to hold the Confederates south of the river.

General Zollicoffer's transfer of the bulk of his army both surprised and concerned the Union commander. Brig. Gen. Jeremiah T. Boyle, commander of the Union post at nearby Columbia, Kentucky, reported to General Thomas: "You cannot drive [Zollicoffer] back with less than 10,000 troops."[7] Zollicoffer's superior, General Albert S. Johnston, was equally surprised and concerned by the move. On December 2, Zollicoffer had reported to Johnston that he "was now building a transport to enable me to cross the river."[8] Eight days later Zollicoffer received a dispatch from Johnston informing him of his commander's surprise and dismay at the move. This dispatch may have also contained an order for Zollicoffer to move his men back across the river. Unfortunately the dispatch no longer exists, but General Zollicoffer's reply gives a clear idea of what it contained. "Your two dispatches of the fourth reached me last night," wrote Zollicoffer to Johnston. "I infer from yours that I should have not crossed the river, but it is now too late. My means of recrossing is so limited, that I could hardly accomplish it in the face of the enemy."[9]

Unwilling (or unable) to withdraw his men, Zollicoffer set his soldiers to fortifying the area and building cabins for a winter camp. Due to a lack of tools and unusually wet weather, the work progressed slowly. While most of the soldiers had completed their cabins by Christmas, work on the fortifications was still far from complete. Throughout this time Zollicoffer continued to request reinforcements and supplies. He eventually received both. On December 26, Capt. Hugh L. W. McClung's Tennessee artillery company arrived at Mill Springs with six guns, and on January 7, 1862, a small stern-wheeler named the *Nobel Ellis* arrived with supplies from Nashville.

Disturbed by Zollicoffer's bold move, Johnston ordered Gen. George Bibb Crittenden, Zollicoffer's immediate superior, to take command of the Confederate army at Mill Springs. General Crittenden, a native Kentuckian, was the son of prominent Kentucky Senator John J.

General George Bibb Crittenden. Kentucky-born and son of Sen. John J. Crittenden, George Crittenden broke ranks with his illustrious father and joined the Confederate army. When Crittenden's Confederate forces were crushed at the Battle of Mill Springs, so was his military career. *Library of Congress*

Crittenden and a graduate of West Point. General Johnston hoped Crittenden's presence would resolve the threatening situation facing Zollicoffer. Arriving on January 3, 1862, Crittenden was surprised to find Zollicoffer's army still on the north bank of the river. He also discovered that the wet weather had turned the Cumberland River into a torrent that destroyed most of the rafts and barges the Confederates had used to make the crossing. His most disturbing discovery was that the entrenchments on the north bank were, by Crittenden's estimation, woefully incomplete and incapable of withstanding an assault.

Union General Schoepf, a trained military engineer, was more impressed with what he was able to observe of the Confederate position, and in a dispatch to General Thomas on January 7, 1862, he gave a detailed description of the works:

> At Mill Springs the Rebel force is represented as numbering 3,000 at which point they have constructed earthen fortifications upon three sides, the north angle of the square being fortified by the precipitous bluffs of the Cumberland river. The area embraced within said fortifications cannot be less than 400 acres, making a line to be defended of 1/2 miles. The fortifications on the north side of the river extend across a narrow neck of land between the main Cumberland River and White Oak Creek, and consists of entrenchments about 1 mile in length.
>
> The timber upon the north of the entrenchments for a distance of three fourths of a mile has been thrown so that there is no approach except by a narrow road in front, while the hope of a flank movement is futile as the precipitous bluffs of the Cumberland upon the east and those of White Oak Creek upon the West render a flank movement of infantry impossible.[10]

Crittenden ordered the fortifications strengthened. Entries in Zollicoffer's order book show this work continued through January 17, two days before the Mill Springs battle.[11] Having done what he could to strengthen his position, all General Crittenden could do was wait for the river to subside so that he could recross the army to the safety of the south bank.

When General Thomas learned of the crossing of the Cumberland by Zollicoffer's forces, he decided to strike the isolated Confederates. Thomas ordered Schoepf to march his command out of Somerset and meet him west of a small tributary of the Cumberland River called Fishing Creek. Thomas and his force left Lebanon on December 30 1861, marching toward Zollicoffer's camp only forty miles away. This march should have only taken a few days, but the wet weather that had been so bothersome to the Confederates now turned its wrath on the Union columns. After Thomas's troops turned onto the Somerset Road at Columbia, rain began and continued unabated for the next ten days.

The roads turned into an ocean of mud. The march became a trial of strength for Thomas's army that lasted two and one-half weeks. Captain Judson Bishop of the 2nd Minnesota Infantry described the march: "The next ten days were spent alternately in short but tedious marches in mud and slush and rain and in waiting for the wagons to come up, so about half the nights and days the troops, without shelter, were lying in woods or fields along the roadside."[12] On January 17, the head of Thomas's exhausted army arrived at the small hamlet of Logan's Crossroads, just nine miles north of the Confederate camp at Beech Grove.

Located in southwestern Pulaski County, Kentucky, Logan's Crossroads (named for William Logan a well-to-do farmer who owned a large amount of land in the area) was nothing more than a road crossing with a few log houses erected in the midst of open fields, surrounded by heavily wooded hills and ravines. His men tired and hungry, and the rear of his column eight miles west at Cain's Store, Thomas decided to stop at Logan's Crossroads and rest his men. He would wait for Schoepf to join him there.

Thomas's troops set up their camps along the Somerset-Columbia Road with Thomas's headquarters pitched near the intersection of the Jamestown and Somerset-Columbia roads. In order to guard against a surprise attack by the Confederates, Thomas posted the 4th Kentucky Infantry and the 1st Ohio Light Artillery near the crossroads facing south, with the 10th Indiana Infantry and three companies of the 1st Kentucky Cavalry posted one-half mile south of the crossroads on the Mill Springs Road.

Meanwhile, General Schoepf was contending with the heavy weather in getting his troops to their rendezvous with Thomas. After slogging their way west from Somerset, Schoepf's forces found that the rain had turned Fishing Creek, a small tributary of the Cumberland, into a raging torrent. Not until January 18, after an extremely difficult and dangerous crossing, was Schoepf able to cross three infantry regiments and one artillery battery. Leaving orders for the rest of his troops to follow as soon as possible, Schoepf marched his men toward Logan's Crossroads. Arriving at Thomas's camp on the evening of the January 18, Schoepf and Thomas began making plans for an attack on the Confederate position.

While the Union generals were making plans for his destruction, General Crittenden was trying to decide what to do with his army. Aware that Thomas was at Logan's Crossroads and Schoepf was marching to join him, Crittenden knew he must decide whether he should retreat across the river, defend his Beech Grove position, or attack. Until early on January 18 it appeared that Crittenden had determined to recross the river. But by that evening, after receiving incorrect information that Schoepf was unable to cross Fishing Creek and join Thomas, Crittenden changed his mind and called a council of war. He divided his small army into two brigades, the first under General Zollicoffer, and the second under Brig. Gen. William H. Carroll, who had recently arrived with one regiment of reinforcements. Crittenden formulated a plan to leave camp that night and launch a surprise attack on the Union camps before daylight. He intended to destroy Thomas's column before Schoepf could reinforce it. In the event the Southerners became confused during the battle, Crittenden designated "Kentucky" as the password his men would use to recognize each other. Crittenden later reported that all of his commanders agreed with the decision to attack. Others would state that Zollicoffer objected to the plan and that both Generals Crittenden and Carroll were drunk during the council of war. These charges, though never proven, would eventually cost both men dearly.

At midnight on a cold Sunday, January 19, 1862, in a rare winter thunderstorm, the 4,000-man Confederate army formed up on the road and began marching north toward the camp of the Union army composed of about equal numbers. General Zollicoffer's First Brigade (15th Mississippi, 19th Tennessee, 20th Tennessee, 25th Tennessee, and Rutledge's Artillery) led the march, with General Carroll's Second Brigade (17th Tennessee, 28th Tennessee, 29th Tennessee, 16th Alabama, and McClung's Battery) bringing up the rear. "The night was dark and cold and the bitter winds drove the sleet and rain in our faces," remembered W. J. Worsham of the 19th Tennessee, "yet on we went, plodding in the gloom and mud to the front. . ."[13] Another Tennessean, T. H. Moore of the 25th Tennessee Infantry, described the mud as "between one to 18 inches deep." At about daylight (6:00 a.m.) on January 19, the head of the Confederate column encountered the vedettes of the Union 1st Kentucky Cavalry near a small creek known as

Timmy's Branch about one and one-half miles south of the main Union camp. After exchanging a few shots, the Union horsemen fell back to the pickets of the 10th Indiana. The Battle at Logan's Crossroads, or more popularly, Mill Springs, was underway.

Upon encountering the Union horsemen, General Zollicoffer quickly deployed Companies E and G of the 15th Mississippi as skirmishers of the advance brigade. Lt. James R. Binford of the 15th Mississippi Infantry recalled that "[b]oth companies had been thoroughly drilled as Zouave skirmishers, being deployed about eight paces apart, advanced in beautiful order and were soon under fire from the skirmishers sent out by the 10th Indiana."[14] After falling back about one-quarter mile, the Union pickets made a brief stand in and around a small log house on the west side of the Mill Springs Road, giving the Union forces in camp more time to prepare for battle. The skirmishers from the 15th Mississippi charged and drove the Union pickets from the cabin back to their skirmish line, which had formed on top of a large hill to the north. Zollicoffer rapidly deployed his brigade into line of battle. He placed Col. D. H. Cummings's 19th Tennessee Infantry west of the Mill Springs Road, and supported it with the 25th Tennessee under Col. S. S. Stanton. The 15th Mississippi, commanded by Col. E. C. Walthall, was placed in the center of the developing line east of the road, while the 20th Tennessee Infantry under Col. Joe A. Battle was dispatched to hold the far right of the Confederate front.

The Confederate line pushed forward up the hill to where the skirmishers of the 10th Indiana Infantry and 1st Kentucky Cavalry had formed. Alerted by the gunfire, Lt. Col. William Kise of the 10th Indiana informed the commander of the Second Brigade, Col. Mahlon D. Manson, of the attack and quickly formed his regiment and marched to the support of the skirmishers. Reaching the battlefield, Colonel Kise reported that "a Regiment of Rebels were advancing in line of battle and their treasonable colors were seen flaunting in the breeze."[15] Kise divided his command by placing five companies of the 10th Indiana on the west side of the road and the remaining companies on the east side. Once deployed, the Hoosiers opened fire on the advancing Confederates.

When they reached the top of the hill recently evacuated by the Union skirmishers, the Confederates moved to attack the forming Union line. The skirmishers of the 15th Mississippi quickly rejoined their regiment on the east side of the road, while the 19th Tennessee continued up the west side of the road, pushing the retreating Union skirmishers through heavy woods until they engaged the 10th Indiana across a ravine in the woods. Capt. A. M. Rutledge's Tennessee Light Artillery was positioned on a hill east of the road, but only fired a few shots during the battle for fear of hitting their own troops. The 15th Mississippi and 20th Tennessee moved up the east side of the Mill Springs Road in an effort to flank the 10th Indiana. After crossing an open field, the Mississippians and Tennesseans plunged into a wooded area, where they encountered a deep ravine. The ravine, coupled with the constant rain, slowed the Confederate advance and led to confusion within the Confederate ranks.

When the Confederates finally emerged from the heavy terrain onto the edge of an open field, the 15th Mississippi sighted a body of troops to their left. As it turned out, the soldiers belonged to the 1st Kentucky Cavalry, but the rain, fog, and smoke made it impossible for the Mississippians to distinguish whether they were friend or foe. Lt. James Binford of the 15th Mississippi described the scene:

> Colonel Walthall cried out and asked who are you? They replied Kentuckians. We fellows insisted they had said 'Kentucky' (the password Crittenden had designated) so Walthall taking the flag and walking about eighty yards in front, accompanied by Lt. Harrington of Company C, again demanded to know who they were. Their reply was a volley which killed Lt. Harrington. Colonel Walthall turned and walked back to the regiment, looking like the proud and brave game-cock he was, remarked 'now I think you know who they are.'[16]

Convinced that the enemy was in front of them, the Confederates on the east side of the road moved forward to engage the enemy extending their line to the north.

While Walthall was determining who was in front of him, the 4th Kentucky Infantry under Col. Speed Fry arrived on the battlefield from the Union encampment. Colonel Manson galloped back to inform General Thomas of the attack and, while so doing, found the 4th Kentucky formed on the road awaiting orders. Manson ordered Fry to

Colonel Speed Smith Fry

A Boyle County, Kentucky native, Fry was a pre-war lawyer in Danville. He raised the 4th Kentucky (Union) Infantry and is reputed to have fired the shot at the Battle of Mill Springs that killed Gen. Felix Zollicoffer.

Library of Congress

---

take a position in the woods ahead. Unsure of exactly what this order meant, Fry marched his men south toward the sound of the battle. Arriving on the battlefield and unable to locate a suitable position for his regiment, Colonel Fry, in his own words, spotted:

> an elevated point in the field on the left of the road, filed my regiment to the left through a fence, and formed my line of battle parallel with and near to it, under a heavy and galling fire from the enemy, who were concealed in a deep ravine at the foot of the hill and posted on the opposite hill, distant about 250 yards. Their line extended around the ridge at the head of the ravine and onto the hill occupied by me and within 50 yards of my right, covered throughout its entire extent by the fence separating the field from the woodlands and by the timber and thick growth thereto. The engagement at once became very warm. Finding I was greatly outnumbered and the enemy being under cover, I ordered my men to the opposite side of the fence in our rear. . .[17]

Noticing that the 10th Indiana on his right was heavily engaged, Fry moved two companies from his left flank and placed them near the Mill

Springs Road, where the contending lines were only fifty yards apart. That move connected the 4th Kentucky with the 10th Indiana. Those two outnumbered regiments would hold the Confederates back for the next hour.

Unaware that additional Union troops had arrived on the field, General Zollicoffer noticed elements of the 19th Tennessee engaged with troops to the north and west of the Mill Springs Road. He was sure these troops were part of his own brigade, and that due to the smoke, rain, and confusion of battle, his men were killing one another. Zollicoffer quickly ordered the 19th Tennessee to cease firing, and guided his mount down the road ordering the other units to follow suit. A brief lull in the battle ensued. Colonel Fry of the 4th Kentucky decided to take this opportunity to ride to his right and make sure his right flank was not exposed. Reaching the right of his regiment, Fry rode out from behind the fence along which his men had formed and galloped a few feet down the road to get a better look at the Confederate position. Within minutes Fry met a mounted officer whom he assumed to be a superior Union officer. Fry described the encounter:

> As I neared the road I saw an officer riding slowly down the road on a white horse and within twenty paces of my regiment. His uniform was concealed, except for the extremities on his pantaloons, which I observed were of the color worn by Federal officers, by a long green overcoat. His near approach to my regiment, his calm manner, my close proximity to him, indeed everything I saw led me to believe he was a Federal officer belonging to one of the Federal regiments just arriving. So thoroughly was I convinced that he was one of our men, I did not hesitate to ride up to his side so closely that our knees touched. He was calm, self possessed, and dignified in manner. He said to me we must not shoot our own men, to which I replied, of course not. I would not do so intentionally, then turning his eyes to the left and pointing in the same direction he said those are our men. I could not see the men from my position but I now suppose that they were there.
>
> I immediately moved off to the right of my regiment, perhaps some fifteen or twenty paces from the spot on which I had met him, his language had convinced me more than ever that he was a Federal officer. How it is that he did not discover that I was one I cannot tell, as my uniform was entirely exposed to view, having nothing on to conceal it. As soon as I reached my regiment, I paused, turning my horse a little to the left, and across the road, I looked back to see what was going on, when to my great

> surprise another officer, whom I had not seen rode out from behind a large tree near the place of my meeting with the first officer and, with pistol in hand, leveled it directly at me, fired, paused for a moment, doubtless to observe the effect of his shot. Instead of striking the object to which it was aimed, the ball struck my horse just above the hip, making a flesh wound.[18]

Realizing that he had been conversing with an enemy officer, Fry wheeled in the saddle and fired his pistol at him while his regiment opened fire. General Zollicoffer and his reckless aide were killed instantly, their bodies falling into the mud on the Mill Springs Road. The corpses would remain there throughout the battle. Later, advancing Union forces removed Zollicoffer's body from the road to avoid it being trampled upon, and placed it under a large white oak tree nearby.

Demoralized by the death of General Zollicoffer, unable to return the galling fire they were receiving from the Union lines and no one having countermanded Zollicoffer's order to cease fire, the men of the 19th Tennessee retreated from the field in confusion. Col. D. H. Cummins, who now commanded the first brigade upon the death of Zollicoffer, ordered the 25th Tennessee forward to plug the hole in the line. In spite of being thrown into some confusion by the retreat of the 19th Tennessee through its ranks, the 25th Tennessee moved forward and stabilized the Confederate front west of the Mill Springs Road.

Up to this point, General Carroll's Second Brigade had not been engaged. Deployed in line of battle behind the brow of the hill east of the road near Rutledge's artillery, Carroll's troops had been standing in reserve while Zollicoffer's brigade had been fighting. General Crittenden ordered two regiments from the Second Brigade forward. The 29th Tennessee moved out to support the 15th Mississippi and 20th Tennessee on the Confederate right, while the 28th Tennessee advanced to assist the 25th Tennessee on the Confederate left west of the Mill Springs Road. Once these reinforcements arrived, Crittenden ordered the line to advance.

One and one-half hours after being informed of the attack by Colonel Manson, General Thomas arrived on the battlefield. Thomas later explained to Manson that the delay had been caused by his difficulty in squeezing into his new general's uniform. Riding to a high point were he could see the battle (along a ridge in what is now the Mill

Springs National Cemetery), Thomas quickly took control of the situation. He sent two regiments, the 2nd Minnesota Infantry and 9th Ohio Infantry, down the Mill Springs Road to relieve the hard-pressed 4th Kentucky and 10th Indiana. Realizing that the Confederates were attempting to flank the Union left east of the road, Thomas sent Batteries B and C of the 1st Ohio Light Artillery, along with the 12th Kentucky Infantry and the 1st and 2nd Tennessee Infantry (Union), to bolster the Union left.

While Thomas's reinforcements made their way to the battlefield, Crittenden ordered his Confederates to advance. Angered by the death of General Zollicoffer and by the words of Colonel Fry, who had at one point in the battle stood upon the rail fence near his men and challenged the Confederates to "come out and fight like men," the 15th Mississippi and 20th Tennessee charged out of the ravine. In two lines the Confederates advanced across a cornfield as they closed on the 4th Kentucky. Lt. James Binford of the 15th Mississippi described the charge:

> Our boys rose with a yell and charged them. Going in front of the company I was leading at the time, I soon got to the fence and there from ten to twenty yards was the enemy line falling back. . . . Our entire line, putting their guns through the cracks of the fence fired into them with ball and buckshot, and the scene that followed defied description. The screams and groans, officers cursing and begging, trying to rally their men. . . . Lt. Freeman of company B jumped up on the fence and called for company B to follow, but just at that time another fresh regiment arrived.[19]

The fresh regiment was the 2nd Minnesota, which arrived just as the 4th Kentucky, its ammunition exhausted, was giving ground and about to break. After firing several volleys at the Confederate line crossing the cornfield, the 2nd Minnesota and 4th Kentucky attacked the Confederates who had taken position behind the rail fence. The struggle became close and desperate, with soldiers on both sides firing their muskets at one another from opposite sides of the same fence. Col. Horatio Van Cleve, commander of the 2nd Minnesota, wrote: "We were so close on them that one of the men had his beard and whiskers singed by the fire of one of the muskets; another caught hold of one of their

"Only a fence between us." The 2nd Minnesota Infantry attacks the 15th Mississippi Infantry through the rain and fog at the Battle of Mill Springs, January 19, 1862. *Courtesy of the artist, Robert J. Cull*

---

muskets and jerked it through the fence; Two stood and fired at each other, their muskets crossing, both fell dead."[20]

One of the men to die during this desperate fighting was Samuel Parker of the 2nd Minnesota. Samuel's brother, Albert, wrote that "[Samuel] died charging bravely on the enemy, from a bayonet wound in the left groin, which passed through his kidneys."[21] Such close-quarter fighting could not last long, and after about thirty minutes the Confederates began to pull back from the fence. About this time the two artillery batteries sent by General Thomas to bolster the Union left arrived on the flank of the Confederates and opened fire. The guns caught many of the Confederates in the open. The Confederates fell back in the face of this heavy fire to the south edge of the field, where they took cover behind piles of fence rails and stacks of hay and kept up a steady fire.

While the this action was taking place east of the road, the 9th Ohio Infantry arrived to reinforce the 10th Indiana on the west side. The Union right was now stablized. Observing the hard fighting on the Union left, General Thomas sent the left wing of the 10th Indiana to the far left to reinforce the 4th Kentucky and 2nd Minnesota. After the Hoosiers helped repel the attack, they countermarched and rejoined the right wing on the west side of the road.

By this time the Confederate advance had ground to a halt. The failure of Crittenden's men to press the attack was due in large part to the new percussion muskets carried by the Union infantry; the Confederates were mostly armed with obsolete flintlocks, weapons rendered nearly useless by the rain. James L. Cooper of the 20th Tennessee recalled: "the rain was descending in torrents and our flintlock muskets were in bad condition; not one in three would fire. . . Mine went off once during the action, and although I wiped the 'pan' and primed a dozen times it would do so no more."[22] In his after-action report, General Carroll wrote that "during the engagement I saw a number of men walking deliberately away from the field of action for no other reason that their guns were wholly useless."[23] Unreliable weaponry, coupled with the fact that the two regiments sent to support the advance could not fire for fear of hitting their comrades and thereupon withdrew, doomed the Confederate advance.

With his lines secure and reinforcements reaching the field, General Thomas at about 9:00 a.m. ordered the Union army to attack all along the line. The Union attack west of the road was led by the 9th Ohio, a regiment of German-speaking soldiers from Cincinnati. Made up of many veterans from the German revolutions of 1848, the 9th Ohio was the only Union regiment that could boast of battle experience. After ordering the men to fix bayonets, Maj. Gustav Kammerling led the 9th Ohio forward in one of the few successful bayonet charges of the war, yelling: "If it gets too hot for you, shut your eyes my boys—Forward!"[24]

Already demoralized by the death of their leader and their inability to use their muskets, the entire Confederate left broke and ran before the Union bayonet charge reached their lines. Simultaneously, the 12th Kentucky Infantry and 1st and 2nd Tennessee Infantry (Union) launched a flank attack on the Confederate right. Surrounded on three sides and in

The Battle of Mill Springs

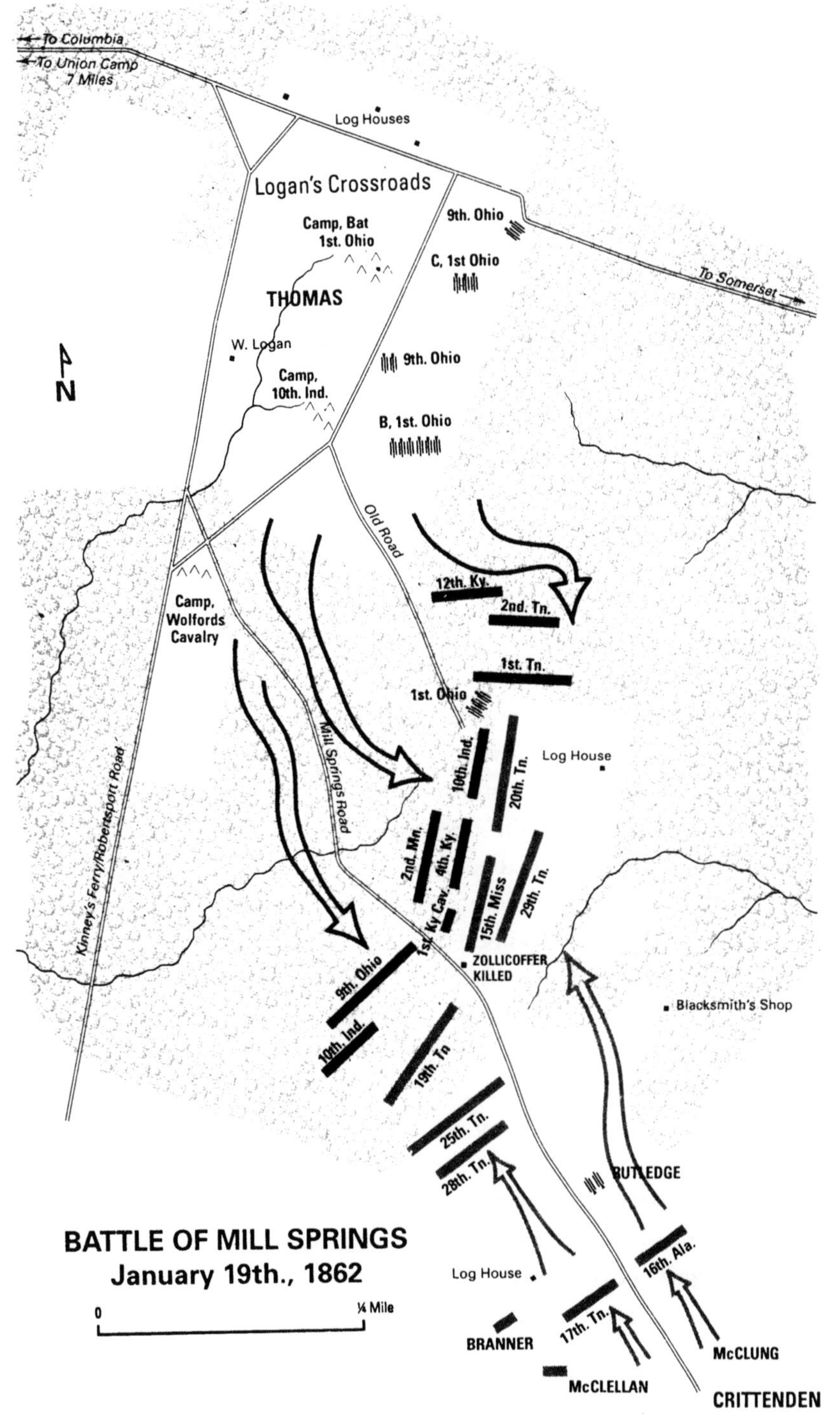

danger of being cut off, the 15th Mississippi and 20th Tennessee broke and retreated in confusion. Lt. Bailie Peyton Jr. of Company A, 20th Tennessee, tried to rally his men. Unsuccessful, Peyton found himself alone and in front of the advancing Union line. Capt. Judson Bishop of the 2nd Minnesota remembered Peyton: "One Lieutenant, as the firing ceased, stood a few paces in front of Company I of the Second, and calmly faced his fate. His men had disappeared and he was called upon to surrender. He made no reply, but raising his revolver fired into our ranks with deliberate aim, shooting Lieutenant Strout through the body. Further parley was useless, and he was shot dead were he stood."[25] Although Lt. Tenbroeck Strout survived the wound, the bullet was lodged so close to his spine that it could not be removed. The ball finally took Strout's life in 1880 when he died from lead poisoning. The lifeless body of Bailie Peyton, Jr. was carried from the field and returned to his father, a well known Unionist from Nashville, Tennessee. It was recorded that the senior Peyton expressed deep sorrow that his son had died a rebel, but he was comforted by the fact he had not died a coward.

With most of his force routed and retreating from the field, General Crittenden ordered the balance of Carroll's Second Brigade—the 17th Tennessee, 16th Alabama, and McClung's Battery—forward to save the Confederate army from destruction. The Tennesseans moved forward down the front slope of the hill on the west side of the road, while the Alabamians advanced on the east side. The troops offered a brief but desperate stand, holding the oncoming Union troops at bay long enough for the routed Confederate units to escape down the road toward the Confederate camp. Outnumbered, alone, and hard-pressed, Carroll's men retreated in confusion from the field, following the rest of the Confederates back to Beech Grove. The Battle of Mill Springs was over.

With his own forces disorganized and many units running low on ammunition, General Thomas did not immediately pursue the beaten Confederates. Only after being issued ammunition and with the arrival of all of Schoepf's force from Somerset did the Union army move in pursuit. A reporter from the *Cincinnati Commercial* noted that the road to Beech Grove "was strewn with abandoned paraphernalia including, guns, blankets, coats, haversacks and everything else that impeded flight."[26] Slowed by muddy roads and occasional stands made by

Confederate cavalry covering the retreat, the pursuing Union troops did not arrive in front of the Confederate entrenchments until dusk. With darkness fast approaching, Thomas decided to rest his men and assault the camp at daylight. Thomas deployed his artillery on three hills overlooking the Confederate camp with orders to shell it all night.

Most of the beaten Confederates had staggered back to their camps by about 3:00 p.m., well in advance of their pursuing enemy. General Crittenden rallied his regiments as fast as possible and deployed them in the fortifications to meet an expected Union assault. A meeting with his officers convinced Crittenden to recross the river under cover of darkness. In what in retrospect seems like a "Dunkirk-style" operation, the little steamboat *Nobel Ellis* worked throughout the night carrying demoralized and panic-stricken soldiers to safety on the south bank. Several times that night the Union artillery opened up on the little boat. Fortunately for the fleeing Confederates, the Union cannoneers were unable to hit their target. Due to the need for haste and lack of means of crossing the river, the Confederates were compelled to abandon everything except what they could carry. Even with this sacrifice, the *Nobel Ellis* did not leave the north bank with its final load until daybreak, January 20, 1862. Its duty completed, the Confederates set fire to the boat to prevent its capture.

As the last Confederates were arriving on the south bank of the Cumberland River, Thomas's soldiers were moving forward to attack Beech Grove. Instead of a battle, however, the Unionists found the Confederate camp abandoned. Equipment was strewn about everywhere, and numerous guns, provisions, regimental flags, and ammunition had also been left behind. On the north river bank, at the ferry crossing, the Union soldiers found horses with saddles still on them, horses hitched to wagons, all of the Confederate artillery, and numerous wounded soldiers, all waiting their turn to be ferried across the river. The Confederate winter cabins at Beech Grove held unfinished letters left on camp tables with pen and ink bottles in place, warm meals sitting on the tables, and a treasure-trove of other personal items. James Baker of the 1st Ohio Light Artillery wrote: "I have heard of soldiers plundering an enemy camp, but now I know what it means. . . . We have taken some of the nicest clothing I ever saw, broadcloth coats worth from five to twenty dollars apiece. I got a satin vest worth five dollars, a shirt worth a dollar and a half, a silver handled stiletto, besides a number of other things."[27]

As one portion of Thomas's army was plundering the Confederate camps, another was engaged in collecting the wounded and interring the dead on the battlefield. A northern newspaper reporter described the horrific scene:

> In the woods and along the roads the scene was dreadful. One body was placed in sitting posture with his back leaning against a tree, the hands crossed in his lap and his lips slightly parted. The ball had entered his left breast just above the region of the heart. Another laid on his side with his head and arms thrown back: the ball had cut away part of his skull over his left eye. . . Another man had a ball through his right hand, breaking two bones. He had done it up himself with a wet bandage, and with his other hand he was carrying one corner of a stretcher with a wounded man. Carrying another corner of the same stretcher, was a man with his face covered in blood. . . A large number of the dead were shot in the head. One was shot directly in the eye and the brain was oozing from the wound. . . One Rebel had a ball through his neck which destroyed the power of speech. . . Several of the dead were old and grey-headed men. A dark complexioned man with a heavy black beard was lying on the ground with a broken thigh. . . An elderly man sat with his back against a stump, with a ball directly through the center of his head at the base of the brain. There was a ghastly grin upon his countenance—his eyes were stretched widely open and staring wildly into vacancy, while his breath was rapid, deep, and heavy. His was a living death, death for he was senseless. . . In these fields of suffering, the freshness of death seemed to fill the whole atmosphere.[28]

The Union dead were taken back to their camps at Logan's Crossroads. They were buried in individual graves, identified by wooden markers bearing the fallen soldier's name and unit. With the exceptions of the bodies of General Zollicoffer and Lieutenant Bailie Peyton, the bodies of the Confederates were buried in shallow mass graves around the battlefield near were they fell in battle. Zollicoffer's body had been discovered by advancing Union troops even before the battle was over. After removing the body from the road and placing it under a nearby tree, the Union soldiers began to take souvenirs from it. Cutting buttons and pieces of cloth from Zollicoffer's uniform, some even yanked hair from his head as mementos. Learning of these deprivations, General Thomas ordered a guard posted over the corpse and later had it brought into camp and embalmed before sending it back through the lines.

A few days after the battle, both commanders reported their casualties. According to General Thomas, his command suffered 39 killed and 207 wounded, while his counterpart, General Crittenden, reported 125 killed, 309 wounded, and 95 captured or missing. Both men underestimated their losses. Recent research puts the Union killed at 55, and the Confederate dead at 148.

After clearing the battlefield of wounded and dead and removing all the abandoned equipment from the Confederate camp, General Thomas sent a portion of his army under General Schoepf to pursue the retreating Confederates south of the river. The weather and bad roads cut short the pursuit and Schoepf returned after only following the Confederates as far as Monticello, Kentucky. In order to prevent the use of the area by Confederate forces should they return, Thomas ordered the 19th Kentucky Infantry to destroy the fortifications and burn the cabins at Beech Grove, while he and the bulk of his army moved to Somerset. Unable to move into East Tennessee because of the weather and bad roads, Thomas and his army returned to Lebanon and from there moved west to take part in other operations.

During the time the Union army was looting the Beech Grove camp and burying the dead, Crittenden's Confederates were retreating south into Tennessee. Having left most of their equipment and provisions behind in their crossing of the river, the Southerners suffered greatly during the retreat. Colonel Woods of the 16th Alabama described the retreating force: "The army as it stretched along the road looked like a great funeral procession, and indeed it was for a great many poor fellow who, exhausted and crazed, fell by the wayside and perished."[29] On January 26, 1862, Crittenden's weary and hungry army arrived at Gainsboro, Tennessee, where it received much needed supplies. By February 17, General Crittenden reported his men ready for duty again. Many of his regiments would see their next action at Battle of Shiloh, and some would come back to Kentucky in the fall of 1862 and fight at Perryville.

News of the Battle of Mill Springs created extraordinary excitement in both the North and the South. The Union had its first significant victory of the war. Eastern Kentucky was now firmly in Union hands and East Tennessee was open for Union invasion (although the Union army would be unable to take advantage of the situation until the fall of 1863). Newspapers throughout the North declared the battle a brilliant victory, and Thomas and his army received a personal thanks from President Lincoln. Thomas's long service to the Union would include a dogged defensive stand at Chickamauga that saved the Army of the Cumberland, a feat which earned him the nickname, "The Rock of Chickamauga."

The defeat at Mill Springs, coupled with the subsequent losses the following month of Forts Henry and Donelson, forced the Confederates to evacuate Kentucky and much of central Tennessee, including Nashville. Triggered by the Mill Springs fiasco, this series of setbacks ultimately led to the Battle of Shiloh. Public opinion targeted Generals Crittenden and Carroll as scapegoats for the disaster at Mill Springs. While Zollicoffer was given a hero's funeral on February 2 in Nashville, Crittenden and Carroll were charged with being drunk during the battle. Although these charges were never proven, both men were ultimately stripped of command and faded from the pages of the war.

While the Battle of Mill Springs had a important effect on the war's strategic situation in the west, it also had long-lasting effects on the citizens of Kentucky and the area known as Logan's Crossroads. The retreat of the Confederate troops from Kentucky allowed the pro-Union groups to consolidate their power and ensure that Kentucky would remain in the Union. This show of power—and the string of Confederate defeats in the west—convinced most undecided Kentuckians that the South could not regain Kentucky or win the war. Kentucky would never be the source of manpower and support the South had hoped it would be.

The impact of the battle on the citizens of Logan's Crossroads was dramatic and personal. Local families hid in caves or at nearby homes of friends and family while the battle raged around them; none actually witnessed the battle. However, when they returned they found their homes full of wounded and dying soldiers, and scores of bodies in need of burial.

One story forms a fitting footnote to the battle. The Confederate dead had been buried by Union soldiers in mass graves on the field. Unfortunately, the burial pits were so shallow that the bodies began surfacing within a few days. The armies were long gone, so the gruesome task of reinterring the bodies was left to the local citizens. One man decided to make his three sons, Van, The' and Silas, help bury the soldiers in order to let them experience the brutality of war up close and personal. Silas, who was only ten at the time, left an account of his efforts:

> After the battle nobody knew what to do; the bodies were all covered with ice and everyone was running around crying. Father hitched the mules up to a dirt scoop and dug three long trenches to place the bodies in. The bodies were frozen to the ground and we had to take shovels and pry them from the ground. . . We stacked the bodies in the wagon like firewood, legs, hands, and arms were in odd postures and some bodies did not have all of their parts. The bodies were then placed in the trenches and covered.[30]

Silas and his brothers would have nightmares for years. The experience affected the family so deeply they eventually moved from the area. It was too late for Van, however. Haunted by the ghastly images he had seen, Van went insane and killed his brother The'. He spent the rest of his life in an insane asylum in Danville, Kentucky, as much a casualty of the battle as any soldier who fell on the field.

* * *

The Opposing Forces at Mill Springs

(Also known as Logan's Cross Roads and Fishing Creek[31])

January 19, 1862

UNION

Brig. Gen. George H. Thomas

Second Brigade, Col. Mahlon D. Manson
10th Ind., Lt. Col. William C. Kise
4th Ky., Col. Speed S. Fry (w)
10th Ky., Col. John M. Harlan
14th Ohio, Col. James B. Steedman
Brigade loss: k, 19; w, 127 = 146
(The two latter regiments were engaged only in the pursuit of the enemy.)

Third Brigade, Col. Robert L. McCook (w)
2d Minn., Col. Horatio P. Van Cleve
9th Ohio, Major Gustave Kammerling
Brigade loss: k, 18; w, 61 = 79

Twelfth Brigade, Acting Brig. Gen. Samuel P. Carter
12th Ky., Col. William A. Hoskins
1st Tennessee, Col. Robert K. Byrd
2d Tennessee, Col., J.P.T. Carter
1st Ky. Cavalry, Col. Frank Wolford
Brigade loss: k, 3; w, 19; m, 15 = 37

Artillery:
Battery B, 1st Ohio, Capt. Dennis Kenny, Jr.
9th Ohio Battery, Capt. Henry S. Wetmore

Camp Guard:
Michigan Engineers and Mechanics
Companies D, F, and K, Lieut. Col. K. A. Hunton
38th Ohio, Company A, Capt. Charles Greenwood

Brig. Gen. Albin Schoepf joined Thomas on the evening of the battle, after the fighting had ceased, with the 17th, 31st, and 38th Ohio.

The total Union loss was killed, 40; wounded, 204; and captured or missing, 15 = 259

CONFEDERATES

Maj. Gen. George B. Crittenden

First Brigade, Brig. Gen. Felix K. Zollicoffer (k), Col. D. H. Cummings
15th Miss., Lieut. Col. E. C. Walthall
19th Tenn., Col. D.H. Cummings, Lieut. Col. Francis M. Walker
20th Tenn., Col. Joel A. Battle
25th Tenn., Col. S. S. Stanton (w)
Tenn. Battery, Capt. A. M. Rutledge
Independent Co. Tenn. Cav., Capt. W. S. Bledsoe
Independent Co. Tenn. Cav., Capt. T. C. Sanders
Brigade loss: k, 98; w, 265; m, 66 = 429

Second Brigade, Brig. Gen. Wm. H. Carroll
16th Ala., Col. Wm. B. Wood
17th Tenn., Lieut. Col. T.C.H. Miller
28th Tenn., Col. J.P. Murray
29th Tenn., Col. Saml. Powell (w), Major Horace Rice
Tenn. Battery (2 guns), Capt. Hugh L.W. McClung
4th Battalion Tenn. Cav., Lieut. Col. B.M. Branner
Brigade loss: k, 28; w, 46; m, 29 = 103

Reserve:
5th Battalion Tenn. Cav., Lieut. Col. George R. McClellan

The total Confederate loss was killed, 125; wounded, 309; and captured or missing, 99 = 533

NOTES

1. Letter of Abraham Lincoln to Orville H. Browning, September 22, 1862, Roy P. Basler, *et al.*, eds., *The Collected Works of Abraham Lincoln*, 9 Vols. (New Brunswick, N.J., 1953-55) 4:535.

2. Raymond E. Myers, *The Zollie Tree* (Louisville, Ky., 1964), 60.

3. *The War of the Rebellion : A Compilation of the Official Records of the Union and Confederate Armies*, 128 vols. (Washington, D.C., 1880-1901) (hereinafter cited as *O.R.*) (all citations are to Series I), 7:686-687.

4. *Ibid.,* 787.

5. *Ibid.*

6. *Ibid.,* 475.

7. *Ibid.,* 487.

8. *Ibid.,* 10.

9. *Ibid.,* 753.

10. *Ibid.,* 536-537.

11. Zollicoffer's Order Book", Museum of the Confederacy Collections, Richmond, Va.

12. Judson W. Bishop, *The Story of a Regiment, Being a Narrative of the of the Second Regiment Minnesota Veteran Volunteer Infantry* (St. Paul, Minn., 1890), 34.

13. W. J. Worsham, *The Old Nineteenth Tennessee Regiment, CSA, 1861-1865* (Knoxville, Tenn., 1902), 36.

14. James R. Binford, "Recollections of the 15th Mississippi Infantry, CSA," Henry Patrick Papers, Mississippi Dept. of Archives and History Collections, Z, 215, vol. 5.

15. *O.R.*, 7:90 .

16. *Binford,* "Recollections of the 15th Mississippi Infantry, C.S.A.", 16.

17. *O.R.*, 7:87.

18. J. H. Battle, W.H. Perrine, and G.C. Kniffin, *Kentucky: a History of the State* (Louisville, Ky., 1885), 393.

19. *Binford,* "Recollections of the 15th Mississippi Infantry, C.S.A.", 17.

20. St. Paul *Pioneer and Democrat*, Feb. 2, 1862.

21. Minnesota *State News*, Feb. 1, 1862.

22. William Alderson, ed., "The Civil War Diary of Captain James Litton Cooper, September 30, 1861, to January, 1865," *Tennessee Historical Quarterly*, 15 (June, 1956), 146.

23. *O.R.*, 7:114.

24. Constantin Grebner, *"We Were The Ninth" A History of the Ninth Regiment, Ohio Volunteer Infantry April 17 1861, to June 7, 1864,* trans. and ed. Frederic Trautman (Kent, Ohio, 1987), 84.

25. Judson W. Bishop, *The Mill Springs Campaign* (St. Paul, Minn., 1890), 67.

26. *Cincinnati Commercial*, Jan. 20, 1862.

27. Letter of James Baker to Father, *History of Newago Co Michigan, Civil War Veterans*, (no publisher, no date), 80 .

28. E. G. Squire, ed., *Frank Leslies Pictorial History of the War of 1861* (New York, N.Y., 1880), 275.

29. James E. Saunders, *Early Settlers of Alabama* (New Orleans, La., 1899), 192.

30. Gray & Pape, Inc., *Preservation Plan for the Mill Springs Battlefield, Wayne and Pulaski Counties, Kentucky* (Cincinnati, Ohio, 1997), 47.

31. Robert Underwood Johnson and Clarence Clough Buel, eds., *Battles and Leaders of the Civil War*, 4 vols. (New York, N.Y., 1887), 1:392.

Lowell H. Harrison

The Government of Confederate Kentucky

Although the summer elections in 1861 showed strong Unionist sentiment in the state, a sizeable minority of Kentuckians were pro-Confederate. With sentiment so divided, the state's decision to declare its neutrality during the early days of the war made sense, although from a constitutional viewpoint a state had no more right to declare neutrality than it had to secede. President Abraham Lincoln recognized the importance of his native state in the developing struggle. "I think to lose Kentucky is nearly the same as to lose the whole game," he wrote Orville Browning. "Kentucky gone, we cannot hold Missouri, nor, as I think, Maryland. These all against us, and the job on our hands is too large for us. We would as well consent to a separation at once, including the surrender of the capital."[1]

Kentucky was relatively a larger and more important state in the 1860s than she has been during the twentieth century. Neutrality was supported by the Unionists as a means of preventing the calling of a secession convention and of allowing time for the Unionists to consolidate their strength. The summer elections for members of the Federal House of Representatives and the members of the General Assembly demonstrated their success. By late summer the pro-Confederates were the main advocates of neutrality; it might keep Kentucky from throwing its strength behind the Union. That forlorn hope ended in early September when Confederate forces occupied Columbus and other towns in the southern part of the state and Union troops poured into the northern part of the state.[2]

Some impatient Confederates had already left the state to join the Confederate States of America, and Camp Boone in northern Tennessee had received a substantial number of Kentucky volunteers. The number of exiles increased as neutrality ended, and such prominent pro-Confederates as the recent Vice-President John C. Breckinridge hastened southward to avoid arrest. The Kentucky military and civilian exiles, embarrassed by their state's decision to remain in the Union, sought some way to rectify that mistake. Missouri Confederates had organized a state government when Missouri had remained loyal to the United States, and that government seemed likely to be admitted into the Confederacy. Why couldn't pro-Confederate Kentuckians follow the same path?

Such Southern theorists as John C. Calhoun had formulated a theory and procedure by which they claimed a state could exercise its sovereign powers and nullify an act of the Federal government or even secede from the Union. One of the first comprehensive statements of that theory had been in the Kentucky Resolutions of 1798 and the Kentucky Resolution of 1799. The theory held that such a momentous decision was too important to be left to a legislature whose members might have been elected earlier when other issues were more important. The role of the legislature was to call for a convention whose members would be elected on that specific issue. Such delegates represented the sovereign will of the people—which in effect meant all white males old enough to vote. There was some disagreement as to whether the vote of the convention was final or whether it should be ratified by the voters in a special election.

The August 5 election for the Kentucky General Assembly resulted in Unionist majorities of 76-24 in the House and 27-11 in the Senate. Thereafter, Gov. Beriah Magoffin's vetoes were routinely overridden. Obviously, the Frankfort legislature that had consistently refused to call a convention could not now be expected to do so. While information is lacking for the origins of the movement to create a Confederate government of Kentucky, John C. Breckinridge and George Washington Johnson were among the leaders. In an "Address to the People of Kentucky" on October 8, 1861, Breckinridge declared flatly that "The United States no longer exists. The Union is dissolved." The states had

Governor George W. Johnson. A native of Scott County, Kentucky, Johnson was a lawyer, farmer and legislator before the war. Chosen governor of Confederate Kentucky, Johnson was mortally wounded in the Battle of Shiloh while serving as a private soldier. *Kentucky Historical Society*

reserved to themselves all powers not delegated to the Federal government, and they certainly had not delegated to it the power to destroy the states as it was attempting to do. "In the wreck of the Federal system, she [Kentucky] exists as an independent Commonwealth, with the right to choose her own destiny." Like many others, Breckinridge decided "to resist the invaders who have driven us from our homes." To defend their sacred rights, "I exchange, with proud satisfaction, a term of six years in the Senate of the United States for the musket of a soldier."[3] Less than a month later, on November 2, 1861, Breckinridge was commissioned a brigadier general in the Confederate army.

George Washington Johnson shared Breckinridge's beliefs. A wealthy Scott County farmer who also owned a large Arkansas cotton plantation, he was a devout believer in state's rights. As the sectional controversy intensified, Johnson saw the Union he loved being destroyed by such radical groups as the new Republican party. When every effort at compromise failed, he argued that Kentucky should secede and join the Confederacy. She would probably be joined by one or more of the other slave states still in the Union, and that would create such an equal balance of power between the sections that both sides would avoid war. His fifty years and a crippled arm seemed to preclude military service, but Johnson fled the state to avoid arrest. When Kentucky's neutrality ended and Confederate troops moved into the southern part of the state, Johnson came to Bowling Green as a volunteer aide to Brig. Gen. Simon B. Buckner.[4]

Breckinridge, Johnson and like-minded Kentuckians decided that a Confederate government of Kentucky would rally support for the Southern cause and give a cloak of legitimacy to their efforts. General Albert Sidney Johnston, commander of the far-flung Confederate Military Department No. 2, was skeptical of their plan. His son and biographer wrote that his father realized from the outset that he might not be able to hold Kentucky, and he foresaw the dangers and difficulties that would confront Kentuckians who had declared for such a government if the Confederate army had to withdraw from the state. He also saw problems with such a state government if it was forced into exile.[5] But Johnston could not voice such doubts openly, and the planners of a Confederate government of Kentucky proceeded with their scheme.

A planning conference held in Odd Fellows Hall in Russellville on October 29-30, 1861, attracted some 63 delegates from 34 counties. Most of them attended because of their interest in the proposal, not as a result of elections. Henry Cornelius Burnett (Trigg County) was elected chairman, and George W. Johnson introduced resolutions that directed the convention's work. This convention made two major decisions. Denying the authority of the Frankfort government, it affirmed that the people had "an inalienable and indefeasible right to alter, reform, or abolish their government, in such manner as they may think proper." Then, because Governor Magoffin could not call a legislative session free of Federal dominance to provide for a sovereignty convention, they called for a convention to meet in Russellville on November 18. Its purpose would be the passage of an ordinance "severing forever our connections with the Federal government, and to adopt such measures, either by the adoption of a provisional government or otherwise, as in their judgment will give full and ample protection to the citizens in their persons and property, and secure to them the blessings of constitutional government." A ten-man committee, which included Breckinridge and Johnson, was appointed to implement the resolutions.[6]

The 216 delegates from 61 counties who attended the November convention forced a move into larger facilities at the Baptist-sponsored Bethel College that had closed in the spring of 1861 because of the war.[7] Some elections of delegates had taken place, perhaps in military units that had strong representation from a county. George Johnson presented a plan for action, presumably the work of the planning committee established in October, and he was made chairman of a ten-man committee to report business for the convention to consider. Again, the recourse of the delegates was to the fundamental right of revolution possessed by all mankind, "against perfidious and despotic government." (Of course this right of revolution did not apply to slaves.)

That evening the delegates jumped the gun by approving the organization of a provisional government without waiting for the committee to report. Dissension developed on the morning of November 19 when H. C. Burnett, reporting for a majority of the committee on business, moved that the creation of a provisional government be postponed until January 8, 1862, when the convention would reconvene. The incomplete convention record does not indicate why some members wanted to postpone action. They may have hoped that some miraculous solution would be found to the nation's crisis during the next several weeks. Some members, troubled by their largely self-constituted membership, may have wanted time to secure a more representative membership.

The minority report from the committee called for the presentation of a plan for a provisional government at the morning session on November 20. Spirited debate was cut off by a motion for the previous question, but then another debate broke out over how the vote was to be cast. The convention had not established a procedure for voting: should it be by individuals or by representative districts? Their decision was to use representative districts, and the minority report calling for immediate secession was approved unanimously, although many delegates wanted to wait until January.[8]

Thus on November 20, 1861 the Russellville Convention declared Kentucky absolved from allegiance to the United States. The committee also presented the draft of a short constitution establishing a provisional government until such time as a permanent one could be set up after a free election. This provisional government would seek admission into the Confederate States of America on an equal basis with its existing members. The plan called for a governor and a council of ten members, one from each of the Congressional districts in 1860. Necessary officials were to be appointed by the governor with the consent of the council. Only an auditor and treasurer were specified in the constitution. The governor's salary was set at $2,000 per year.

All members of the government were required to take this oath: "I, [name], do solemnly swear (or affirm) in the presence of Almighty God and upon my honor that I will observe and obey all laws passed by the Provisional Government of Kentucky, so help me God." Bowling Green was designated as the state capital, but with admirable foresight the constitution added that "the Governor and Council shall have power to meet at any other place that they may consider appropriate." As soon as the constitution was adopted the convention elected George Johnson governor and the ten members of the council. Three commissioners were appointed to seek admission into the Confederacy: William Preston (Louisville), W. E. Simms (Bourbon County), and Henry C. Burnett (Trigg County). For some unexplained reason, Dr. Luke P. Blackburn of Mississippi (a Kentuckian until he moved south in 1846) was invited to accompany the commissioners to Richmond. Before adjourning, the delegates signed the document that they had adopted.[9]

Some difficulties were encountered in filling the posts in the new government. Such prospects as John C. Breckinridge and Humphrey Marshall had accepted Confederate commissions, and Richard Hawes rejected the auditor's position to become a brigade commissary in Marshall's command.[10] Robert McKee, a journalist who had been secretary of both conventions, became secretary of state, and Theodore Legrand Burnett became the first secretary of the treasury. Burnett resigned on December 17 when he was elected to the Confederate Provisional Congress and was replaced by John Quincy Burnam of Warren County. Another Warren Countian, Josiah Pillsbury, became auditor when Hawes refused the post.[11]

Johnson was a popular choice for governor. Born in Scott County in 1811, he had earned three degrees from Transylvania University but soon abandoned a legal practice in favor of the life of a farmer-planter. He refused public office after three elections (1838, 1839 and 1840) to the state House of Representatives, but retained an intense interest in public affairs. Johnson headed the Committee of Sixty that seized Cassius M. Clay's *True American* press in Lexington in 1845. Johnson saw slavery as a state issue with which the Federal government had no right to interfere. He opposed secession when Lincoln was elected, for the Republicans could not have a majority in Congress for at least two years, and a compromise might be reached before then. Johnson, who asserted that a state could not be held in the Union against its will, worked diligently to maintain Kentucky's neutrality during the summer of 1861. "I have been run nearly to death," he wrote his wife Ann from Louisville on July 9, 1861. He was preparing to go to Richmond, Virginia, to secure President Jefferson Davis's assurance that the Confederacy would respect Kentucky's neutrality. His hopes for a peaceful settlement faded after the Union victories in the summer elections and the failure of a Peace Convention in Frankfort on September 10. Johnson fled southward to avoid arrest, then made his way to Bowling Green. He resigned as volunteer aide to General Buckner when he was elected governor, and moved to another house to show the separation between the civilian state government and the Confederate military establishment.[12]

In truth, the Kentucky Confederate government had power only within the Confederate lines in the southern part of the state, and many of the people within that area were Unionists who resisted the government as far as they dared. In an address to the people of Kentucky issued on November 26, Johnson blamed abolitionists for disrupting the Union and predicted that it could never be restored. His permanent solution was the existence of two nations bonded by free trade. He would be glad to relinquish his position as governor to Beriah Magoffin, the governor in Frankfort, if Magoffin could escape from virtual imprisonment.[13]

Although Magoffin was pro-Confederate, he denounced the "self-constituted" Russellville Conventions and their product; their actions simply did not represent the will of the majority of Kentuckians. Joint resolutions of the General Assembly also denounced the "effort to subvert and overturn the civil government of the State, and substitute a military despotism in its stead, by an insignificant and factious minority in opposition to the often expressed and well known will of an overwhelming majority of its citizens."[14]

The day after he became governor, Johnson wrote President Davis about Kentucky's desire to join the Confederacy. Because the Kentuckians had not been allowed to express their desires through a convention, they had had to appeal to the inalienable right "to destroy any government whose existence is incompatible with the interests and liberty of society. . . . There is no incompatibility between the right of secession by a State and the ultimate right of revolution by the people," Johnson argued. "The one is a civil right, founded upon the Constitution; the other is a natural right, resting upon the law of God." Surely, the Confederate States of America would not reject their plea for admission. "We come to you now, when it is honorable to do so, to offer you our assistance in a common cause while peril surrounds us both and to share with you a common destiny."[15]

President Davis was troubled by the request, for the Kentucky procedure was irregular when measured against the careful procedures followed by the Confederate states. But the admission of a Confederate State of Missouri earlier in November had set a precedent, and the addition of Kentucky to the Confederate cause could be of great value. Davis may also have had some sentimental attachment to the state of his birth in which he received much of his education before entering West Point. He recommended Kentucky's admission into the Confederacy on November 25 with the statement that "there is enough of merit in the application to warrant a disregard of its irregularity."[16] Some members of Congress shared the president's doubts, but they also saw the potential value of having Kentucky in their confederation. On December 10, 1861 the Confederate Congress enacted "That the State of Kentucky be, and is hereby, admitted a member of the Confederate States of America, on an equal footing with the other States of this Confederacy."[17]

The pertinent question, however, was how effective would this provisional government be? The council had its first meeting in Bowling Green on Thursday, November 21 with six members present. Willis B. Machen from the First District was elected president. The usual procedure was for a morning session beginning at ten o'clock with an afternoon session on about half the days. Night sessions were held occasionally. The council used the usual legislative procedures despite its small size, and several standing committees were established.[18]

This government soon had differences with the Richmond government over the status of Kentuckians who joined the Confederate army. On December 4, 1861, the council authorized the raising of twenty companies of volunteer infantry for at least one year's service. The results were disappointing. Most young men preferred the cavalry, and many of them expected to start as captains. The Confederate authorities wanted a national army, not separate state forces. On February 3, 1862, Secretary of War Judah P. Benjamin called upon each state to supply troops equal to 6% of its 1860 white population. Kentucky should supply 46,000 men who would serve for three years or the duration of the war. "Under the peculiar circumstances in which Kentucky is placed and the difficulties which embarrass her authorities, I cannot hope that you will be able at present to meet this call," Benjamin admitted, but he predicted that "but a short period will elapse ere the soil of Kentucky will be freed from the oppression of the invader."[19] The provisional government was in exile before anything could be done to meet the demand, and the number of Kentuckians who fought for the Confederacy was less than the assigned quota.

Finances were also a major problem. Even loyal Confederates avoided taxes if they could. Only limited public monies could be found and General Johnston was careful to avoid interference with private funds. The provisional government hoped to use the $1,000,000 voted by the Confederate Congress in August, 1861, to support the Confederate cause in Kentucky, but President Davis ruled that the money could not be used once Kentucky became a member of the Confederacy. Instead, in January, 1862 the Congress appropriated $2,000,000 in treasury notes to support the Kentucky provisional government, its expenditure being subject to the president's approval.[20]

One act of the council attempted to meet the shortages of both money and guns. White males aged 18 to 45 who did not volunteer for military service were required to turn in a gun to a county officer. A man who had no gun and had taxable property worth $500 had to pay $20 or be fined $50. The pacifist Shakers at South Union who were trying to maintain a neutral stance sent their only two guns to Russellville. They were allowed to retain "the most indifferent one."[21]

On December 14 the council provided for the election of ten representatives to the provisional one house Congress. They had short terms, for the provisional Congress ended on February 17, 1862, and the initial session of the First Confederate Congress met the next day. In the two-house Congress Kentucky had two senators and twelve representatives, based on one for each 50,000 inhabitants counted in the 1860 census. Election day—the first Wednesday in November—had passed before the provisional Kentucky government was formed, so the governor and council scheduled an election for January 22, 1862. Because of "obvious difficulties" voters were allowed to vote a general ticket for all positions and to vote in any Kentucky county in which they were on election day. The soldier vote was probably larger than the civilian total.[22]

The provisional government also made a number of appointments to minor offices vacated as the Confederate forces entered the state. Such changes created some postwar problems. For example, would a marriage performed by a Confederate justice of the peace be valid after the war? (In 1865 the Kentucky attorney-general ruled that such marriages were legal.) Wayne County became Zollicoffer County to honor the Confederate general who had died at Mill Springs on January 19, 1862. The work of the provisional government was frustrated by the failure of the Confederate troops to continue their initial advance and the Unionism of the majority of Kentuckians.

Governor Johnson sorely missed his family, although he occasionally saw his son Madison (Matty) who was riding with John Hunt Morgan in his forays along the Green River. But Johnson remained true to the cause to which he had committed himself. "Never will I submit or compromise the question," he wrote Ann on January 23, 1862.[23] But by then the tenure of the government in Kentucky was coming to an end. The fall of Fort Henry on the Tennessee River on February 6, 1862 and the impending Union attack on Fort Donelson on the Cumberland River made the Confederate army's position in Kentucky untenable. General Johnston had long been aware of the weakness of his Kentucky front, and realized that his stay in the state might be brief. Still, he accepted the state government that was formed and cooperated with it. On February 8, after consulting with Gens. P. G. T. Beauregard and William J. Hardee, Johnston decided that he would have to withdraw south of the Tennessee River before giving battle. The Confederate evacuation of Bowling Green and the surrounding area began on February 11. Despite miserable weather—South Union reported three inches of snow—most of the troops were in Nashville by February 15.[24]

Governor Johnson hoped that the defeats would arouse the South to make the effort necessary to achieve victory. He asked Ann if she would send their fifteen year old son Junius to him so that the lad could later feel that "he too did something in the field for our glorious revolution."[25]

The *New Orleans Picayune* of March 12, 1862, reported that the Provisional Government of Kentucky "were with Gen. Crittenden's brigade; the capital of Kentucky now being located in a Sibley tent, near the headquarters of that general." Governor Johnson concluded that the retreat from Kentucky was a strategic necessity that would be only temporary. His faith in General Johnston never faltered, and when it was rumored in March that Johnston proposed to give the command to General Beauregard, he wrote Johnston a vigorously worded protest: "We are in the right place, at the right time, and the proudest victory of the war awaits you, unless you commit suicide, by yielding up the command of your army when it most needs energy and an active head. *You must not do this*."[26]

Below the Tennessee River the Confederates turned on their enemy and on Sunday morning, April 6, 1862, achieved surprise when they attacked Gen. Ulysses S. Grant's army at Shiloh. On the first day Governor Johnson served as a volunteer aide to Gen. John C. Breckinridge, who commanded the Reserve Corps. When the First Kentucky Brigade became separated from Breckinridge, Johnson assisted Col. Robert P. Trabue. After his horse was killed under him, Johnson refused another mount and joined Capt. Ben Monroe's Company E of the Fourth Kentucky Infantry, CSA. "They are my friends and relatives," he explained, and wanted to share the battle with them. That night he was sworn in as a private in Company E.[27]

The next afternoon as the Confederates fought to halt the sweeping Union counterattack, Johnson was hit in the right thigh and abdomen by bullets. He suffered unattended on the bloody battlefield until the morning of April 8, when he was seen by a fellow Mason, Union Gen. Alexander McDowell McCook, commander of the Second Division of the Army of the Ohio. Johnson was treated on the hospital ship *Hannibal*, but the body wound proved fatal. The first Confederate governor of Kentucky died on April 9 without sending a message to Ann: "My wife knows how well I love her, and she needs no message." But in one of his last communications he tried to explain his motives for his participation in the war. "I wanted personal honor and political liberty and constitutional state government, and for these I drew the sword." Union friends sent his body, packed in salt, home to Kentucky, where even political foes mourned his death.[28]

The provisional constitution allowed the council to fill the vacancy, and it soon selected sixty-five year old Richard Hawes, a Virginia-born

Monument at the graves of Governor George W. Johnson and his wife in the Georgetown Cemetery, Georgetown, Kentucky. *Editor's Collection*

---

lawyer and businessman. Active in Whig politics, Hawes had served in both the General Assembly and Congress. As the Whig party dissolved in the 1850s, Hawes became a Democrat and supporter of John C. Breckinridge in 1860. Hawes saw his beloved Union being destroyed by Northern radicals and blamed the Republicans for starting the war. Active in the State's Rights party in Kentucky, he fled southward when neutrality ended in September 1861. Despite his age he was commissioned a major and assigned to Brig. Gen. Humphrey Marshall's

A rarely seen tintype of Governor Richard Hawes. A Bourbon County, Kentucky lawyer before the war, Hawes was named governor of Confederate Kentucky after the Battle of Shiloh. Sworn in on the State Capitol steps in front of a large crowd on October 4, 1862, during the invasion of Kentucky, Hawes fled a few hours later at the approach of Union troops. *Kentucky Historical Society*

command as a brigade commissary. Hawes was not present at the Russellville Conventions, and declined the office of auditor in the Provisional Government. Hawes proved to be a somewhat troublesome subordinate. Ignoring the army's chain of command, he sometimes wrote directly to Confederate authorities. In January, 1862, Governor Johnson requested him to come to Bowling Green, but a bout of typhoid fever delayed his departure. When he reached the council at Corinth, Mississippi, he took the oath of office on May 31, 1862, and became the second and last governor of Confederate Kentucky.[29]

In the absence of the official records of the exiled government after it left Kentucky, we know all too little about its operations during the rest of the war. By December 22, 1862, when Hawes requested "passports" from the secretary of war, several changes had occurred in the membership of the council. One must assume that changes probably continued to take place during the rest of the war. Hawes added to the burdens of President Davis by recommending Kentuckians for various military and civilian positions, many of them well above the entry level.[30]

The persistent hope of the exiles was to return to Kentucky. Their hope became brighter in the summer of 1862. On July 16, John Hunt Morgan wired General Kirby Smith from Georgetown: "I am here with a force sufficient to hold all the country outside Lexington and Frankfort. These places are garrisoned chiefly with Home Guards. . . . The whole country can be secured, and 25,000 or 30,000 men will join you at once."[31] Braxton Bragg, who had become head of the Army of the Mississippi as of June 27, 1862, wanted to move against Nashville, defeat the Union army in central Tennessee, then consider a move into Kentucky. To ensure success, he needed the cooperation of Maj. Gen. Edmund Kirby Smith who commanded the Department of East Tennessee. When they conferred in Chattanooga on August 1, Kirby Smith insisted that "our true policy" was "to strike at Kentucky." As long as their forces were not united, Kirby Smith, infected with the fatal Confederate desire for independent command, would not be under Bragg's direct supervision. Bragg allowed Kirby Smith to seize the initiative, and Smith moved out of Knoxville on August 14. Bypassing the strong Union force holding Cumberland Gap, he crossed into southeastern Kentucky. Smith wrote Bragg from Barbourville six days later that forage was so inadequate in that area that he must either return to Tennessee or advance toward Lexington. Because he believed a retreat would be "disastrous to our cause in Kentucky," Smith advanced into the Bluegrass.[32]

The council endorsed the invasion of Kentucky in a letter of August 18 to President Davis, and it sent H. C. Burnett to Richmond to urge the government to order John C. Breckinridge, Humphrey Marshall, and Simon B. Buckner back into their native state to encourage enlistments. On August 27 the council resolved that Governor Hawes should confer with President Davis about ways to expedite the establishment of a Confederate government in Kentucky that would raise military forces to help win the war. Hawes did confer with Davis, and they must have agreed then that the provisional government should follow the Confederate armies into Kentucky.[33]

Kirby Smith's incursion, however, created a problem for Bragg. Without Smith's men, Bragg was not strong enough to challenge Don Carlos Buell's Union army. If Bragg did not move, Kirby Smith might be trapped between Buell and the Union forces being assembled along the Ohio River. On August 27 Bragg's troops began moving from Chattanooga toward Sparta, Tennessee, where they would be between Buell and Kirby Smith. Thereafter Bragg advanced into Kentucky. Bypassing heavily fortified Bowling Green, he passed through Glasgow to Munfordville, where he halted to capture a Federal force of over 4,000 men.[34] Bragg apparently assumed that when the Confederate armies combined they would crush Buell as he retreated northward to protect his supply line. Some critics have contended that Bragg should have hastened to capture Louisville, an important river port and manufacturing center, before Buell could reach it. But Louisville was never Bragg's goal, and his delays at Sparta and Munfordville allowed Buell to catch up with him. Bragg tentatively offered battle at Munfordville, although Kirby Smith still had not joined him, but Buell slipped by and moved on to occupy Louisville, where the Kentucky government had fled. Once the immediate threat of battle with Buell passed, Bragg turned aside to the Bardstown area and dispersed his army to help alleviate his dwindling supply situation.

Using only part of his strength, Kirby Smith almost annihilated a poorly trained Union force of some 6,500 near Richmond on August 30.[35] He occupied Lexington on September 2 and Frankfort the following day—the only Union state capital captured by Confederates during the Civil War. The *Richmond* (Virginia) *Dispatch* of September 8 reported that "we think we may safely say that the day of Kentucky's deliverance from the hateful thrall of abolition despotism has brightly dawned."

Bragg was not as optimistic. The general was discouraged by the failure of Kentuckians to join the Confederate armies. The recruits were fewer than half the Confederate losses, and Bragg wrote Adjutant General Samuel Cooper on September 25 that "Unless a change occurs soon we must abandon the garden spot of Kentucky to its cupidity."[36] The best hope appeared to be to install the provisional government in Frankfort, then let it apply the conscription law that the Confederate Congress had enacted in April, 1862. Neglecting other responsibilities, Bragg and Kirby Smith met in Lexington on October 2. The next day they went by train to Frankfort for the elaborate ceremonies planned for the installation of Governor Hawes.

A considerable crowd braved rain on October 4 to observe the procession that Kirby Smith led to the capitol. Inside, the crowd overflowed the hall of the House of Representatives and the rotunda. Humphrey Marshall spoke, then Bragg introduced Hawes and promised to respect and protect the civil power of the state. Hawes spoke confidently of his plans as governor of the state. He promised to call a convention at the earliest possible moment to provide for a permanent government to replace the provisional one. "It is now a truth and a fact," he asserted, "that the late Union cannot be restored." Despite what the Unionists had claimed, the abolition of African slavery had become the purpose of the United States. Emancipation, he said "would be the most unmitigated curse which could be inflicted upon the slave race," and it would "crush and desolate the planting States." The great purpose of his government, Hawes assured his fellow Kentuckians, was "to restore our Commonwealth to the true basis of constitutional liberty."[37]

Such hopes were soon proved futile. While Buell's major columns advanced toward Bardstown on October 1, the divisions of Joshua W.

The Old State Capitol Building in Frankfort, Kentucky. Inside the Capitol, Richard Hawes was sworn in as governor of Confederate Kentucky on October 4, 1862. *Editor's Collection*

Still and Ebenezer Dumont moved on the Shelbyville Road toward Frankfort. They were within artillery range of Frankfort by early afternoon on October 4, and by 4:00 p.m. Bragg, Kirby Smith and the provisional government had left town. The banquet scheduled for that evening and other inaugural ceremonies were abandoned. After the inconclusive Battle of Perryville on October 8, the Confederate forces withdrew from the state, and the provisional government of Kentucky returned to exile.

The governor and councilmen had little to do on a day-by-day basis, and they scattered to places where they could earn a living or be supported by friends and relatives until called into session by the governor. Hawes was in Athens, Tennessee on December 30, 1862, when he called for a meeting in that town on January 15, 1863. The treasurer and auditor were also asked to attend.[38] Governor Hawes continued to send suggestions and recommendations to members of the Confederate government, but he had little success in his determined efforts to get his former commander, Humphrey Marshall, removed from his independent command.[39] Although Hawes was embarrassed by his inability to meet the requests of President Davis for troops and supplies, he remained optimistic about the future. He wrote Davis on March 4, 1863, that "our cause is steadily on the increase." He was sure that another invasion of Kentucky would produce better results than had the one in 1862.[40]

Hawes was also chagrined by the continued search for some $45,000 that had been sent from a bank in Columbus to Memphis during the Confederate occupation of southern Kentucky. No one, including Hawes, seemed to know precisely what had happened to it.[41] In 1864, the governor tried to obtain the $1,000,000 that the Confederate Congress had voted in August of 1861 to assist the Confederates in Kentucky. But Davis, again displaying his skill in legalistic argument that infuriated many, rejected Hawes's request: Kentucky, he argued, had lost any claim to the money when it was admitted into the Confederacy.[42]

In 1864 Hawes was living at Nelly's Ford, a small settlement about 100 miles west and slightly northwest of Richmond, Virginia. A sister, Mrs. Kitty Coleman, lived there, and after his election as governor Mrs. Hawes and daughter Hetty were able to get there through the Union lines. Daughter Clara later joined them. Hawes could get to Richmond whenever necessary. As late as September 16, 1864, he was still dreaming of another strike against Union forces in eastern Kentucky.[43]

During the summer of 1864, Hawes received disturbing charges against Brig. Gen. John Hunt Morgan, the most admired hero of Kentucky Confederates. A number of his unit commanders had been concerned by Morgan's leadership after his escape from a Northern prison in 1863, and Col. R. A. Alston, commander of the 9th Tennessee Cavalry Regiment, alleged that during the unauthorized and disastrous raid into Kentucky in June 1864, "the conduct of our command . . . was such as to disgrace the country and cause a man to blush at the name of Confederate soldier." Having failed to secure punishment for the officers and men involved in the outrages, Alston appealed to Hawes to assist in bringing about an investigation. Others had also appealed to Confederate authorities, and on August 30 Morgan was suspended from command pending the meeting of a court of inquiry in Abingdon,

Virginia, on September 10. The court never met, for Morgan was killed by Union troops in Greenville, Tennessee, on September 4.[44]

The Confederate States of America collapsed in the spring of 1865, and the provisional government of Kentucky died with it. In the absence of records, we must assume that the state government simply dissolved. The fate of Confederate leaders was uncertain for a time, and Hawes remained at Nelly's Ford until the summer of 1865, when he decided it was safe to return to Bourbon County. On September 18 he appeared before the clerk of the Federal district court in Louisville and swore that "I will henceforth faithfully support, protect and defend the Constitution of the United States, and the Union of the States thereunder; and that I will in like manner abide by and faithfully support all laws and proclamations which have been made during the existing rebellion with reference to the emancipation of slaves." When he received a presidential pardon, Hawes resumed his legal practice. He was elected to the Bourbon County Court and then as master commissioner of the Common Pleas and Circuit Court; he remained in office until his death on May 25, 1877. In 1869, Hawes issued a ruling that part of the Freedman's Bureau Act did not apply to Kentucky. The Act applied only to states that had been in rebellion and, the last governor of Confederate Kentucky declared, Kentucky had never left the Union.[45]

NOTES

1. Lincoln to Orville H. Browning, Sept. 22, 1861, in Roy S. Basler, *et al.*, eds., *The Collected Works of Abraham Lincoln*, 9 vols. (New Brunswick, N.J., 1953-55), 4:532.

2. Kentucky politics during this period are best described in E. Merton Coulter, *The Civil War and Readjustment in Kentucky* (Chapel Hill, N.C., 1926).

3. Frank Moore, ed., *The Rebellion Record: A Diary of American Events*, 11 vols. (New York, N.Y., 1864-68), 3:254-59. The best biographies of Breckinridge are William C. Davis, *Breckinridge: Statesman, Soldier, Symbol* (Baton Rouge, La., 1974) and Frank H. Heck, *Proud Kentuckian: John C. Breckinridge* (Lexington, Ky., 1976), but see also James C. Klotter, *The Breckinridges of Kentucky*, 1760-1981 (Lexington, Ky., 1986), chapters 8-10.

4. Lowell H. Harrison, "George W. Johnson and Richard Hawes: The Governors of Confederate Kentucky," *Register of the Kentucky Historical Society*, 79 (Winter, 1981),

3-11; Mrs. William H. Coffman, comp., "Letters of George W. Johnson." in *ibid.*, 40 (October, 1942), 337-43.

5. William Preston Johnston, *Life of Gen. Albert Sidney Johnston* (New York, N.Y., 1879), 381.

6. The brief minutes of this convention are in Moore, ed., *Rebellion Record*, 3:259-61.

7. Alvin Fayette Lewis, *History of Higher Education in Kentucky* (Washington, D.C., 1899), 173-178.

8. "Proceedings of the Convention held at Russelville Nov. 18th, 19th & 20th," Manuscript Department, The Filson Club (Louisville). The "Proceedings" are followed by the council minutes up to January 1, 1862 when they cease abruptly.

9. *Ibid.*

10. Marshall's commission was dated October 30, 1861; Breckinridge's was November 2, 1861. Lowell H. Harrison, "Humphrey Marshall," in William C. Davis, ed., *The Confederate Generals*, 6 vols., (Garden City, N.Y., 1991), 4:158-59; William C. Davis, "John Cabell Breckinridge," in *ibid.*, 1:126-27.

11. Inventory for the Robert McKee Papers, Alabama Department of Archives and History (Montgomery, Alabama); Burnam Family Papers, Manuscripts, The Kentucky Library (Western Kentucky University); Thirtieth Anniversary Edition, *Bowling Green Times-Journal*, Feb. 12, 1913.

12. Harrison, "Governors of Confederate Kentucky", 3-14; Johnson to Ann, July 9, 1861, in "Johnson Letters", 339.

13. *Bowling Green-Nashville Daily Courier*, Nov. 29, 1861.

14. Magoffin to Editor, *Louisville Journal*, Dec. 13, 1861, in *Frankfort Daily Yeoman*, Dec. 17, 1861; *Journal of the House of Representatives*, Nov. 29, 1861, 338-39.

15. Governor Johnson to President Davis, Nov. 21, 1861, in *The War of the Rebellion: A Compilation of the Official Records of the Union and Confederate Armies*, 128 vols. (Washington, D.C., 1880-1901) (hereinafter cited as *O.R.*), IV, 1 (1):743-47.

16. *Ibid.*, 755-56.

17. *Ibid.*, 780.

18. The council minutes to January 1, 1862 provided details on the functioning of this government.

19. Benjamin to Johnson, *O.R.*, I, 7:857.

20. Johnson to Robert W. Johnson, Jan. 3, 1862, in *ibid.*, I, 52 (2):249-50, Act to Aid Kentucky, 261-62; *Bowling Green-Nashville Daily Courier*, Dec. 2, 1861; *Nashville Patriot*, Dec. 3, 1861.

21. Louisville *Daily Democrat*, Jan. 24, 1862; Arndt Mathias Stickles, *Simon Bolivar Buckner: Borderland Knight* (Chapel Hill, N.C., 1940), 112; Eliza Calvert Hall, "Bowling Green and the Civil War," *Filson Club History Quarterly*, 11 (October, 1937), 244; Julia Neal, ed., *The Journal of Eldress Nancy* (Nashville, Tenn., 1963), 4-29.

22. Council minutes, Dec. 30, 1861.

23. "Johnson Letters", 345-46.

24. Charles P. Roland, *Albert Sidney Johnston: Soldier of Three Republics* (Austin, Tx., 1964), 289-90; Benjamin Franklin Cooling, *Forts Henry and Donelson: The Key to the Confederate Heartland* (Knoxville, Tenn., 1987) is an excellent account of that campaign. Neal, ed., *Journal of Eldress Nancy*, 29.

25. Johnson to Ann, Feb. 15, 1862, "Johnson Letters": 346-47. Ann refused to let Junius join his father, but in the summer of 1864 the youth slipped through Union lines to join John Hunt Morgan. Brother-in-law Colonel J. Stoddard Johnston insisted that Junius enroll in the Virginia Military Institute. He did participate in the Battle of New Market, Virginia. John Hunt Morgan to W. Preston Johnston, Aug. 3, 1864, *O.R.*, I, 39 (2):750; "Johnson Letters", 340-41.

26. Johnson to Johnston, March 26, 1862, quoted in Johnston, *Johnston*, 551.

27. Undated clipping in postwar *Glasgow Times*, in Johnson Family Papers (The Filson Club); *Louisville Evening Post*, Oct. 17, 1899, in "Johnson Letters,", 351-52; Report of Colonel Robert P. Trabue, April 15, 1862, *O.R.*, I, 10 (1):614, 618.

28. James S. Jackson to Ann Johnson, April 12, 1862; the Rev. James F. Jacquess to Ann Johnson, April 15, 1862; death message of George W. Johnson, all in Johnson Family Papers (The Filson Club); A. McDowell McCook to H.V. Johnson, June 20, 1894, "Johnson Letters", 349-51; Ed. Porter Thompson, *History of the Orphan Brigade* (Louisville, Ky., 1898), 520; *Louisville Daily Journal*, April 15, 17, 1862; *Covington Journal*, April 26, 1862.

29. Harrison, "Governors of Confederate Kentucky", 28-32.

30. Several of Hawes's requests and recommendations are in the National Archives, RG 109.

31. *O.R.*, I, 16 (2):733-34.

32. The best recent accounts of the 1862 Kentucky campaign are Kenneth A. Hafendorfer, *Perryville: Battle for Kentucky* (Utica, Ky, 1991) and James Lee McDonough, *War in Kentucky: From Shiloh to Perryville* (Knoxville, Tenn., 1994), but see also Thomas L. Connelly, *Army of the Heartland: The Army of Tennessee, 1861-1862* (Baton Rouge, La, 1967).

33. Burnett to Davis, Aug. 22, 1862, *O.R.*, I, 16 (2):771; council to Davis, Aug. 18, 1862, in *ibid.*, 771-72; Davis to Hawes, Sept. 12, 1862, in *ibid.*, 814.

34. The unusual affair at Munfordville is described in Lowell H. Harrison, "'Should I Surrender?'—A Civil War Incident," *Filson Club History Quarterly*, 40 (October, 1966), 297-306.

35. The first detailed study of this battle is D. Warren Lambert, *When the Ripe Pears Fell: The Battle of Richmond, Kentucky* (Richmond, Ky, 1996).

36. Bragg to Cooper, Sept. 25, 1862, *O.R.*, I, 16 (2):876.

37. Bragg's remarks, Hawes's speech, broadside in Hawes Papers, Special Collections, University of Kentucky.

38. Hawes to McKee, Dec. 30, 1862, Robert McKee Papers.

39. Hawes to Davis, Jan. 8, 1863, *O.R.*, I, 20 (2):490.

40. *O.R.*, IV, 2:417-18.

41. Several letters concerning the missing funds are in the Hawes Papers, Special Collections, University of Kentucky.

42. Davis to Hawes, Jan. 21, 1864, *O.R.*, I, 52 (2):604-05.

43. *Reminiscences of Maria Jane Southgate Hawes* (N.p., 1986), 7. This pamphlet was written in 1882.

44. Alston to Hawes, Aug. 11, 1864, *O.R.*, I, 39 (1):77-80; Special Orders 205, Aug. 30, 1864, in *ibid.*, 80; James A. Ramage, *Rebel Raider: The Life of General John Hunt Morgan* (Lexington, Ky., 1986), 229-42.

45. Copy of Hawes's oath; Acting Assistant Secretary of State to Hawes, Sept. 21, 1865, Hawes Papers, Special Collections, University of Kentucky. The 13th amendment to the United States Constitution was not ratified until December 18, 1865. Kentucky ratified it, and the 14th and 15th amendments, in 1976.

D. Warren Lambert

The Decisive Battle of Richmond

August 29-30, 1862

As Civil War battles go, the military action fought in Madison County, Kentucky, between Kingston and Richmond on August 29 and 30, 1862, was not a large engagement. This fact, coupled with Gen. Robert E. Lee's stunning victory at Second Manassas in Virginia on the same two days, accounts for why the Battle of Richmond has been largely ignored by historians. Its obscurity is both ironic and undeserved, for the battle boasts several unique aspects, including a higher percentage of total loss in the Union army in killed, wounded and prisoners, than either side suffered in any other single engagement of the war.

Strategically, the outcome of the Richmond fight was the virtual obliteration of Union power in central Kentucky.[1] At the same time, Lee was moving his army into Maryland, and England and France seemed as close as they ever would be to considering intervention on the side of Southern independence. Thus, this largely overlooked Confederate victory—the most complete success Southern arms ever won west of the Appalachians—helped usher in what one historian later described as "the one brief space in Confederate history that was pure sunshine."[2]

The Battle of Richmond was the first Southern success in the invasion of Kentucky in the late summer of 1862 by the armies of Gen. Braxton Bragg and Maj. Gen. Edmund Kirby Smith. The victory followed a disastrous spring and early summer for the Confederacy west of the Appalachians. Now, however, opportunities seemed to abound.

The superior Union strength was dissipated into several separate commands over an expansive theater of operations. The primary Union

General Edmund Kirby Smith. Smith's Provisional Army of Kentucky crushed a Union force south of Richmond, Kentucky, but was never able to join Gen. Braxton Bragg's army to effectively hold the Bluegrass State. *Library of Congress*

force, Maj. Gen. Don Carlos Buell's Army of the Ohio, was in northern Alabama moving slowly northeast toward Chattanooga along the Memphis & Charleston Railroad. Buell's sloth-like advance gave Bragg time to move his army almost 800 miles by rail from Tupelo, Mississippi, to Chattanooga, where he would have the option of either moving against Buell or striking north into central Tennessee. If Bragg could coordinate his movements with Gen. Kirby Smith, whose independent command in Knoxville included about 12,000 Confederates, the liberation of Nashville and an invasion of Kentucky seemed inviting possibilities.

The details of the Kentucky invasion plan were broadly agreed to in a meeting between Smith and Bragg in a Chattanooga hotel room on July 31. Smith proposed that the two generals coordinate the movements of their armies with an eye toward capturing Middle Tennessee "and possibly Kentucky." Smith agreed to cooperate with Bragg and to "cheerfully place my command under you subject to your orders." Their enthusiasm for the thrust into Kentucky was encouraged by Col. John Hunt Morgan, a dashing Kentucky cavalry leader who had just returned from a spectacular raid in the Blue Grass State. Central Kentucky, Morgan told the two generals, was seething with secessionist feeling. Bragg liked the simple and sensible plan, which called for using the two Southern armies (his own and Smith's) like pincers to lure Buell to his destruction. As Bragg moved his army north through Tennessee and central Kentucky, Smith would knock out a small Union post holding Cumberland Gap on the border of Tennessee and Kentucky. They would then join forces in Kentucky, capture the state's capital, and install a pro-Confederate government. Unfortunately, the plan was weakened from the start by Smith's independent command status; thus, neither Bragg nor Smith was in command of the invasion.

To assist Smith with the reduction of Cumberland Gap, Bragg gave him some of his best units, including four brigades from Texas, Arkansas, and Tennessee, which would form two divisions under Gens. Thomas J. Churchill and Patrick R. Cleburne. Although Kirby Smith had written to Bragg that there was "yet time for a brilliant summer campaign," his idea of it did not include helping Bragg in Tennessee or Kentucky.[3] Exercising his independence of command, on August 14

Smith marched out of Knoxville, passed through gaps in the mountains west of the Union position at Cumberland Gap (where the Union commander was his West Point classmate, Brig. Gen. George Washington Morgan), and by August 18 was over the border at Barbourville, Kentucky. Smith believed the Union force at the gap was too well fortified to capture, but not strong enough to come out and face his much larger force in the field.

Smith's decision to avoid a fight at Cumberland Gap left him with few options other than to continue deeper into Kentucky. The country around him was "poor as Job's turkey" and, contrary to Morgan's boasts, the locals viewed secessionists with hostility. Their attitude was typified by the response received from one of Smith's troopers from a member of a family sitting on a porch. "Where does this road go?" inquired the cavalryman. "Don't go nowhere, dammit, it stays right here."[4] Forage was also lacking around Barbourville, but there would be plenty in the Kentucky Bluegrass, and John Hunt Morgan had promised all those Southern sympathizers, whom Kirby Smith felt he could not abandon. On August 20, Smith notified President Jefferson Davis that he had ordered General Morgan to meet him in Lexington, Kentucky on September 2.[5]

With the addition of Bragg's brigades, Kirby Smith had about 18,000 men in four divisions. Three of them, Churchill's, Cleburne's, and Gen. Harry Heth's, contained about 3,000 men each, or roughly half of Smith's total force. The other 9,000 men were organized in one large division under Brig. Gen. Carter L. Stevenson, about the same size as the Union garrison at Cumberland Gap. Unwilling to leave such a large force in his rear unattended, Kirby Smith left Stevenson's men behind to keep an eye on the Federals.

On August 26 he started Churchill's and Cleburne's divisions north toward Big Hill and Richmond, while Heth's remained near Barbourville awaiting reinforcements and the army's wagon train. Churchill's Division consisted of two brigades, Texas and Arkansas troops under Cols. T. J. McCray and Evander McNair, with an attached Arkansas battery under Capt. John T Humphreys. Cleburne also had two brigades, one from Tennessee and one from Arkansas under Cols. Preston Smith and Benjamin J. Hill, respectively, with attached artillery

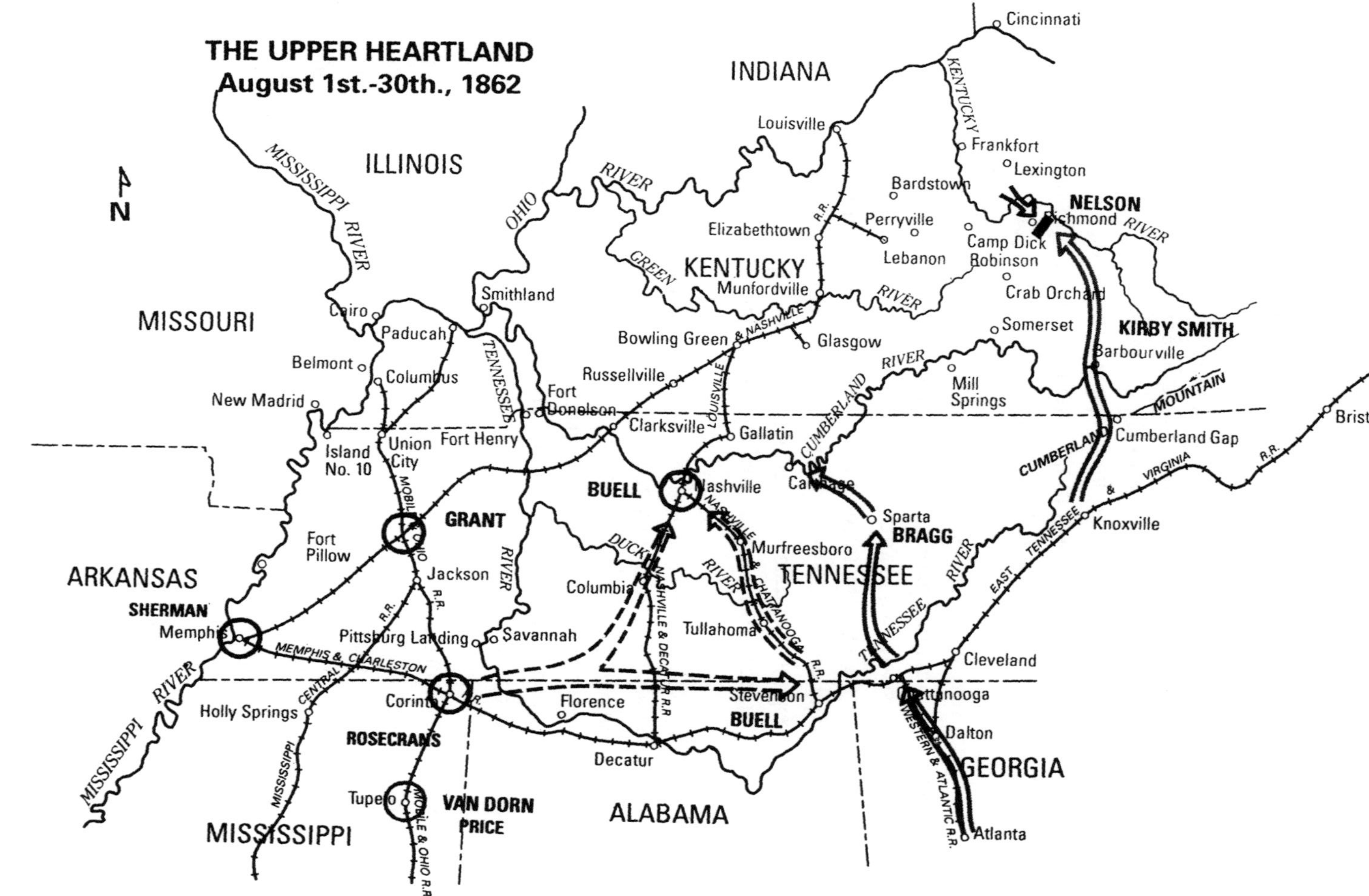
THE UPPER HEARTLAND
August 1st.-30th., 1862
N
MISSOURI
ILLINOIS
INDIANA
KENTUCKY
TENNESSEE
ARKANSAS
MISSISSIPPI
ALABAMA
GEORGIA
MISSISSIPPI RIVER
OHIO RIVER
TENNESSEE RIVER
CUMBERLAND RIVER
GREEN RIVER
DUCK RIVER
KENTUCKY RIVER
CUMBERLAND MOUNTAIN
SHERMAN
GRANT
ROSECRANS
VAN DORN
PRICE
BUELL
BRAGG
KIRBY SMITH
NELSON
Memphis
Holly Springs
Fort Pillow
New Madrid
Island No. 10
Belmont
Columbus
Cairo
Paducah
Union City
Fort Henry
Fort Donelson
Smithland
Jackson
Corinth
Tupelo
Pittsburg Landing
Savannah
Florence
Decatur
Columbia
Clarksville
Russellville
Bowling Green
Nashville
Gallatin
Tullahoma
Murfreesboro
Stevenson
Carthage
Sparta
Chattanooga
Dalton
Atlanta
Cleveland
Knoxville
Cumberland Gap
Barbourville
Bristo
Glasgow
Munfordville
Elizabethtown
Louisville
Perryville
Lebanon
Bardstown
Mill Springs
Somerset
Camp Dick Robinson
Crab Orchard
Richmond
Lexington
Frankfort
Cincinnati
MISSISSIPPI CENTRAL R.R.
MEMPHIS & CHARLESTON R.R.
MOBILE & OHIO R.R.
NASHVILLE & DECATUR R.R.
NASHVILLE & CHATTANOOGA R.R.
LOUISVILLE & NASHVILLE R.R.
WESTERN & ATLANTIC R.R.
EAST TENNESSEE & VIRGINIA R.R.

batteries, one from Tyler, Texas, under Capt. James P. Douglas, and the other the Marion (Florida) Light Artillery under Capt. John M. Martin. With John Hunt Morgan's cavalry well to the west, the army was screened by another horse brigade under Col. John S. Scott, comprised of the 1st Louisiana, 1st Georgia, and a company of the Kentucky Buckner Guards.

The roads from Barbourville to Big Hill were through almost impassable mountains; the weather was dry, the temperature was in the 90s, and water was almost unobtainable. The infantry outran their own supply wagons and lived on roasting ears and apples from the little farms they passed. They had obtained some salt in Barbourville, and joked that the "C.S.A." stamped on their belt buckles—those that had them—stood for "corn, salt and apples."[6]

Though a terrible march, the two lead divisions made it in three days, infused with an enthusiasm for their cause compared to that of a religious revival or Cromwell's army. The miserable heat was having its effect. When Smith's infantry reached Big Hill and tangled with a Union cavalry unit there, somebody—whether Union or Confederate is not recorded—shot a little slave girl off a gatepost she had climbed to watch the soldiers pass by.[7]

Supplies were only a small part of the problem facing the Confederates. Smith's unilateral thrust into central Kentucky wrested control of the campaign away from Bragg and made it doubly difficult for the two armies to coordinate their movements. With Kirby Smith now so far north of him, Bragg moved his Army of the Mississippi out of Chattanooga, feinted toward Nashville, and started north into Kentucky. Buell, with his Union army in Tennessee thus outflanked, was forced to do likewise.

The dual Confederate thrust created a high level of panic in Kentucky. In July, Gen. Jeremiah Tilford Boyle, military commandant of the state, had bombarded Washington with agitated telegrams during John Hunt Morgan's cavalry raid in Kentucky. Boyle's alarms had prompted Lincoln to telegraph his General-in-Chief, Henry Halleck, "They are having a stampede in Kentucky. Please see to it."[8] Morgan's threat to Union control, however, had been minimal; Bragg's and Smith's armies posed a real danger.

General Horatio G. Wright

Wright was Commander of the Military Department of the Ohio at the time of the invasion of Kentucky in 1862.

Library of Congress

As Buell's army marched north through Tennessee, he sent one of his division commanders, Maj. Gen. William "Bull" Nelson, north to command a growing collection of men styled the Army of Kentucky. This "army," about 6,500 strong in two divisions, was comprised almost entirely of green troops recently called up by the alarmed governors of Indiana and Ohio. General Horatio Wright, commanding the recently created Department of the Ohio from his headquarters in Cincinnati, had little confidence in the new recruits. An army can't be formed in a few days, he warned Washington. "If you say go, they go, but I shall not expect success except by chance." Wright ordered Nelson to Lexington with the intention of meeting the advancing Confederates along the defensible Kentucky River.

General Lew Wallace, who would later become famous as the author of the classic *Ben Hur*, was temporarily in charge of the deployment of the green recruits until Nelson arrived. Uncertain of where Kirby Smith was headed, Wallace dispatched troops south to Lancaster. Three regiments, the 12th and 66th Indiana, and 95th Ohio, all under the temporary command of Col. William H. Link of the 12th Indiana, were also marched southeast toward Richmond, Kentucky. The 7th Kentucky Union Cavalry under Col. Leonidas K. Metcalfe was

General William "Bull" Nelson. Born in Mason County, Kentucky, and a prewar naval officer, Nelson established Camp Dick Robinson in Garrard County, Kentucky, in August, 1861. He commanded a large force of newly-raised regiments at the disastrous Battle of Richmond, and was shot down at the Galt House Hotel in Louisville a month later by fellow Union officer, Gen. Jefferson C. Davis. *Library of Congress*

ordered to scout south of Link's regiments toward Kingston and Big Hill.

On August 23, Cassius M. Clay, noted Kentucky emancipationist just called home from Russia where he had been American minister, rushed south to Lexington when he heard of Kirby Smith's approach. Since Clay held a major general's commission and was a native of Madison County, he persuaded Wallace to give him two regiments still in Lexington, the 18th Kentucky and 69th Indiana Infantry, together with a section of Michigan artillery. Clay advanced this force as far as the beetling palisades of the Kentucky River north of Richmond.

As Wright had realized and Clay seemed to appreciate, the Kentucky River was by far the best defensive line the Union had to stop Kirby Smith. Nelson, who arrived within a few hours, however, threw away its advantages by removing Clay from command and sending his pair of regiments and artillery on to Richmond to join the forces gathered there under Colonel Link. Nelson was probably reluctant to risk working with an inexperienced subordinate major general with a temper as bad as his own. Nelson's decisions, however, triggered a Union deployment exactly where Kirby Smith hoped to meet the enemy, i.e., below the Kentucky River.

Of the other units available to him, Nelson kept some in Lexington and others in the area of Lancaster and Danville west of Richmond, where a concentration would threaten Kirby Smith's flank if he dared to move farther north. This dispersion of forces, however, came too late to deter Smith, who had already told John Hunt Morgan to meet him in Lexington; Smith had already decided to risk a direct advance into the Bluegrass.

As Nelson was dispatching his men, Scott's Confederate cavalry was screening Smith's movement north. Scott's troopers had ridden into Kentucky through Monticello and Somerset, scattering several Union units on the way. They also captured a number of wagons bound for Cumberland Gap and reached Big Hill on August 23, well ahead of their infantry. Without the benefit of reliable intelligence concerning Kirby Smith's advance, Union authorities had started a wagon train from Richmond to Cumberland Gap, escorted by Metcalfe's 7th Kentucky (Union) Cavalry and a battalion of Lt. Col. John C. Chiles' 3rd (Union)

Tennessee Infantry, which George W. Morgan had sent up to meet it. Metcalfe attacked the approaching Southerners, but Scott's two small mountain howitzers utterly panicked the untrained and undisciplined 7th Kentucky Cavalry. The Tennessee infantry barely covered the resulting disastrous rout. Lew Wallace, when he heard the details of the action, described it as "most disgraceful."[9] After capturing the wagon train Scott rode on to Richmond and demanded its surrender, but Colonel Link refused. Because Scott could not force a decision with just his cavalry, he withdrew south of Big Hill to await the arrival of Kirby Smith's infantry.

Nelson arrived in Lexington on August 24, relieved Wallace of his administrative responsibilities, and began shuffling about what troops he had available in central Kentucky. Union commanders at Lebanon, Cynthiana, and Cincinnati were being notified to send any units they could to Richmond. Wright's earlier instructions to Nelson, while not offered as an absolute order, were more in line with what Cassius M. Clay had planned: "If enemy is in force get your troops together, and do not risk a general battle at Richmond unless you are sure of success. Better fall back to a more defensible position, say the Kentucky River, than to risk much." Nelson, however, was going to fight Smith south of the river line.[10]

However, with Cumberland Gap threatened and Buell's army now outflanked to the north, nobody was sure of Kirby Smith's location or intentions. Nelson thought Scott's Southern cavalry had retreated south all the way to London. A civilian from Barbourville, however, sent him an alarming report that 18,000 Confederates were north of that town (It is interesting to note that the report was the correct size of Kirby Smith's army, but half of it, Stevenson's 9,000-man division, was still south of Cumberland Gap watching George W. Morgan.) With some of his strength in Lancaster and with four regiments ordered to the area around Danville to cover his left flank, Nelson had ordered three infantry regiments to move from Nicholasville to Richmond. This force was composed of Col. Thomas J. Lucas's 16th Indiana, Lt. Col. John R. Mahan's 55th Indiana, and Lt. Col. Melville D. Topping's 71st Indiana, with Lt. Byron D. Paddock's section of Battery F of the 1st Michigan Artillery. Nelson also dispatched Clay's former regiments, Col. William

A. Warner's 18th Kentucky and Lt. Col. Harman J. Korff's 69th Indiana, from Clay's Ferry to Richmond, where they were to join the three regiments already there under Colonel Link.

On August 25, Nelson sent two of his cavalry regiments back to Nicholasville with orders to ride south and see if they could locate any hostile movement. The troopers rode to Crab Orchard and through Mt. Vernon, reconnoitering west and south of Big Hill just as Kirby Smith's infantry was approaching that place. Late on the night of August 28, the Union cavalry forwarded a good estimate of the growing Confederate strength in the area. The report was addressed to Nelson in Richmond, but the general had already departed for Lexington. As a result, he did not get word of the enemy concentration in his front. This failure of field intelligence would have vast consequences. Had Nelson known that Kirby Smith's army was in strength near Big Hill, he very probably would have handled his forces—which were divided between Danville, Lancaster, and Richmond—in a different manner the following day.[11]

By the 27th of August, Nelson had organized the regiments he now had in Richmond into two brigades. Both of his brigadiers, Gens. Mahlon D. Manson and Charles Cruft, were from his former division in Don Carlos Buell's army; both were also political appointees without any field experience. Manson's First Brigade was made up of Lucas's 16th, Mahan's 55th, Korff's 69th, and Topping's 71st Indiana, and an improvised unit of Michigan artillery. The Second Brigade under Cruft included Link's own 12th and Morrison's 66th Indiana, Warner's 18th Kentucky, and McMillen's 95th Ohio, with another Michigan artillery battery attached.[12] Nelson's cavalry consisted of a brigade of three regiments and a battalion-size detachment from another. Only two of these units, Metcalfe's 7th Kentucky and the battalion-size detachment under Lt. Col. Reuben J. Munday of the 6th Kentucky, would actually be involved in the forthcoming fight at Richmond. Nelson's own brigade commanders had little confidence in their soldiers. Of his own brigade, Cruft wrote in his final report an estimate that probably described the whole army: "It was a sad spectacle for a soldier to look at these raw levies and contemplate their fate in a trial at arms with experienced troops."[13]

The next day, August 28, Nelson traveled back to Lexington. His journey was probably prompted by the lack of any telegraph line between there and Richmond, which left him out of direct contact with his other forces in central Kentucky. General Manson, the commander of Nelson's First Brigade, assumed command in Nelson's absence. When he left Richmond, however, Nelson compounded his mistake of remaining below the Kentucky River by ordering Manson to stay where he was instead of starting west to join Nelson's planned concentration at Lancaster. Although Nelson had directed Manson to report to his headquarters in Richmond, he left before Manson arrived. The order to remain in Richmond was relayed through Nelson's adjutant; Manson was not to move in any direction without the now-absent commanding general's permission.[14]

The next day was August 29. Nelson notified Horatio Wright that "Kirby Smith's game is now clear. He will assail Buell in left and rear."[15] This conclusion prompted Nelson to concentrate his forces southwest of Richmond at Lancaster, which would put him on the flank of Kirby Smith's expected move back toward Buell in Tennessee. Regardless of the direction Kirby Smith moved, if the Union force at Richmond were shifted to Lancaster, Nelson would have 16,000 men there. Kirby Smith, he believed, would never bypass such a large force if he came straight up toward the Bluegrass. Under the circumstances it was a sensible enough speculation, but it was wrong.

On the day Nelson informed Wright that Kirby Smith meant to "assail Buell in left and rear," Patrick Cleburne's Division marched to the top of Big Hill, sixteen miles south of Richmond. Thomas Churchill's Division was stretched out on the road behind Cleburne. It was in incredible accomplishment. In three days of grueling marching through the mountains over virtually impassable roads, and with almost no water anywhere, Kirby Smith's Confederates had covered the weary miles from Barbourville through Raccoon Springs to London and then Hazel Patch, some of them going even farther by way of Manchester or Mt. Vernon. "[R]agged, bare footed almost starved, marching day and night, exhausted [from] want of water," Smith wrote, "I have never seen such suffering, and there is not a complaint, not a murmur. Such fortitude, patriotism and self control has never been surpassed by any army that ever existed."[16]

Scott's cavalry had passed back up the Old State Road and were now in front of the infantry, scouting past Kingston toward the Lancaster Pike west of Richmond and the Irvine Pike east of it. His skirmishes with Union forces along the Lexington Turnpike during the last week of August seemed to indicate the enemy was assembling around Richmond. If so, Kirby Smith was anxious to bring on a fight now, far below the strong line of the Kentucky River.

Scott's information did not overly concern Smith. True, Union troops had been driven off Big Hill on August 23 and others seemed to be gathering ahead of him in Richmond. Smith, however, either assumed or was informed by civilian sympathizers that these men were green levies, and his move from Barbourville had been so rapid that the Union commanders were probably unaware of the strength of his army. Otherwise, he later wrote, they would have "opposed us in the passes and strong positions of the Cumberland mountains or would have posted themselves along the high bluffs and precipices of the Kentucky River, where they could have successfully resisted the passage of even a greatly superior force."[17] It was now apparent they were going to do neither, and instead risk fighting him somewhere on the flatlands between Big Hill and the Kentucky River, where his veteran troops could fight to maximum advantage. Smith thus ordered Cleburne to advance several more miles on the Richmond Road and camp for the night until Churchill's brigades reached him. Scott's cavalry was sent ahead to scout out the enemy positions.

As Smith pondered his options a few miles to the south, Manson's First Brigade of Nelson's army was bivouacked two miles below Richmond, with Cruft's Second Brigade men in camp on a line circling the town cemetery to its east and south. The two generals had taken command of their units only three days before. Cruft lamented that his men "could but indifferently execute some of the simplest movements in the manual of arms" and "knew nothing whatever of company or battalion drill."[18] On the morning of August 29, some of Manson's cavalry, Munday's 6th Kentucky and a remnant of Metcalfe's 7th Kentucky, stumbled into the Confederate advance not far north of Big

Hill. Munday sent back a report to Manson, which reached him at eleven that morning, and Manson relayed it to Nelson, sending one copy to Lexington and another to Lancaster, adding with what in his final report sounds like a touch of asperity, "not having been informed at which place you might be found." For some unexplained reason, it took nearly sixteen hours for this message to reach Nelson.[19]

By two that afternoon the cavalry informed Manson that 4,000 or 5,000 Confederates were marching toward Kingston, an accurate assessment if the Union riders had been far enough south to see some of Churchill's Division tramping behind Cleburne's, but too high if they had only spotted Cleburne's brigades. Either way, the report left Manson with no option other than to disregard Nelson's order not to move in any direction without permission. To retreat in the face of what might have proved to be a smaller force, Manson wrote years after the war, would have made him seem a coward. "The only question for me now to determine was whether I should allow the enemy to attack me in camp or whether I should advance to meet him."[20] In addition, a ridge a mile and one-half south of his bivouac towered above the surrounding terrain. If Manson remained where he was, the advancing enemy would occupy the high ground and dominate his position. When he received the cavalry report at 2:00 p.m., Manson later explained, "It did not take me a moment to decide."[21]

Thus the general ordered his brigade forward to occupy the higher ground. Some of Scott's Confederate cavalry rode up on his left but was driven off by his improvised sections of Michigan artillery. As he advanced to take the ridge, Manson discovered that it dominated the terrain as far south as Rogersville. Although Manson may have made a mistake risking an advance rather than giving up Richmond and falling back to the Kentucky River, his men were now in a tactically stronger position.

Initially, Manson felt good about his prospects. The Confederate horsemen faded back out of the range of his artillery and an advance of a few of his companies resulted in the capture of a handful of prisoners, some horses, and one of Scott's mountain howitzers. This easy "victory" lulled Manson into thinking that he had met and defeated a force of infantry, cavalry, and artillery. From the ridge he advanced his brigade the short distance to Rogersville and went into camp there for the night after sending what remained of Metcalfe's 7th Kentucky Cavalry south past Kingston to reconnoiter.

Uneasy with the enemy so near, however, Pat Cleburne formed his Southern infantry in a line of battle near the present road junction of U.S. Highway 421 and Kentucky 1016 at Bobtown. After instructing his officers to form their troops accordingly if an alarm was sounded, he dismissed his men and left a small rearguard deployed on both sides of the Richmond Road. Within a short time and in pitch blackness Metcalfe's Union troopers chased Scott's cavalry into Cleburne's prepared position. The Southern gunfire repulsed the troopers nearly as badly as they had been routed at Big Hill,[22] and the fighting on August 29 came to an end. Smith learned of the encounter and that the Union troops were wholly inexperienced later that night. Convinced that his proper course of action was indeed a march on Lexington, he ordered Cleburne to attack the next morning.

Metcalfe promptly reported the action near Bobtown to Manson about 11:00 p.m., and Manson sent an order back to Cruft at Richmond to picket the roads running east and west of town (the Irvine and Lancaster Pikes) and to be ready to march south to support Manson in the morning. Cruft had already sent a reconnaissance out the Irvine Pike when he heard the cannon fire to the south that afternoon. The detachment chased off some of Scott's cavalry troopers who had ridden that far north. Unable to learn anything more, Cruft let his men bed down at 10:00 p.m. with orders to sleep on their arms.[23]

The next morning, August 30, Manson's men awoke at 4:00 a.m., made their coffee, and tried to find water to fill their canteens. Within a short while a line of men was seen advancing north through early dawn light up the road through Kingston. Cavalry videttes were spread out well in front of the advancing foot soldiers. The troops were Cleburne's Division, with General Hill's Brigade and Douglas's Texas Artillery Battery in the vanguard. Preston Smith's Brigade marched immediately in their rear. Now too far south of a town he would have done better not to try to defend at all, Manson sent orders back to Richmond for Cruft to join him. As the courier rode off, Manson began deploying his own brigade into a defensive line one mile beyond Rogersville just south of

Mt. Zion Church south of Richmond, Kentucky. On either side of the church Union forces established lines of battle which were broken by persistent Confederate attacks on August 30, 1862. The church still shows scars from artillery fire. *Editor's Collection*

Mt. Zion Christian church, a handsome brick building on high ground facing the Richmond Road (Old State Road) from the west and about five and one-half miles below Richmond.

While his artillery bombarded the head of Cleburne's column, Manson organized his defense. The 55th Indiana was deployed east of the road, the 69th west of it and south of the church, and the 71st behind the 55th in reserve. When Manson's artillery opened fire, Cleburne deployed his division east of the Richmond Road and along the Irvine-Lancaster Pike, which ran east and west just north of Kingston. Hill's Brigade was placed in front behind the crest of a low hill, with Preston Smith's 500 yards behind it. Douglas's Texas battery unlimbered at the center of Hill's line and promptly replied to the Union guns.[24] Cleburne's Florida battery was also thrust forward in the line after a near-disastrous advance into the range of Manson's skirmishers because of a misunderstanding of the orders.[25] As the infantrymen on both sides formed into lines of battle in stifling heat, the concussion of the artillery fire spread through the ground in all directions, shaking ripe pears off trees four miles away at a little settlement called Bear Wallow.[26]

Kirby Smith reached the front about 7:30 a.m. Although he approved of Cleburne's dispositions, Smith told him not to risk a direct advance against Manson's strong position until Churchill's brigades arrived on the field. Smith's plan was to advance one of Churchill's brigades against Manson's right flank. When Churchill was in position to attack there, Cleburne would then advance Hill's brigade east of the road against Manson's center, with Preston Smith's either behind it or sliding off to the east to attack Manson's left flank.

An attack against his left flank was exactly what Manson feared from the first, and this led him to make a series of disastrous mistakes. During the methodical counter-battery fire which followed Kirby Smith's order to Cleburne to wait until Churchill was ready to attack, the last of Manson's four regiments, Lucas's 16th Indiana, arrived on the road from Rogersville. Manson squeezed these Hoosiers into the center of his line between the 55th and 69th Indiana regiments. This adjustment extended the Union left flank (east of the Richmond Road) beyond Cleburne's right. During the two hours it took for Churchill's leading brigade under Col. Thomas H. McCray to get into position facing Mt. Zion Church, Cleburne simply stayed where he was, telling his artillery to "fire slowly and not waste a round."[27]

McCray's Brigade was nearing the church about 10:00 a.m. when an increasingly hot exchange of skirmish fire in the woods east of the road convinced Kirby Smith and Cleburne that Manson was preparing a flanking action against their right. To counter it, Cleburne moved the 154th Tennessee Infantry, the regiment farthest to the right of Preston Smith's reserve line, east and forward to extend Hill's front.[28] This maneuver, in turn, confirmed Manson's fears that the enemy planned to turn his left flank. Unbeknownst to Manson, McCray's Confederates were forming at Mt. Zion Church for their advance against Manson's right flank.

Manson was making his decisions from a position with the 55th Indiana at the center of his line. A trick of the terrain led him into a series of disastrous tactical errors. West of where the Irvine-Lancaster Pike crossed the Richmond Road ran a little creek called Hayes Fork. About a mile in that direction was a big cornfield, north of which a ravine led straight toward Mt. Zion Church. None of this was visible from Manson's position. Increasingly worried about what was happening on his left front, Manson ordered the 71st Indiana forward from its reserve position to support the lines in front. Through some misunderstanding the regiment initially moved in the wrong direction (west toward the Richmond Road) and did not reach the left front for almost half an hour.[29] There were already three companies of skirmishers ahead of his left front and flank, driving Cleburne's skirmishers back in the woods. In order to stop the Union advance, Cleburne moved Col. Lucius E. Polk's consolidated 13th and 15th Arkansas Infantry, which formed the right flank of General Hill's line, over to support the 154th Tennessee.

This action served to confirm Manson's fears for his left, and he in turn moved all but three companies of Colonel Korff's 69th Indiana away from Mt. Zion Church beyond the 16th Indiana at precisely the same time McCray's Southern brigade was forming to attack Korff's original position on the right. Korff sent out two companies as skirmishers in front of his new position. There were already three other companies from Manson's other regiments deployed in front of the main line. These men traded an increasing fire with Cleburne's skirmishers while Manson's whole front line east of the road—the 55th, 16th, and 69th Indiana—advanced to within about one hundred yards of Cleburne's line, where they engaged in a deadly fire with the consolidated 13th and 15th Arkansas and the 154th Tennessee. The Federal advance only served to convince the Confederates that Manson was making "a bold and well-conducted attempt . . . to turn Cleburne's right."[30]

To counter this flanking action, Cleburne ordered the balance of Preston Smith's brigade to move out from behind Hill's front line, march to the right, and when far enough into the woods, swing into a ninety-degree angle to the end of Manson's line. By overloading his left Manson had triggered the response he feared the most, an attack against that portion of his front. He was still unaware McCray was moving to strike the opposite end of his line, which apparently he ignored.[31]

As Manson's troops advanced, Cleburne rode over to see if Preston Smith's men were getting into position for their flanking operation. He had started back toward Hill's Brigade, which he apparently meant to personally lead straight ahead toward Manson's center, when McCray attacked the Union right at the church and Preston Smith hit Manson's left. On the way, Cleburne stopped to talk to Colonel Polk, who had been wounded, and was himself hit by a ball which took out four jaw teeth and forced him to turn the division over to Preston Smith.[32] Colonel Alfred J. Vaughan of the 13th Tennessee Infantry moved up to command Smith's Brigade. Richmond was Cleburne's first battle with an independent command at divisional level, and he had handled his troops well.

Manson, for the next fatal half-hour, would not. Preston Smith's brigade nimbly executed Cleburne's wishes by forming the ninety-degree angle on the flank of Manson's regiments, achieving a deadly enfilade from which they began blasting the Union lines with massive volleys. As the raw Union soldiers began to break, Manson ordered the 71st Indiana to fix bayonets and charge forward into the rear of the 16th, thus throwing both regiments into complete confusion. Oral history in Madison County has it that Manson was drunk at this stage of the battle, a judgment supported by the statement of a corporal in the 69th Indiana, who said that the general was "drunk as a lord and crazy as a loon."[33] It was at this juncture of the battle, with Manson's entire brigade dissolving into something close to chaos, that General Charles Cruft's brigade, led by Col. William McMillen's 95th Ohio Infantry, began arriving on the field.

Cruft had waited at Richmond as long as he dared. Manson's messenger had not been able to find him, and Cruft's own courier could not find Manson on the field. To his credit, Cruft had simply marched south toward the sound of the guns.[34] The appearance of Cruft's men was surely welcomed by Manson, who ordered the 95th Ohio to charge Humphreys's Arkansas Battery, which was unlimbering on the west side of the road to support McCray's advance against Mt. Zion Church. The only way McMillen could assault the Southern guns, however, was to march his regiment squarely in front of McCray's Brigade, which was then pouring out of the ravine toward the church. Manson's order should never have been given and was obviously based upon a misunderstanding of the tactical situation unfolding on the Union right flank; McMillen should have questioned the order. Instead, he guided his Ohioans as Manson directed and McCray's Confederates blasted them from the flank. The fire tore into the 95th Ohio, which lost 250 killed, wounded, and captured in a few minutes.[35]

As McMillen's bloodied regiment fell back in confusion, Cruft's next unit, the 18th Kentucky, formed just east of the Richmond Road and established a line behind which Manson's broken units could reform. Meanwhile, the Confederates continued to advance. General Hill drove his brigade in line up the road while Preston Smith's [Vaughn's] brigade formed a line facing north after its enfilade of Manson's left. The 18th Kentucky, with great bravery and determination in the ninety-six degree heat, held long enough for the battered regiments in front of it to escape. Then the Manson's entire force fled north up the road toward Richmond. "[T]he whole thing," Cruft lamented, "was fast becoming shameful." The initial engagement had been a disaster for the Unionists.[36]

About a mile north of Rogersville and two miles north of the first battle line was the handsome farm residence of State Senator R. J. White. Cruft still had two regiments that had not yet been engaged, the 12th and 66th Indiana, and he moved them back past Rogersville to the west side of the road opposite White's farm. Cruft cobbled together a new line with the reformed 95th Ohio positioned just west of the road. The 66th Indiana extended the line west, followed by the 18th Kentucky and 12th Indiana. As Cruft was falling back to form a new line, Manson covered his dissolving front with some of his cavalry and artillery near Rogersville. Then, he gathered his three battered regiments into line east of the road and about 300 yards behind Cruft's new position not far from where he had repulsed Scott's cavalry the previous afternoon.

McCray's Confederates followed the Union retreat west of the Richmond Road and formed in front of Cruft's new line. Preston Smith, commanding Cleburne's entire division, sent Hill's Brigade up the east side of the road toward Manson's new line, with Smith's own brigade under Alfred Vaughan forming on its flank. It was about 12:30 p.m., while Manson and Cruft were watching the gray brigades in front of them forming to advance, that a courier from Lexington rode up and handed Manson an order from General Nelson. The directive, which should have been sent two or three days earlier, instructed Manson not to fight at Richmond at all, but to march west to Lancaster![37] Nelson had

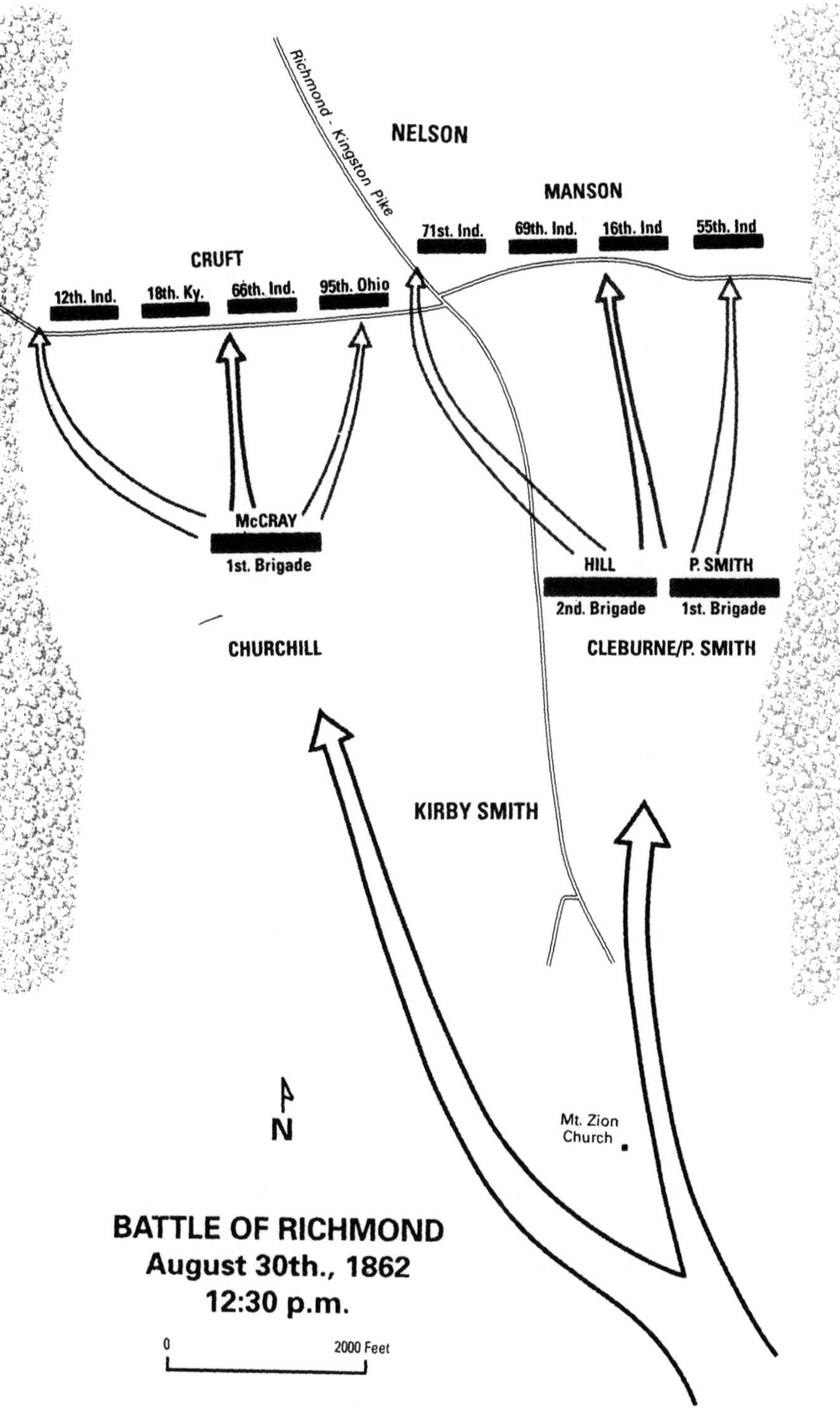
Richmond - Kingston Pike
NELSON
MANSON
71st. Ind.
69th. Ind.
16th. Ind
55th. Ind
CRUFT
12th. Ind.
18th. Ky.
66th. Ind.
95th. Ohio
McCRAY
1st. Brigade
HILL
P. SMITH
2nd. Brigade
1st. Brigade
CHURCHILL
CLEBURNE/P. SMITH
KIRBY SMITH
N
Mt. Zion
Church
BATTLE OF RICHMOND
August 30th., 1862
12:30 p.m.
0
2000 Feet

sent the message ten hours earlier at 2:30 a.m., when he received at Lexington's Phoenix Hotel Manson's copy of Munday's cavalry report dispatched the previous day.

Within five minutes the Confederates advanced, McCray's Southerners leading the way toward Cruft's reformed line. Though Cruft had earlier lamented the lack of training in his brigade, his soldiers held their position with remarkable firmness, driving back McCray's first assault. Some of Cruft's troops next to the road (perhaps from the 95th Ohio) launched their own counterattack. The Confederates, taking refuge behind a thickly overgrown fence, held their fire until the charging Federals closed to within a deadly range and then blasted them with volleys that drove them back "in the wildest confusion and disorder."[38] Farther west, however, the rest of McCray's regiments managed to turn Cruft's right flank, and again the Union position on that side of the road collapsed.

With Cruft's line falling back, Manson slowly withdrew his regiments on the Union left. His wise action prevented Hill's and Vaughan's brigades from doing any more than firing a few volleys in his general direction. The Confederate advance continued apace, and in places the Union lines held firm for a time, temporarily driving the enemy back. By 2:00 p.m. however, the entire Union force was little more than a disorderly mob. Some of Manson's regiments were down to one-half or one-third of their morning strength; others had virtually ceased to exist. The Confederates—McCray on the left, Hill in the center and Vaughan on the right—relentlessly pushed forward. With both flanks advancing ahead of the center, the Southern front assumed the form of a broad triangle, with the retreating Union troops melting away at the base.[39]

Manson and Cruft worked furiously to retain and regain unit cohesion as their men fell away to the north. Despite their deficiencies in discipline and training, utter exhaustion, and lack of water, some of the men responded. By the time they approached the site of Manson's former bivouac south of Richmond, the generals decided to make another stand. The new position was being organized when a sudden cheer erupted along the line: General "Bull Nelson, the army's commanding general, had arrived on the field.

Richmond, Kentucky Cemetery. Among these tombstones were formed the last Union lines of battle on August 30, 1862. *Editor's Collection*

After sending Manson the order at 2:30 a.m. to take the army to Lancaster, Nelson had started there himself. When he arrived in the middle of the morning Manson and Cruft were nowhere to be seen. The sinister rumble of artillery off to the east, however, convinced Nelson to ride to Richmond as fast as he could. Later, he bitterly accused Manson of disobeying his order to avoid a fight. Manson countered by claiming he had not received the order until the fighting was well underway. Whatever words passed between the two officers when they met on the field is not recorded, but Nelson immediately decided that he did not like the terrain there and ordered the troops to fall back to the edge of Richmond.[40]

The Union Army of Kentucky had numbered that morning about 6,500 men. By the time Nelson arrived, only some 2,200 to 2,500 men were still available for action. Nelson established these remnants in a line running from the Irvine Pike on the east through the Richmond cemetery to the west. None of the regiments were able to field their original strength, and the 71st Indiana was down to two single companies of about thirty men each.

As the Unionists were forming their last line of the day, Kirby Smith let his Confederates rest for about an hour. His men were almost as enervated as the Federals. The fight had been going on for some eight hours and had covered miles of ground under an unrelenting sun. The lack of water also took its toll. Still, Smith knew that the battle was his for the taking. He had already sent Scott's cavalry on a wide sweep west and then north around Richmond. Scott's objective was to cut off the expected Union retreat along the Lexington and Tates Creek Pikes, and catch a fleeing wagon train of Union supplies. The heavy earlier fighting west of the road at White's Farm had left McCray's men completely fought out. They were allowed to fall back and were replaced by Churchill's remaining fresh brigade under Col. Evander McNair. General Hill's brigade continued to man the center of the line, while Colonel Vaughan's brigade, with one regiment held back out of the fight, held the right. Once his line was reorganized and his men rested, Kirby Smith ordered a general advance. His strength this late in the day was probably about 4,000 men.

The soldiers waiting for Smith's men in the new Union line running through the Richmond cemetery were not quite as green as they had been earlier that day. The pair of drubbings they had received taught them a great deal about combat, and they were prepared to put some of it to good use. Union artillery opened first, firing shells and then canister at the approaching enemy. The drifting smoke and dust caught and held the setting sun's rays, which assumed a blood-red hue. General Nelson rode from regiment to regiment, inspiring the men while threatening them with bodily injury if they did not perform their duty. He also promised reinforcements that did not exist. "Boys!" the giant Nelson roared while hitting some skulkers with the flat of his sword, "if they can't hit me they can't hit anything."[41]

Perhaps Nelson's entreaties worked; certainly the experience gained that morning helped. Holding firm, the Union troops delivered a withering fire into the Southern ranks, exacting more casualties than they had in either of the previous stages of the fighting. Their valiant effort, however, was not enough. Kirby Smith's Confederates moved

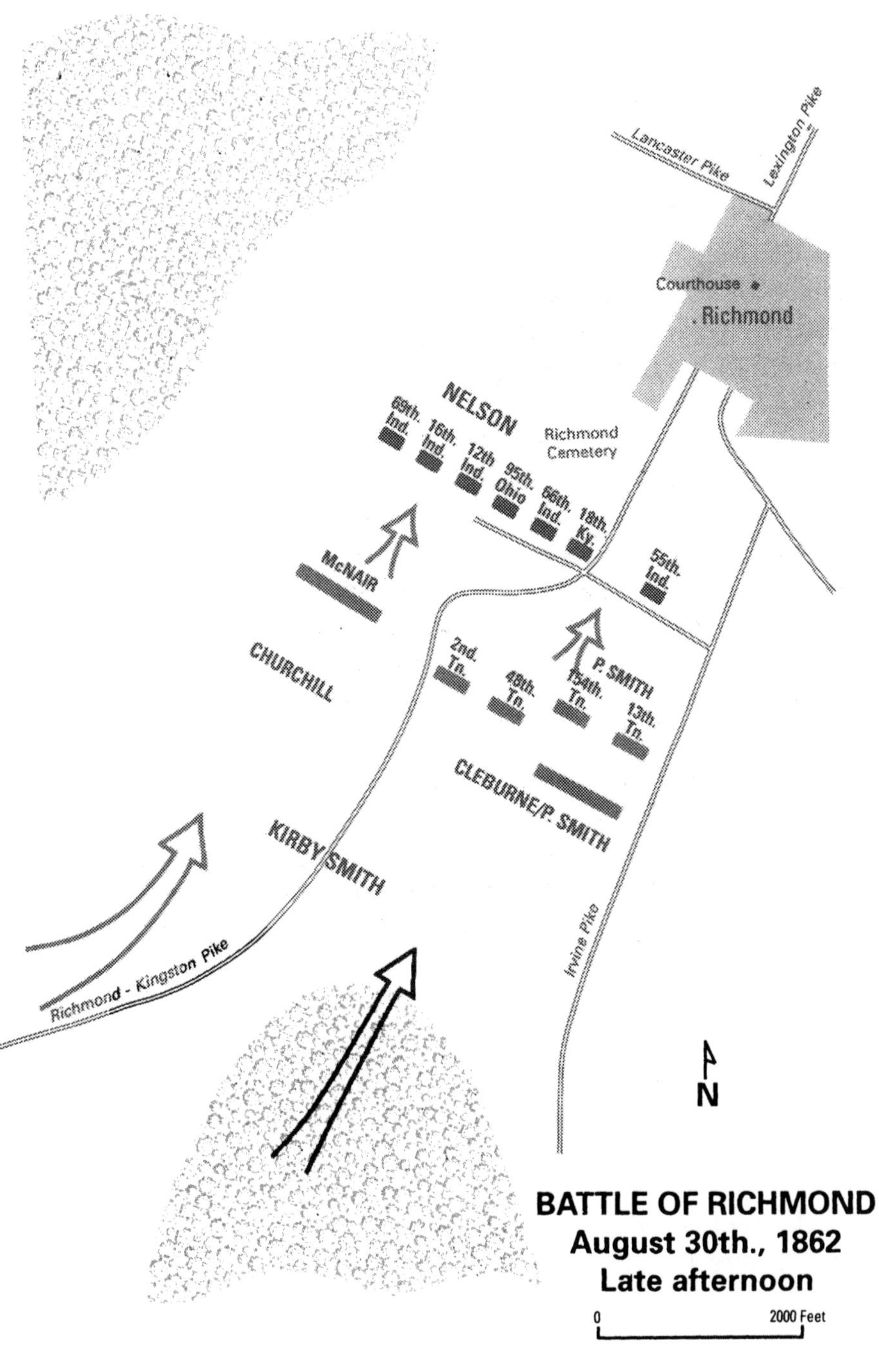
Lancaster Pike
Lexington Pike
Courthouse
Richmond
NELSON
Richmond Cemetery
69th. Ind.
16th. Ind.
12th Ind.
95th. Ohio
66th. Ind.
18th. Ky.
55th. Ind.
McNAIR
CHURCHILL
2nd. Tn.
48th. Tn.
154th. Tn.
P. SMITH
13th. Tn.
CLEBURNE/P. SMITH
KIRBY SMITH
Irvine Pike
Richmond - Kingston Pike
N
BATTLE OF RICHMOND
August 30th., 1862
Late afternoon
0
2000 Feet

forward through the hail of fire and delivered a thunderous volley. Nelson's men held their ground and responded in kind. Another Southern volley ripped through their lines, killing and maiming men and sending others running for the rear. Nelson was shot down when a pair of lead slugs smashed into his thigh. With the bullets whizzing past, General Cruft dismounted to examine his wounded horse. After climbing back on the animal he shouted, "Remember Indiana!" By this time McNair's Brigade had swept around Nelson's right flank and Vaughn's regiments were enveloping his left. A third crashing volley was delivered, and the thinning blue line broke apart. The remnants of Nelson's small army fell back in utter disorganization through the streets of Richmond and onto the Lexington Road.

It was there that Kirby Smith's unpleasant surprise awaited them. Aligned across the road, Scott's troopers shot down a good many of the men in the milling procession trying desperately to reach the Kentucky River line. By the hundreds they surrendered, holding their muskets (those who still had them) over their heads, the standard Civil War gesture that meant, "don't shoot, brother, come and get me." There were so many prisoners that Scott himself could not give Kirby Smith an accurate estimate of how many he had captured. The cavalryman simply reported that he "had a ten acre lot full."[43]

Somehow Nelson, with the help of an aide, managed to mount a horse and get away. Manson, with a small rearguard composed of officers separated from their regiments, tried to escape toward the Kentucky River but was soon taken prisoner.[42] Only 800 or 900 Federals managed to escape by way of Winchester, Clay's Ferry, Valley View, or the mouth of Jack's Creek. Nelson's army officially lost 206 killed and 844 wounded, a total of 1,050. As a percentage of those engaged, Union losses for the Battle of Richmond matched Shiloh and Antietam. In addition to the killed and wounded, Nelson's force also suffered 4,304 missing (the final count of prisoners was 4,303). Kirby Smith's losses, almost universally underestimated because he did not include the figures for McCray's brigade, were 98 killed, 492 wounded and eight missing. These figures did not include his artillery or cavalry.[44]

Main Street (looking east), Lexington, Kentucky, 1860. General William Nelson occupied the Phoenix Hotel (at center-right) when the fighting south of Richmond, Kentucky began. After the battle, Gen. Edmund Kirby Smith's army occupied Lexington. *University of Kentucky Special Collections*

Blame for the Union disaster at Richmond can be laid squarely at the feet of Generals Nelson and Manson. Nelson's decision to travel north to Lexington on August 28 (two days before the battle) because of its better telegraph connections is understandable, as is his hesitation regarding where to concentrate his forces. However, he should have heeded

General Wright's message about making the Kentucky River his primary line of defense, and he should have kept Manson in Richmond better informed of his intentions. Manson's decision to engage raw troops against seasoned veterans while routinely failing to protect his flanks demonstrated his tactical unfitness for command. None of the culpability for the humiliating defeat rested with the Kentucky, Indiana, and Ohio soldiers. Although green and led by inexperienced company and field officers, their final stand in the Richmond cemetery by about one-third of their original number demonstrated great bravery and a willingness to engage a numerically superior enemy.

The Confederates were competently led from first to last by their more experienced commanders who, if they did nothing of Napoleonic brilliance, made effective use of their veteran soldiers and the advantages of the terrain. Cleburne's handling of his division was exceptional. Kirby Smith's failure, as well as Braxton Bragg's, would come later when the two generals clumsily scattered their forces across central Kentucky in a spectacular failure to follow up the decisive Richmond victory. For a brief while before Braxton Bragg allowed General Buell to advance to Louisville, there was virtually nothing to oppose the Southerners in central Kentucky. A better coordination between Bragg and Smith might have pulled large numbers of Union troops from the Mississippi Valley north to defend the Midwest, leaving Lincoln's government with nothing to show for fifteen months of hard fighting.

Vast military opportunities lay before Kirby Smith and Braxton Bragg in the Bluegrass of Kentucky, much like the ripe pears shaken off the trees at Bear Wallow south of Kingston by the thundering artillery. Considering the possibilities of what a coordinated campaign might have accomplished, it must be said that they failed to reap the harvest.

* * *

The Opposing Forces at the Battle of Richmond, Kentucky

(August 29-30, 1862)

UNION

Provisional Army of Kentucky
Maj. Gen. William "Bull" Nelson

Cavalry Brigade, *Brig. Gen. James S. Jackson
Battalion (Cos. A, B, C, D & E), 6th Kentucky Cavalry Regiment, Lt. Col. Reuben J. Munday
7th Kentucky Cavalry Regiment, Col. Leonidas K. Metcalfe
*9th Kentucky Cavalry Regiment, Col. Richard T. Jacob
*9th Pennsylvania (sometimes mistakenly listed as Tennessee) Cavalry Regiment, Col. Edward C. Williams

First Infantry Brigade, Brig. Gen. Mahlon Dickerson Manson
Improvised Battery, part of Battery F, 1st Regiment Michigan Light Artillery, borrowed from Cruft's Second Brigade (see below) with part of Battery G, 1st Regiment Michigan Light Artillery from George W. Morgan's command at Cumberland Gap, Lt. Edwin O. Lanphere
Detachment 3rd (later 7th Veteran Volunteer) Kentucky Infantry Regiment, * Col. Theophilis Toulmin Garrard
Detached battalion, 3rd Tennessee Infantry Regiment, Col. Leonidas Houk, Lt. Col. John C. Chiles
16th Indiana Infantry Regiment, Col. Thomas J. Lucas
55th Indiana Infantry Regiment, Lt. Col. John R. Mahan
69th Indiana Infantry Regiment, Lt. Col. Harman [Hermann?] J. Korff
71st Indiana Infantry Regiment, Lt. Col. Melville D. Topping

Second Infantry Brigade, Brig. Gen. Charles Cruft
Battery F, 1st Regiment Michigan Light Artillery, Lt. Luther F. Hale
12th Indiana Infantry Reg., Col. William H. Link
66th Indiana Infantry Regiment, Maj. Thomas G. Morrison / Capt. John F. Baird

* Astericks indicate that the individual or unit, though assigned as indicted, was not present at the Battle of Richmond on August 29-30, 1862.

18th Kentucky Infantry Regiment, Col. William A. Warner / Maj. Frederick G. Bracht
95th Ohio Infantry Regiment, Col. William Linn McMillen

Union losses: killed, 206; wounded, 844; captured or missing, 4,303 = 5,353

Confederate

Provisional Army of Kentucky, Maj. Gen. Edmund Kirby Smith
(after August 25, 1862, Confederate Army of Kentucky)

Cavalry Battalion, Cos. A, E & F, 1st Florida Cavalry, Capt. Footman, attached directly to army headquarters.
Headquarters Escort, Georgia Cavalry, Capt. Nelson

Cavalry Brigade, Col. John S. Scott
1st Louisiana Cavalry Regiment, Col. John S. Scott / Lt. Col. James O. Nixon
1st Georgia Cavalry Regiment, Col. James Jefferson Morrison
Company Kentucky Buckner Guards, Capt. Garnett
Detachment 3rd Tennessee Cavalry Regiment, Col. James W. Starnes, joined Brigade on August 27
* 2d Kentucky Cavalry Regiment, Col. John Hunt Morgan

* First Infantry Division, Brig. Gen. Carter Littlepage Stevenson
* Second Infantry Division, Brig. Gen. Henry Heth

Third Infantry Division, Brig. Gen. Thomas James Churchill

First Brigade, Col. Thomas H. McCray
10th Texas Regiment Dismounted Cavalry, Col. C. R. Earp
11th Texas Regiment Dismounted Cavalry, Col. J. C. Burks
14th Texas Regiment Dismounted Cavalry, Col. Matthew Duncan Ector
15th Texas Regiment Dismounted Cavalry, Lt. Col. James A. Weaver
31st Regiment Arkansas Sharpshooters, Col. Thomas H. McCray / Maj. J.W. Clark

Second Brigade, Col. Evander McNair
Humphrey's Battery Arkansas Artillery, Capt. John T. Humphreys

1st Arkansas Dismounted Rifles, Col. Daniel H. Reynolds / Col. Robert W. Harper
2d Arkansas Dismounted Rifles, Col. Harris Flanagin / Col. J.A. Williamson
4th Arkansas Infantry Regiment, Col. Evander McNair / Lt. Col. Henry C. Bunn
4th Arkansas Battalion, Maj. J[esse] A. Ross
30th Arkansas Infantry Reg,, Col. C[harles] J. Turnbull

Fourth Infantry Division, Brig. Gen. Patrick Ronayne Cleburne / Col. Preston Smith, as Acting Brig. Gen.

First Brigade, Col. Preston Smith, P.A.C.S. / Col. Alfred Jefferson Vaughan
Marion (Florida) Light Artillery Battery, Capt. John M. Martin
12th and 47th Tennessee Infantry Regiments, consolidated at Richmond under Col. Lipscomb P. McMurray
13th Tennessee Infantry Regiment, Col. Alfred Jefferson Vaughan / Lt. Col. William E. Morgan
154th Senior Tennessee Infantry Regiment, Col. Edward Fitzgerald / Lt. Col. Michael Magevney, Jr.

Second Brigade, Col. Benjamin Jefferson Hill
Battery 1st Texas Artillery, Capt. James Postell Douglas
13th and 15th Arkansas Infantry Regiments, consolidated at Richmond under Col. Lucius Eugene Polk
2d Tennessee Infantry Regiment Provisional Army (see 35th Tennessee Infantry Regiment below)
35th Tennessee Infantry Regiment, formerly the 5th (above) in the Provisional Army, Col. Benjamin J. Hill / Lt. Col. Joseph A. Smith
48th Tennessee Infantry Regiment, Col. George H. Nixon / Lt. Col. T. R. Hughs
Company of Sharpshooters

Total Confederate losses: killed, 98; wounded, 492; captured or missing, 10 = 600

NOTES

1. Shelby Foote calls the battle the nearest in the entire war to being a Cannæ. Shelby Foote, *The Civil War: A Narrative*. 3 vols. (New York, N.Y., 1958), 1:650.

2. Nathaniel W. Stephenson, *The Day of the Confederacy: A Chronicle of the Embattled South* (New Haven, Conn., 1920), 43.

3. *The War of the Rebellion: A Compilation of the Official Records of the Union and Confederate Armies*, 128 vols. (Washington, D.C., 1880-1901) (hereinafter cited as *O.R.*) (all citations are to Series I), 16 (1):734. The exact understanding, or lack of it, between Bragg and Kirby Smith is explored in such works as Grady McWhiney, *Braxton Bragg and Confederate Defeat*, 2 vols. (New York, N.Y., 1969), 1:269-70; Joseph Howard Parks, *General Edmund Kirby Smith, C.S.A.* (Baton Rouge, La., 1954), 202; and Kirby Smith's own post-war account, E. Kirby Smith, "The Kentucky Campaign," typescript of a paper on the Kentucky Campaign, E. Kirby Smith Papers, #404, Southern Historical Collection, University of North Carolina Library, Chapel Hill (hereinafter cited as "Kentucky Campaign"), 4-5. In 1868, Smith categorically said that he came into Kentucky on his own without any agreement with Bragg. See "Glimpses of a Visit to Richmond and the Madison County Fair," by J. C. Craddock, August 1868, reprinted in the *Kentucky Explorer* (July) and August 1995, 47.

4. Alberta and Carson Brewer, *Valley So Wild: A Folk History* (Knoxville, Tenn., 1975), 156.

5. *O.R.*, 16 (2):766.

6. Capt. John W. Lavender, C.S.A., *They Never Came Back: The Story of Co. E., Fourth Ark. Inf., C.S.A.* (Pine Bluff, Ark., 1956), 104.

7. Gladys Gilbert McCray, whose grandparents knew the family that owned the slave girl, personal interview with the author, June, 1984, notes in the author's possession.

8. *O.R.*, 16 (1):738.

9. *Ibid.*, 884.

10. *Ibid.*, 908.

11. The commander of the cavalry reconnaissance, Brig. Gen. James S. Jackson, having sent the information concerning the size of Kirby Smith's army, later said he was "astounded" when notified that there was fighting at Richmond. *O.R.*, 16 (1):910.

12. Of the eight regimental commanders at the beginning of the battle, three, Topping, Link and Warner would be killed in action or fatally wounded.

13. *O.R.*, 16 (1):918-19.

14. M. D. Manson, letter to State Sen. R. J. White of Kentucky, *Louisville Courier-Journal,* April 6, 1878, 2.

15. *O.R.*, 16 (1):449.

16. Kirby Smith, letter to Cassie Smith, from Camp near Richmond, Aug. 29, 1862, Kirby Smith Papers, Southern Historical Collection, University of North Carolina Library.

17. Kirby Smith, "Kentucky Campaign," 7-8; Paul F. Hammond, "Campaign of General E. Kirby Smith in Kentucky, in 1862," *Southern Historical Society Papers*, 50 vols. (Richmond, Va., 1876-1919) (hereinafter cited as *SHSP*), 9 (1881), 249-50.

18. *0.R.*, 16 (1):918.

19. *Ibid.*, 911.

20. Manson to White, *Louisville Courier-Journal*, 2.

21. *0.R.*, 16 (1):911.

22. *Ibid.*, 949; Robert M. Frierson, Nashville, Tenn., "Gen. E. Kirby Smith's Campaign in Kentucky," *Confederate Veteran*, 1 (August, 1893), 295.

23. *O.R.*, 16 (1):919, 926, 928.

24. Sam Thompson, diary, in Lucia Rutherford Douglas, ed., *Douglas's Texas Battery, CSA* (Tyler, 1996) (hereinafter cited as Thompson, diary), 197, 198.

25. Cleburne sent the order from somewhere along the IrvineLancaster Pike, which ran east and west, telling the Florida battery to take position near a brick house west of where the Irvine-Lancaster Pike crossed the Old State Road. The battery commander, Capt. John M. Martin, however, was on the old State Road, which ran north and south, and thought the order meant a brick house past the crossroads in front of him as he came north, the first building fitting that description being 1000 yards ahead of the Confederate line. Jim. R.S. Cox, Account published in the *Indianapolis Journal*, in Frank Moore, ed., *The Rebellion Record: A Diary of American Events*, 11 vols. (New York, N.Y., 1864-1868), 5:418. Cox was a Second Lieutenant in Co. F, and Adjutant of the Regiment; Thompson, diary, 198: Hammond, "Campaign of General Smith," *SHSP*, 250.

26. McCray Interview. She was a descendant of a family which fled from Kingston to Bear Wallow during the battle.

27. *O.R.*, 16 (1):945.

28. *Ibid.*

29. E. B. Allen, Capt. Commanding Detachment, 71st Regiment Indiana Volunteers, to W.H. Fairbanks, A.A. Genl., camp near Louisville, Sept. 8, 1862, Edward B. Allen Collection SC10, Folder 2, Indiana Historical Society, Indianapolis. This document appears to be intended as the official regimental report for the battle; Oliver Haskell, Private in Co. A., 71st Indiana Infantry, autographed diary, SC 707, vol. 3, Indiana Historical Society, Indianapolis, Indiana.

30. Thompson, diary, 199; *O.R.*, 16 (1):934.

31. For an opinion that by this time Manson did know of McCray's movement, see Lieutenant General Joseph Wheeler, "Bragg's Invasion of Kentucky," *Battles and Leaders of the Civil War*, 4 vols. (New York, N.Y., 1884, 1888), 3:5.

32. There are a number of different accounts of the details of the wound. Undoubtedly the most reliable is Cleburne's own, *O.R.*, 16 (1):946.

33. Richard Manifee Hunt, "First Battle at Richmond, Kentucky During the Civil War," typed manuscript, Richard M. Hunt Papers, Archives, U.S. Army Military History Institute, Carlisle Barracks, Pa.

34. *O.R.*, 16 (1):942.

35. J. B. Armstrong, Acting Lieutenant Colonel, 95th Ohio Infantry, Supplementary Report to the Governor, in Moore, ed., *Rebellion Record*, 5:412.

36. *O.R.*, 16 (1):920.

37. *Ibid.*, 945-46.

38. W. L. Gammage, Brigade Surgeon, Fourth Arkansas Infantry, *The Camp, The Bivouac, and the Battle Field*, (Selma, Ala., 1864, reprint edition Little Rock, Ark., 1958), 44.

39. Moore, ed., *Rebellion Record*, 5:417.

40. *O.R.*, 16 (1): 909, 921.

41. Thomas D. Clark, *A History of Kentucky* (Lexington, Ky., 1954), 321; Nathaniel Southgate Shaler, *Kentucky: A Pioneer Commonwealth* (Boston, Mass., 1885), 292; "Telmah," "Another Account," *Cincinnati Gazette*, Sept. 5, 1862, reprinted in Moore, ed., *Rebellion Record*, 5: 421. *Rushville* (Ind.) *Jacksonian*, Sept. 10, 1862, 2.

42. Howell Carter, *A Cavalryman's Reminiscences of the Civil War* (New Orleans, L.A., [1900]), 38.

43. *O.R.*, 16 (1): 939; Moore, ed., *Rebellion Record*, 5:419; Foote, *The Civil War*, 1:652.

44. *O.R.*, 16 (1): 909, 936, 943.

Kent Masterson Brown

Munfordville: The Campaign and Battle Along Kentucky's Strategic Axis

Throughout the early months of the Civil War, Abraham Lincoln and his War Department repeatedly urged Union commanders in Kentucky to direct operations against East Tennessee.[1] Politically, the idea had merit, given East Tennessee's animus against secession. History proved, however, that Lincoln's idea was neither the key to holding Kentucky nor to penetrating the lower South.

After Maj. Gen. Don Carlos Buell assumed command of the Department of the Ohio (which included all Union troops in Kentucky) on November 15, 1861, he recognized the great *geographical* axis up which the lower South could be penetrated by Union forces. Commenting on the movement of Union troops up the Tennessee and Cumberland Rivers (both rivers flow north through Kentucky) against Gen. Albert Sidney Johnston's defense lines across southern Kentucky, General Buell, on February 5, 1862—the eve of the surrender of Fort Henry—wrote to Maj. Gen. Henry W. Halleck: "I think it is quite plain that the center of the enemy's line—that part which you are now moving against—is the decisive point of his whole front, as it is also the most vulnerable."[2]

Indeed, no geography was ever more favorable to a modern invading army than was Kentucky's to the Union army in early 1862. What made it so were the Tennessee and Cumberland Rivers. The Tennessee, navigable all the way from its mouth at the Ohio River to the Muscle Shoals at Decatur, Alabama, and the Cumberland, navigable from its mouth at the Ohio River to and beyond Nashville, Tennessee, cut the Confederate defense lines in Kentucky not more than twenty miles apart.

It was along this geographical axis that Gens. Henry W. Halleck and Ulysses S. Grant ruptured General Johnston's Confederate defenses in the winter of 1862.

But there was another element to this great axis, and it was man-made: the Louisville & Nashville Railroad. The L&N was new in 1862. Chartered in Kentucky in 1850, the railroad had taken nine years to construct its 185-mile line between Louisville, Kentucky and Nashville, Tennessee. The first train ran between the two cities on October 27, 1859; regular schedules were established by October 31.[3]

From Louisville, the L&N ran south to Shepherdsville and then to Lebanon Junction where a spur line connected the main stem with the town of Lebanon, Kentucky about thirty-seven miles east. From Lebanon Junction the main stem of the railroad continued south and southwest to Elizabethtown, Munfordville, Horse Cave, Cave City, Bowling Green, and Franklin, Kentucky, before crossing into Tennessee some seventy miles east of where the Cumberland River cut the state line. In Tennessee, the railroad proceeded to Gallatin and then turned west to Nashville.[4]

The L&N connected with the Memphis, Clarksville & Louisville Railroad at Bowling Green, Kentucky, providing passage to Clarksville, Tennessee, and then all the way to Memphis and the Mississippi River by way of the Memphis & Ohio Railroad. At Nashville the L&N connected with the Central Alabama Railroad which ran to Decatur, Alabama, and the Nashville & Chattanooga Railroad, which ran to Stevenson, Alabama. Both Decatur and Stevenson were junctions on the great Memphis & Charleston Railroad, the longest east-west rail line in America, linking Memphis and Chattanooga and points east, by way of the East Tennessee & Georgia Railroad, the East Tennessee & Virginia Railroad, and the Virginia & Tennessee Railroad, all the way to Petersburg, Virginia.[5]

By 1862, the L&N was a most important transportation and communication artery. For Union forces holding Kentucky, the L&N was their principal means of supply and reinforcement, and its telegraph wires, their principal means of communication. To Confederates—after they were forced to relinquish Kentucky—the L&N was their principal target. To retake and hold Tennessee or any portion of Kentucky necessitated, at a minimum, denying Union forces access to the L&N Railroad. For the Confederates to retake Kentucky would require them being supplied by rail from Nashville. Thus, the L&N was critical. Consequently, from the very beginning of the war every bridge on the 185-mile roadbed was protected by troops and elaborate defensive works. In every respect, from the time General Buell's Army of the Ohio seized Nashville after General Johnston's Confederate army evacuated it upon the fall of Forts Henry and Donelson in February, 1862, the L&N Railroad became the axis upon which Kentucky was held or upon which it could be retaken. Buell used the L&N to seize Nashville. Once his army occupied Nashville, the L&N became the principal means by which his divisions were supplied from Louisville. The L&N telegraph wires formed the principal means by which Buell communicated with his supply base at Louisville and points north.[6]

And no location on the L&N line was more critical than the Green River bridge at Munfordville, Kentucky. The town of Munfordville in Hart County, a growing cluster of log and frame houses, brick churches and a number of somewhat impressive brick dwellings showing an advancement from its frontier origins, had about two hundred citizens in 1862. There, the Green River runs below high and precipitous bluffs. Munfordville was built above the north bank of the river, with the little village of Woodsonville above the south bank, just across the waterway. For years, the two towns were connected only by a ferry.[7]

With the coming of the L&N, the "viewscape" changed dramatically. The L&N line ran about one mile west of Munfordville. To cross the deep gorge of the Green River, the L&N called upon the nationally-known bridge designer Albert Fink. With his assistance, a massive bridge was constructed over the river in 1857. The bridge was held up by three principal cut stone piers of enormous proportions. Between the piers and below the roadbed were intricate iron trusses, which were known as "Fink Bridge Trusses." The bridge, including its approaches, was over 1,800 feet long and, at center pier, stood over 115 feet above the Green River. The bridge cost $165,000 to construct.[8]

To destroy the Green River bridge would shut down the railroad for months. So critical was the protection of the bridge at Munfordville that it may be safely said that it was under continuous protection by military forces every single week of the four-year war.[9]

At the beginning of the war, when Gen. Albert Sidney Johnston's Confederate lines extended across southern Kentucky, Maj. Gen. Simon Bolivar Buckner's troops seized the bridge on September 18, 1861, in an effort to block any Union advance down the L&N line. When Union troops entered Kentucky's heartland in December 1861, General Buckner tried to destroy the bridge before he withdrew back to Bowling Green, but only the southern pier was damaged.[10]

Union Maj. Gen. Alexander McDowell McCook's forces seized Munfordville and the bridge on December 10, 1861. McCook immediately ordered work parties to repair it. To protect the bridge and its work parties from Confederate forays from the south, General McCook assigned Col. August Willich and his German-speaking 32nd Indiana Infantry to secure the south end of the structure and lay a pontoon bridge across the river between Munfordville and Woodsonville.[11]

In one of the first actions of the war in Kentucky, Willich's regiment was attacked by Confederate horsemen on December 17, 1861. The 8th Texas Cavalry—or, as it was popularly known, "Terry's Texas Rangers"—struck about two miles south of the bridge at a place along the L&N tracks called Rowlett's Station. Willich's Hoosiers repulsed the raiders.[12]

General McCook then ordered the construction of more elaborate defenses for the bridge. Rifle pits were constructed on either side of the tracks along the bluffs on the south bank of the river, and a two-story log stockade was built on the west side of the tracks at the southern end of the bridge. Such is how the bridge would be defended by Union forces for nearly four years of war. Although McCook's Corps soon moved to Nashville to join in the developing offensive against Johnston's Confederate army, Munfordville was left with sufficient troops to protect the Green River bridge.[13]

Munfordville and the Green River bridge could not escape the ravages of war very long. After all, it was the most vulnerable link in the great axis by which Kentucky was held or could be seized, and to the Confederacy, the retaking of Kentucky remained a principal objective of

General Braxton Bragg. As commander of the Army of the Mississippi, the dyspeptic and contentious Bragg engineered one of the most remarkable movements of large bodies of troops in military history when he invaded Kentucky. His indecisiveness once in the Bluegrass State, however, proved disastrous to the campaign. *Library of Congress*

the war. After the Battle of Shiloh on April 6 and 7, 1862, the death of Gen. Albert Sidney Johnston and the subsequent removal of Johnston's successor, Gen. P. G. T. Beauregard, the L&N Railroad and its Green River bridge at Munfordville would again occupy center stage in the tragic national drama.

Assigned to replace Beauregard after Shiloh was Gen. Braxton Bragg, a hero of the Mexican War and division commander at Shiloh. Bragg has been described as "remarkably intelligent" and upright, but he "was possessed of an irascible temper and was naturally disputatious." A skillful planner, Bragg had an unfortunate reputation for being irritable and prone to vacillation. His men would never grow to like him.[14]

The battered Confederate Army of the Mississippi, then about 45,000 strong, had withdrawn from its base at Corinth, Mississippi—the site of the junction of the Memphis & Charleston Railroad and the Mobile & Ohio Railroad—and marched south to Tupelo on the Mobile & Ohio in the face of a growing Union army under Maj. Gen. Henry W. Halleck of nearly 125,000 men.[15] At Tupelo, Bragg, new to command, was pressured by Maj. Gen. Don Carlos Buell's Union Army of the Ohio, which had joined in the Battle of Shiloh on the night of April 6 after marching from Nashville. Buell's army was now part of Halleck's combined force at Corinth. Bragg claimed that Buell's movement against him at Tupelo "threatened the very heart of our country, and was destined, unless checked immediately, to sever our main line of communication between East and West." After sending one of his divisions to East Tennessee pursuant to orders from the War Department, Bragg determined to move his army to Chattanooga in order to maintain his communications with Richmond, and "there oppose this dangerous combination of the enemy."[16]

Using the Mobile & Ohio Railroad, Bragg boarded all of his infantry on freight trains at Tupelo in July 1862 and transported them south to Mobile, Alabama. From Mobile, the soldiers traveled on the Mobile & Great Northern and the Alabama & Florida Railroads northeast to Montgomery, Alabama, then on the Montgomery & West Point and Atlanta & West Point Railroads east to Atlanta, Georgia. There, Bragg's foot soldiers boarded Western & Atlantic Railroad freight cars and were hauled north to Chattanooga, where they arrived in early August. It was the largest, longest, and most complex movement of troops by means of rail in history. Bragg's artillery, cavalry, and baggage trains were sent across northern Alabama and arrived at Chattanooga a few days after the infantry.[17]

Bragg met in Chattanooga with Gen. Edmund Kirby Smith, commander of the Department of East Tennessee. The two determined on a combined operation to retake Middle Tennessee and invade Kentucky. General Smith returned to Knoxville and commenced a movement toward Cumberland Gap after receiving two more brigades—Brig. Gen. Patrick R. Cleburne's and Brig. Gen. Preston Smith's—from Bragg's army. Bypassing Cumberland Gap, Kirby Smith moved up the old Wilderness Road toward central Kentucky. His advance included a decisive engagement at Richmond on August 29 and 30, 1862, where he demolished Maj. Gen. William "Bull" Nelson's Union Provisional Army of Kentucky. Smith then proceeded to Lexington, the heart of central Kentucky.[18]

In the meantime, General Bragg set his own Army of the Mississippi in motion. On August 28, Bragg's columns moved across Walden's Ridge and headed into the Cumberland Mountains toward Nashville. When Bragg reached Middle Tennessee he discovered that his old adversary, General Buell's Army of the Ohio, in response to the alarm brought about by Kirby Smith's operations in Kentucky, had marched from Corinth, Mississippi, to Nashville. Buell's army was fortifying the city and again using the L&N to secure supplies from, and to communicate with, Louisville.[19]

In response, Bragg moved his army onto the Louisville and Nashville turnpike and headed toward Glasgow, Kentucky, the site of the terminus of a twenty-mile spur line to the main stem of the L&N. It was a difficult march. Tennessee and Kentucky had been suffering under a severe drought which was now in its third month. The road was ankle-deep in dust and forage was scarce. With Bragg threatening his rail communications, Buell marched his men north on dusty roads alongside the L&N toward Bowling Green. Just up the tracks, not more than forty-one miles from two contending armies, was the Green River bridge at Munfordville.[20]

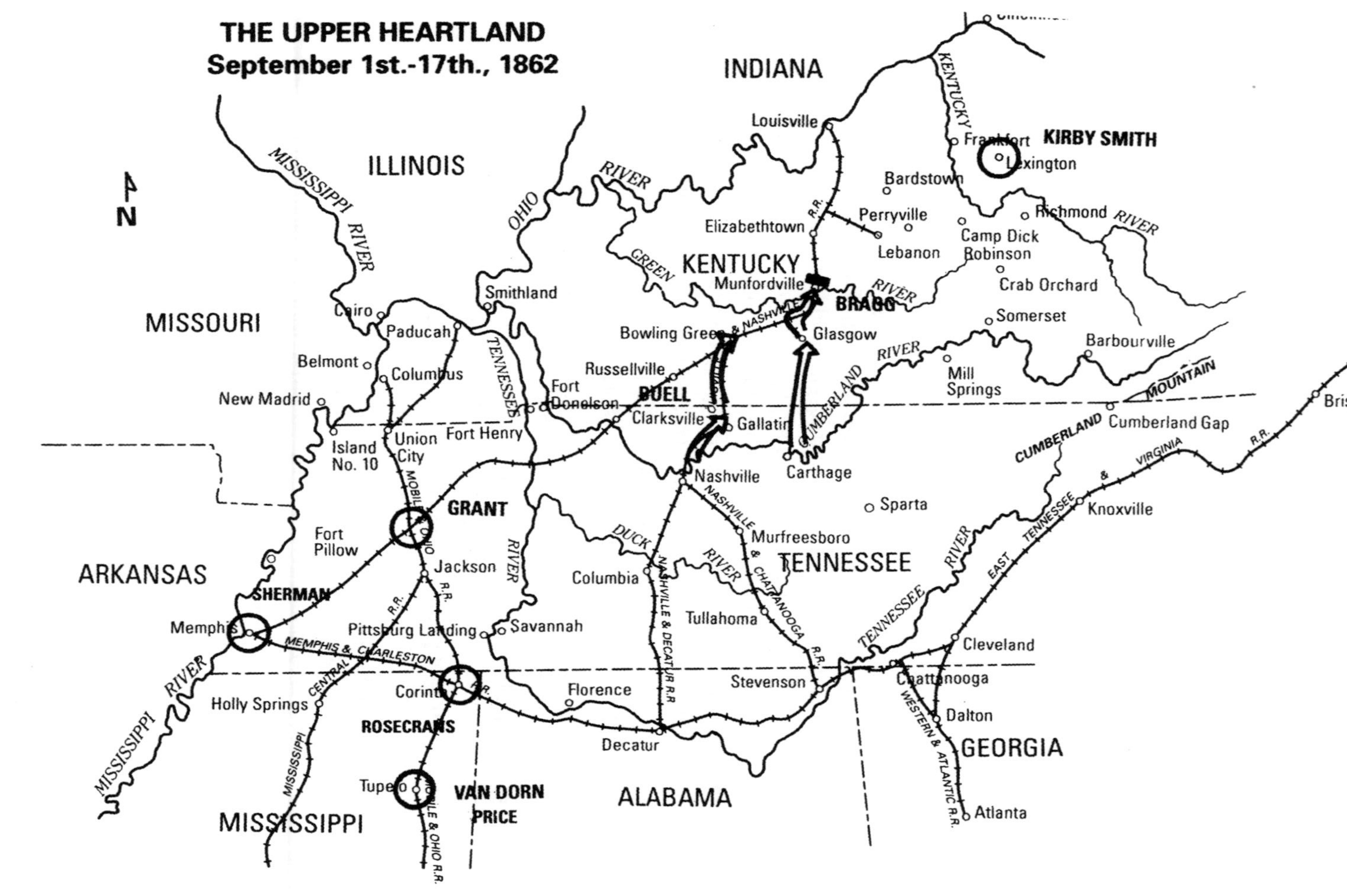
THE UPPER HEARTLAND
September 1st.-17th., 1862
N
ILLINOIS
INDIANA
MISSOURI
ARKANSAS
KENTUCKY
TENNESSEE
MISSISSIPPI
ALABAMA
GEORGIA
MISSISSIPPI RIVER
OHIO RIVER
TENNESSEE RIVER
CUMBERLAND RIVER
GREEN RIVER
KENTUCKY RIVER
DUCK RIVER
CUMBERLAND MOUNTAIN
Cairo
Paducah
Smithland
Louisville
Elizabethtown
Munfordville
Bowling Green
Russellville
Belmont
Columbus
New Madrid
Island No. 10
Union City
Fort Henry
Fort Donelson
Clarksville
Gallatin
Nashville
Glasgow
Carthage
Sparta
Murfreesboro
Tullahoma
Columbia
Stevenson
Chattanooga
Cleveland
Dalton
Atlanta
Knoxville
Cumberland Gap
Barbourville
Somerset
Mill Springs
Crab Orchard
Camp Dick Robinson
Lebanon
Perryville
Bardstown
Frankfort
Lexington
Richmond
Memphis
Fort Pillow
Holly Springs
Jackson
Corinth
Tupelo
Pittsburg Landing
Savannah
Florence
Decatur
SHERMAN
GRANT
ROSECRANS
VAN DORN
PRICE
BUELL
BRAGG
KIRBY SMITH
MEMPHIS & CHARLESTON
MISSISSIPPI CENTRAL R.R.
MOBILE & OHIO R.R.
NASHVILLE & DECATUR R.R.
NASHVILLE & CHATTANOOGA R.R.
WESTERN & ATLANTIC R.R.
EAST TENNESSEE & VIRGINIA R.R.

Colonel John T. Wilder

New York-born and an Indiana industrialist when the war began, Wilder held Munfordville for nine days during the approach of Gen. Braxton Bragg's army, finally surrendering after one of the most bizarre "reviews" of enemy positions in military history.

Library of Congress

Thus far Bragg was satisfied. "Without firing a gun," he wrote, "we had compelled the evacuation of Northern Alabama and Middle Tennessee south of the Cumberland."[21] Indeed he had. But in Louisville, the northern terminus of the L&N, Union forces were mobilizing to resist the invasion. New troops were pouring into the city from Illinois, Indiana , Ohio, and other states in response to the crisis.[22]

A very nervous Maj. Gen. Jeremiah T. Boyle, commander of the Department of Kentucky, followed these events from his Louisville headquarters. Bragg's invading army appeared to be moving straight up the main stem of the L&N. General Buell's Union army was moving astride the L&N toward Bowling Green, racing toward Louisville. Buell was relying upon the railroad line for communications and support.[23]

Boyle desperately needed someone to take command of the skeleton Union forces at Munfordville before Bragg reached the Green River bridge. He turned to a thirty-two year old colonel from Greensburg, Indiana, who was in Louisville getting ready to take new recruits back to join his 17th Indiana Infantry, which was then marching north with Buell's army. His name was John T. Wilder.[24]

Wilder was no professional soldier. Raised in the Catskill Mountains of New York, Wilder had moved with his family to Columbus, Ohio, when he was nineteen. He obtained a job at a foundry in Columbus where he learned drafting and mill-wrighting. In 1857 he moved to Greensburg, Indiana, where he opened a foundry and invented and built hydraulic machinery. By 1861 he had become a nationally known expert in hydraulics. At the outbreak of the war, Wilder raised a company of artillery. He even cast his two six-pound guns at his own foundry. Wilder's dreams of artillery service vanished when his company of men were mustered in as Company A, 17th Indiana Infantry. Within months, Wilder was promoted to lieutenant colonel and then colonel of the 17th Indiana. He and his regiment were with the Army of the Ohio at Shiloh, but arrived on the battlefield too late on April 7 to enter the fighting.[25]

Wilder took command of the garrison at Munfordville on September 8. Assembled at the Green River bridge was an odd complement of newly-recruited volunteers and regulars: the 67th Indiana Infantry under Col. Frank Emerson and 89th Indiana under Col. Charles D. Murray; Company H, 2nd Battalion, 18th United States Infantry; Companies C and K, 74th Indiana Infantry; sixty unarmed men from the 33rd Kentucky Infantry under Capt. Cyrus J. Wilson; and four guns of Lt. Henry Watson's 13th Battery, Indiana Light Artillery. To this assortment of troops Wilder added 204 new recruits from his own 17th Indiana, who had traveled with him down the L&N tracks from Louisville aboard freight cars. In all, Wilder had 2,122 men to protect the Green River bridge. Coming up the road from Glasgow following the L&N main stem, however, was Gen. Braxton Bragg's Army of the Mississippi, about 24,000 strong, veterans of nine months of campaigning and battle-hardened at Shiloh.[26]

Wilder faced enormous obstacles from the outset. His men had only one day's rations and many of them had no arms at all. Wilder sent out foraging parties and urgently sought reinforcements, arms, ammunition, and equipment. In a matter of days the garrison had collected from the surrounding countryside enough forage for ten days, and Wilder was informed by telegraph from Louisville that reinforcements would be on the move soon.[27]

The colonel's greatest discomfort was the nearness of a powerful enemy. Only one day after he assumed command at Munfordville, Wilder learned that the four-hundred fifty foot long and forty-six foot high L&N bridge over the Salt River at Shepherdsville had been partially burned by a roving contingent of Confederate cavalry from Col. John Hunt Morgan's command. It was obvious to Colonel Wilder that if the garrison at Munfordville were to protect the Green River bridge, larger and more imposing fortifications were needed.[28]

Under Wilder's direction and that of the 15th Indiana's Capt. Frank White, Union soldiers began reconstructing the earthworks protecting the bridge along the south bluff of the Green River. The two-story log stockade at the south end of the bridge, about 125 yards west of the tracks, was strengthened. The stockade was used as an observation tower for enemy movements south of Munfordville as well as a defensive bastion for infantry. Surrounding the stockade was a long, arching rifle trench, which was also improved. A rifle trench extending east of the tracks for the better part of 700 yards was constructed. Wilder wanted the works improved for the use of his artillery. Thus, the left end of the long rifle trench was secured on high ground near the Green River Baptist Church above Woodsonville with Fort Craig, a polygon earthwork consisting of four artillery *lunettes* and capable of being held by 300 men.[29]

When finally built, Wilder's earthworks stood in places ten feet high. In front of all the works Wilder opened deep ditches eight feet wide. In the fields approaching the defensive line, Wilder placed improvised *abatis*. He felled trees from the dense woods along the river and from wood lots bordering farmyards and laid them, entangled branches and all, in the open fields in front of the works along with heavy brush and logs to stall any approaching enemy column. Wilder's earthworks and their approaches protecting the Green River bridge were formidable.[30] To prevent surprise, Wilder ordered the unarmed men of Captain Wilson's 33rd Kentucky to spread out in the fields alongside the L&N tracks and the turnpike for miles south of the defenses to provide warning of the approach of any Confederate force and to gather intelligence. Elements of the 89th Indiana Infantry took up skirmish positions in the fields ahead of the works.[31]

Events moved rapidly. On September 12 General Bragg's army entered Glasgow and cut off the approaches to Cave City and the L&N from use by Buell's army, which was then between the Tennessee border and Bowling Green. Bragg quickly moved astride the L&N and rested his road-weary and tattered army, sensing he would soon have to repel Buell along the L&N corridor.[32]

Bragg reconnoitered the country ahead of him while his army rested. He appreciated the fact that the L&N, as a life line to the Union forces in Kentucky, depended upon the Green River bridge remaining intact. Upon instructions from Bragg, Gen. Jones Withers, commander of the army's reserve division, ordered Gen. James R. Chalmers to move his leading brigade of Mississippians ahead. At 8:00 p.m., behind a small detachment of cavalry commanded by Lt. G. T. Banks, Chalmers moved his brigade along with its baggage and ordnance trains forward on the dusty turnpike astride the L&N to Cave City.[33]

James Ronald Chalmers, like his counterpart Colonel Wilder, was only thirty-two years old. Born in Halifax County, Virginia, Chalmers had moved to Holly Springs, Mississippi, with his family as a young boy. Chalmers studied at South Carolina College, graduating in 1851. He returned to Holly Springs where he was admitted to the bar two years later. Chalmers served as district attorney at Holly Springs and, in the secession crisis, was elected a delegate to the convention which passed the ordinance

General James R. Chalmers

His hard-fighting Mississippi brigade assaulted the Union works at Munfordville in a manner described by Gen. Braxton Bragg as "injudicious and unauthorized."

Library of Congress

taking Mississippi out of Union. The Virginia native entered Confederate service as colonel of the 9th Mississippi Infantry. He served with that regiment at Pensacola, Florida, in early 1862 after the fall of the Union garrison there at the beginning of the war. Elevated to the rank of brigadier general, Chalmers assumed command of a brigade of Mississippi regiments in April 1862, which he led with conspicuous gallantry at the Battle of Shiloh. On the battle's first day Chalmers's "High Pressure Brigade," as it came to be known, participated in six major assaults against the Union left flank. The brigade suffered 82 men killed and another 343 wounded, but captured more than 1,600 Union soldiers.[34]

Those veteran Mississippi commands were still serving with Chalmers on the evening of September 12, and included the 7th, 9th, 10th, 29th, and Blythe's (44th) Mississippi Infantry regiments, along with Richards's Battalion of Mississippi Sharpshooters and Ketchum's Alabama battery of artillery, commanded by Lt. James C. Garrity. Clad in all kinds of butternut-dyed attire and wearing broad-brimmed hats of every kind and description, the Mississippians kept up the march even though most were barefooted. Although worn and sick from exhausting campaigns and thinned by battle, the six Mississippi infantry units were among the best fighters in the Army of the Mississippi.[35]

Chalmers's Brigade marched eleven miles, reaching Cave City at 11:30 p.m. The town was taken completely by surprise. The L&N depot, together with its telegraph office and the post office, were quickly seized to prevent any outgoing communications to Union forces up the tracks. Chalmers called upon Sgt. Samuel Bradford, 1st Louisiana Infantry—who had been detailed to Chalmers's staff as a telegrapher—to establish telegraphic communications with Louisville. Bradford tapped out messages at Cave City as though he was the regular L&N telegrapher in an attempt to convince Union authorities that all was well there. Messages intercepted by Bradford revealed the presence of a sizable Union force at Munfordville with more men on the way.[36]

On the morning of Saturday, September 13, General Chalmers ordered a reconnaissance along the L&N toward Munfordville. His scouts discovered a mill up the tracks near Horse Cave containing a considerable quantity of wheat. Chalmers directed the 10th and Blythe's

Soldiers of Company B, 9th Mississippi Infantry, at Pensacola, Florida in late 1861. These soldiers in Gen. James R. Chalmers's Brigade assaulted Fort Craig near Munfordville. Note the wide variety of garments, broad-brimmed hats and accouterments. *Library of Congress*

(44th) Mississippi regiments forward to seize and grind the wheat for his hungry troops.[37]

Although Chalmers's location was not known by Union commanders in Louisville, the presence of Bragg's main army at Glasgow had already had a profound effect upon them. At about 7:00 p.m. on September 13, while Chalmers's Brigade held Cave City and his men were grinding flour in Horse Cave, Union Gen. Charles C. Gilbert in Louisville called upon Col. Cyrus L. Dunham and his 50th Indiana Infantry to proceed at once to Munfordville to bolster Colonel Wilder's small command. Colonel Dunham was in Louisville with six companies of his newly-raised regiment as part of Indiana Governor Oliver P. Morton's response to the invasion alarm. Given one company (Company K of the 78th Indiana Infantry) in addition to his own men, Dunham and his contingent of 446 troops, with five day's rations, boarded an L&N train at 11:00 p.m. at the Louisville depot and headed south to Munfordville.[38]

Chalmers learned of the order for Colonel Dunham to reinforce Colonel Wilder soon after the directive was issued. Sergeant Bradford had intercepted the message from Union headquarters at the Cave City L&N depot. Two hours later, Chalmers received more valuable information from Col. John C. Scott, whose cavalry brigade, accompanied by five mountain howitzers from Gen. Edmund Kirby Smith's army, was operating in the area in an effort to establish communications with Bragg. According to Scott, the Union force at Munfordville was only 1,800 strong and consisted of largely raw troops. Scott also reported that the telegraph between Munfordville and Louisville had just been severed by his men. Scott informed Chalmers that he had already challenged Colonel Wilder's resolve that afternoon. The cavalryman had approached the Union works by following the north side of the river from Greensburg and had demanded Wilder's surrender. Wilder had "peremptorily refused." Scott intended to attack the Union forces at Munfordville early the next morning and requested Chalmers's cooperation in the attempt.[39]

With hardly a moment's hesitation Chalmers determined to move ahead with his brigade to Scott's assistance. Leaving all his baggage and a sufficient force behind to protect Cave City, Chalmers moved his brigade, along with its ordnance trains, forward at 10:00 p.m. The Mississippians marched twelve dusty miles astride the L&N through Horse Cave to a position just south of Wilder's defensive works at Munfordville.[40]

Union Colonel Dunham and his men were also on the move. Chugging down the L&N tracks at a slow rate of speed, Dunham's train moved ever deeper into the area where Confederate raiding parties had been active. The Salt River bridge had been repaired enough to use, but that was little consolation to the engineer. Dunham, impatient with his timidity, climbed into the engine cab and instructed the engineer to speed up the train. The nervous operator opened the throttle on the wood-burning engine. The train crossed Bacon Creek, about seven miles north of Munfordville, and stopped to take on more wood. Colonel Dunham ran from car to car, alerting the men to stand by their arms in anticipation of an attack. He returned to the engine and the train slowly chugged ahead. After proceeding about one mile, the locomotive struck a rail which had been undermined by Confederate raiders (probably Colonel Scott's cavalrymen), slid to one side and fell off of the roadbed. The coupled freight cars followed suit, turning over and crashing into the ground and one another. Oddly enough, not a single soldier was seriously injured.[41]

Colonel Dunham climbed out of the hissing engine and helped extricate his men from the wrecked cars. The Hoosiers were formed in a battle line along the tracks while skirmishers were sent into the woods bordering the railroad to protect the troops from ambush. When no enemy troops were found, Dunham ordered his men to march to Munfordville on the double-quick. It was about 3:00 a.m., Sunday, September 14.[42]

While Dunham and his infantry were approaching Munfordville from the north, General Chalmers's Confederates were marching toward the town from the south. All along the way the Mississippians met frantic civilians fleeing south on foot and in all sorts of wagons loaded with personal possessions. The Union forces at Munfordville, claimed some of the civilians, were stronger than Chalmers had been led to believe. A dense ground fog, however, eliminated any hope of an effective reconnaissance of the Union works.[43]

Chalmers's vanguard was composed of Maj. W. C. Richards's Battalion of Sharpshooters. As Richards's men passed Rowlett's Station, one and one-half miles south of Colonel Wilder's line of works, they ran headlong into skirmishers from Col. Frank Emerson's 89th Indiana Infantry, deployed along the south side of the turnpike near the L&N tracks. The first Union volley knocked Major Richards from his horse with a severe wound. One of his company commanders assumed command as firing rippled up and down the line. The Hoosiers, however, held on stubbornly and refused to yield their ground.[44]

The sudden outbreak of gunfire convinced Chalmers to order Col. Thomas W. White's 9th Mississippi and Col. E. L. Walthall's 29th Mississippi forward to support Richards. Lieutenant Garrity's battery rumbled along the road behind them, with the 10th Mississippi bringing up the rear. The skirmishers of the 89th Indiana, under the tactical direction of Maj. George Cubberly, slowly withdrew in the face of the approaching columns of Mississippi infantry.[45]

Garrity's guns unlimbered about one thousand yards south of the Union works along an elevation west of the tracks known locally as Lewis's Hill. While Garrity's four guns raked the Hoosier columns, the 9th and 29th Mississippi regiments formed in lines of battle and fired several volleys at the retreating enemy.[46] The Union skirmishers suddenly found themselves nearly surrounded, and Colonel Emerson yelled for the men to fall back. As the Union line withdrew, the first streaks of daylight broke through the fog, dust, and acrid gun smoke which blanketed the dark fields ahead of the Union field works. It was 5:30 a.m.[47]

Garrity's artillery fire appeared to be effective. Heavy columns of flame and smoke arose from near the railroad bridge. That, coupled with the steady withdrawal of the Union skirmishers, led Chalmers to believe that Wilder's Union forces were abandoning their lines. It was difficult to tell, however, for the fog, dust, smoke and lingering darkness continued to obscure Chalmers's view.[48]

Nevertheless, the aggressive Chalmers decided to move quickly. He ordered one section (two guns) of Garrity's battery under Lieutenant Garrity himself, along with the 9th and 29th Mississippi regiments, to move to the right of the battlefield, where they formed along a hill nearly one thousand yards in front of Fort Craig. Garrity soon opened fire on the bastion.[49] The left section of Garrity's battery was ordered to limber up and moved farther down Lewis's Hill toward the works in front of the stockade protecting the southern approach to the bridge. Colonel Robert Alexander Smith was directed by Chalmers to move his 10th Mississippi toward the bank of the Green River in front of the left section of Garrity's battery and advance against the works in front of the reinforced stockade. Blythe's (44th) Mississippi regiment, under Lt. Col. James Moore, was kept in reserve to protect the ordnance train.[50]

As these dispositions were taking place, Captain Watt E. Strickland of Chalmers's staff rode up to Colonel Smith. "Colonel, the general orders you to charge."

Smith found little comfort in the news, for neither of the regiments on the Confederate right—the 9th and 29th Mississippi—were in place to engage the enemy. "To charge now before the right is ready will draw upon me the concentrated fire of the enemy," he declared. "Will it not be too soon?"

"No," replied Strickland, "the general says, charge now."

"The duty is mine," Smith shot back, "[but] the responsibility belongs elsewhere." Smith deployed his 10th Mississippi in two battle lines beneath its flapping, star-crossed Polk flag. With rolling drums, he ordered the men forward and spurred his mount toward the Union works.[51]

Looking again to his right, Chalmers ordered Lieutenant Garrity's two-gun section and the 9th and 29th Mississippi regiments forward to the Woodson House, about two hundred yards from Fort Craig. The infantrymen were ordered to keep under cover while the artillery pounded away at the fort and its defenders. Determined to strengthen the attack on his right, Chalmers ordered Col. W. H. Bishop's 7th Mississippi to follow the 9th and 29th regiments and halt within supporting distance. Richards's Sharpshooters kept up a lively fire from the *abatis*-strewn fields in front of Colonel Wilder's defenses. By now it was 6:30 a.m.[52]

As Bishop was guiding his 7th Mississippi troops to the right, Colonel Robert Alexander Smith, holding the extreme left of Chalmers's line, bravely led his 10th Mississippi across the fields toward the stockade. The patrician colonel was a remarkable man. Born in Edinburgh, Scotland in 1836, he emigrated to America at the age of fourteen in 1850, settling with his older brother James in Jackson, Mississippi. At the outbreak of the war, Robert helped raise a company of militia and was elected captain. His first duty had been to escort Jefferson Davis to the capital at Montgomery, Alabama. When it reached Pensacola, Florida, Smith's company became Company D, 10th Mississippi Infantry. Smith was elected colonel of the regiment before the Battle of Shiloh where, on Sunday, April 6, his gallant leadership won the undying admiration of his Mississippians. Now he was yelling for his men to advance again on a Sunday through a storm of gunfire toward the Union works at Munfordville.[53]

Smith's men dropped rapidly as Union bullets began finding their marks. His horse was shot from beneath him. Undaunted, the brave colonel stood up, waved his sword, and led his men forward on foot. He soon reached a beech log *abatis* in front of the Union rifle trench protecting the stockade. As he was urging his men on, Smith was struck in the abdomen by rifle fire. The wound was found to be mortal, and he was carried from the field by Sgt. Maj. William French and Capt. George Dobson of his staff, along with his black servant, Henry, to a house in the rear which had been converted into a field hospital.[54]

As Smith's line crested against the log works, General Chalmers ordered Blythe's (44th) Mississippi regiment forward to support them. Lt. Col. James G. Bullard, a cadaverous-looking man fanatically dedicated to both "the cause" and Colonel Smith, assumed command of the 10th Mississippi. Bullard's luck, however, proved no better than his dying superior's. Within minutes he was shot in the face and killed. J. M. Walker, a mere captain, assumed command of the 10th Mississippi. The brief assault left thirteen men killed and ninety-five wounded.[55]

Like the 10th Mississippi, Blythe's (44th) Mississippi regiment was riddled with gunfire as soon as it appeared within range of the Union works. Regimental commander Lt. Col. James Moore, advancing behind the center of the line, was shot down. Major John C. Thompson was on the right of the regiment when he heard his commander had fallen. Thompson guided his mount to the center of the line and found Moore on the ground, mortally wounded. Thompson ordered the men to lie down

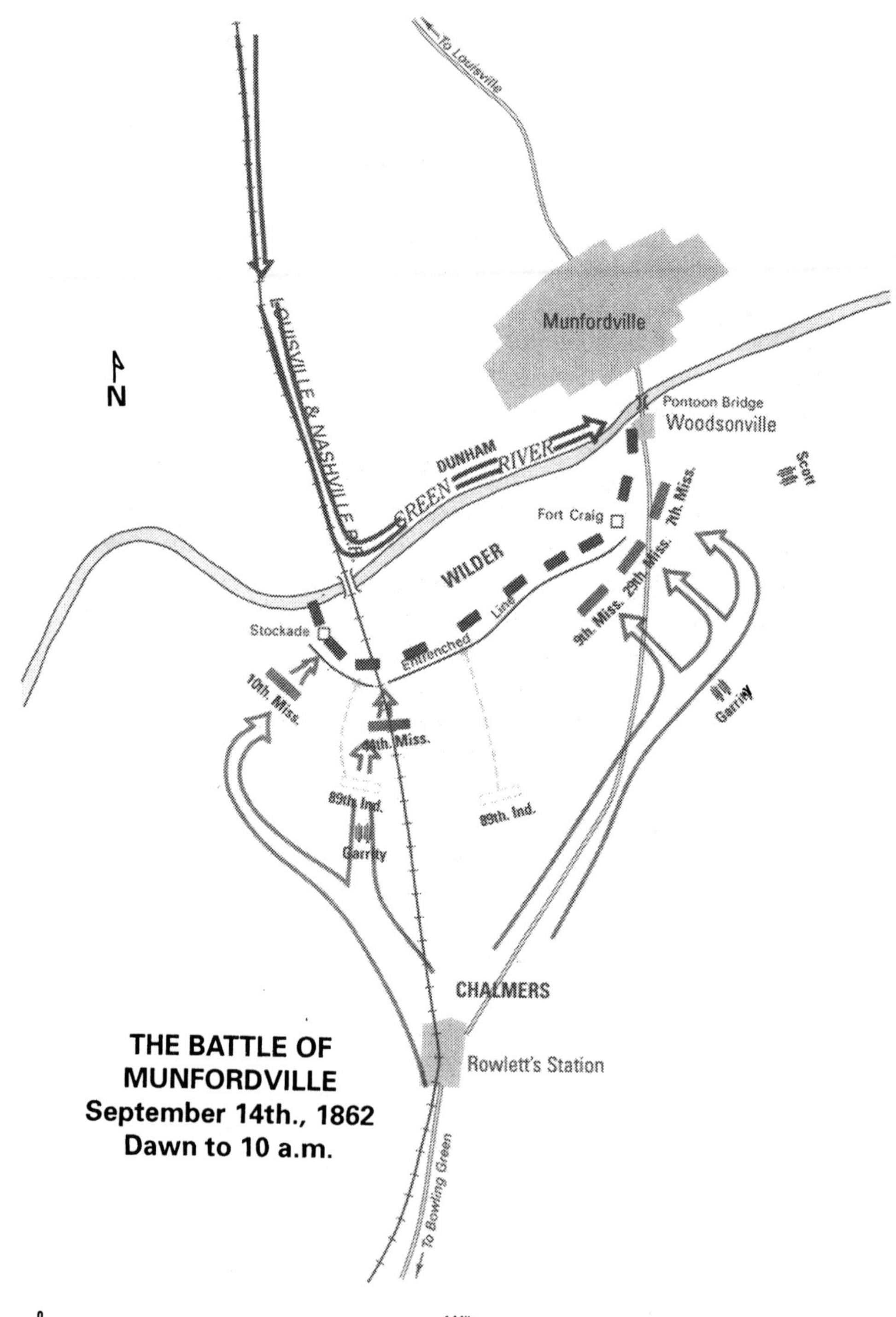
To Louisville
Munfordville
N
LOUISVILLE & NASHVILLE R.R.
Pontoon Bridge
Woodsonville
DUNHAM
GREEN RIVER
Scott
Fort Craig
7th. Miss.
WILDER
29th. Miss.
9th. Miss.
Stockade
Entrenched Line
10th. Miss.
Garrity
44th. Miss.
89th. Ind.
89th. Ind.
Garrity
CHALMERS
THE BATTLE OF MUNFORDVILLE
September 14th., 1862
Dawn to 10 a.m.
Rowlett's Station
To Bowling Green
0
1 Mile

to get out of the way of the gunfire and make the Union troops believe they had retreated in the dense smoke. In less than thirty minutes Blythe's regiment lost four killed and thirty-eight wounded.[56]

Wilder's men barely held on in the face of Chalmers's piecemeal attacks. His four artillery pieces fired grape and canister into the faces of Chalmers's Mississippians, while his infantrymen let loose heavy volleys. Major Augustus H. Abbott of the 67th Indiana Infantry was killed while bravely standing on the parapet, his hat in one hand and drawn sabre in the other, urging the men to stand to their works. So heavy was the Confederate gunfire that Abbott's regimental flag was riddled with 146 bullet holes and the staff struck eleven times. Wilder, steadying his men, scanned the north bank of the river for relief.[57]

Help for Colonel Wilder was nearby. After their harrowing journey by train and by foot, Colonel Dunham and his Hoosier reinforcements were finally only three or four miles from Munfordville. A civilian warned Dunham of the nearness of Col. John Scott's Southern cavalry. Dunham ordered his men to detour through woods, cornfields and ravines to elude the enemy. His force reached the Green River just downstream from the railroad bridge and opposite the stockade. The gunfire on the bluffs was thunderous but, above the din, Wilder's Hoosier and Kentucky troops yelled and cheered at the arrival of the reinforcements. Dunham ordered his men upstream to the pontoon bridge at Woodsonville. A detachment of Scott's cavalry attempted to block the crossing of the river, but Dunham brought his men into battle line and fired a series of volleys at the horsemen. The way was soon cleared, and Dunham raced his Hoosiers across the pontoon bridge to join their fellow Union soldiers, who were bravely resisting the Confederate assaults.[58]

Colonel Dunham and his men entered the fort, where they were met by Colonel Wilder. Recognizing that Dunham was his senior in rank, Wilder offered him command of the Union forces. Dunham, however, wisely refused. The battle was in progress, and he did not want to disrupt the chain-of-command established by Wilder during the crisis.[59]

Unlike his Union counterpart, General Chalmers displayed marked confusion in his decision-making on the battlefield. He was having second thoughts about sending Colonel Smith's 10th Mississippi

The Battle of Munfordville. Artist Henri Lovie's drawing from *Frank Leslie's Illustrated Newspaper* accurately shows the attack of what appears to be either the 29th or 7th Mississippi Infantry regiments through the *abatis* of felled trees against Union forces at Fort Craig. Note the distant Louisville & Nashville Railroad bridge over the Green River, the objective of the Confederate attack. *New York Public Library*

forward against the stockade and its rifle trenches. After ordering the 9th and 29th Mississippi regiments on the right to move closer to Fort Craig, Chalmers considered countermanding his orders to Smith and sending him to the opposite end of the line with the idea of launching a massive assault with all of his regiments against Colonel Wilder's exposed left flank at Fort Craig. It was now too late for that. Smith had already fallen mortally wounded, and his regiment was being torn to pieces in front of the stockade. Instead, Chalmers ordered the 7th, 9th and 29th Mississippi regiments forward against the Union left at Fort Craig. He hoped this assault would score a breakthrough and take the pressure off of the beleaguered 10th Mississippi and Blythe's (44th) Mississippi regiments.[60] With the 7th Mississippi on the right, the 9th Mississippi on the left and the 29th Mississippi in the center, the long column moved out from its cover behind the Woodson House and marched toward Fort Craig behind a line of skirmishers. Flags flapped overhead and drums rolled. The Mississippians yelled.[61]

Colonel Wilder's Union troops were prepared. Anticipating an attack against the bastion fort, they had set fire to the Green River Baptist Church to avoid it being used by the Confederates to snipe at the troops in the fort. Heavy smoke from the burning church covered the battlefield. As the three Mississippi regiments approached the works and unleash a series of volleys, the Union defenders returned fire from behind their high breastworks. Chalmers soon discovered that the left flank of his advancing line was "in the air," and the open fields gave the defenders a clear line of fire into the exposed left of the 9th Mississippi. As both sides traded volleys, Chalmers shifted the 9th to the right flank, where it took up a position in rear of the 7th Mississippi for an advance against the fort from the direction of the river.[62]

The attack reached a point only twenty-five yards from the ditch in front of Fort Craig when artillery shells began to explode within the Confederate ranks. The men were ordered to halt and about-face, their officers believing a Union battery had gotten in their rear. Unfortunately for the Southerners, the battery doing the damage belonged to Colonel Scott's cavalry brigade, which was positioned some distance to the east of Fort Craig. Unable to penetrate the strong Union line of works, Chalmers ordered his men to fall back out of range of Wilder's gunfire.

One hundred fourteen officers and men in the three Mississippi regiments had fallen in the hapless assault, some due to friendly fire. Like all else that morning, confusion and indecision undermined success for Chalmers's Brigade. It was now about 9:30 a.m.[63]

Realizing that his force was not strong enough to carry the Union lines, Chalmers sent Maj. J. B. Morgan of the 29th Mississippi forward under a flag of truce. Major Morgan tendered to Wilder a note demanding that he surrender unconditionally.[64] Wilder would have none of it. The Union commander quickly scribbled a reply peremptorily refusing to surrender, and informed Chalmers that he had been reinforced. He would, however, allow Chalmers to remove his dead and wounded if he wished to do so. Chalmers accepted Wilder's generous offer. Chalmers had lost thirty-five men killed and 250 wounded, including three regimental commanders and eleven commissioned officers. It had been a bloody morning. Wilder reported the loss of seventy-two officers and men. Borrowing shovels from the Union defenders, Chalmers's fatigue parties buried their dead on the field and conveyed their wounded to hospital sites at Rowlett's Station. The ghastly work continued through the night and into the morning of Monday, September 15.[65]

Colonel Wilder's men had held their position. Thus far, the Green River bridge remained secure. When General Bragg heard the news of Chalmers's disastrous attack, he referred to it as "unauthorized and injudicious; but the conduct of the troops and commander in action reflects credit on both, and adds but another proof to the many of their distinguished gallantry."[66]

Chalmers's failure, however, meant Bragg had to seize the Union position at Munfordville; he could not move any farther into Kentucky with such a sizable Union position in his rear or on his flank. Of more importance, he could not allow the L&N Railroad to continue operating for the benefit of General Buell's army. Bragg, therefore, determined to move his Army of the Mississippi northward astride the L&N Railroad to seize the Green River bridge and its Union defenders.

With the battle over, Colonel Dunham assumed command of the Union forces on September 15. He quickly set his men to work improving the entrenchments. Wagons were sent back to the train which wrecked the day before to retrieve all the rations and ammunition which it carried. Luckily, loyal Union citizens of Munfordville had secreted the rations and ammunition to prevent their capture by the Confederates. Dunham sent out details to repair the telegraph wires to Louisville, and mounted messengers were sent up the L&N tracks toward Louisville asking for reinforcements.[67]

The results of Dunham's efforts were obvious by nightfall. From Lebanon Junction, reinforcements were sent by rail to Munfordville. Arriving at the Green River under cover of darkness was the 60th Indiana Infantry under Col. Richard Owen; Lt. George Conaway's Company I, 28th Kentucky; the 68th Indiana Infantry under Col. Edward A. King; and six pieces of artillery of Capt. Andrew Konkle's Battery D, 1st Ohio Light Artillery.[68]

There was also movement south of Munfordville. In response to General Chalmers's appeals, the 28th Alabama Infantry under Col. John W. Frazer and Col. A. J. Lythgoe's 19th South Carolina Infantry, both of Col. Arthur M. Manigault's Brigade, Jones Withers's reserve division, were marching from Cave City on the double-quick. Behind them, all of General Bragg's Army of the Mississippi was on the move up the turnpike paralleling the L&N tracks, over 24,000 strong. Farther down the L&N Railroad tracks, Gen. Don Carlos Buell's Union Army of the Ohio finally reached Bowling Green.[69]

At 9:30 a.m. on September 16, the leading elements of Bragg's army, the 28th Alabama and 19th South Carolina, reached Rowlett's Station.[70] Colonel Dunham had ordered Company A, 60th Indiana, followed by Companies A, B, H and G, 50th Indiana, along with Company K, 78th Indiana, forward as skirmishers to resist the Confederate advance. All day long the sound of gunfire alternately increased and slackened in the fields south of the Green River bridge. The Indiana skirmishers held on even though casualties mounted. With each passing hour, though, more of Bragg's army arrived on the field until his entire force faced Dunham's little command protecting the Green River bridge.[71]

Among the hard-fighting divisions that arrived along the hills and fields near Rowlett's Station was the one commanded by Maj. Gen. Simon Bolivar Buckner, part of Maj. Gen. William J. Hardee's wing of

General Simon Bolivar Buckner. Born in Hart County, Kentucky, Buckner negotiated the surrender of Union forces holding his hometown of Munfordville, Kentucky. He was elected Governor of Kentucky after the war. *Library of Congress*

the Army of the Mississippi. Buckner had been in command only a brief while, for he had only recently been released from Fort Warren prison after his capture at Fort Donelson the previous February. What made General Buckner's presence so unique was that he was born and raised in Hart County, Kentucky, not more than seven miles from Munfordville. Born in 1823 in a spacious log home named "Glen Lily," Buckner spent his boyhood in Munfordville, often with a young friend named Thomas John Wood. (In a sad bit of irony, at the very moment Buckner's Division approached Rowlett's Station, Thomas Wood, now a major general in the Union Army, was bringing his division into Bowling Green with Buell's Army of the Ohio.) Buckner graduated from West Point in 1840 and made a distinguished record for himself in the Mexican War. On the eve of the Civil War, he led the pro-Southern Kentucky State Guard. Refusing a command in the Union Army, Buckner was commissioned a brigadier general in the Confederate Army on September 14, 1861. The Kentuckian had once held the Green River bridge while commanding forces under Gen. Albert Sidney Johnston. He had even tried to destroy it in December 1861. Now he was back, approaching his old home town at the head of a division of infantry trying to recapture his home state.[72]

General Bragg determined to take the Union defenses of the Green River bridge by storm. General Buckner appealed to General Hardee to intercede and employ an alternate plan, hoping to save his hometown from destruction and the army from further loss of men. Buckner wanted to mass the army in front of and around the Union works in hopes that the show-of-force would cause the Union commander to capitulate. Buckner finally appealed to Bragg, who agreed to the arrangement. Bragg's wing commander, Gen. Leonidas Polk, was ordered to move his divisions across the Green River east of Munfordville and encircle the Union forces on the north. Hardee's command, including Buckner's Division, spread out along the hills and fields south of the Green River, facing Dunham's defenses. Within hours, Munfordville and the Green River bridge were invested.[73]

Between 5:00 and 6:00 p.m., a flag of truce was observed approaching the Union lines. Wilder was directed by Dunham to receive it. The messenger handed Wilder a note from Bragg, which Wilder tendered to Dunham. Bragg informed his opposite that he was surrounded by an overwhelming force with all hopes of reinforcements cut off. Bragg demanded the surrender of the Union forces to prevent the useless loss of life, or the works would be taken by storm. The colonel's first reaction was to refuse, but Wilder demanded he reconsider. Dunham asked Bragg for a cessation of hostilities while the demand was considered. A cease fire was agreed upon until 9:00 p.m., and Dunham called a council of war among his senior regimental commanders. Gathered together behind the Union defensive works were Colonel Wilder; Colonel Dunham; Col. Edward A. King, 68th Indiana; Col. Richard Owen, 60th Indiana; Col. Frank Emerson, 67th Indiana; Col. Charles Murray, 89th Indiana; and Capt. Andrew Konkle, Battery D, 1st Ohio Light Artillery.[74]

Finding the wires miraculously reopened along the L&N, Dunham quickly telegraphed Gen. Charles C. Gilbert in Louisville, informing him that the enemy had been held, but that fresh columns were moving against Munfordville. Dunham also informed Gilbert that he would hold out as long as possible. Incredibly, a message was soon returned from General Gilbert relieving Colonel Dunham of command and ordering him to turn over the garrison to Colonel Wilder. Dunham continued the council of war. In the end, Wilder, Dunham, King, Owen, Emerson, Murray and Konkle agreed to surrender—but only if some competent officer could observe the enemy's strength to verify Bragg's representations.[75]

Once the conference was concluded, Dunham followed his orders and turned the command over to Wilder. He then telegraphed Gilbert informing him of his action, and that he would not fight under the command of a junior officer (Wilder) except as a soldier in the trenches. Gilbert promptly telegraphed Dunham that he was under arrest, and ordered him to report to Colonel Wilder as such.[76]

At about 2:00 a.m. on September 17, a blindfolded Union officer was escorted into General Buckner's presence. He was none other than Col. John T. Wilder. The Union colonel informed Buckner that he had come through the lines in order to get advice about surrendering. "I come to you to find out what I ought to do," said Wilder. Buckner was startled. "It appealed to me at once," remembered Buckner years afterward. "I wouldn't have deceived that man under those circumstances for anything."[77]

"Colonel," Buckner replied, "I cannot advise you about that, you are in command of your troops, and you must decide for yourself what you ought to do; but I will give you some facts for which I pledge my honor as a soldier and a gentleman: At this moment you are surrounded by a force of not less than twenty-two thousand men [there were more than twenty-four thousand]. There are in position about eighty to one hundred pieces of artillery, those on the south side commanding your position in reverse; they have orders to open fire at daylight. It is for you to judge how long your command would live under that fire."[78]

Colonel Wilder looked very solemn, recalled Buckner. For about five minutes he said nothing, contemplating his predicament. "Well," Wilder finally replied, "it seems to me, General Buckner, that I ought to surrender."

"No, Colonel," Buckner snapped back, "you appealed to me, and I must tell you frankly everything that I think a soldier ought to do. You need not tell me the strength of your army; I know what it is. You need not tell me that, because it would be wrong, but I pretty well know what it is. You are the judge of whether you could live under the fire that is to be opened on you; but if you have information that would induce you to think that the sacrificing of every man at this place would gain your army an advantage elsewhere, it is your duty to do it."[79]

Wilder denied he had any such information, but he asked to observe the Confederate lines in order to verify for himself the situation represented by Buckner. Buckner agreed, and the two officers rode along the Confederate lines, viewing the massed infantry columns and artillery batteries. It had to be the most bizarre review of troops of the entire war. In the end, Wilder, satisfied about the truth of Buckner's statements, simply stated: "I believe I will surrender."

"If that is your conclusion," replied Buckner, "I will take you to General Bragg."[80]

At Bragg's headquarters, discussions hit a snag. Wilder wanted his men paroled, given their personal effects and four days' rations, and allowed to go to the Ohio River after giving up all arms, ammunition and government supplies. "Such terms are unheard of, and cannot be considered," snapped an irritated Bragg. "We have men and guns enough in position to crush you out of existence without losing a man." The disputatious Bragg dismissed the Union colonel from his presence.[81]

"This is willful murder," said General Buckner.

"That if it was," replied Wilder, "he had to commit it."

General Buckner admonished Wilder to stay where he was and returned to Bragg's tent. After a few minutes he rejoined Wilder and explained that the surrender terms had been left to him. The two officers agreed on the terms of surrender.[82]

In the early morning of September 17, Bragg and his commanders received the surrender of Wilder's Union force at Rowlett's Station. It was a formal occasion. Wilder marched his weary command—over 4,000 officers and men—out of the works protecting the Green River bridge. The captives tramped down the Louisville and Nashville Turnpike and lined up, one unit after the other, facing the heavy columns of Confederate infantry, artillery and cavalry. Each unit simultaneously laid down arms in formal surrender. They were then paroled, given captured rations, and led back up the turnpike for the long march back to Louisville.[83]

Sadly, on that very day in far away Maryland, General Buckner's wife's brother, Union Col. Henry Walter Kingsbury, was mortally wounded leading his 11th Connecticut Infantry across Antietam Creek near the lower stone bridge in an effort to turn back Gen. Robert E. Lee's invasion at the Battle of Antietam. Buckner would spend much of the rest of his life trying to settle Kingsbury's estate.[84]

Munfordville and the Green River bridge were now in Confederate hands. Bragg, using all of the Union earthworks, readied his army for the approach of Buell's Union legions, just down the L&N tracks. From his headquarters, a jubilant Bragg telegraphed a message to President Davis in Richmond informing him of the glorious victory and that his "junction" with Gen. Edmund Kirby Smith's army was now "complete." Of course, no junction of the two armies had been effectuated at all.[85]

And what was General Bragg to do now? Should he turn and fight General Buell's approaching Union army before it reached Louisville? Or, should he move east to join forces with Kirby Smith? Bragg chose

Troops from Gen. Don Carlos Buell's Army of the Ohio crossing the Barren River near Bowling Green, Kentucky in September, 1862. Francis T. Miller, *Photographic History of the Civil War*, 1:211

the latter option. Of all the decisions of his wartime career, Bragg regretted that one the most. On September 22, he moved his army north from Munfordville toward Hodgenville and Bardstown. Buell took full advantage of Bragg's strategic blunder and raced his men unmolested up the L&N Railroad to Louisville, where his army was reinforced and re-equiped. "Here," wrote Gen. Basil W. Duke after the war, "was the first exhibition of [Bragg's] vacillation, that fatal irresolution, which was to wither the bright hopes his promises and his previous action had aroused." Bragg, who never linked up with Kirby Smith in Kentucky, was finally forced to give battle to Buell's reinforced army outside of Perryville on October 8, 1862. After that bloody day, Bragg gave up Kentucky and returned to Tennessee.[86]

But before Bragg ever left Munfordville, he ordered the Green River bridge destroyed. Under the supervision of General Buckner—and with the help of some of the local citizens of Munfordville who helped build the great bridge in 1857—the span was set afire, and its flaming roadbed and wooden supports crashed into the river.

Buell's army arrived at Munfordville after Bragg's Confederates evacuated the town. Once again, the bridge (or what was left of it), was in Union hands. It would remain under Union control until the end of the war. The L&N called upon Albert Fink again, and the bridge was repaired by November 1, 1862. The great strategic axis would be used to support the Union Army again when it entered Nashville following Bragg's hasty withdrawal from Kentucky, and to support Union armies in their conquest of the lower South from late 1862 until the war's end.[87]

* * *

The Opposing Forces at Munfordville, KY[88] *

(September 14 to September 17, 1862)

UNION

ARMY OF THE OHIO

Command at Munfordville
Col. John T. Wilder / Col. Cyrus L. Dunham

* 17th Indiana Infantry (detachment of 204 recruits), Col. John T. Wilder
* 50th Indiana Infantry, Companies A, B, D, F, G, and H, Col. Cyrus L. Dunham
60th Indiana Infantry , Col. Richard Owen
* 67th Indiana Infantry, Col. Frank Emerson, Maj. Augustus H. Abbott (k)
68th Indiana Infantry, Col. Edward A. King
* 74th Indiana Infantry, Companies C and K
* 89th Indiana Infantry, Col. Charles D. Murray
28th Kentucky Infantry, Company I, Lt. George W. Conaway
* 33rd Kentucky Infantry (detachment of 60 men), Capt. Cyrus J. Wilson
34th Kentucky Infantry, Company G
* 18th United States Infantry, Company H, 2nd Battalion
* 13th Battery, Indiana Light Artillery (detachment of 4 guns), Lt. Tyler A. Mason

* Asterisks denote unit actually engaged in battle on September 14, 1862.

1st Ohio Light Artillery, Battery D, Capt. Andrew Konkle
* 78th Indiana Infantry, Company K, Maj. Samuel T. Wells
* Louisville Provost Guard, one company of cavalry, Lt. Henry Watson

The total Union loss was: killed, 15; wounded, 57;
captured or missing 4,076 = 4,148.

CONFEDERATE

ARMY OF THE MISSISSIPPI

Second Brigade, Reserve Division, Right Wing,
Brig. Gen. James R. Chalmers
* 7th Mississippi Infantry, Col. W. H. Bishop
* 9th Mississippi Infantry, Col. Thomas W. White
* 10th Mississippi Infantry, Col. Robert A. Smith (mw), Lt. Col. Bullard (k), Capt. J. M. Walker, Maj. James Barr, Jr.
* 29th Mississippi Infantry, Col. E. L. Walthall
* Blythe's (44th) Mississippi Infantry, Lt. Col. James Moore (k), Maj. J. C. Thompson
* Mississippi Battalion of Sharpshooters, Maj. W. C. Richards (w), Capt. O. F. West
* Ketchum's Battery, Lt. James Garrity

Attached
28th Alabama Infantry, Col. John W. Frazer
19th South Carolina Infantry, Col. A. J. Lythgoe

Cavalry Brigade, Col. John S. Scott
* 1st Louisiana Cavalry Regiment, Col. John S. Scott / Lt. Col. James O. Nixon
* 1st Georgia Cavalry Regiment, Col. James Jefferson Morrison
* Company, Kentucky Buckner Guards, Capt. Garnett
* Detachment 3rd Tennessee Cavalry Regiment, Col. James W. Starnes (joined the brigade on August 27)
2d Kentucky Cavalry Regiment, Col. John Hunt Morgan (assigned to Col. Scott's brigade, but not present at Munfordville)

The total Confederate loss was: killed, 35; wounded, 251 = 286.

NOTES

1. R. M. Kelly, "Holding Kentucky for the Union," Robert Underwood Johnson and Clarence Clough Buel, eds., *Battles and Leaders of the Civil War*, 4 vols. (New York, N.Y., 1888; reprint ed., New York, N.Y., 1956) (hereinafter cited as *Battles and Leaders*), 1:377-386.

2. *Ibid.*, 386.

3. Maury Klein, *History of the Louisville & Nashville Railroad* (New York, N.Y., 1972), 4, 5-17.

4. *Ibid.*

5. Robert C. Black, III, *The Railroads of the Confederacy* (Chapel Hill, N.C., 1952), 72, 141.

6. Klein, *History of the Louisville & Nashville Railroad*, 29-36.

7. Hal Engerud, *The History of the Seige of Munfordville September 14-17, 1862* (Munfordville, Ky., 1984; 1997 ed.), 6.

8. Klein, *History of the Louisville & Nashville Railroad*, 10, 13.

9. *Ibid.*, 27-36.

10. Kelly, "Holding Kentucky for the Union," 379-386. Interestingly, a current Munfordville landowner, William Seymour, Sr.'s, ancestors helped build the Green River bridge. His two great uncles, Abner David Lewis and John Martin Key, were detailed by General Buckner to help blow up the bridge in 1861. Gray & Pape, Inc., *The Battles for the Bridge: A Civil War Resources Preservation Plan, Hart Co., Ky.* (Cincinnati, Ohio, 1998), 9; Klein, *History of the Louisville & Nashville Railroad*, 30.

11. Kelly, "Holding Kentucky for the Union," 386; John W. Coons, *Indiana at Shiloh: Report of the Commission* (Indianapolis, Ind., 1904), 123-127; Thomas B. Van Horne, *History of the Army of the Cumberland*, 3 vols. (Cincinnati, Ohio, 1875), 1:64-66. Colonel Willich's regiment was part of Brig. Gen. R.W. Johnson's Sixth Brigade of McCook's Second Division, Army of the Ohio.

12. Coons, *Indiana at Shiloh*, 123-127; Van Horne, *History of the Army of the Cumberland*, 1:64-66.

13. Van Horne, *History of the Army of the Cumberland*, 1:66-67; Klein, *History of the Louisville & Nashville Railroad*, 30-31.

14. Ulysses S. Grant, *Personal Memoirs of U.S. Grant*, 2 vols. (New York, N.Y., 1886), 2:86; Stanley F. Horne, *The Army of Tennessee* (Norman, Okla., 1959), 155.

15. Horne, *The Army of Tennessee*, 146-156; Joseph Wheeler, "Bragg's Invasion of Kentucky," *Battles and Leaders*, 3:1.

16. *The War of the Rebellion: A Compilation of the Official Records of the Union and Confederate Armies,* 128 vols. (Washington, D.C., 1880-1901) (hereinafter cited as *O.R.*) (all citations are to Series I), 16 (1):1088-1089.

17. *Ibid.*, 1089; Black, *The Railroads of the Confederacy*, 180-184.

18. *O.R.*, 16 (1):1089; Wheeler, "Bragg's Invasion of Kentucky," 2-7; and see: D. Warren Lambert, *When the Ripe Pears Fell: The Battle of Richmond, Kentucky* (Richmond, Ky., 1995).

19. *O.R.*, 16 (1):1089-1090; Wheeler, "Bragg's Invasion of Kentucky," 8-9.

20. *Ibid.*

21. *O.R.*, 16 (1):1090.

22. Don Carlos Buell, "East Tennessee and the Campaign of Perryville," *Battles and Leaders*, 3:44-45.

23. Jeremiah Tilford Boyle was born in what is now Boyle County, Kentucky in 1818. Educated at Centre College, Princeton and Transylvania University, he practiced law in Danville, Kentucky before the war. Appointed brigadier general in 1861, Boyle served as a brigade commander at Shiloh, and, on May 27, 1862, Secretary of War Edward M. Stanton directed him to "take command of the forces in Kentucky... on account of his intimate knowledge of the requirements of the service in his State...." Ezra J. Warner, *Generals in Blue* (Baton Rouge, La., 1964), 40.

24. *O.R.*, 16 (1):959-960; Glenn W. Sunderland, *Lightning at Hoover's Gap: The Story of Wilder's Brigade* (New York, N.Y., 1969), 19.

25. Sunderland, *Lightning at Hoover's Gap*, 19; Coons, *Indiana at Shiloh*, 103.

26. *O.R.*, 16 (1):959, 961. One of the strangest organizations in Wilder's command was the 33rd Kentucky Infantry. It was "thrown together from various commands" at Munfordville on September 13, 1862. Companies A and B were actively recruited at Bowling Green for the 35th Kentucky Infantry. Company C was recruited for the 7th Kentucky Cavalry, but its captain refused because of an injustice done him and asked to be assigned to the 33rd. Wholly unarmed when the regiment was made part of Wilder's force, the men were put to good use on picket and scout duty. Commonwealth of Kentucky, *Report of the Adjutant General of the State of Kentucky* (*Union*), 2 vols. (Frankfort, Ky., 1867) (hereinafter cited as *Report of Adjutant General*), 2:316-317.

27. *O.R.*, 16 (1):959-960.

28. *Ibid.* The attack on the Salt River bridge was conducted by Capt. John Hutchinson with four companies of the 2nd Kentucky Cavalry and two howitzers which left Lexington, Kentucky on the mission on about September 3, 1862. Hutchinson forced the surrender of 150 Union troops, partially burned the bridge and destroyed the stockade. Basil W. Duke, *History of Morgan's Cavalry* (Bloomington, Ind., 1960), 238-239.

29. *O.R.*, 16 (1):961, 974-975-976, 987.

30. *Ibid.*, 975-976, 987.

31. *Ibid.*, 960; *Report of Adjutant General*, 2:316-317.

32. *O.R.*, 16 (1):973, 1090.

33. *Ibid.*

34. Clement A. Evans, ed., *Confederate Military History*, 16 vols. (Wilmington, N.C., 1987), 9:244-245; Bobby Roberts and Carl Moneyhon, *Portraits of Conflict: A Photographic History of Mississippi in the Civil War* (Fayetteville, Ark., 1993), 94-95.

35. *O.R.*, 16 (1):973-980.

36. *Ibid.*, 973-974; Andrew B. Booth, ed., *Records of Louisiana Confederate Soldiers and Louisiana Confederate Commands*, 3 vols. (Spartanburg, S.C., 1984), 1:82.

37. *O.R.*, 16 (1):974.

38. *Ibid.*, 963.

39. *Ibid.*, 974.

40. *Ibid.*

41. *Ibid.*, 963-964; Klein, *History of the Louisville & Nashville Railroad*, 34.

42. *O.R.*, 16 (1):963-964.

43. *Ibid.*, 975.

44. *Ibid.*, 975, 989.

45. *Ibid.*, 975, 982, 985, 987-988, 989.

46. *Ibid.*, 975, 982.

47. *Ibid.*, 960.

48. *Ibid.*, 975.

49. *Ibid.*

50. *Ibid.*

51. Evans, ed., *Confederate Military History*, 9:476.

52. *O.R.*, 16 (1):975-976.

53. Evans, ed., *Confederate Military History*, 9:475-477.

54. *Ibid.*; *O.R.*, 16 (1):976, 987-988.

55. *O.R.*, 16 (1):976, 982; Roberts and Moneyhon, *Portraits of Conflict*, 41.

56. *O.R.*, 16 (1):976, 987-988.

57. *Ibid.*, 960.

58. *Ibid.*, 963-964.

59. *Ibid.*, 964.

60. *Ibid.*, 976.

61. *Ibid.*, 976-977.

62. *Ibid.*

63. *Ibid.*, 977.

64. *Ibid.*

65. *Ibid.*, 961, 977, 982.

66. *Ibid.*, 980.

67. *Ibid.*, 964.

68. *Ibid.*, 964-965; Edwin H. High, *History of the Sixty-Eighth Regiment Indiana Volunteer Infantry, 1862-1865* (Indianapolis, Ind., 1902), 14-16.

69. *O.R.*, 16 (1):983, 988-989.

70. *Ibid.*

71. *Ibid.*, 965.

72. Evans, ed., *Confederate Military History*, 11:259-260.

73. Arndt M. Stickles, *Simon Bolivar Buckner: Borderland Knight* (Chapel Hill, N.C., 1940), 200-201.

74. *Ibid.*; *O.R.*, 16 (1):965-966.

75. *O.R.*, 16 (1):966.

76. *Ibid.*

77. Stickles, *Simon Bolivar Buckner*, 201.

78. M. B. Morton, "Last Surviving Lieutenant General," *Confederate Veteran*, 17 (February, 1909), 85. Marmaduke B. Morton, the managing editor of the *Nashville Banner*, journeyed to General Buckner's residence, "Glen Lily," near Munfordville, in 1909, and personally interviewed the general. A stenographer and photographer accompanied Morton. All the quotes referenced herein were those uttered by General Buckner as he recollected the events of September 16 and 17, 1862.

79. *Ibid.*

80. *Ibid.*

81. *Ibid.*

82. *Ibid.*

83. *O.R.*, 16 (1):962.

84. Mary Elizabeth Sergent, *They Lie Forgotten* (Middletown, N.Y., 1986), 152-156.

85. *O.R.*, 16 (1):968.

86. *Ibid.*, 1090; Basil W. Duke, "Bragg's Campaign in Kentucky, 1862," *Southern Bivouac*, 1 (June, 1885), 167.

87. Klein, *History of the Louisville & Nashville Railroad*, 34-35.

88. *O.R.*, 16 (1):961, 977, 982.

Kenneth W. Noe

"Grand Havoc": The Climactic Battle of Perryville

I was in every battle, skirmish and march that was made by the First Tennessee Regiment during the war, and I do not remember a harder contest and more evenly fought battle than that of Perryville. . . . Both sides claimed victory—both whipped. . . . Such obstinate fighting I never had seen before or since.

Sam Watkins, "*Co. Aytch*"[1]

Sam Watkins's memoir, celebrated once again as a result of Ken Burns's television series *The Civil War*,[2] remains perhaps the most honest rendering of the spirit of that terrible conflict. Watkins was in the thick of the fighting in the war's Western theater, but he remembered Perryville—"This grand havoc of battle," as he once called it—as his hardest fight.[3]

Yet, beyond the borders of the Bluegrass State, Perryville, or Chaplin Hills as many participants termed it, remains largely ignored, a neglected battle. Perhaps the timing of the fight, after the shocking carnage at Shiloh but weeks before the better known bloodletting on Stone's River, accounts for it. Or, as historian James McDonough suggested, Stonewall Jackson and Robert E. Lee's legendary Virginia campaigns of 1862, climaxing on Antietam Creek, displaced Perryville from contemporary interest and modern memory. Certainly historian Thomas Connelly made a convincing case that the Western theater of the war as a whole has been ignored. Whatever the reason, the Battle of Perryville continues to receive surprisingly little attention from historians. Only one modern volume tracks the battle as a whole, while McDonough's examination of Gen. Braxton Bragg's Kentucky

Campaign dispenses with Perryville in less than three chapters. Clearly, there is more for historians to consider on the bloody banks of Doctor's Creek.[4]

In October 1862, Perryville, Kentucky, was a small town of a few hundred people, nestled amid the bluegrass farms and rolling hills of central Boyle County. The town straddled the Chaplin River, which together with its tributaries would dramatically shape the battle to come. The river meandered roughly northward through Perryville and about two-and-a-half miles beyond before abruptly turning to the southwest. Here Walker's Bend formed a narrow, thumb-shaped peninsula before the river eventually turned northward again. Doctor's Creek branched off the Chaplin southwestward from Walker's Bend. About a mile and a half southward, near the home of "Squire" Henry P. Bottom, Bull Run entered Doctor's Creek from the south.[5] Significantly, most of these waterways had run dry after a three-month drought in the region, leaving only stagnating scum-covered pools in what had been creeks and river beds. Perryville's supply of water, however meager, would figure prominently in the days ahead.[6]

A system of roads defined Perryville as well and they also would frame the battle. The Springfield-Danville Road ran east-west through the town, while the Harrodsburg-Lebanon Road bisected Perryville from the northeast to the southwest. The Mackville Road ran northwesterly from Perryville, crossing Doctor's Creek at Squire Bottom's house. About a mile to the west, it crossed the Benton Road, the latter then running toward the northeast at the Chaplin River.[7]

Both the road network and the tributaries of the Chaplin River attracted two contending armies to Perryville. Gen. Edmund Kirby Smith's August 1862 incursion from East Tennessee, climaxing at the Battle of Richmond; Braxton Bragg's subsequent march from Chattanooga into Middle Tennessee and then Kentucky; and Gen. Don Carlos Buell's pursuit of Bragg had brought war back to Kentucky in August. In Louisville, during the last week of September, the exhausted veteran units of Buell's Army of the Ohio, joined by four divisions of raw, barely-trained (if drilled at all) Midwestern recruits, rested, refitted, and gaped in astonishment as one of their generals (Gen. Jefferson C. Davis) murdered another (Gen. William "Bull" Nelson). Meanwhile,

General Don Carlos Buell, commander of the Union Army of the Ohio during the Perryville Campaign. *Library of Congress*

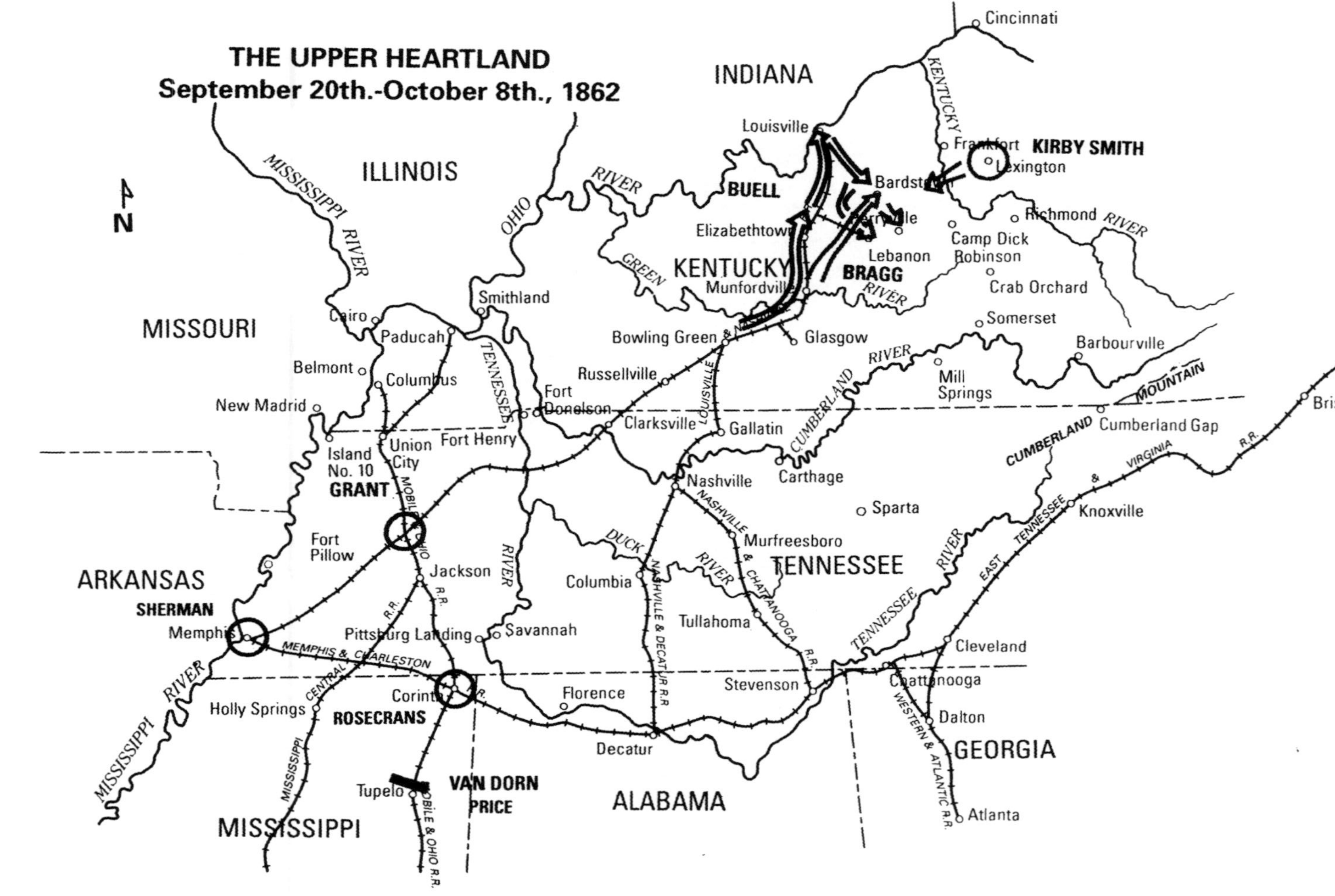
THE UPPER HEARTLAND
September 20th.-October 8th., 1862
N
ILLINOIS
INDIANA
MISSOURI
KENTUCKY
ARKANSAS
TENNESSEE
MISSISSIPPI
ALABAMA
GEORGIA
MISSISSIPPI RIVER
OHIO RIVER
GREEN RIVER
KENTUCKY RIVER
TENNESSEE RIVER
CUMBERLAND RIVER
DUCK RIVER
CUMBERLAND MOUNTAIN
BUELL
BRAGG
KIRBY SMITH
GRANT
SHERMAN
ROSECRANS
VAN DORN
PRICE
Cincinnati
Louisville
Frankfort
Lexington
Richmond
Elizabethtown
Lebanon
Camp Dick Robinson
Crab Orchard
Munfordville
Somerset
Barbourville
Glasgow
Bowling Green
Smithland
Cairo
Paducah
Belmont
Columbus
New Madrid
Russellville
Fort Donelson
Mill Springs
Clarksville
Gallatin
Island No. 10
Union City
Fort Henry
Cumberland Gap
Nashville
Carthage
Sparta
Knoxville
Fort Pillow
Jackson
Murfreesboro
Columbia
Memphis
Pittsburg Landing
Savannah
Tullahoma
Cleveland
Stevenson
Florence
Holly Springs
Dalton
Decatur
Tupelo
Atlanta
LOUISVILLE
MEMPHIS & CHARLESTON
MISSISSIPPI CENTRAL R.R.
NASHVILLE & DECATUR R.R
NASHVILLE & CHATTANOOGA R.R.
EAST TENNESSEE & VIRGINIA R.R.
WESTERN & ATLANTIC R.R.

Buell barely maintained command in the face of President Abraham Lincoln's growing disenchantment, largely because of Gen. George H. Thomas's refusal to take command in the midst of a campaign.[8]

Thirty-five miles to the south, Bragg's "jaded and footsore"[9] Confederate Army of the Mississippi had straggled into Bardstown. Concerned with the want of supplies and reinforcements, frustrated with Kirby Smith's independence, and particularly discouraged by the failure of Kentuckians to troop to his colors as promised by Kirby Smith and others, Bragg had grown increasingly pessimistic about his campaign. Convinced that conscription was the last alternative to abandoning the effort entirely, Bragg rode for Frankfort on September 28, leaving Gen. Leonidas Polk in command. Bragg planned to confer with Kirby Smith before installing Richard Hawes as Kentucky's Confederate governor, a necessary precursor to a state-wide draft.[10]

While Bragg and Kirby Smith met on October 1, the Army of the Ohio marched out of Louisville. As two divisions feinted toward Frankfort, Buell's main force made for Bardstown and Bragg's army on three separate roads, byways soon enveloped in clouds of dust and strewn with the belongings of the straggling "fresh fish." The feint worked, as Bragg remained convinced until the end of the looming battle that the bulk of Buell's army was driving on the state capital at Frankfort. While Bragg had hoped to unite the two Rebel hosts at Frankfort and crush the Federal threat in what historians Herman Hattaway and Archer Jones have called "a bold Napoleonic concentration," Polk, pressed on three roads by Buell's genuine advance, disobeyed orders and retreated toward Danville. Bragg then planned a concentration at Harrodsburg. Finally, still convinced that the bulk of the Yankee army lay toward Frankfort, Bragg ordered a concentration at Versailles. Even that fell through as reports came in from Polk regarding a Union force approaching Gen. William J. Hardee's Corps, which had advanced to Perryville. Poor reconnaissance, divided command, garbled communication, independent subordinates, and his own pessimism had combined to confuse Bragg and stymie him at every turn. At length, on October 7, an increasingly concerned Bragg, worried but still convinced that most of Buell's force lay to the north, ordered Polk to gather the army at Perryville and attack the "mystery" force without delay. Bragg then rode for Perryville himself, where in the morning he expected to find most of his hastily assembled force crushing an isolated fragment of Buell's army. By the time he arrived on the morning of October 8, the battle had begun—but not in the manner Bragg desired.[11]

All day on October 7, Confederate cavalry skirmished with Buell's thirsty columns as they neared Perryville on the Mackville, Springfield, and Lebanon roads. Three of Bragg's four divisions were then at or coverging on Perryville; the fourth, under Gen. Jones Withers, fatefully had already passed through Perryville and was moving away toward the north under Bragg's orders, toward the planned concentration with Kirby Smith. Hardee, the first in Perryville, deployed his corps in a north-south line west of town. Notably, Gen. St. John R. Liddell's Arkansas brigade was placed about a mile west of town on Bottom Hill, just east of Bull Run near the Springfield Pike, where the Arkansans could control both the Springfield and Mackville roads as well as the vital water. Liddell then advanced the 7th Arkansas to Peters Hill, about three-quarters of a mile further west.[12]

Out on the Springfield Pike, Buell's Third Corps, under Gen. Charles C. Gilbert, began arriving in the vicinity of Perryville about dark, the first of three Union corps to reach the scene. Buell wrote orders for an attack to begin at 10:00 a.m. the next morning. Not long before midnight, he also ordered his officer of the day, brigade commander and local Kentuckian Gen. Speed S. Fry, to take a regiment forward on picket. Two companies of the 10th Indiana, acting as skirmishers, slipped past the Arkansans on Peters Hill and crept almost a mile beyond, to the Samuel Bottom House, before falling back under fire. Fry reported that pools of water lay in the bed of Doctor's Creek, clearly visible in the bright moonlight; he also noted that the Rebels guarded it in force. Buell's parched army desperately needed that water, and he assigned Gen. Philip H. Sheridan's division the task of wresting it from the Confederates.[13]

Acting under orders from Gilbert and Sheridan, Col. Daniel McCook's brigade advanced across the creek a few minutes after three o'clock and drove the 7th Arkansas from Peters Hill and back toward Liddell's main line on Bottom Hill. After daybreak, Liddell launched a counterattack, his artillery pounding the Federals on Peters Hill and the

Yankee cannoneers returning fire. About an hour and fifteen minutes later, Liddell sent two regiments forward. Despite great effort, the Confederates of the 5th and 7th Arkansas regiments were unable to retake the hill, the Johnnies falling back to a strip of woods between the two hills. Sheridan, arriving on the scene with two additional brigades, steadily pressed the Confederates in the trees, finally sending in elements of Lt. Col. Bernard Laiboldt's brigade to clear the woods. Laiboldt's Missourians accomplished their task and more, pressing on toward Liddell's outnumbered main line on Bottom Hill. After a stand-up fight of about twenty minutes, Liddell withdrew under orders from Polk, and Sheridan occupied Bottom Hill.[14] He held it only briefly before Gilbert recalled the isolated Federals back to Peters Hill and ordered Sheridan to "limit himself to . . . defense" until otherwise ordered.[15] By 11:00 a.m. on what was becoming a bright, sweltering day, the fighting had played out.

As Sheridan secured and then surrendered Bottom Hill, Buell was resting at his headquarters at the Dorsey House on the Springfield Pike, recovering from a fall from his horse. The Union army commander was concluding that his attack of the day was finished as well. By 10:00 a.m.—the planned hour for commencing the assault—Buell had heard from neither Gen. Alexander McD. McCook's First Corps, still out on the Mackville Pike, nor Gen. Thomas L. Crittenden's Second Corps on the Lebanon Road. There was enough blame to go around. The corps commanders had received their orders only well after midnight; inexplicably McCook did not begin marching until 5:00 a.m. and Crittenden's corps tarried until nearly 7:00 a.m. Thus, by 11:00 a.m., with McCook's corps finally moving into position on Gilbert's left but with still no word from Crittenden on the right, Buell postponed the attack until the next morning. Believing that he faced most, if not all, of Bragg's army, Buell concluded that he needed his entire force to counter the Rebels.[16]

Buell's chagrin, however, hardly matched Braxton Bragg's fury. Bragg arrived in Perryville from Harrodsburg around 10:00 a.m. expecting to find a victory in progress. In his most recent dispatch, Polk had promised him that he would attack "vigorously." Instead, when Bragg arrived he discovered that Polk had changed his mind yet again

General Thomas L. Crittenden. A Kentuckian and a son of Senator John J. Crittenden of Kentucky, General Crittenden commanded the Second Corps of Gen. Don Carlos Buell's Union Army of the Ohio during the Perryville Campaign. *Library of Congress*

and had decided "to adopt the defensive-offensive, to await the movements of the enemy, and to be guided by events as they developed." Accordingly, Polk had aligned his men west of town for defense, not an attack, placing the divisions of Gens. Simon Bolivar Buckner, J. Patton Anderson, and Benjamin Franklin Cheatham, respectively, in a north to south configuration. Colonel John A. Wharton's cavalry brigade guarded the right flank, while Col. Joseph Wheeler's horsemen protected the left.[17]

Bragg exploded with indignation, finding both Polk's timidity and the actual arrangement of troops wanting. Accordingly, he undertook his own reconnaisance, which uncovered a serious blunder. Polk had failed to secure his right flank, giving the Federals an opening to turn the entire Confederate army. As Bragg aide J. Stoddard Johnston remembered it, to the right of Buckner "and extending to the forks of the creek, there was a gap, which already the enemy was aiming to possess . . . and it was not long before the enemy effected a lodgement on a portion of the bluff with his sharpshooters, while on the slope beyond the creek could be seen long lines of his infantry, with their glistening bayonets, as if preparing for an advance. It was evident that with the enemy in this position, we could make no fight. . . ."[18]

What Bragg and Stoddard Johnston had seen were two of the three brigades of Gen. Lovell H. Rousseau's division of McCook's corps, not preparing for an assault but rather moving into their assigned positions on the Union left for Buell's about-to-be aborted attack. However, as Johnston indicates, Bragg was convinced that the Union line was shifting to the north in order to flank his army through the "gap" Polk had left. In response, Bragg determined to shift further northward himself and launch a turning movement of his own. The Union force had to be smashed before Bragg led the army back to the north, where it would confront, he still believed, Buell's main force. Accordingly, Bragg ordered General Cheatham's Division to pull out of line on the left, double-quick two miles through Perryville, and reform on the extreme right.[19] After an artillery bombardment, set to begin thirty minutes after noon, Polk would send in Cheatham's Division brigade by brigade, "in echelon from the right." If all went as planned, Cheatham

General Lovell Harrison Rousseau. Born in Lincoln County, Kentucky, and a pre-war lawyer and state senator, Rousseau resigned from the Senate in the spring of 1861 to raise Union troops. At Perryville, his division held the right flank of Gen. A. McD. McCook's First Corps, Army of the Ohio. *Library of Congress*

would roll up the presumably exposed Union left flank. Hardee then would advance his divisions to finish the job.[20]

Cheatham was in position by noon, despite sporadic but generally harmless Union fire, and four batteries of Confederate artillery opened up at 12:30 p.m. as scheduled. The attack, however, did not begin, and after an hour, the artillery duel had all but petered out. Bragg, once again furious over the corruption of his battle plans, dispatched staff officers and finally confronted Polk himself on the Confederate right. Polk, he soon learned, had wisely delayed the assault after learning from Colonel Wharton that the Union line was being extended even more to the left with newly-arriving troops. This Federal extension was composed of Gen. James S. Jackson's division of raw recruits, forming to the left of Rousseau in a position to control the water of the Chaplin River. Still determined to flank the Yankees and win the day, Bragg decided to shift Cheatham further north, into Walker's Bend, even though that would necessiate some of Cheatham's men climbing the sheer bluffs of the riverbank before forming into line and attacking. To fill the gap that resulted between Cheatham and Hardee, Bragg placed two of Anderson's brigades, Gen. John C. Brown's and Col. Thomas M. Jones's, as well as Gen. S. A. M. Wood's brigade of Buckner's Division. Finally, to clear the bluffs of Federal pickets, Bragg dispatched Wharton's cavalry. Seeing the gray horsemen, Union General McCook dismissed them as nothing more than a force threatening his train. The time was about 2:00 p.m.[21]

"Give 'em hell boys," Cheatham shouted. "Give it to 'em boys," the pious Bishop Polk added, "give 'em what General Cheatham says!" The attack was on. The Confederates crossed the Chaplin, struggled up the bluff, fifty feet high in some spots, and formed their lines eight hundred yards from the surprised Federals on the hills beyond. After a brief respite, across undulating ground and over stone fences, the brigade of Gen. Daniel S. Donelson, Andrew Jackson's nephew, advanced "as if on dress parade," with a Rebel yell and the battle cry "Victory!" on their lips. Donelson's orders were to flank the brigade presumably holding the far Union left, which was Col. George P. Webster's brigade. However, as Donelson's Tenneseans closed on the Union line, "firing as they ran" with Col. John Savage's 16th Tennessee pulling ahead into the lead, they ran into a hellish fix. Instead of flanking the Yankees, they charged headlong into a previously unknown Union force, Gen. William R. Terrill's brigade of Jackson's division, more green troops who had just arrived to extend the blue line further northward and seize control of the

General Benjamin Franklin Cheatham. A hard-fighting, hard-drinking Tennessean who commanded a division of Tennessee and Georgia regiments in Gen. Braxton Bragg's army, Cheatham delivered the opening attack against what Bragg thought was the extreme Union left flank. *Library of Congress*

precious water. Captain Samuel J. Harris's 19th Indiana Battery of Webster's brigade, Terrill's infantrymen, and especially Lt. Charles C. Parsons's new, eight-gun battery, assigned to Terrill, mowed down the Rebels as they poured into a "slight trough-like depression" below their line. Caught in a crossfire of balls, grapeshot, and cannister, Donelson was in grave danger, and his line twitched in fear and confusion.[22] "It is yet a wonder to me that any man in our Regiment escaped death. . . ," C. H. Clark of the 16th Tennessee wrote. "If you wish to know how a soldier feels in such a battle as that, you must ask someone else. I cannot explain, but I had no hope of getting out alive."[23]

Donelson's first reaction was to charge the tormenting new battery. Cheatham, however, ordered Donelson to maintain his attack as originally directed. General Alexander P. Stewart's Confederate brigade would swing to Donelson's aid from his left, while to his right Gen. George E. Maney's reserve brigade—including Sam Watkins's 1st Tennessee—would neutralize Parsons's Battery and its support. Shifted right and then drawn up in line, Maney's first line of three regiments, unobserved by the Federals, at about 2:30 p.m. suddenly emerged from the trees to face Parsons's guns. General James S. Jackson, standing with Lieutenant Parsons, immediately ordered the artillery captain to respond to the new threat. Parsons's artillery decimated Maney's regiments with canister, and the gray line stalled at a vine-covered rail fence at the base of the open knob.[24]

As General Maney's adjutant, Thomas Malone, remembered it, "I told [Maney] that I didn't think our position could be maintained. . . I told him I believed that our only chance was to take those guns."[25] Maney agreed. Riding among his men until his horse was felled, and then walking, Maney steadied his brigade and launched another effort, which ground to a halt halfway up the hill. The men continued their fire from prone positions. "Most of the bullets went over our heads," one Union soldier wrote his wife, "and sounded like bees running away in the hot summer air overhead."[26]

Two balls hit General Jackson in the right breast as he stood next to Parsons's Battery; he died nearly instantly. Almost at the same moment, the green 123rd Illinois, supporting the battery, "saw the elephant," broke, and ran. Another Union regiment that had double-quicked to

General James S. Jackson was born in Fayette County and practiced law before the war in Hopkinsville, Kentucky. He was killed at Perryville on the extreme left flank while commanding a division of raw Union troops in Gen. A. McD. McCook's First Corps, Army of the Ohio. Both of Jackson's brigade commanders, Gen. William R. Terrill and Col. George P. Webster, were also killed during the battle. *Library of Congress*

Parsons's aid, the 105th Ohio, picked up the fight to the battery's left despite such rawness that they could not form a proper line. After about fifteen minutes, however, the Ohioans began to fall back under orders from General Terrill, a former artilleryman in the old army who according to at least some reports had spent most of the fight as an *ad hoc* member of one of Parsons's gun crew.[27] The Buckeyes as well as Parsons's cannoneers finally retreated, "not in verry good order as we were like to be surrounded," according to one Ohioan,[28] as Maney's dogged soldiers charged bayonets and finally topped the hill. The Federals managed to save only one gun. Terrill, having spiked his 12-pound Napoleon after one final shot, formed a new line along a fence 60 yards in the rear.[29]

Watching with Bragg from a cedar strewn bluff with "a perfect view of the battle-field," Stoddard Johnston, "with a feeling of horror," recalled "the sight which presented itself to view from our position. It was a square, stand-up, hand-to-hand fight." From his vantage point, Bragg could see Maney's Tennesseans and Georgians crash over the crest of the hill. To their left, Donelson's and Stewart's brigades continued to press against Col. Leonard A. Harris's brigade of Rousseau's division, although making less headway. And to the left of Cheatham's Division, Bragg and his entourage also could see Hardee's corps open its act in the drama.[30]

Hardee, as noted above, was to pitch into the Federals after Cheatham began his attack. Accordingly, after Donelson's initial attack, Col. Thomas M. Jones's untried Mississippians went into action against the right regiments of Colonel Harris's Union brigade. At about 2:30 p.m., Capt. Charles L. Lumsden's Alabama Battery, in support of Jones, opened up on the blue line three hundred yards in the distance. Captain Peter Simonson's 5th Indiana Battery responded. At about 3:00 p.m. Jones's three regiments crossed Doctor's Creek, passed the Widow Bottom house, and attempted to close on the Yankees. Such an assault required descending into a deep valley before charging the hill held by Colonel Harris. Like Donelson before him, as they entered the hollow Jones's men became ripe targets for Union double-shotted cannister and minie balls. Unable to face the galling fire, the shattered Missisippians were forced to fall back after a few minutes. Almost out of ammunition

The drawing of the Battle of Perryville from *Harper's Weekly* shows Col. Leonard A. Harris's brigade, with Capt. Peter Simonson's 5th Indiana Battery, preparing to receive a Confederate attack (probably from Gen. Daniel S. Donelson's or Col. Thomas M. Jones's brigades) on the afternoon of October 8, 1862. *Kentucky Historical Society*

This 1885 view looks west toward the positions of Cols. Leonard A. Harris's and George P. Webster's Union brigades (along the distant ridgeline) at Perryville, as the attacking Confederates in Gen. Daniel S. Donelson's Brigade observed them. The log crib in the foreground is possibly that of the Widow Bottom's. *U.S. Army Military History Institute*

and under heavy fire from Lumsden's Battery, Simonson's battery fell back as well, toward the Russell House.[31]

To Jones's left, the attack launched by Gen. Bushrod R. Johnson's six-regiment brigade was going even worse. Johnson's Brigade approached Doctor's Creek and the Squire Bottom house, moving toward the right portion of McCook's line of battle. Then, Johnson attempted a complex, parade ground manuever, an oblique wheel to the left. The net effect was a breakdown in his first line, as the four regiments involved spun off in different directions. While the 37th Tennessee plowed straight ahead into the skirmishing 10th Ohio of Col. William H. Lytle's brigade, the 44th Tennessee angled off to the southwest. Under fire from Simonson's battery as well as another, the men of the 44th fixed bayonets and charged the latter artillery battery. Unfortunately, the guns belonged to Capt. Cuthbert H. Slocomb's 5th Washington Artillery, a Confederate battery attached to Gen. Daniel W. Adams's Brigade. Even more incredibly, a second Johnson regiment, the 25th Tennessee, also charged the elite Confederate gunners. Instead of trying to draw order from the chaos, Johnson added to it by sending in his second line. Eventually, four of Johnson's regiments—the two that had charged Slocomb's Battery stayed to support it—fought their way to the stone fences along the Mackville Road to the right of the Squire Bottom house. On their own—neither Johnson nor Buckner were on the scene—Johnson's regiments shifted steadily to the left toward the Bottom House and then up the hill, passing the dwelling, before being driven back by first the 3rd Ohio, then the 15th Kentucky of Lytle's brigade, firing from behind cornstalks and stone fences on the hill above. As the fighting intensified, a stray Confederate shell from Slocomb's Battery struck the Bottom barn, setting it on fire and adding to the confusion by covering the field with heat and smoke.[32]

"It seemed as if all hell had broken loose," remembered John Beatty of the 3rd Ohio. "The air was filled with hissing balls; shells were exploding continuously, and the noise of the guns was deafening; finally the barn at the right took fire, and the flames bursting from roof, windows, doors, and interstices between the logs, threw the right of the regiment into disorder. . . ."[33] Ultimately, however, the strength of the

The Squire Henry P. Bottom House, Perryville, 1885. The brigades of Gens. Patrick Cleburne and Daniel W. Adams swept through these yards (where the 5th Company of the Washington Artillery unlimbered to rake the Union lines) in their attacks against the position of Gen. William Lytle's brigade along Loomis's Heights. *U.S. Army Military History Institute*

Union position, coupled with the fact that the Confederates were running low on ammunition, forced Johnson's grayclads to fall back.

Through most of this action, Johnson's Brigade had been supported on its left by Adams's Louisiana Brigade; by now, about 3:00 p.m., those Confederates approached Lytle's flank. Adams's unimpeded presence near the Squire Bottom house was largely due to another breakdown in the Union chain-of-command. Originally stationed at the Springfield Road, Adams had to pass directly in front of Phil Sheridan's division in order to come to Johnson's support. Yet Sheridan did nothing to stop the Confederates. His inaction has puzzled historians ever since. Historian James McDonough credibly suggests that "Little Phil," already upbraided once in the morning for exceeding his orders on Peters Hill, refused to move again without positive instructions from Gilbert, his corps commander. McDonough's explanation has merit. When Sheridan finally did something to answer McCook's frantic calls for help—he advanced Capt. Henry Hescock's Battery G, 1st Missouri Artillery, with supporting infantry to enfilade the Confederates—Gilbert countermanded the order. Just as importantly, Sheridan and Gilbert believed, or at least convinced themselves, that a major Rebel assault was approaching their lines. So they let Adams pass, and then watched as McCook's corps was steadily cut to pieces. As it turned out, the major Confederate threat that Sheridan feared involved only Col. Samuel Powell's vastly outnumbered brigade of Anderson's Division. Led by Anderson himself, Powell's Brigade of four regiments unknowingly was preparing to attack Gilbert's entire corps, convinced that only a small Union force occupied the area around Peters Hill.[34]

Here the situation stood roughly an hour and a half after the Confederate attack began. In Gilbert's front, Powell's little brigade was preparing to make a costly and futile charge against four times as many Federals. McCook was in much greater trouble. On his right, despite Jones's repulse and the miscues and confusion that had marked Bushrod Johnson's initial attack, Hardee continued to apply pressure on Lytle's and Harris's brigades. Even worse, on McCook's left, Cheatham's men had smashed through Terrill's brigade and were now boring down on McCook's second line of defense. There, Webster, joined by some of Terrill's soldiers and more significantly by Col. John C. Starkweather's

The Battle of Perryville

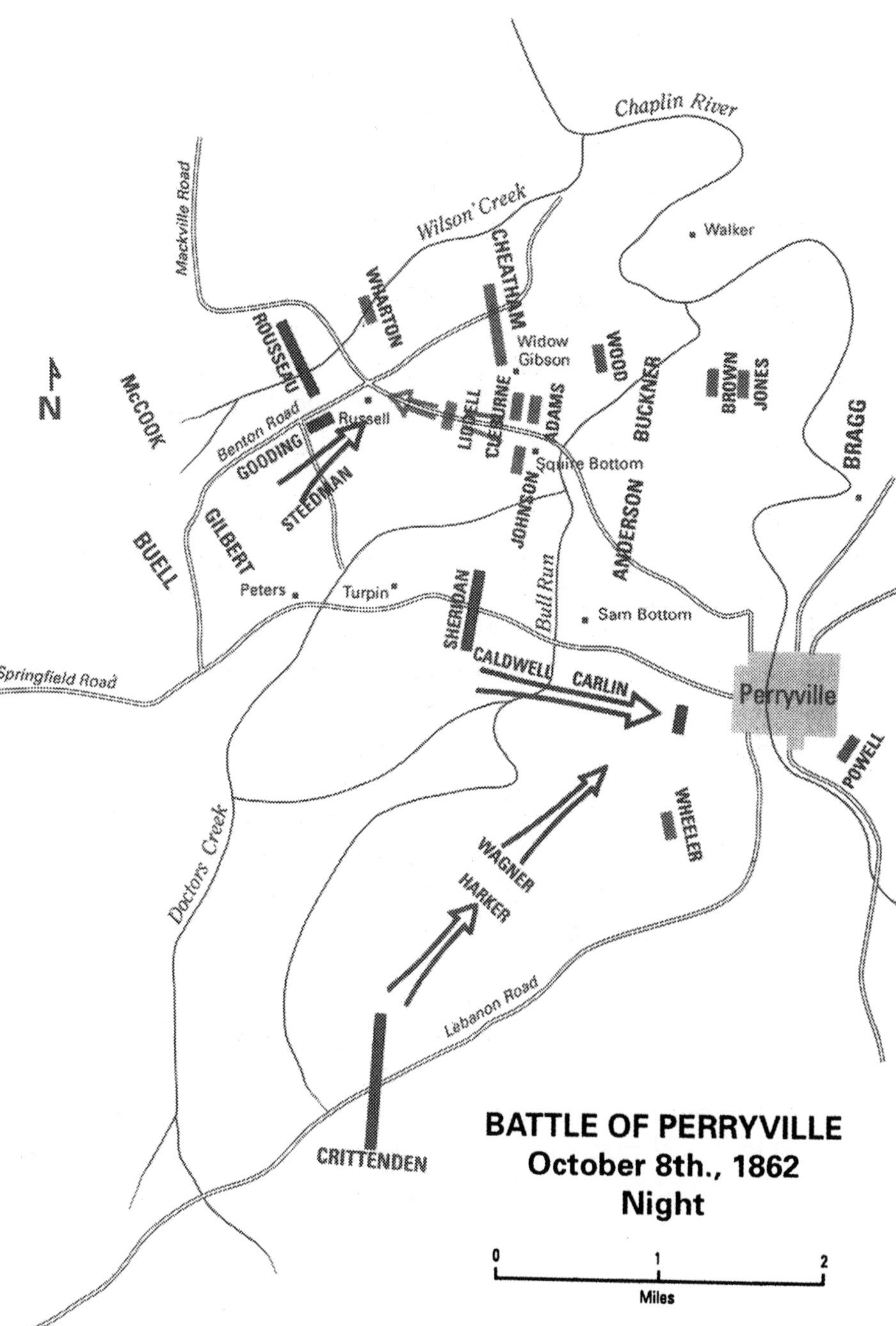
Chaplin River
Wilson Creek
Mackville Road
CHEATHAM
WHARTON
ROUSSEAU
Widow Gibson
WOOD
BUCKNER
BROWN
JONES
Walker
N
McCOOK
Benton Road
Russell
LIDDELL
CLEBURNE
ADAMS
GOODING
STEEDMAN
Squire Bottom
JOHNSON
ANDERSON
BRAGG
GILBERT
BUELL
Peters
Turpin
SHERIDAN
Bull Run
Sam Bottom
Springfield Road
CALDWELL
CARLIN
Perryville
POWELL
WHEELER
WAGNER
HARKER
Doctors Creek
Lebanon Road
CRITTENDEN
BATTLE OF PERRYVILLE
October 8th., 1862
Night
0
1
2
Miles

veterans, occupied the high ground above the Benton Road. Delayed that morning and left behind by an impatient General Jackson, Starkweather's men had marched to the sound of the guns. They had arrived just in time, at just the right place, to save the day.[35]

The five hundred yards between the knoll where Parson's guns had been lost and the ridge Starkweather now held included a cornfield and then the Benton Road where it passed the Widow Gibson house. Starkweather had posted the 21st Wisconsin in the cornfield, but as Terrill's panicked men fled to the safety of Starkweather's guns, some of the Wisconsin men followed and then the others were forced to retire. On the hill, General Rousseau rode down the line, his hat upon his sword. "Now, boys," he cried out, "you will stand by me, and I will by you, and we will whip —— out of them!" On came the Rebels, who poured through the cornfield and across the road, where most were checked in a crossfire of Union balls and especially artillery fire from Capt. Asahel K. Bush's 4th Indiana Battery and Capt. David Stone's 1st Kentucky Battery. The 1st Tennessee however surged forward and engaged in a hand-to-fight for Bush's battery before falling back as well.[36]

Blunted, Colonel Maney called for one more effort, with help from Stewart on the left. Lieutenant William B. Turner's Mississippi Battery, as well as Capt. William W. Carnes's Tennessee Battery of Donelson's Brigade, pounded the Union position as the 8th and 51st Tennessee, moving with Carnes's gunners, attempted to flank the Union line. The Confederate guns took their toll; among those to die was General Terrill, mortally wounded by shrapnel as he rallied his men. As his own artillery horses began to fall, Starkweather ordered his guns to the rear. Then, at about 4:00 p.m., the Confederate tide again swept up the hill. Led by the 1st Tennessee, which again seized two of Bush's guns, the Rebels surmounted the ridge only to be raked again by Stone's battery and what was left of Bush's. Vicious hand-to-hand fighting ensued. Perhaps Sam Watkins, one of Maney's veterans, described the bloody climax best:

> It was death to retreat now to either side. Our Lieutenant-Colonel Patterson halloed to charge and take their guns, and we were soon in a hand-to-hand fight—every man for himself—using the butts of our guns and bayonets. One side would waver and fall back a few yards, and would

> rally, when the other side would fall back . . . and yet the battle raged. . . . The very air seemed full of stifling smoke and fire which seemed the very pit of hell, peopled by contending demons."[38]

Unfortunately for Watkins and his fellow Southerners, Union numbers and Confederate casualties combined to favor Starkweather. At about sunset, the Federals drove the Confederates back down the hill. Maney's gallant brigade was broken.[37]

On Maney's left, Generals Stewart's and Donelson's "contending demons" were in no better shape. With the two brigades intermingling in the fight, the Confederates also had continued to push in that sector against a tenacious Union defense. At about 4:00 p.m., Polk ordered Donelson to attack again with what was left of his brigade in support of Stewart. Desperately, the Confederates surged toward what had been Colonel Webster's line and beyond to the next hill, part of that same ridge where Starkweather and Maney battled. It was to no avail, as Harris's infantry and artillery stemmed the tide and forced the Confederates back. Like Maney's troops, Donelson's and Stewart's regiments were decimated; Cheatham's Division was done for the day.[39]

Confederate victory, if it were to come, would have to be won by Hardee's men fighting just to the south. On his right, to replace Jones's retreating men, Hardee sent in Gen. John C. Brown's fresh, largely untried brigade of Mississippians and Floridians against Harris's right. Crossing the treacherous ground that had bedeviled Jones, Brown met the same fate, his men chewed up in the deep ravine in front of Harris's blue line. Brown at least had helped in the battering process directed against Harris's brigade, which finally had to fall back itself.[40]

Hardee's most important effort, however, was massing at the same time to Brown's left. There, Bushrod Johnson's attack largely had miscarried and by 3:30 p.m. most of his men had fallen back for want of ammunition. Adams's Brigade, however, was having more success against Lytle's Federals. At this juncture, Hardee ordered in Gen. Patrick R. Cleburne's Brigade, veterans of the recent Battle of Richmond. Double-quicking to the Bottom House, Cleburne's fresh men swept past the house and up the hill, driving back at last Lytle's flank despite being hit from the rear by friendly fire from Capt. Henry C. Semple's Alabama Battery. Lytle attempted to form a new line along the

Mackville Road, but upon seeing Harris's retreat toward the Russell House, he had to fall back again, and at that moment his ranks began to give way in disorder. In the confusion, Lytle himself was wounded and captured. Together, Adams's and Cleburne's brigades rolled toward the Russell House and what they hoped would be the final destruction of a Union corps.[41]

In the mounting chaos near the Russell House, Generals McCook and Rousseau—the latter having just arrived from the action on the Union left—struggled to rally Lytle's and Harris's fleeing men and form a line of defense around the Russell House. McCook also had cast deperately for help, but so far, he was disappointed. He had dispatched aides both to Buell and to Gen. Albin Schoepf, who commanded Gilbert's reserve division. Schoepf, confronted with McCook's hurried request, referred it to Gilbert, who was then at Buell's headquarters. Gilbert in turn referred the aide to Buell himself, and the aide reported to the Union commander between 3:30 and 4:00 p.m. By his own admission, Buell was "astonished"[42] by the news, which he found hard to believe. While the noise of battle had increased in volume at his headquarters—he had given orders "to stop that useless waste of powder"—Buell had had no idea that McCook's corps was in the midst of a grand battle. Tricked by the atmospheric phenomenon of "acoustic shadow," which muffled sound, and constrained by their own limitations as well, Buell and Gilbert had spent the afternoon in sublime ignorance. Now confronted by reality—but still unable to absorb all of it—Buell ordered McCook to hold his ground and directed Gilbert to dispatch two brigades to assist McCook.[43] As historian Kenneth Hafendorfer has noted, sending only two brigades suggests that Buell still refused to believe the totality of the report.[44] Indeed, as late as 8:30 that evening, Buell could write Crittenden that "The First Corps . . . has been very heavily engaged. The center and left gained ground, but the right of it yielded a little." Clearly, Buell had never comprehended the scale of the day's struggle.[45]

Gilbert promptly compounded the error, ordering only Col. Michael Gooding's brigade to McCook's assistance. Schoepf remained on his corps' left, protecting the flank if McCook was overrun. Part of Gilbert's seeming timidity can be attributed to his belief that a major Rebel force

A company of the 21st Michigan Infantry. These men saw their first combat at Perryville as part of Col. Nicholas Greusel's Brigade, Gen. Philip H. Sheridan's division, Gen. Charles C. Gilbert's Third Corps, Army of the Ohio. Their appearance is typical of Union soldiers during the invasion of Kentucky in 1862. *National Archives*

was massing to assail his lines. As noted above, Sheridan was convinced that Powell's Confederate brigade comprised only the tip of a treacherous gray iceburg. At about 4:00 p.m., Patton Anderson ordered Powell toward Peters Hill, unaware that a Union corps awaited him. As the Southerners approached, Sheridan's artillery commenced a devastating fire. Against four-to-one odds, Powell's men bravely drove close to the enemy line, panicking Sheridan enough to convince him to call for more help. Ultimately, however, the weight of numbers and the superior Union position were no match for Powell's Confederates, who were in Sheridan's words "'whipped . . . like hell'" and driven back within an hour. Powell fell all the way back to Perryville itself, pursued by Col. William P. Carlin's brigade of Gen. Robert B. Mitchell's division, which later was joined by two additional brigades. All that prevented the Federals from taking the town and appearing in Bragg's rear was Gilbert, who after ordering an all-out assault—"'now is the time to push everything'"—changed his mind and called back Carlin's advance. Only an artillery duel followed, lasting until night.[46]

Meanwhile, the decisive moment approached near the Russell House. As he steadied his men and called for more artillery, McCook saw Adams and Cleburne approaching about 600 yards away. Moreover, a third Confederate brigade, Gen. S. A. M. Wood's reserves, appeared to Cleburne's right, under orders from Hardee to assist Cleburne. Adams, on the Confederate left, bore down particularly on the Union flank. However, Adams soon found himself under fire from an unexpected source—the artillery of Sheridan's division, relieved of their own defense after Powell's repulse. Facing strong resistance and caught in a crossfire, Adams fell back, leaving Cleburne's and Wood's men to continue bearing down on Col. George Webster's brigade, which had been in line to the rear of Rousseau until ordered into the fray by McCook. As that Union brigade began to fall back, Webster was shot from his horse and killed.[47]

It was about 6:30 in the evening. Night had fallen, yet victory still seemed within Bragg's grasp. In fact, the moment had passed him by, and his breakthrough was about to collapse. First, Cleburne pulled up, fought out and all but out of ammunition. Without their wounded commander, Wood's men rushed on, cutting through the remanants of

The Battle of Perryville

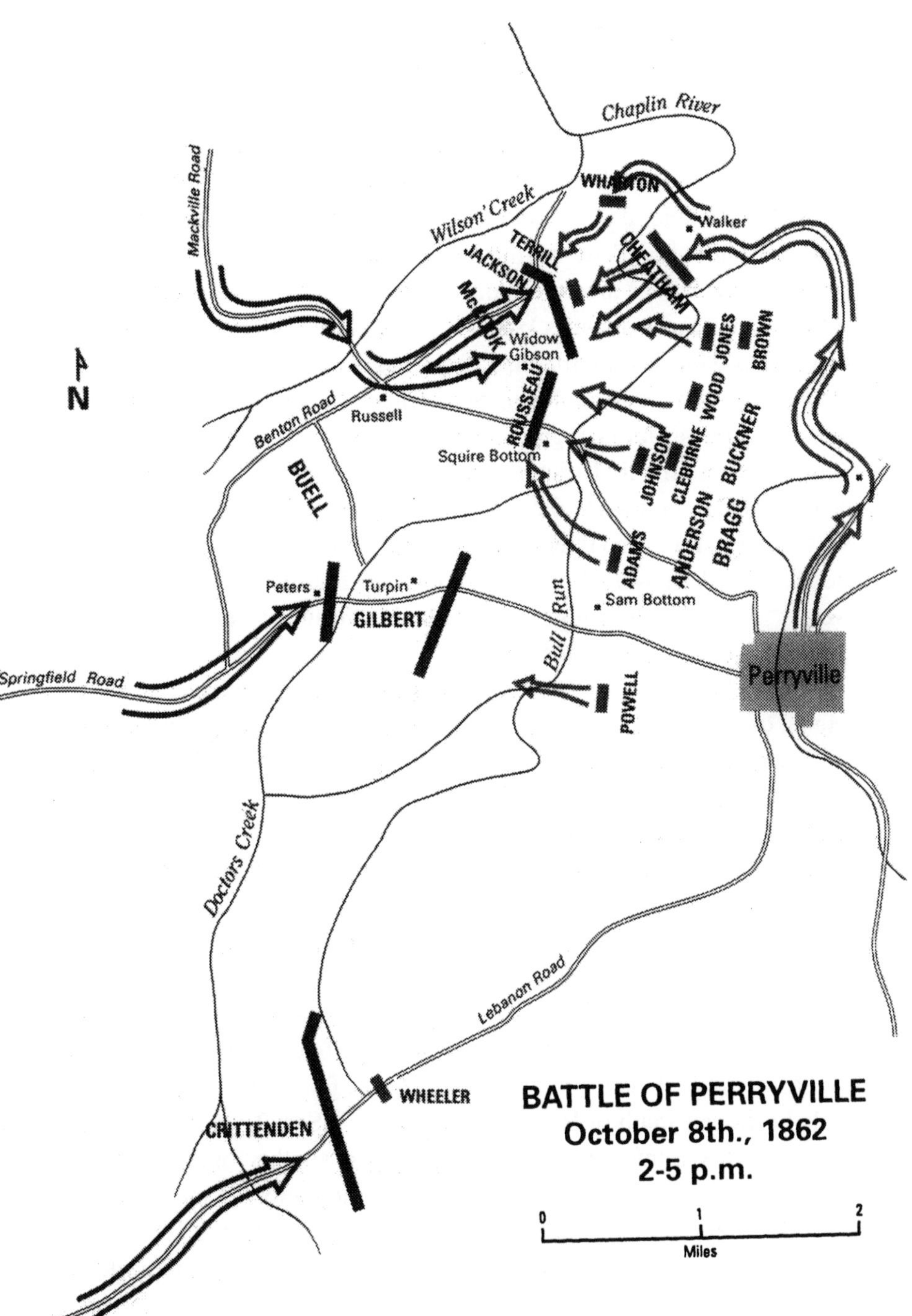
Chaplin River
Mackville Road
Wilson' Creek
Walker
TERRILL
JACKSON
CHEATHAM
Widow Gibson
JONES
BROWN
ROUSSEAU
WOOD
Russell
Benton Road
BUELL
Squire Bottom
JOHNSON
CLEBURNE
BUCKNER
ANDERSON
BRAGG
ADAMS
Peters
Turpin
GILBERT
Bull Run
Sam Bottom
Springfield Road
Perryville
POWELL
Doctors Creek
Lebanon Road
WHEELER
CRITTENDEN
N
BATTLE OF PERRYVILLE
October 8th., 1862
2-5 p.m.
0
1
2
Miles

Webster's brigade and past the Russell House, where they unexpectedly encountered a fresh Union force. Colonel Gooding's brigade of Gilbert's corps, under orders from Gilbert, had double-quicked to the sound of firing, arriving just in time to relieve McCook's exhausted warriors. As the two brigades fought it out, reinforcements raced to provide help. General St. John R. Liddell's regiments, which had helped start the fight out on Peter's Hill so many hours before, groped through the growing darkness toward Wood, using muzzle flashes as guideposts. Liddell's men arrived just as Wood's troops were falling back and took their places. Under a full moon, a desperate hand-to-hand fight ensued. The conditions were so confusing that General Polk was nearly captured after ordering a Union regiment to hold its fire. As Gooding's line collapsed, more timely Union reinforcements appeared, the "Pea Ridge men" of Gen. James B. Steedman's brigade of Schoepf's division. Advancing as far as the intersection of the Mackville and Benton roads, Liddell halted. It was about 7:30 p.m.; the Battle of Perryville was over.[48] "The moon rose higher," Stoddard Johnston remembered, "and lit up the ghastly faces of the dead. . ."[49]

As the firing died down, Braxton Bragg and his lieutenants held a council of war. Convinced that he had won a victory, Bragg nonetheless noted the high number of casualties. More importantly, Bragg finally realized that he would soon face Buell's entire army. Wheeler's cavalry had kept Crittenden's corps occupied throughout the day far to the southwest, but on the morrow, the battered Army of the Mississippi would face three unbloodied veteran Union divisions. Left with few options, Bragg determined to abandon the field around midnight and move his outnumbered force to Harrodsburg, where a junction at last could be made with Kirby Smith. Bragg's army slipped quietly away during the night, taking as many wounded and burying as many of the dead as possible. Buell followed the next day. On October 10, another battle beckoned south of Harrodsburg along the Salt River, but despite Kirby Smith's reinforcement, Bragg declined another opportunity to fight for Kentucky, as did Buell. To the consternation of many of his generals, Bragg retreated to his supply depot at Bryantsville. There, he made the final decision to abandon Kentucky altogether and fall back to Tennessee. Buell's army half-heartedly followed. As early as October

17, Buell was ready to break off the pursuit and make for Nashville. His timid pursuit resulted in his sacking on October 24 and replacement by Gen. William S. Rosecrans. Both Bragg and Buell were roundly criticized by civilians and soldiers alike—many even accused them of being conspiring brothers-in-law—but while Bragg had the support of his president (if hardly anyone else), Buell did not.[50]

While armies marched and generals quarreled, and while the weather turned rainy and cold, Perryville itself became a vast charnal house. According to accepted casualty lists, 1,355 men were killed at Perryville, 5,486 soldiers (including apparently at least one woman, attached to an Alabama regiment) were wounded, and 766 remained missing, totaling 7,607 casualties. These figures are certainly understatements. After the battle, nearly every available building in a ten mile radius housed the wounded and dying; most of the dead men lay about the battlefield for as long as a week. Many of the wounded later were housed in nearby towns like Danville and Harrodsburg, and as far away as Louisville and southern Indiana. The lack of water not only worsened the suffering of the wounded, but some doctors could not wash their hands for two days, which meant infection and more death in the days to come. Meanwhile, the horrors of the field deeply affected those who saw it. Indeed, any historian studying the Battle of Perryville will soon note that while solid accounts of the fight itself are not always easy to come by, descriptions of the hospitals and field are ubiquitious. Many soldiers were appalled by the horrible disfigurement of bodies, many naked due to pillaging, while others noted that the corpses of decomposing Confederates blackened more quickly, a phenemonenon now attributed to diet but at the time blamed on alleged pre-battle cocktails of whiskey and gunpowder. Federals and impressed locals, black and white, buried dead soldiers and chased away the hogs that returned repeatedly to uproot graves and eat the remains, until the hogs themselves died of poisoning.[51] A correspondent of the *New Albany* (Indiana) *Daily Ledger* reported that "In many places the dead are piled in shallow ravines and pits, and only slightly covered with earth, and the first heavy rain is likely to wash away this slight covering. The effluvia emitted from these graves is said to be horrible."[52]

Such was the wreckage of Kentucky's "grand havoc of battle," the last major battle on Kentucky soil. As the two armies marched toward another murderous confrontation at Murfreesboro, where Cheatham again would unleash his fury on McCook's corps, they left in their wake a state held firmly in Union hands (although the dream of a Confederate Kentucky still refused to die for many Southerners). Union soldiers had at least that with which to console themselves; Confederates in the end had only their valor.

* * *

The Opposing Forces at Perryville, KY[53]

(October 8th, 1862)

UNION

ARMY OF THE OHIO
Maj. Gen. Don Carlos Buell
Maj. Gen. George H. Thomas, second in command

Escort: Anderson (Pa.) Troop, Lieut. Thomas S. Maple; 4th U.S. Cav. (6 co's), Lieut. Col. James Oakes. Escort loss: m, 1
Unattached: 7th Pa. Cav. (4 co's), Maj. John E. Wynkoop
Loss: w, 4; m, 3 = 7

FIRST ARMY CORPS, Maj. Gen. Alexander McD. McCook

THIRD DIVISION, Brig. Gen. Lovell H. Rousseau
Staff loss: m, 1

Ninth Brigade, Col. Leonard A. Harris
38th Ind., Col. Benjamin F. Scribner
2d Ohio, Lieut. Col. John Kell
33d Ohio, Lieut. Col. Oscar F. Moore (w and c), Maj. Frederick J. Lock
94th Ohio, Col. Joseph W. Frizell
10th Wis., Col. Alfred R. Chapin
5th Ind. Battery, Capt. Peter Simonson

Brigade loss: k, 121; w, 419, m, 51 = 591

Seventeenth Brigade, Col. William H. Lytle (w and c)
Col. Curran Pope (m w)
42d Ind., Col. James G. Jones
88th Ind., Col. George Humphrey
15th Ky., Col. Curran Pope
3d Ohio, Col. John Beatty
10th Ohio, Lieut. Col. Joseph W. Burke
1st Mich. Battery, Capt. Cyrus O. Loomis
Brigade loss: k, 193; w, 606, m, 23 = 822

Twenty-eighth Brigade, Col. John C. Starkweather
24th Ill., Capt. August Mauff
79th Pa., Col. Henry A. Hambright
1st Wis., Lieut. Col. George B. Bingham
21st Wis., Col. Benjamin J. Sweet
4th Ind. Battery, Capt. Asahel K. Bush
1st Ky. Battery, Capt. David C. Stone
Brigade loss: k, 170; w, 477; m, 109 = 756

Unattached:
2d Ky. Cav. (6 co's), Col. Buckner Board
A, C, and H, 1st Mich., Eng'rs and Mech's, Maj. Enos Hopkins
Unattached loss: w, 18; m, 4 = 22

TENTH DIVISION, Brig. Gen. James S. Jackson (k)
Staff losses: k, 1

Thirty-third Brigade, Brig. Gen. William R. Terrill (k), Col. Albert S. Hall
80th Ill., Col. Thomas G. Allen
123d Ill., Col. James Monroe
Detachments 7th and 32d Ky. and 3d Tenn., Col. Theophilus T. Garrard
105th Ohio, Col. Albert S. Hall
Parsons's (improvised) Battery, Lieut. Charles C. Parsons
Brigade loss: k, 100; w, 336; m, 91 = 527

Thirty-fourth Brigade, Col. George Webster (k)
80th Ind., Lieut. Col. Lewis Brooks
50th Ohio, Col. Jonah R. Taylor, Lieut. Col. Silas A. Strickland

98th Ohio, Lieut. Col. Christian L. Poorman
121st Ohio, Col. William P. Reid
19th Ind. Battery, Capt. Samuel J. Harris
Brigade loss: k, 87; w, 346; m, 146 = 579

SECOND ARMY CORPS, Maj. Gen. Thomas L. Crittenden

FOURTH DIVISION, Brig. Gen. William S. Smith

Tenth Brigade, Col. William Grose
84th Ill., Col. Louis H. Waters
36th Ind., Lieut. Col. O.H.P. Carey
23d Ky., Lieut. Col. J.P. Jackson
6th Ohio, Lieut. Col. Nicholas L. Anderson
24th Ohio, Lieut. Col. Frederick C. Jones
H, 4th U.S. Art'y, Lieut. Samuel Canby
M, 4th U.S. Art'y, Capt. John Mendenhall

Nineteenth Brigade, Col. William B. Hazen
110th Ill., Col. Thomas S. Casey
9th Ind., Col. William H. Blake
6th Ky., Col. Walter C. Whitaker
27th Ky., Col. C.D. Pennebaker
41st Ohio, Lieut. Col. George S. Mygatt
F, 1st Ohio Art'y, Capt. Daniel T. Cockerill

Twenty-second Brigade, Brig. Gen. Charles Cruft
31st Ind., Lieut. Col. John Osborn
1st Ky., Lieut. Col. David A. Enyart
2d Ky., Col. Thomas D. Sedgwick
20th Ky., Lieut. Col. Charles S. Hanson
90th Ohio, Col. Isaac N. Ross
B, 1st Ohio Art'y, Capt. William E. Standart

Cavalry
2d Ky. (4 co's), Lieut. Col. Thomas B. Cochran

FIFTH DIVISION, Brig. Gen. Horatio P. Van Cleve

Eleventh Brigade, Col. Samuel Beatty

79th Ind., Col. Frederick Knetler
9th Ky., Lieut. Col. George H. Cram
13th Ky., Lieut. Col. J.B. Carlile
19th Ohio, Lieut. Col. E.W. Hollinsworth
59th Ohio, Col. James P. Fyffe

Fourteenth Brigade, Col. Pierce B. Hawkins
44th Ind., Col. Hugh B. Reed
86th Ind., Col. Orville S. Hamilton
11th Ky., Lieut. Col. S.P. Love
26th Ky., Col. Cicero Maxwell
13th Ohio, Col. Joseph G. Hawkins

Twenty-third Brigade, Col. Stanley Matthews
35th Ind., Col. Bernard F. Mullen
8th Ky., Col. Sidney M. Barnes
21st Ky., Col. S. Woodson Price
51st Ohio, Lieut. Col. Richard W. McClain
99th Ohio, Lieut. Col. John E. Cummins

Artillery:
7th Ind., Capt. George R. Swallow
B, Pa., Lieut. Alanson J. Stevens
3d Wis., Capt. Lucius H. Drury

SIXTH DIVISION, Brig. Gen. Thomas J. Wood

Fifteenth Brigade, Brig. Gen. Milo S. Hascall
100th Ill., Col. Frederick A. Bartleson
17th Ind., Lieut. Col. George W. Gorman
58th Ind., Col. George P. Buell
3d Ky., Lieut. Col. William T. Scott
26th Ohio, Maj. Chriss M. Degenfield
8th Ind. Battery, Lieut. George Estep

Twentieth Brigade, Col. Charles G. Harker
51st Ind., Col. Abel D. Streight
73d Ind., Col. Gilbert Hathaway
13th Mich., Lieut. Col. Frederick W. Worden
64th Ohio, Col. John Ferguson

65th Ohio, Lieut. Col. William H. Young
6th Ohio Battery, Capt. Cullen Bradley

Twenty-first Brigade, Col. George D. Wagner
15th Ind., Lieut. Col. Gustavus A. Wood
40th Ind., Col. John W. Blake
57th Ind., Col. Cyrus C. Hines
24th Ky., Col. Louis B. Grigsby;
97th Ohio, Col. John Q. Lane
10th Ind. Battery, Capt. Jerome B. Cox
Brigade loss (40th Ind.): w, 2

Unattached:
B, E, I, and K, 1st Mich., Eng's and Mech's, Col. William P. Innes
1st Ohio Cav. (detachment), Maj. James Laughlin

THIRD ARMY CORPS, Maj. Gen. Charles C. Gilbert

FIRST DIVISION, Brig. Gen. Albin Schoepf

First Brigade, Col. Moses B. Walker
82d Ind., Col. Morton C. Hunter
12th Ky., Col. William A. Hoskins
17th Ohio, Col. John M. Connell
31st Ohio, Lieut. Col. Frederick W. Lister
38th Ohio, Lieut. Col. William A. Choate

Second Brigade, Brig. Gen. Speed S. Fry
10th Ind., Col. William C. Kise
74th Ind., Col. Charles W. Chapman
4th Ky., Col. John T. Croxton
10th Ky., Lieut. Col. William H. Hays
14th Ohio, Lieut. Col. George P. Este
Brigade loss: k, 4; w, 7 = 11

Third Brigade, Brig. Gen. James B. Steedman
87th Ind., Col. Kline G. Shryock
2d Minn., Col. James George
9th Ohio, Lieut. Col. Charles Joseph
35th Ohio, Col. Ferdinand Van Derveer

18th U.S., Maj. Frederick Townsend
Brigade loss: w, 6; m, 8 = 14

Artillery
4th Mich., Capt. Josiah W. Church
C, 1st Ohio, Capt. Daniel K. Southwick
I, 4th U.S., Lieut. Frank G. Smith
Artillery loss: w, 1

Cavalry
1st Ohio (detachment), Col. Minor Milliken

NINTH DIVISION, Brig. Gen. Robert B. Mitchell

Thirtieth Brigade, Col. Michael Gooding
59th Ill., Maj. Joshua C. Winters
74th Ill., Lieut. Col. James B. Kerr
75th Ill., Lieut. Col. John E. Bennett
22d Ind., Lieut. Col. Squire I. Keith (k)
5th Wis. Battery, Capt. Oscar F. Pinney
Brigade loss: k, 121; w, 314; m, 64 = 499

Thirty-first Brigade, Col. William P. Carlin
21st Ill., Col. John W.S. Alexander
38th Ill., Maj. Daniel H. Gilmer
101st Ohio, Col. Leander Stem
15th Wis. Col. Hans C. Heg
2d Minn. Battery, Capt. William A. Hotchkiss
Brigade loss: w, 10

Thirty-second Brigade, Col. William W. Caldwell
25th Ill., Lieut. Col. James S. McClelland
35th Ill., Lieut. Col. William P. Chandler
81st Ind., Lieut. Col. John Timberlake
8th Kan. (battalion), Lieut. Col. John A. Martin
8th Wis. Battery, Capt. Stephen J. Carpenter

Cavalry
B, 36th Ill., Capt. Samuel B. Sherer

ELEVENTH DIVISION, Brig. Gen. Philip H. Sheridan

Thirty-fifth Brigade, Lieut. Col. Bernard Laiboldt
44th Ill., Capt. Wallace W. Barrett
73d Ill., Col. James F. Jaquess
2d Mo., Capt. Walter Hoppe (k)
15th Mo., Maj. John Weber
Brigade loss: k, 22; w, 102; m, 1 = 125

Thirty-sixth Brigade, Col. Daniel McCook
85th Ill., Col. Robert S. Moore
86th Ill., Col. David D. Irons
125th Ill., Col. Oscar F. Harmon
52d Ohio, Lieut. Col. D.D.T. Cowen
Brigade loss: k, 7; w, 63; m, 9 = 79

Thirty-seventh Brigade, Col. Nicholas Greusel
36th Ill., Capt. Silas Miller
88th Ill., Col. Francis T. Sherman
21st Mich., Col. Ambrose A. Stevens
24th Wis., Col. Charles H. Larrabee
Brigade loss: k, 15; w, 124; m, 4 = 143

Artillery
I, 2d Ill., Capt. Charles M. Barnett
G, 1st Mo., Capt. Henry Hescock
Artillery loss: w, 3

CAVALRY: *Third Brigade*, Capt. Ebenezer Gay
9th Ky. (detachment), Lieut. Col. John Boyle
2d Mich., Lieut. Col. Archibald P. Campbell
9th Pa., Lieut. Col. Thomas C. James
Cavalry loss: k, 4; w, 13 = 17

The total Union loss was: killed, 845; wounded, 2,851; captured or missing, 515 = 4,211

The Battle of Perryville

Confederate

General Braxton Bragg

ARMY OF THE MISSISSIPPI: Major General Leonidas Polk

RIGHT WING, Maj. Gen. Benhamin F. Cheatham
CHEATHAM'S DIVISION, Brig. Gen. Daniel S. Donelson

First Brigade, Col. John H. Savage
8th Tenn., Col. W.L. Moore
15th Tenn., Col. R.C. Tyler
16th Tenn., Lieut. Col. D.M. Donnell
38th Tenn., Col. John C. Carter
51st Tenn., Col. John Chester
Tenn. Battery, Capt. W.W. Carnes
Brigade loss: k, 68; w, 272; m, 7 = 347

Second Brigade, Brig. Gen. A.P. Stewart
4th Tenn., Col. O.F. Strahl
5th Tenn., Col. C.D. Venable
24th Tenn., Lieut. Col. H.L.W. Bratton
31st Tenn., Col. E.E. Tansil
33d Tenn., Col. W.P. Jones
Miss. Battery, Capt. T.J. Stanford
Brigade loss: k, 62; w, 340; m, 26 = 428

Third Brigade, Brig. Gen. George Maney
41st Ga., Col. Charles A. McDaniel (w), Maj. John Knight
1st Tenn., Col. H. R. Field
6th Tenn., Col. George C. Porter
9th Tenn., Lieut. Col. John W. Buford (w), Major George W. Kelsoe
27th Tenn., Lieut. Col. W. Frierson (w), Maj. A.C. Allen
Miss. Battery, Lieut. William B. Turner
Brigade loss: k, 136; w, 517; m, 34 = 687

CAVALRY BRIGADE, Col. John A. Wharton
1st Ky. (3 co's), ——
4th Tenn., ——
8th Tex., ——

Brigade loss (not separately reported)

LEFT WING, Maj. Gen. William J. Hardee.

SECOND DIVISION, Brig. Gen. J. Patton Anderson
First Brigade: Brig. Gen. John C. Brown (w), Col. William Miller
1st Fla., Col. William Miller
3d Fla., ——
41st Miss., ——
Palmer's Battery, ——
Brigade loss (not separately reported)

Second Brigade, Brig. Gen. Daniel W. Adams
13th La., Col. R.L. Gibson
16th La., Col. D.C. Gober
20th La., Col. Aug. Reichard, Lieut. Col. Leon von Zinken
25th La., Col. S.W. Fisk
14th Battalion La. Sharp-shooters, Major J.E. Austin
5th Co. Washington (La.) Art'y, Capt. C.H. Slocomb
Brigade loss: k, 6; w, 78; m, 68 = 152

Third Brigade, Col. Samuel Powell
45th Ala., ——
1st Ark., ——
24th Miss., Col. William F. Dowd
29th Tenn., ——
Mo. Battery, Capt. Overton W. Barret
Brigade loss (not separately reported)

Fourth Brigade, Col. Thomas M. Jones
27th Miss., ——
30th Miss., ——
37th Miss., ——
Ala. Battery (Lumsden's)
Brigade loss (not separately reported)

THIRD DIVISION, Maj. Gen. Simon B. Buckner
First Brigade, Brig. Gen. St. John R. Liddell
2d Ark., ——
5th Ark., Col. L. Featherston
6th Ark., ——
7th Ark., Col. D.A. Gillespie

8th Ark., Col. John H. Kelly
Miss. Battery (Swett's)
Brigade loss: k, w, and m, 71

Second Brigade, Brig. Gen. P.R. Cleburne (w):
13th Ark., ——
15th Ark., ——
2d Tenn., ——
Ark. Battery (Calvert's)
Brigade loss (not separately reported)

Third Brigade, Brig. Gen. Bushrod R. Johnson
5th Confederate, Col. J.A. Smith
17th Tenn., Col. A.S. Marks
23d Tenn., Lieut. Col. R.H. Keeble
25th Tenn., Col. John M. Hughs
37th Tenn., Col. Moses White
44th Tenn., Col. John S. Fulton
Miss. Battery (Jefferson Art'y), Capt. Put. Darden
Brigade loss: k, 30; w, 165; m, 9 = 204

Fourth Brigade, Brig. Gen. S.A.M. Wood (w)
16th Ala., ——
33d Ala., ——
3d Confederate, ——
45th Miss., ——
15th Battalion Miss. Sharp-shooters, ——
Ala. Battery, Capt. Henry C. Semple
Brigade loss (not separately reported)

CAVALRY BRIGADE, Col. Joseph Wheeler
1st Ala., Col. William W. Allen
3d Ala., Col. James Hagan
6th Confederate, Lieut. Col. James A. Pell
2d Ga. (battalion), Maj. C.A. Whaley
3d Ga., Col. Martin J. Crawford
1st Ky. (6 co's), Maj. J.W. Caldwell
Brigade loss (not separately reported)

Confederate losses: killed, 510; wounded 2,635; missing, 251 = 3,396

NOTES

1. Sam R. Watkins, *"Co. Aytch": A Side Show of the Big Show* (Chattanooga, Tenn., 1902; reprint ed., New York, N.Y., 1962), 61, 63.

2. Ken Burns, *The Civil War* (videocassettes, 9 pts., approx. 60 min. each, Florentine Films in association with WETA-TV, Washington, D.C., 1990).

3. Watkins, *"Co. Aytch"*, 63.

4. James Lee McDonough, *War in Kentucky: From Shiloh to Perryville* (Knoxville, Tenn., 1994); Thomas Lawrence Connelly, *Army of the Heartland: The Army of Tennessee, 1861-1862* (Baton Rouge, La., 1967); Kenneth A. Hafendorfer, *Perryville: Battle for Kentucky*, 2nd ed. (Louisville, Ky., 1991). All three works were consulted throughout. The present essay is based on early research for a projected new history of the battle, to be published by the University Press of Kentucky.

5. Edward Ruger and Anton Kilp, Surveyors and Compilers, "Map of the Battlefield of Perryville Ky.," (Washington, D.C., 1877; reprint, Lexington, Ky., 1979).

6. *The War of the Rebellion: A Compilation of the Official Records of the Union and Confederate Armies*, 128 vols. (Washington, D.C., 1880-1901) (hereinafter cited as *O.R.*) (all citations are to Series I), 16 (1):114, 1024; Luke W. Finley, "The Battle of Perryville," *Southern Historical Society Papers,* 50 vols. (Richmond, Va., 1876-1919) 30 (1902), 242; Charles C. Gilbert, "On the Field of Perryville," Robert Underwood Johnson and Clarence Clough Buel, eds., *Battles and Leaders of the Civil War*, 4 vols. (New York, N.Y., 1888; reprint ed., New York, N.Y., 1956) (hereinafter cited as *Battles and Leaders*), 3:52.

7. Ruger and Kilp Map; *O.R.*, 16 (1):1120.

8. See also *O.R.*, 16 (2):538-39, 542-43, 546, 555, 557-59, 1088-90; Herman Hattaway and Archer Jones, *How the North Won: A Military History of the Civil War* (Urbana, Ill., 1983), 245-56.

9. *O.R.*, 16 (1):1091.

10. In addition to works in this volume, see *O.R.*, 16 (1):1088, 1091, 1109; *O.R.*, 16 (2):876, 880, 886; Joseph Wheeler, "Bragg's Invasion of Kentucky," *Battles and Leaders*, 3:1-13; Connelly, *Army of the Heartland*, 234-46; McDonough, *War in Kentucky*, 1-200; Grady McWhiney, "Controversy in Kentucky: Braxton Bragg's Campaign of 1862," *Civil War History,* 6 (1960), 16-25.

11. *O.R.*, 16 (1):524, 613, 640, 1024, 1087, 1091-1107, 1109-10; *O.R.*, 16 (2):566, 570-71, 575-80, 896-97, 898, 900, 901-6, 912, 917, 919-20; Wheeler, "Bragg's Invasion of Kentucky," 14-15; Connelly, *Army of the Heartland*, 245-62; McWhiney, "Controversy in Kentucky," 25-32; Hattaway and Jones, *How the North Won*, 257.

12. *O.R.*, 16 (1):1087; William J. Hardee, Report, Dec. 1, 1862, Filson Club Historical Society, Louisville, Ky (hereinafter cited as Filson).

13. *O.R.*, 16 (1):219, 233, 1024, 1074; Henry J. Aten, *History of the Eighty-Fifth Regiment, Illinois Volunteer Infantry* (Hiawatha, Kan., 1901), 34-35; Maurice Marcoot, *Five Years in the Sunny South: Reminiscences of Maurice Marcoot, Late of Co "B," 15th Reg. Missouri Veteran Volunteer Infantry From 1861 to 1866* (no publisher, no date), 16; Philip H. Sheridan, *Personal Memoirs of P.H. Sheridan*, 2 vols. (New York, N.Y., 1888), 193-94.

14. *O.R.*, 16 (1):219, 238-41, 1025, 1081, 1083-84, 1110; Janet B. Hewett, et. al., eds. *Supplement to the O.R. of the Union and Confederate Armies*, (Wilmington, N.C., 1994), 3 (1):278-79; Allen L. Fahnestock Diary, Oct. 8, 1862, Peoria Public Library, Peoria, Ill., photocopy in 86th Illinois file, Perryville State Historical Site, Perryville, Ky. (hereinafter cited as PSHS); Julius B. Work Diary, Oct. 8, 1862, Ohio Historical Society, Columbus, Oh. (hereinafter cited as OHS); J.R. Kinnear, *History of the Eighty-Sixth Regiment Illinois Volunteer Infantry, During Its Term of Service* (Chicago, Ill., 1866), 12-13; Marcoot, *Five Years in the Sunny South*, 16; Whitelaw Reid, *Ohio in the War: Her Statesmen Generals and Soldiers*, 2 vols. (Cincinnati, Ohio, 1895), 2:314-15; Sheridan, *Personal Memoirs*, 194; Nixon B. Stewart, *Dan. McCook's Regiment, 52nd O.V.I.: A History of the Regiment, Its Campaigns and Battles. From 1862 to 1865* (Claysville, Oh., 1900), 26-27.

15. Gilbert, "On the Field of Perryville," *Battles and Leaders*, 3:53.

16. *O.R.*, 16 (1):62, 74, 89, 96, 344, 526-27, 1025; *O.R.*, 16 (2):580-81, 587-88.

17. *O.R.*, 16 (1):1087, 1092-93, 1096, 1109-1110 (first quotation, 1092; second quotation, 1110); McWhiney, "Controversy in Kentucky," 32.

18. J. Stoddard Johnston, "Battle of Perryville," J. Stoddard Johnston Papers, Filson.

19. *O.R.*, 16 (1):1044; David Biggs, "Incidents in Battle of Perryville," *Confederate Veteran*, 33 (1925), 141; B.F. Cheatham, "The Battle of Perryville," *Southern Bivouac*, 1 (Apr. 1886), 704; Gilbert, "On the Field at Perryville," *Battles and Leaders*, 3:53-54; J. Stoddard Johnston, "Battle of Perryville," Filson; Thomas H. Malone, *Memoir of Thomas H. Malone* (no publisher, 1928), 128; Marcus B. Toney, *The Privations of A Private* (Nashville, Tenn., 1905), 42.

20. *O.R.*, 16 (1):1120-21; McDonough, *War in Kentucky*, 233.

21. *O.R.*, 16 (1):90, 1039-40, 1062, 1110, 1121; W.W. Carnes, "Artillery at the Battle of Perryville," *Confederate Veteran*, 33 (1925), 8; J. Stoddard Johnston, "Battle of Perryville," J. Stoddard Johnston Papers, Filson; John H. Savage, *The Autobiography of John H. Savage* (Nashville, Tenn., 1903), 118-19; Wheeler, "Bragg's Invasion of Kentucky," *Battles and Leaders*, 3:16.

22. *O.R.*, 16 (1):90, 104, 1060, 1062, 1064-65; Atlanta *Confederacy*, Nov. 13, 1862; *Confederate Veteran*, 5 (1897), 435; *Knoxville Register*, Oct. 18, 1862; Gilbert, "Bragg's Invasion of Kentucky," ch. 5; *Southern Bivouac*, 1 (Jan. 1886), 466; Thomas A. Head, *Campaigns and Battles of the Sixteenth Regiment, Tennessee Volunteers, In the War Between the States, with Incidental Sketches of the Part Performed by Other Tennessee Troops in the Same War, 1861-1865* (Nashville, Tenn., 1885), 95-96 (third

quotation, 96); Kurt Holman, "Revised Location of Parson's Battery," unpublished paper, PSHS; Johnston, "Battle of Perryville," J. Stoddard Johnston Papers, Filson (first quotation); Edward Rennolds, *A History of Henry County Commands* (Jacksonville, Fla., 1904; reprint ed., Kennesaw, Ga., 1861), 45-48 (second quotation, 45); Savage, *Autobiography*, 118-21; James R. Thompson, "Hear the Wax Fry," (typescript, 1966, PSHS), 9; Angus Waddle, Camp Near Perryville, Ky., to Sister, Oct. 11, 1862, Angus Waddle Letters, Missouri Historical Society, Columbia, Mo.; J.J. Womack, *The Civil War Diary of Capt. J.J. Womack* (McMinnville, Tenn., 1961), 62-63.

23. C.H. Clark, "The Civil War Articles of C.H. Clark" typescript, 16th Tennessee file, PSHS, 27.

24. *O.R.*, 16 (1):294, 1060, 1064-65, 1113-14, 1115, 1116, 1118; Malone, *Memoir of Thomas H. Malone*, 128-30; Toney, *Privations of a Private*, 42-44; Reid, *Ohio in the War*, 566; Christopher Lossing, *Tennessee's Forgotten Warriors: Frank Cheatham and His Confederate Division* (Knoxville, Tenn., 1989), 67. Kurt Holman, current manager of the Perryville Battlefield State Historic Site, questions the impact of Parsons's battery. Noting a higher concentration of case shot and common shell than canister in archaeological digs in the area where the 16th Tennessee was cut to pieces, Holman suspects that perhaps as many as four other batteries further back in line may have zeroed in on the Tennesseans. See Holman, Perryville, Ky., to Kenneth W. Noe, May 9, 1997, Author's Collection.

25. Malone, *Memoir of Thomas H. Malone*, 129.

26. *O.R.*, 16 (1):1113; Paul M. Angle, ed., *Three Years in the Army of the Cumberland: the Letters and Diary of Major James A.Connolly* (New York, N.Y., 1969), 21.

27. *O.R.*, 16 (1):1026, 1060, 1066-67; Joshua Ayre, "The Civil War Diary of Joshua Ayre," transcribed by James Glauser, 105th Ohio file, PSHS; John Holbrook Morse, "Civil War: The Letters of John Holbrook Morse 1861-1865," ed. by Bianca Morse Federico and Betty Louise Wright (Washington, D.C., 1975), typescript, 63; Bliss Morse, Danville, Ky., to Mother, Oct. 14, 1862, Blis Morse Papers, OHS; Reid, *Ohio in the War*, 566; Robert B. Taylor Diary, Oct. 8, 1862, microfilm 1146) Kentucky Historical Society, Frankfort, Ky.; Albion W. Tourgee, *The Story of a Thousand* (Buffalo, N.Y., 1896), 116-23.

28. Morse, "Civil War," 63.

29. *O.R.*, 16 (1):1065; Malone, *Memoir of Thomas H. Malone*, 129-31; Morse, "Civil War," 64; Arthur Howard Noll, ed., *Doctor Quintard: Chaplain C.S.A. and Second Bishop of Tennessee, being His Story of the War (1861-1865)* (Sewanee, Tenn., 1905), 57, 59; Tourgee, *Story of a Thousand*, 121-23; Hattaway and Jones, *How the North Won*, 258-59. "Perfectly unmanned and broken-hearted," Parsons lamented to his captain "'I could not help it, captain; it was not my fault.'" *O.R.*, 16 (1):1061.

30. Johnston, "Battle of Perryville," J. Stoddard Johnston Papers, Filson.

31. *O.R.*, 16 (1):1049, 1055-56, 1120-21; Daniel H. Chandler, "History of the 5th Ind. Battery," 19, Daniel H. Chandler Collection, Indiana State Library, Indianapolis,

Ind.; Ormond Hupp, *My Diary* (no publisher, no date), 23, microfilm, Indiana Historical Society; Robert A. Jarman Manuscript, Mississippi Dept. of Archives and History, Jackson, Miss; Henry M. Kendall, "The Battle of Perryville," *Military Order of the Loyal Legion of the United States, Commandery of the District of Columbia, War Papers,* 2 (no publisher, 1902), 379-381; Robert Kohlsdorf, Camp Near Louisville, Ky., to A.M. Thompson, Nov. 1, 1862 (typescript), 10th Wisconsin file, PSHS; B.F. Scribner, *How Soldiers Were Made; or The War as I Saw It Under Buell, Rosecrans, Thomas, Grant and Sherman* (New Albany, Ind., 1887), 58-59.

32. *O.R.*, 16 (1):69-71, 1057-58, 1121, 1124-26, 1128, 1129, 1130-31, 1132; *Supplement to the O.R.*, 3 (1):280; John Beatty, *The Citizen-Soldier; or, Memoirs of a Volunteer* (Cincinnati, Ohio, 1879), 178-79; William P. McDowell, "Reminiscences of the Battle of Perryville, Ky." Talks Before the Filson Club Collection, Filson; Reid, *Ohio in the War*, 79; McDonough, *War in Kentucky*, 260.

33. Beatty, *The Citizen-Soldier*, 178.

34. *O.R.*, 16 (1):240, 528, 1072, 1082, 1122-23; L.G. Bennett and William M. Haigh, *History of the Thirty-Sixth Regiment Illinois Volunteers During the War of the Rebellion* (Aurora, Ill., 1876), 251-52; William F. Dowd, "Recollections," Thomas J. Ford, *With The Rank and File* (Milwaukee, Wis., 1898), 6-7; Charles Lewis Francis, *Narrative of a Private Soldier in the Volunteer Army of the United States, Durig a Portion of the Period Covered by the Great War of the Rebellion of 1861* (Brooklyn, N.Y., 1879), 56-57; William H. McCardle Papers, Mississippi Dept. of Archives and History, Jackson, Miss.; McDonough, *War in Kentucky*, 267-71; Sheridan, *Personal Memoirs*, 196-97.

35. *O.R.*, 16 (1):294, 1045, 1060.

36. *Ibid.,* 1045-46, 1113-14, 1115, 1116-17, 1118; Edward Ferguson, "The Army of the Cumberland Under Buell," *Military Order of the Loyal Legion of the United States, Commandery of the State of Wisconsin, War Papers* (n.p., 1891), 428-30 (quotation, 429); Leo M. Kaiser, ed., "Civil War Letters of Charles W. Carr of the 21st Wisconsin Volunteers," *Wisconsin Magazine of History,* 43 (Summer 1960), 269-70; Tourgee, *Story of a Thousand*, 124-26

37. *O.R.*, 16 (1):1026, 1114, 1115, 1116-17, 1118; Carnes, "Artillery at the Battle of Perryville, Ky.," *Confederate Veteran,* 33 (1925), 8; Connolly, *Three Years in the Army of the Cumberland*, 21-22; Joseph C. Haddock, "Historical Sketch of the 4th Indiana Battery," 16-17, Joseph C. Haddock Collection, Indiana Historical Society, Indianapolis, Indiana; D.C. Stone, Near Crab Orchard, Ky., to Sir, Oct. 17, 1862, Battery A, Kentucky Artillery Collection, Union Artillery—Primary Sources, Kentucky Military History Museum, Frankfort, Ky.; *Valparaiso Republic*, Nov. 13, 1862; Malone, *Memoir of Thomas H. Malone*, 131-33; L.B. McFarland, "Maney's Brigade at the Battle of Perryville," *Confederate Veteran* 30 (1922), 467-68; Toney, *Privations of a Private*, 43-44; Tourgee, *Story of a Thousand*, 126.

38. Watkins, *"Co. Aytch"*, 62-63.

39. *O.R.*, 16 (1):1046; Savage, *Autobiography of John H. Savage*, 120-22; Edwin H. Rennolds, *A History of Henry County Commands Which Served in the Confederate States Army, Including Rosters of the Various Companies Enlisted in Henry County, Tennessee* (Jacksonville, Fla., 1904; reprint ed., Kennesaw, Ga., 1961), 46-49.

40. *O.R.*, 16 (1):1049-50; William A. Bryant, Bryantsville, Ky., to Mother, Oct. 11, 1862, 3rd Florida file, PSHS; Kendall, "The Battle of Perryville," 9; Scribner, *How Soldiers Were Made*, 58-59.

41. *O.R.*, 16 (1):70, 1047, 1123; *Supplement to the O.R.*, 3 (1):280-81; Beatty, *The Citizen-Soldier*, 178-79; Irving A. Buck, *Cleburne and His Command* (New York, N.Y., 1908), 66-71; *Cincinnati Daily Enquirer*, Oct. 17, 1862; *Daily Evansville Journal*, Oct. 16, 21, 1862; "The 'Fighting' Forty-Eighth Tennessee Regiment," *Southern Bivouac*, 2 (Feb. 1884), 246-49; Jill K. Garrett, transcriber, *Confederate Diary of Robert D. Smith* (Columbia, Tenn., 1975), 33-34; James G. Jones, Camp at Tyree Springs, Tenn., to Oliver Morton, Nov. 24, 1862, Regimental Correspondence of the Adjutant General of Indiana, 42nd Indiana, Indiana State Archives, Indianapolis, Ind.; S.F. Horrall, *History of the Forty-Second Indiana Volunteer Infantry* (no publisher, 1892), 152-53; George Morgan Kirkpatrick, *The Experiences of a Private Soldier of the Civil War* (Chicago, Ohio, 1924; reprint ed., Indianapolis, Ind., 1973), 14-16; *Princeton* [Ind.] *Clarion*, Oct. 25, 1862; Kurt Holman, Perryville, Ky., to Kenneth W. Noe, May 9, 1997, Author's Collection.

42. *O.R.*, 16 (1):564, 1023, 1040, 1047.

43. *Ibid.*, 11, 51, 91, 102, 284, 345 (quotations, 284).

44. Hafendorfer, *Perryville*, 289.

45. *O.R.*, 16 (1):536. See also pp. 345, 1025-26.

46. *Ibid.*, 94, 283, 655, 1072-73, 1077-79, 1082 (quotations, 283); Theodore C. Blegen, ed., *The Civil War Letters of Colonel Hans Christian Heg* (Northfield, Minn., 1936), 145-46; L.W. Day, *Story of the One Hundred and First Ohio Infantry* (Cleveland, Ohio, 1894), 53-55; William F. Dowd, "Recollections," William H. McCardle Papers, Mississippi Dept. of Archives and History, Jackson, Miss.; *Montgomery Directory*, 1866, 97-98, Confederate Regimental History Files, 45th Alabama Infantry Regiment, Alabama Dept. of Archives and History, Montgomery, Ala.; *Montgomery Daily Advertiser*, Nov. 24, 1864; W.E. Patterson Memoir, Western Historical Manuscript Collection, Columbia, Mo.; Daniel E. Sutherland, ed., *Reminiscences of a Private: William E. Bevens of the First Arkansas Infantry, C.S.A.* (Fayetteville, Ark., 1992), 99. Twenty-five years later, Sheridan continued to grossly exaggerate the threat to his lines. See his *Personal Memoirs*, 196-97.

47. *O.R.*, 16 (1):1041, 1061, 1082; *Cincinnati Daily Commercial*, Oct. 24, 1862; Joseph P. Glezen Diary (microfilm), Oct. 8, 1862, Indiana State Library, Indianapolis, Ind.; Paul E. Rieger, annotator, *Through One Man's Eyes: The Civil War Experiences of a Belmont County Volunteer, Letters of James G. Theaker* (Mount Vernon, Ohio, no date), 13-14.

48. *O.R.*, 16 (1):98-99, 132, 137, 655, 1041-42, 1047, 1075-76, 1079-80, 1121; Patton Anderson, Near Shelbyville, Tenn., to Henry C. Semple, June 10, 1863, Confederate Artillery Batteries: Lumsden's Battery-Waters' Battery, Alabama Dept. of Archives and History, Montgomery, Ala.; Buck, *Cleburne and His Command,* 70; *Confederate Veteran* 8 (1900), 73; "Co. Aytch" [Sam Watkins], "An Adventure of General Leonidas Polk at the Battle of Perryville," *Southern Bivouac,* 2 (1884), 403; A.M. Crary, *The A.M. Crary Memoirs and Memoranda* (Herington, Kan., 1915), 74-76; William Sumner Dodge, *A Waif of the War; or, The History of the Seventy-Fifth Illinois Infantry, Embracing The Entire Campaigns of the Army of the Cumberland* (Chicago, Ill., 1866), 44-45; Luke W. Finley, "The Battle of Perryville," *Southern Historical Society Papers,* 30 (1902), 244-246; Garrett, ed., *Confederate Diary of Robert Smith*, 33; Constantin Grebner, *"We Were the Ninth": A History of the Ninth Regiment, Ohio Volunteer Infantry April 17, 1861, to June 7, 1864*, trans. and ed. Frederic Trautman (Kent, Ohio, 1987), 115; A.S. Hamilton, Huntsville Ala., to S.A.M. Wood, Mar. 25, 1863, Sterling A.M. Wood Papers, Alabama Dept. of Arhives and History, Montgomery, Ala.; Glenn W. Sunderland, *Five Days to Glory* (South Brunswick, N.J., 1970), 58-60; L.B. Williams, ed., "The 33rd Alabama Regiment in the Civil War" (typescript), 25-29, Alabama Dept. of Archives and History, Montgomery, Ala.; L.B. Williams, *A Sketch of the 33rd Alabama Volunteer Infantry Regiment and its Role in Cleburne's Elite Division of the Army of Tennessee 1862-1865* (no publisher, no date), 14-16.

49. "Battle of Perryville," J. Stoddard Johnston Papers, Filson.

50. *O.R.*, 16 (1):1029, 1093-94; *O.R.*, 16 (2):597-601, 605-08, 611-14, 618-19, 621-22, 624, 626-27, 634, 636-38, 640-42, 931, 951-52; Thomas Lawrence Connelly and Archer Jones, *The Politics of Command: Factions and Ideas in Confederate Strategy* (Baton Rouge, La., 1973), 59-78; Gary Donaldson, "'Into Africa': Kirby Smith and Braxton Bragg's Invasion of Kentucky," *Filson Club History Quarterly,* 61 (1987), 463; Finley, "Battle of Perryville," 246; Johnston, "Battle of Perryville," J. Stoddard Johnston Papers, Filson; McDonough, *War in Kentucky*, 304-17; C.C. Gilbert, "Bragg's Invasion of Kentucky," *Battles and Leaders*, 3: Ch. 6; *Southern Bivouac,* 1 (1883), 551-56; McWhiney, "Controversy in Kentucky," 34-43; A.C. Quisenberry, "The Confederate Campaign in Kentucky, 1862: The Battle of Perryville," *Register of the Kentucky Historical Society,* 17 (1919), 34-38; Wheeler, "Bragg's Invasion of Kentucky," *Battles and Leaders*, 3:17-25. Buell's conduct was investigated later in the winter by a military commission, and the controversy dragged on for many years after the war. See *O.R.*, 16 (1):6-728.

51. Daniel H. Chandler, "History of the 5th Indiana Battery," p. 25, Daniel H. Chandler Collection, Indiana State Library, Indianapolis, Ind.; *Cincinnati Daily Commercial*, Nov. 17, 1862; *Indianapolis Daily Journal*, Oct. 24, 1862; Bliss Morse, Danville, Ky., to Mother, Oct. 15, 1862, Bliss Morse Papers, Ohio Historical Society, Columbus, Oh.; *New Albany* [Ind.] *Daily Ledger*, Oct. 15, 21, 22, 28, 20, Nov. 16, 1862; *Princeton* [Ind.] *Clarion*, Oct. 25, 1862; Lora Parks Diary, PSHS; Sarah E. Philips, "Disaster at Perryville: The Aftermath of the Bloodiest Battle in Kentucky," unpublished

paper, PSHS; John Sipe, Crab Orchard, to Sallie, Oct. 16, 1862, Civil War Regimental History—38th Infantry, Indiana State Library, Indianapolis, Ind.; William Spencer, Camp Near Perryville, Ky., to Sister, Oct. 11, 1862, William and Joseph Spencer Letters, Ohio Historical Society, Columbus, Oh.; Thomas C. Thoburn, "My Experiences During the Civil War" (typescript), 98th Ohio File, PSHS;

52. *New Albany Daily Ledger*, Oct. 25, 1862.

53. Robert Underwood Johnson and Clarence Clough Buel, eds., *Battles and Leaders of the Civil War*, 4 vols. (New York, N.Y., 1887), 3:29-30.

Wiley Sword

General Patrick R. Cleburne:

Earning His Spurs as a Field Commander in Kentucky, 1862

Patrick Cleburne couldn't talk! For a youthful Irishman, it seemed a fate worse than death. While in the act of talking to a wounded officer, a rifle ball had struck his left jaw, smashed several of his lower teeth and passed out through his open mouth. The bleeding was so profuse and the pain so excruciating that in a few minutes, later wrote Cleburne, I was deprived of "the powers of speech, and [this] rendered my further presence on the field worse than useless."[1]

Cleburne was referring to the unfortunate wound he received at Richmond, Kentucky on August 30, 1862, during one of the Western Confederacy's most complete limited engagement victories of the war. Yet by that point in the Battle of Richmond, Kentucky, Cleburne didn't really need to talk. Despite the debilitating wound and Cleburne's subsequent absence from the field, that bold victory was due in large measure to his earlier tactical dispositions. As such, it was an early indication of the skill that was ultimately to identify Patrick R. Cleburne as one of the Confederacy's best combat generals.

Although in recent years Pat Cleburne has received significant attention, he remains trapped in the shadow of many larger-than-life Southern Civil War heroes. This is unfortunate, for his story is one of the most fascinating, if tragic, of the war.

General Patrick Ronayne Cleburne. A native of Ireland, Cleburne rapidly rose in rank during the war because of his remarkable abilities as a commander, not the least of which was his consummate tactical skill first shown at the battles of Richmond and Perryville. *Library of Congress*

Various writers and historians have told of Cleburne's major role in defeating William Tecumseh Sherman on North Missionary Ridge at Chattanooga, his stout defense of Rinngold Gap during the November 1863 retreat to Dalton, Georgia, and his untimely death while leading a desperate assault at Franklin in 1864.[2] Yet Cleburne's part in the Kentucky fighting of 1862, where he early displayed so much of his great fighting ability, has often been overlooked or underestimated.

The reality of the 1862 Kentucky Campaign was that Pat Cleburne provided much of the tactical expertise that enabled the Confederates to achieve battlefield victories at Richmond and Perryville. Indeed, despite the failings of his senior commanders that resulted in the Confederate army's eventual strategic checkmate and withdrawal, Cleburne had provided much of the basis for an overall campaign victory by his accomplishments on the battlefield.[3] That his role was extraordinary during the Kentucky Campaign was suggested by the formal thanks of the Confederate Congress, which cited Cleburne and three other generals for "the highest order of generalship" at the Battle of Richmond, Kentucky.[4]

What is thus of analytical importance is a close scrutiny of Cleburne's performance in the actions at Richmond and Perryville. In fact, here are to be found some the most revealing aspects of Cleburne's tactical acumen—a quality that made him one of the Confederacy's most capable battlefield generals.

Battlefield tactics played an increasingly important role in mid-nineteenth century warfare, and this factor was one of the most crucial to the outcome of an engagement. Yet so few Civil War generals grasped the evolving lessons of a new era in combat that often the men in the ranks knew as much or more about fighting on a tactical level as did their senior commanders. This incredible circumstance was demonstrated time and time again by the resort to massed frontal attacks in the second, third, and even fourth year of the war. Furthermore, many unit commanders insisted that when entering combat their men stand up and fight the enemy in the open, "toe to toe and eyeball to eyeball," so to speak. This may have been in keeping with the "manful" concept of facing the enemy with "disciplined valor," but it resulted in excessive exposure and, as a result, the wasteful loss of precious lives.[5]

General Bushrod R. Johnson. When Johnson's Tennessee Brigade faltered in its attack at Perryville, Cleburne brought his brigade into action. *Library of Congress*

At Richmond, Kentucky, Cleburne, who was initially in command prior to the arrival of Maj. Gen. Edmund Kirby Smith, aggressively sought to fight the enemy force confronting him from a high hill, but not by means of a traditional frontal attack. Cleburne's maneuvering had brought much of his division into an extended line beyond the enemy's eastern flank. Until ordered not to attack by Kirby Smith who was coming up with reinforcements, Cleburne had nearly completed his preparations for a bold flank attack.[6]

Although he was wounded before this delayed but successful attack began, Cleburne demonstrated in the Richmond fight his tactical sagacity. By observing that the enemy was reinforcing its eastern flank, he correspondingly made plans to quickly strike at the point from which the Union troops were being removed—in addition to the planned flank attack. Accordingly, his tactical alignments were those that proved decisive when the final phase of the first stage fighting began.[7]

Again at Perryville less than two months later, Cleburne displayed battlefield perception and tactical skill. Although reduced to the command of a brigade, Cleburne had an important part in the Confederate battlefield victory. Ordered to support Brig. Gen. Bushrod R. Johnson's attacking brigade, Cleburne was at first operationally restricted by being required to maneuver in the wake of Johnson's troops, who were having difficulty ascending a ridge heavily lined with enemy guns and troops. Yet Cleburne and his men were soon placed in the same grim situation. When called on to advance and reinforce the front line, his brigade was confronted with a severe tactical problem. Cleburne was ordered to make a frontal attack across open and rising ground against thousands of Union troops, many of whom were behind a breast-high stone wall that formed an obtuse angle in their battleline. Because Johnson's soldiers had already been brought to a standstill by a devastating fire, Cleburne would be advancing into a battlefield inertia across fireswept open ground.[8]

Cleburne, following his orders, continued the charge. Observing that the irregular creek bottom in front offered shelter, Clebune ordered his entire brigade to move along the rocky Doctor's Creek defile. Advancing "double time" through this depression, Cleburne's troops were protected from a storm of rifle and artillery fire that "passed harmlessly over us," said Cleburne. Then, taking advantage of a stone wall that ran at right angles to Johnson's and the enemy's flank, Cleburne sent his old regiment, the 15th Arkansas, under cover of the wall to creep up the hillside and open an enfilading fire on the enemy—all the while "without [they] being . . . exposed."[9]

An 1885 view looking east from Loomis's Heights near the Mackville Pike at Perryville. Cleburne's brigade attacked Gen. William Lytle's Union brigade, which was holding these heights, by moving up the steep slope from Doctor's Creek (in the depression below) and then diagonally (to the left) across these fields. Visibile in the foreground is Squire Henry P. Bottom. *U. S. Army Military History Institute*

By this time, Bushrod Johnson's brigade had taken heavy casualties and were so nearly out of ammunition that they fell back into the adjacent creek bed. This left Cleburne and his brigade with the prospect of carrying out a virtually isolated attack agaist the salient angle portion of the enemy's line. Personally leading the way, Cleburne ordered his brigade forward to take the place of Johnson's brigade.[10]

It was here Cleburne found a tactical opportunity. Fire from the 15th Arkansas along the roadside stone wall, together with a battery firing from the left, had caused the enemy, Col. William H. Lytle's brigade, to drop back from a stone wall running just below the hilltop. Lytle's troops were now directly behind the crest, but firing with renewed energy.[11]

Cleburne did not despair. He deployed a line of skirmishers in front and sent all the brigade's flags forward into this skirmish line. Next he ordered the entire brigade to charge. Although they were soon halted and many fell back when their own Confederate artillery fired into them by mistake—because many of his men were wearing captured Yankee blue pants said Cleburne—the attack was quickly resumed. Clebune then described his calculated assault:

> The moment our flags, carried by the line of skirmishers, appeared above the crest of the hill, the enemy, supposing our [main] line of battle was in view, emptied their guns at the line of skirmishers. Before they could reload, our true line of battle was upon them [and] they instantly broke and fled, exposed to [our] deadly fire.[12]

It had been a display of tactical skill of the highest order. One of his captains later asserted; "it was only such a man as Cleburne who could inspire men to go up against such odds, and win—and he did." From an analytical perspective, the innovative tactical adjustments that Cleburne had made were based upon very sound, logical thinking.[13] In fact, Pat Cleburne had given particular credence to a critical key to winning or losing in battle—the methodology of fighting.

As was revealed at Shiloh and various other early war actions, the exposure of aligned ranks in prolonged close range combat between opposing battlelines was both unwise and intolerably destructive. At Shiloh, the repeated piecemeal (brigade-sized) frontal attacks ordered by Braxton Bragg at the Hornet's Nest and elsewhere were ruinous,

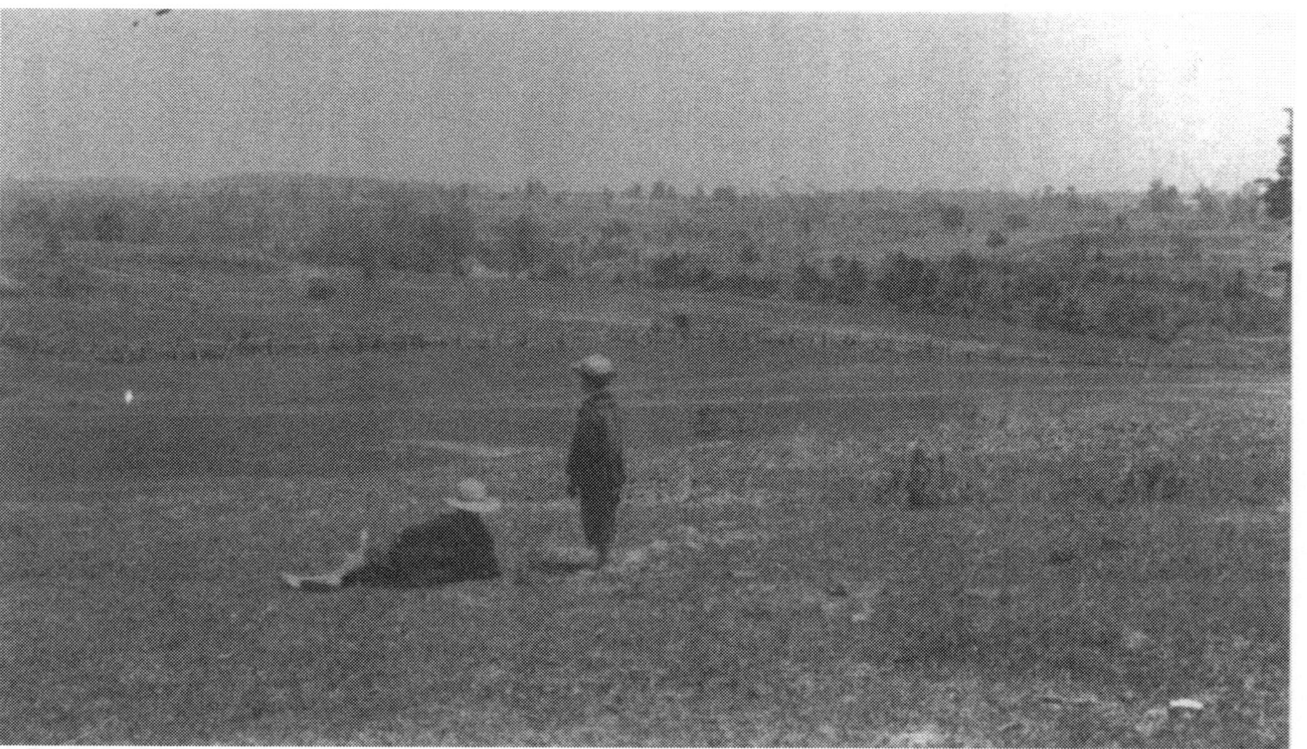

An 1885 view looking northeast from Loomis's Heights of the fields across which Cleburne's brigade attacked as the soldiers in the center of Gen. William Lytle's Union brigade observed them. *U.S. Army Military History Institute*

creating a tactical disaster out of a brilliant strategic operations victory. Cleburne had observed these lessons well. "Shiloh was a battle gallantly won and as stupidly lost," he had bitterly asserted.[14]

As Cleburne had demonstrated at Perryville, if a tactical victory was to be won, an able, enterprising commander must be alert to innovative means to protect his column of assault in order to reach intact the lines of a numerically stronger enemy. Thus, this Kentucky battlefield ploy was no fluke, or the result of mere chance. Beyond Perryville, time and time again, Cleburne avoided the open exposure of his men when in battle and preserved his troops' combat efficacy.[15]

In carefully analyzing the various factors of decisive importance in the fighting of a battle, it is apparent that victory or defeat in a major Civil War encounter often turned on matters of small but critical nature. As an investigation of battle after battle will demonstrate, it was very infrequent in a Civil War engagement that the critical difference was made by the strategic planning of a senior general. Battle's decisive equation not only involved the operational execution of those plans, but more importantly, the tactical expertise that was utilized.

Winning a pitched battle was far more sophisticated than just going out and meeting the enemy on a chosen field, or making a rapid flanking march. The concept that your personal opponent, either a Rebel or Yankee, was an incapable or inferior fighter was disproved early in the war. Thus, if combat success was expected, the factors of time, place, and circumstance had to be interwoven with an effective method and means of fighting—to provide an advantage over an equally determined and capable foe.

Based upon improved weapons technology, the tactical battlefield situation had dramatically changed from the Mexican War era. The minie ball-firing rifle musket—far more accurate and a killer at extended ranges—had made an enormous difference. By 1862 the basic reliance on the battlefield offensive, of overwhelming a targeted point with a massed column, had been proven to be largely impractical. The problem was, attacking columns couldn't often get within effective striking distance without losing too many troops. Heavy casualties generally caused a premature withdrawal, or resulted in insufficient strength for penetration once the enemy line was reached. When compounded by factors of disorganization involving wooded terrain, poor unit-to-unit communications and coordination, and the difficulty of overpowering enemy held fortifications, the successful execution of a direct, large scale attack was more and more improbable as the war progressed.[16]

The dominance of defensive firepower on the field of battle—versus the old reliance on offensive "shock" from a massed column of troops—resulted in many bloody, failed attacks. This was fully traceable to the increased accuracy and volume of musketry, shell fire, and canister. Exposed units were quickly disabled at extended ranges, and the subsequent loss of control and rampant confusion usually resulted in a tactical disaster. Moreover, considering the many "piecemeal" attacks that occurred, the problems of carrying and occupying an enemy position were compounded. Often the absence of sustaining troops required a withdrawal even if the attack was initially successful—or else this opened the door to counterattack. Gen. Braxton Bragg's stubborn reliance on limited or generally isolated attacks at Perryville, the Hornet's Nest at Shiloh, and the assault on the Round Forest at Stone's River, were manifestations of unwise and unperceptive battlefield initiatives. As was evident time after time, the true basis of victory was generally overlooked or ignored.[17]

What was needed was an advantage in fighting; a means to beat the enemy with all of the difficult, technologically sophisticated battlefield factors intermixed. Because the basic fighting unit in a Civil War battle was a regiment (often reduced to the strength of several companies as the war continued), the real test of combat occurred at that level. It was there that overall success or failure was often determined. Not only were the "fighting qualities" of each regiment's soldiers important, but equally so the extent of their exposure [losses], ability to deliver an effective fire [position], and the perceived opportunity of victory [the justification of personal risk by an imminent prospect of winning the fight].[18]

It was a wise commander who understood these critical aspects. By his applied common sense and intelligent grasp of the vital and decisive tactical circumstances of the battlefield, Pat Cleburne emerged as perhaps the most capable higher ranking infantry general of the Western Confederacy.

Not a West Point educated commander—in fact, he was a former British Army enlisted man—Cleburne seemed to know war intuitively, from the soldier's perspective. Hence, he was able to grasp the fighting man's basic problems and capabilities. This was important to understanding the complexities of the modern battlefield. The British army was among the world's most highly trained and disciplined, and Cleburne recognized the need for similar qualities in the Confederate forces he commanded. He also understood the need for the nurturing of the individual soldier as an effective fighting instrument, rather than just an abstract component of massed ranks.[19]

The recognition and utilization of an individual's full capabilities on the battlefield was a key to success. It involved each soldier's preservation, efficacy, and the utilization of his special talents. Cleburne selected the best shots from among his men and formed them into a battalion of sharpshooters. He personally trained the soldiers not only in maneuver, but in sham "battle tactics." He sought and obtained the best weapons for his men—usually Enfield rifle muskets for the infantry and costly Whitworth or Kerr sniper's rifles for the sharpshooters. He insisted on cleanliness and order as a means of fighting disease and sickness, and otherwise instructed his men in practical disciplines learned while in the British army.[20] The results spoke for themselves.

By mid-1863 Cleburne's Division was regarded by many as the army's elite command, an honor deservedly earned by its well demonstrated fighting ability. The famed and fearsome blue banners that Cleburne was allowed to keep for his division, when in 1863 all other flags were replaced by the "national" St. Andrews Cross red battle flag, was but one mark of the immense respect for Cleburne and his men within the Army of Tennessee. As such, Cleburne's superior performance went beyond his powers of combat perception and keen intelligence. It was further rooted in Cleburne's insistence on hard work and repeated practice in various military skills. What made his men such reliable fighters was their high skill level at all aspects of soldiering.[21]

Patrick Cleburne, later termed the "Stonewall Jackson of the West," had carefully developed first his regiment, and then his brigade and division, into elite units. This, of course, involved more than just their intelligent direction in battle. It involved Cleburne's commitment to

Hardee-pattern battleflag (blue field with a silver disc) of the 17th Tennessee Infantry. Although the regiment served in Gen. Bushrod R. Johnson's Brigade at Perryville, it later became part of Cleburne's Division and proudly carried this flag to the end of the war. The crossed guns in the silver disc illustrate the capture of an artillery battery by the Tennesseans. *Editor's Collection*

---

making himself and his soldiers the best that they could be. There were few leaders who exceeded Pat Cleburne in terms of his devotion to excellence, or exhibited a greater personal courage and dedication to duty.[22] The Irish native was born to greatness as a combat leader, later reflected one of his staff officers. From his work ethic to his enormous personal effort, there were few others like him. He was constantly seeking to improve both his men and himself.[23]

Whether on the battlefield or in camp, Cleburne was intent on his soldiers' performance. Fellow brigadier general Basil Duke witnessed Cleburne's non-stop, rigorous training regimen and wrote in admiration, "Cleburne took great interest in everything connected with tactics and personally taught it all. He was occupied from morning until night in superintending squad, company, and battalion drill. I have seen him in the hottest days of August instruct squad after squad in the bayonet exercise until I wondered how any human frame could endure the fatigue that his exertions must have induced."[24]

By his personal involvement, Cleburne sought to impart confidence; a confidence that his men would demonstrate time and time again on many battlefields. Although noted as a disciplinarian, Cleburne saw to it that his men were treated fairly and with justice. Hours of drill and instruction often produced some fatigue, but little other than minor grousing. The men knew it was for their benefit, rather than a "text book" form of punishment.[25]

That practiced battlefield drill and unit conditioning worked in the applied sense was clearly demonstrated during the Kentucky Campaign. During their march over the rugged mountains at the beginning of their journey northward, Cleburne's troops were in the forefront, continually toiling to manhandle wagons and artillery over the roughest of roads. Despite their herculean efforts and subsequent exhaustion, the men of his command were counted on to respond with alacrity when a forced march was necessary to meet the enemy. Their enthusiasiam and healthy conditioning as an outgrowth of Cleburne's leadership played a large role in reaching the Richmond, Kentucky battlefield in both a swift manner and in excellent order.[26]

During the ensuing action, Cleburne's men responded to their well-trained unit commanders just as Cleburne had envisioned—despite his wounding and absence in the later phases of the fighting. The men, as a result, earned further confidence in themselves and placed implicit trust in their unit commanders.

In examining various letters from Cleburne's soldiers, it is unusual to find criticism of their unit level commanders. Instead, any criticism was mostly directed toward the very top—the army's commander, or senior generals. This is a revealing circumstance and speaks in reams of the value of skillful battlefield leadership. Despite battle's awful horrors, men who were intelligently led and protected to the fullest extent possible were among the most efficacious and tenacious in combat. Those officers who utilized refined, common sense, tactically based concepts both offensively and defensively were recognized by the men as leaders who not only deserved their trust but as commanders who could make a critical difference in a battle's outcome.[27]

In the wake of their successes at Richmond and Perryville, a feeling of intense pride permeated the ranks of Cleburne's command. Inspired by Cleburne's leadership, his men soon came to idolize him—often to the point of virtual hero worship. He had led them by personal example and by intelligent reason. The men knew greatness in a commander when they experienced it, and the results were duly reflected in their devoted attitudes toward him.[28] Moreover, Cleburne's personal example as a gritty warrior was the talk of the camp. He had felt his responsibilities so keenly that when wounded at Richmond his first desire was to remain on the field despite being unable to speak. At Perryville, after taking a wound in the foot from a Union artillery shell that killed his prized horse, "Dixie," Cleburne remained with his brigade until the fighting ended. This was only one example of the man's enormous mental and physical discipline.[29]

Particularly revealing of Cleburne's character was his attitude about the prospect of further promotion—just after having been given permanent division command and a major general's commission following Perryville. In the wake of Braxton Bragg's disheartening Kentucky Campaign, and after Stone's River, Cleburne was asked by Bragg for a candid opinion about his competency as the army's commander. In typical fashion, Cleburne replied with firm and honest convictions. Bragg, while possessing a "great capacity for organization," said Cleburne, was not the proper commander for the Army of Tennessee. "You do not possess the confidence of the Army . . . in that degree necessary to secure success," he wrote with admirable truth, but unfortunate political implications.[30]

Despite his skill as a military leader, Cleburne's political vulnerability was always apparent. His sense of right and wrong was always uppermost in his mind. Even when politically denied or rebuffed by his superiors, Cleburne's characteristic attitude was reflected in a favorite adage: "An honest heart and a strong arm should never succumb."[31]

This quality accentuated the man's great worth. By logic Cleburne was able to assess various practical opportunities involving the

Confederacy's war effort. He later raised a key issue and sought to implement his own attendant proposal with a commitment to duty as he saw it—no matter what the personal cost. This involved one of the most explosive emotional issues in the entire Southern Confederacy, and became an important factor in the broad framework of the war.

Because the conflict had become technically sophisticated and resulted in devastating losses in trained personnel that the South generally couldn't replace, there was a glaring need for a new approach to the South's waging of the war. Cleburne was convinced that the course of the war must involve a greater utilization of the South's total available assets. Specifically, he saw the need for more manpower within the "fighting" army, so as to both withstand the rigors of warfare and perpetuate armed resistance to the point of stalemate. This would enable a political solution to an unwinnable military confrontation. It wasn't that the South could not win military victories; it was that those victories would not be decisive, save eroding the North's will to continue the contest.

This realistic appraisal was reflected in Cleburne's controversial proposal to arm the slaves. The South's manpower pool of white soldiers was all but exhausted by late 1863. By seeking to add substantial numbers of blacks to the army's ranks as fighting men—which was a critical military point considering the South's offensive-minded tactical concepts—the prospect of facing the enemy's superior weapons and equipment would be partly counterbalanced. To be confronted with overwhelming numbers and resources was a sure way to lose the war, just as Robert E. Lee belatedly acknowledged in his farewell address to the Army of Northern Virginia in 1865.[32]

Pat Cleburne, as what we would term today a "proactive" military commander, had sought the prospect of leveling the "playing field" of battle. Instead he got despair. Jefferson Davis condemned Cleburne's proposal as outrageous, and suppressed even the mere mention of this matter in army or civilian circles. Of even more dire implication, Cleburne was effectually "blacklisted" from further promotion. Essentially, the Army of Tennessee's ablest infantry commander was prevented from playing a major role in the area where expertise was woefully lacking—conduct of battlefield operations at the senior level.[33]

Cleburne's capacity for upper level command was evident both at Richmond and Perryville, Kentucky, where he sought to fight aggressively but while seeking the maximum protection for his men. In the same sense that Gen. Joseph E. Johnston sought to protect his soldiers during the Atlanta fighting by covering them with strong breastworks, Cleburne advocated the practical conservation of his troops. They were the army's most vital asset, and while it was important to fight hard and well in any given battle, it was also necessary to be able to do so again in the next fight.

Having recognized the critical need to both effecively utilize and preserve his experienced soldiers early in his career, Cleburne had insisted on maneuver in the operational conduct of a battle, rather than the customary resort to direct attack. Also, he had seen to it that his troops were among the most effective and capable of fighting men. But this was not enough. His superiors' mismanagement continued to lose battles and campaigns. As the war ground relentlessly onward, he was among the first to advocate several crucial themes based upon the successful waging of modern warfare.

In contrast to beliefs prevalent in 1861, it was now evident that a single battle was unlikely to end the war. The ablity to destroy an enemy army on a given field had been proved to be negligible, based upon new and complex technological factors. Because the expanded war involved a physical contest waged over a political issue, the long term survival of each Southern army was of the essence in reaching a favorable political solution. This longevity was insured by both the army's preservation and its efficacy. As such, Cleburne's focus after the experiences of Perryville, Stone's River, Chickamauga, Missionary Ridge, and other might-have-been victories, was on both the conservation and procurement of more manpower in order to sustain a prolonged war effort.

Because army commanders such as Braxton Bragg and John Bell Hood were devoted to offensive fighting concepts—usually accompanied with flawed tactics—the prospect of victory from the conduct of battlefield operations by the top echelon was severely lacking in the Army of Tennessee. Further, by Jefferson Davis's stubborn insistence on at first Bragg, and later Hood, as the Army of Tennessee's commander, Cleburne and other "front line" style leaders were confronted with personal disaster—not to mention the sad fate eventually to befall their valiant army.

Through little fault of the men—their extraordinary efforts were a remarkable testimonial to their devotion and exceptional valor—their military efforts were often negated by tactical and operational stupidity at the highest levels. One only has to look at the frightful casualties of the Atlanta fighting and at Franklin to understand the full measure of internal despair. Here the outnumbered Confederate soldiers were compelled to make repeated suicidal frontal attacks in the face of breastworks, repeating rifles, and concentrated artillery.[34]

Through it all, Pat Cleburne supressed feelings of betrayal and did his duty. Just as had occurred in 1862, when his troops marched forth into Kentucky with jubilant hearts and rising spirits, Cleburne sought to inspire his troops during the November 1864 march northward into Tennessee, and devoted his efforts to their excellent performance. If only Jefferson Davis had understood as much as many of Cleburne's private soldiers did about recognizing leadership and the essence of fighting, there might have been a different history to record in the Western theater, if not the war.

Perhaps the most notable attribute of this Irish-born commander was his skill on the tactical battlefield. As had been well demonstrated at Richmond and Perryville in Kentucky, Cleburne's ability to often win against numerical odds and tactical disadvantages was paramount. His full attention was given to small details that made a difference in tactical results. From the utilization of skirmish formations, to the use of sharpshooters who could pick off key enemy officers or wreak havoc with deployed artillery at extended ranges, Cleburne's tactical concepts marked him as a most capable military commander. His early insistence on the preparation of breastworks while on the defensive was a harbinger of the later manner of warfare commonly encountered in the war. Even Cleburne's frequent deceptive masking of artillery with brush and trees (to obtain surprise in delivering close range cannon fire, as at Ringgold Gap) was significant. Also, his effective use of loose order battle lines after encountering the morass at Shiloh was exemplary.

These devices reflected Cleburne's perception of the new order of combat.[35]

Today it is fair to say Pat Cleburne endures as a tactical mastermind of his era. Many senior commanders of the war had been schooled in concepts of engineering and linear tactics, and they continued to struggle in adjusting to the altered tactical realities of the battlefield. Cleburne's ability to get his troops in close proximity of an enemy line with minimal losses reflected his higher capacity as a true student of warfare. His perception of enemy strength or weakness in their battle positions, and his uncanny ability to engage his command with lightning-like speed of manuever was remarkable. In all, it made him the premier performing Confederate commander on many of the war's most crucial Western battlefields.[36]

Despite his many abilities, however, Cleburne knew that in the final analysis his was merely a humble part of the war effort. He understood that the essence of effective warfare rested with his troops. As a commander he might lead and inspire, but beyond this, the soldiers were the key. They were both irreplacable military assets and the means of accomplishment. Cleburne thus had sought to improve his soldiers' capacity, and protect them to the largest extent possible.

While his men were required to fight hard as a common unit with intense fervor and pride, he asked no more of them than he did himself. As part of the inspiration for his soldiers to fight even more fiercely, Cleburne himself routinely shared in their front line exposure, even to the point of personally leading a vital attack—as at Perryville. Accordingly, his applied common sense and logic did not stand in the way of his higher courage in displaying the highest pinnacle of leadership. His troops' confidence in his role as commander was a vital matter to Cleburne. Like various other front line leaders on both sides, Pat Cleburne required no man to go where he himself would not go. The men thus knew that when Cleburne asked them to fight, he was as committed as they. Because his proven valor and leadership was accentuated by a brilliance in the tactical sense, his men had enormous confidence in him as their leader and, perhaps more importantly, in themselves as soldiers. It was this quality, the performance of his men and their great efficacy on the battlefield, that ultimately made

Cleburne's Division the best in the Western army. Fittingly, it was but a mirror reflection of their commander.

In the final analysis, the greatest tragedy of all was that Pat Cleburne's brilliance failed to extend beyond divisional command. Although briefly given temporary corps command in 1864, Cleburne was subsequently politically disenfranchised, and seemingly blacklisted for his suggestion that slaves be enlisted and given their freedom for fighting for the South. Although he remained in command limbo, the ultimate value of this man shines through the clouds of political disfavor cast over him. Even in the strategic realm, the correctness of Cleburne's ideas are apparent today. While there were those who condemned Cleburne for even thinking of upending Southern "tradition, pride, and honor" by arming the South's slaves, from a practical standpoint it was at the time the best possible solution for revitalizing the Confederacy's military effort, and hence prolonging the war. Jefferson Davis's desperate last minute concession (in 1865) to utilize slaves in the army was an ironic testimonial to the worthiness of Cleburne's ideas.[37] Had Cleburne been given a larger role in the war, would the outcome have been different? Probably not, but in the fundamental waging of war it would have made a big difference in Confederate fortunes in the West—where the war was eventually lost.

If a star lost through the waste of internal political dissent, Pat Cleburne remains in the light of modern analysis the premier Confederate infantry commander west of the Appalachians. This is a remarkable testimonial to the military competency of an Irish immigrant, and an ex-British enlisted man. Contrary to the old myth that the best general was to be found only from among the ranks of professionally educated officers, Cleburne's career looms large in the military annals of our nation.

This was perhaps first apparent, like the sparkle of a diamond in the rough, at Richmond and Perryville in Kentucky. That Pat Cleburne's tactical expertise made him among the best was clearly demonstrated in the fall of 1862 to the South's heirarchy—as it was to many others among his contemporaries. Yet, despite his early promotion and subsequent shunted treatment and cruel fate, Cleburne willingly sacrificed it all two years later in the fatal charge at Franklin—for an ideal. Pat Cleburne knew that to do one's duty required a courage and commitment in both word and deed no matter what the ultimate cost.

Perhaps now, after the passage of considerable time has cooled many intense emotions, we can learn from his example.

NOTES

1. United States War Department, *The War of the Rebellion: A Compilation of the Official Record of the Union and Confederate Armies*, 128 vols. (Washington, D.C., 1880-1901) (hereinafter cited as *O.R.*) (all citations are to Series I), 16 (1):946.

2. For a brief review of Cleburne's notable exploits at Atlanta, see Albert Castel, *Decision in the West, the Atlanta Campaign of 1864* (Lawrence, Kan., 1992); for Cleburne's role at Chickamauga, see Peter Cozzens, *This Terrible Sound: The Battle of Chickamauga* (Urbana, Ill., 1992); for Cleburne at Chattanooga and Ringgold Gap, see Wiley Sword, *Mountains Touched With Fire, Chattanooga Besieged, 1863* (New York, N.Y., 1995).

3. For an interpretation of Cleburne's importance in winning at Richmond and Perryville, see Craig L. Symonds, *Stonewall of the West: Patrick Cleburne and the Civil War* (Lawrence, Kan., 1997), 80 ff.

4. *O.R.*, 16 (1):1161.

5. Earl J. Hess, *The Union Soldier in Battle, Enduring the Ordeal of Combat* (Lawrence, Kan., 1997); Gerald F. Linderman, *Embattled Courage, The Experience of Combat in the American Civil War* (New York, N.Y., 1987), 134 ff; Wiley Sword, *Embrace an Angry Wind, The Confederacy's Last Hurrah* (New York, N.Y., 1992), 42 ff.; Larry J. Daniel, *Soldiering in the Army of Tennessee* (Chapel Hill, N.C., 1991), 151-152.

6. *O.R.*, 16 (1):945-946.

7. *Ibid.*

8. *O.R.*, 52 (1):51 ff; see also Howell and Elizabeth Purdue, *Pat Cleburne, Confederate General* (Hillsboro, Tx., 1973), 147 ff.

9. *Ibid.*, Also, see Kenneth A. Hafendorfer, *Perryville: Battle for Kentucky* (Louisville, Ky., 1991), 248 ff.

10. *Ibid.*

11. *Ibid.*

12. *Ibid.*

13. Purdue, *Pat Cleburne*, 148.

14. Wiley Sword, *Shiloh: Bloody April* (New York, N.Y., 1974), 234 ff, 251 ff, 277 ff; Purdue, *Pat Cleburne*, 119.

15. For example, see Cleburne's tactical dispositions at Franklin. Sword, *Embrace an Angry Wind*, 183.

16. Hess, *The Union Soldier in Battle, passim.*

17. *Ibid.*; Sword, *Shiloh: Bloody April*, 251 ff.

18. Hess, *The Union Soldier in Battle, passim.*

19. Purdue, *Pat Cleburne*, 10.

20. *Ibid.*, 120, 185 ff.

21. Purdue, *Pat Cleburne*, 188-189.

22. *Ibid.*, 185 ff, 438.

23. Irving A. Buck, *Cleburne And His Command* (Wilmington, N.C., 1987), 72 ff.

24. Purdue, *Pat Cleburne*, 86-87.

25. *Ibid.*, 89, 185 ff.

26. *O.R.*, 16 (1):944; D. Warren Lambert, *When the Ripe Pears Fell, The Battle of Richmond, Kentucky* (Richmond, Ky., 1995), 28 ff.; J. G. Law, "Advance into Kentucky (diary Aug. 1862)," *Southern Historical Society Papers*, 50 vols. (Richmond, Va., 1876-1919) 12 (1884) 390 ff.

27. Norman D. Brown, ed., *One of Cleburne's Command, The Civil War Reminiscences and Diary of Capt. Samuel T. Foster, Granbury's Texas Brigade, CSA* (Austin, Tx., 1980; For various other soldiers' opinions, see also Howell and Elizabeth Purdue, *Pat Cleburne, Confederate General*, 86-87.

28. Purdue, *Pat Cleburne*, 188.

29. *Ibid.*, 149.

30. *Ibid.*, 182-183.

31. *Ibid.*, 67.

32. *Ibid.*, 267 ff; Buck, *Cleburne And His Command*, 186 ff.

33. *Ibid.*

34. For casualty estimates at Franklin, see Sword, *Embrace an Angry Wind*, 269.

35. Purdue, *Pat Cleburne*, 438.

36. *Ibid.*

37. *Ibid.*, 275-278.

James A. Ramage

General John Hunt Morgan and His Great Raids Into Kentucky

John Hunt Morgan was a quiet, gentle businessman when the Civil War began. Thirty-five years old, he was a Mason, captain of a volunteer fire company, and had been elected to the Lexington, Kentucky town council and school board. He identified with the down-and-out and word spread among the beggars that one could usually get a handout at his hemp factory. Reluctant to fight, he joined the Confederate rebellion five months into the war, only after the Kentucky General Assembly decided for the Union and demanded that his Lexington Rifles Volunteer Infantry company surrender their arms. Driven from Kentucky by Union troops, his factory confiscated and his wife Rebecca recently deceased, Morgan had no children, and in the words of the *Atlanta Commonwealth*, propertyless, "houseless, wifeless, with little to live, love, fight or die for, but the new republic."[1]

Adopting the hit-and-run tactics of guerrilla warfare, Morgan became for the Southern people the "Marion of the War," the primary model for the Partisan Ranger Act that authorized guerrilla bands to raid behind enemy lines. He represented the Southern ideal of the chivalrous knight, the cavalier from the romantic novel come to life. He was six feet tall, 185 pounds, and square shouldered, with a dark mustache, imperial beard and grayish-blue eyes that sparkled with good humor, and he had perfect white teeth and an unforgettable smile. "Did you ever see Morgan on horseback?" inquired his brother-in-law and second-in-command Basil Duke. "If not, you missed one of the most impressive figures of the war. Perhaps no General in either army surpassed him in the striking proportion and grace of his person, and the

General John Hunt Morgan. Born in Huntsville, Alabama, and raised in Lexington, Kentucky, Morgan rose to command a division of cavalry before his death in 1864. *Library of Congress*

ease and grace of his horsemanship . . . always handsomely and tastefully dressed, and elegantly mounted, he was the picture of the superb cavalry officer."[2]

For Kentucky Confederates Morgan embodied the dream of liberating Kentucky from Yankee rule. "AROUSE, KENTUCKIANS!" he proclaimed. "Let the old men of Kentucky, and our noble-hearted women, arm their sons and their lovers for the fight! Better death in our sacred cause than a life of slavery!"[3] Like the Orphan Brigade, the First Kentucky Infantry Brigade in the Confederate army, Morgan's men were exiles, driven from home by the invading Union army. When they raided into Kentucky to recruit and stir the fires of rebellion, Morgan's men carried the hopes of all Kentucky Confederates.[4]

Strategically, Morgan closed the Louisville and Nashville Railroad, the main artery of supply for the Union army in the West, for four and one-half months, and he and other Confederate raiders forced the diversion of over 20,000 Union troops from the front to guard supplies and communications. During the Christmas Raid in 1862, Morgan directly diverted 7,300 first-rate infantry from Gen. William S. Rosecrans's army in the Battle of Stone's River. By the last year of the war the Confederates lost interest in guerrilla raids, but Morgan, in taking the war behind enemy lines into Kentucky, accomplished on a small scale what the Union army under Gen. Ulysses S. Grant eventually achieved with cavalry and infantry raids behind Southern lines.[5]

Morgan's five independent raids into Union-occupied Kentucky incorporated tactics used by special forces today. Morgan's men travelled light; leaving the supply wagons behind, they took no rations or forage but lived off the land; the only wheels were those of the light artillery. The raiders used the fastest, most efficient transportation, the fleetest horses available, many captured from the Union cavalry. When Morgan organized Tom Quirk's company of scouts, they complained of having slow horses. "You'll have better ones in a short time," came Morgan's reply. In the next skirmish, when the enemy line wavered, he shouted to the scouts: "Boys, yonder are those horses I've been promising you. Be very particular how you take them, for you observe that each horse has an armed man upon him."[6] Quirk's scouts and other hand-picked men conducted careful reconnaissance. On the move

General John Hunt Morgan as he looked in the field. Dressed in a black and blue plaid civilian shell jacket, tall cavalry boots and a black felt hat with the brim pinned up on one side, Morgan presented a dashing appearance on his five great Kentucky raids. *University of Kentucky Special Collections*

Morgan used a system of "rolling" videttes, guards thrown out in all directions and checking every crossroad and then leapfrogging to the front when the column appeared. The system was so efficient that the main body was never surprised when moving.[7] And like special forces today, Morgan used psychological warfare to create a feeling of uneasiness and fear in the minds of the enemy. By seeming to be in several places at once and attacking behind the lines where defenses were weak, he caused panic. General Jeremiah T. Boyle, forty-four years old, was a Kentucky native, a lawyer in Danville when the war began. At Shiloh he fought with conspicuous gallantry and was named military commander of the District of Kentucky with headquarters in Louisville. Boyle became one of the most hated men in Kentucky because he arrested and imprisoned Confederate sympathizers and threatened to rule with an iron hand.[8] Therefore, Morgan and his men took great delight in frightening him.

On the First Kentucky Raid in July 1862, Morgan's main body of 867 men came no nearer than Midway, fifty miles from Louisville. Overcome with fear Boyle assumed that Morgan was headed for Louisville with 3,000 men. Calling out the shopkeepers and clerks to march back and forth in front of the Galt House, Boyle feared that the Kentucky rebels would rise and Morgan would conquer the state within a few days. He begged Gov. Richard Yates of Illinois to send troops to Paducah, requested that all forces in Indiana and Ohio be sent to Kentucky, and asked over and over again for reinforcements from Buell's headquarters in Nashville. When he wired Cincinnati Mayor George Hatch pleading, "Send artillery to Lexington and as many men as possible by special train without delay," Secretary of War Edwin M. Stanton in Washington asked, "What means this sudden call on the mayor of Cincinnati to send men and artillery immediately and why have you not advised this Department of the real or supposed necessity for such a step?" Finally Abraham Lincoln told General Halleck in Corinth, Mississippi, "They are having a stampede in Kentucky. Please look to it."[9]

The next summer, when Morgan's men marched into Kentucky on the Great Raid, Union forces along the L&N from Bowling Green to Louisville went on alert. At Muldraugh's Hill, the garrison was called

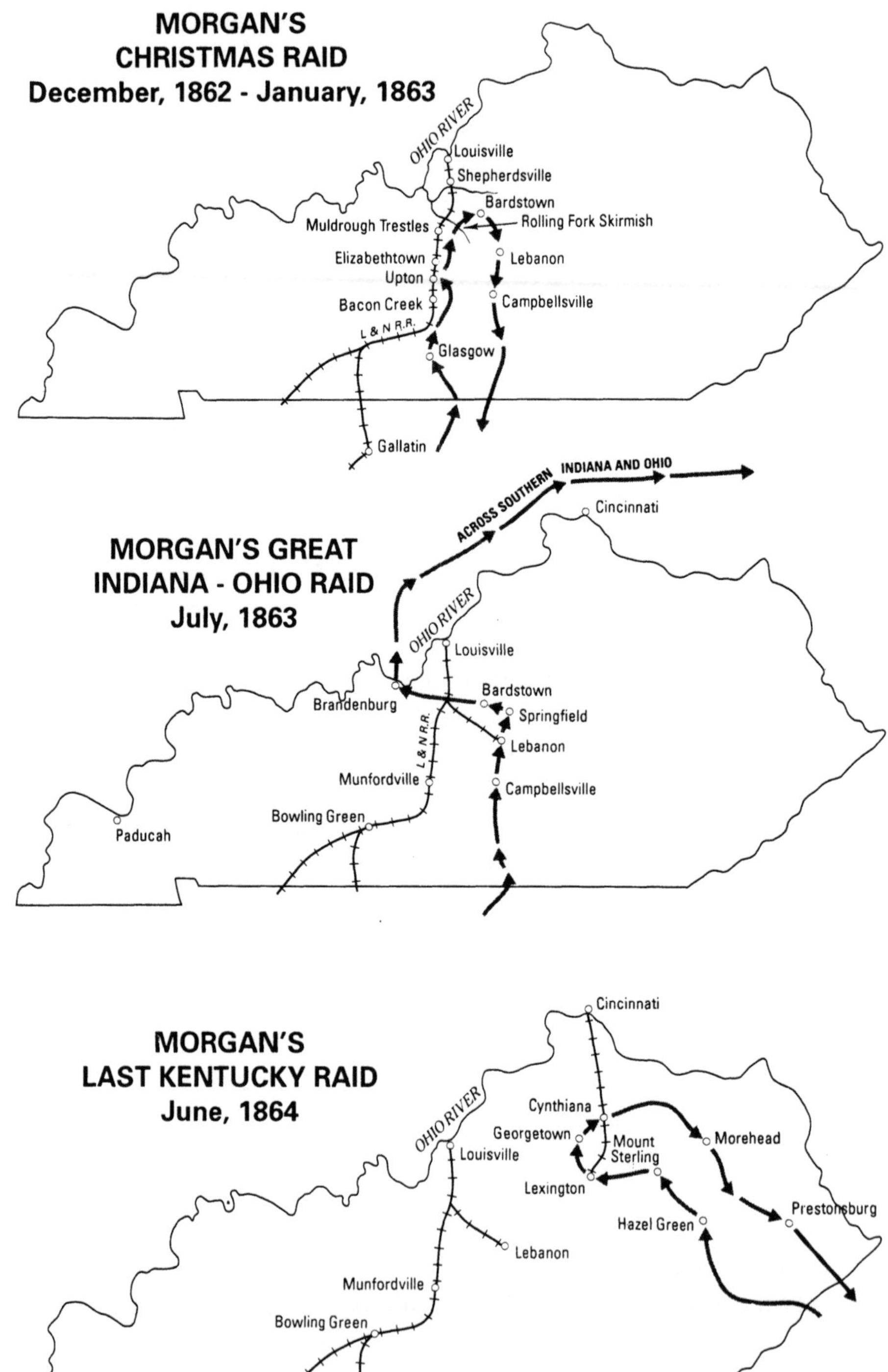
MORGAN'S
CHRISTMAS RAID
December, 1862 - January, 1863
OHIO RIVER
Louisville
Shepherdsville
Bardstown
Rolling Fork Skirmish
Muldrough Trestles
Elizabethtown
Upton
Lebanon
Bacon Creek
Campbellsville
L & N R.R.
Glasgow
Gallatin
MORGAN'S GREAT
INDIANA - OHIO RAID
July, 1863
ACROSS SOUTHERN
INDIANA AND OHIO
Cincinnati
OHIO RIVER
Louisville
Brandenburg
Bardstown
Springfield
L & N R.R.
Lebanon
Munfordville
Campbellsville
Bowling Green
Paducah
MORGAN'S
LAST KENTUCKY RAID
June, 1864
Cincinnati
OHIO RIVER
Cynthiana
Georgetown
Mount
Sterling
Morehead
Louisville
Lexington
Hazel Green
Prestonsburg
Lebanon
Munfordville
Bowling Green

out every morning at 1:00 a.m. and remained in the forts and breastworks until after daylight. "And we kept this up," a soldier complained, "I think, for nearly a week."[10] Boyle controlled himself until a false rumor reached him that Morgan's men were the advance for a general invasion and attack on Louisville by the Confederate army. General Joseph Wheeler's cavalry corps, according to the report, had already crossed Green River, passed through Campbellsville and now occupied Lebanon, sixty miles south of Louisville. "Where will troops be gotten to meet them?" Boyle asked Gen. Ambrose E. Burnside, who was in Cincinnati organizing the new Army of the Ohio to invade east Tennessee. Burnside had withdrawn the troops stationed on the Kentucky-Tennessee border to pursue Morgan. The answer was, there were no forces to stop Wheeler. Now Burnside united in panic with Boyle. "You will, as quietly as possible," he telegraphed Boyle, "remove all the public stores, &c., across the river to Jeffersonville" and defend the city "till the last." Continuing to shore up his own courage and Boyle's as well, Burnside kept sending messages. "You will arm the Indiana Legion Home Guards," ordered Burnside, "and, in fact, every fighting man you can find, and, in case of attack, you must defend the city to the last. I will send a gunboat at once, and will try to leave here on evening train for Louisville."[11] Burnside calmed down and remained in Cincinnati, but with Morgan near, nearly anything seemed possible. Later the same day when Burnside learned that Morgan had captured two Ohio River steamboats at Brandenburg, he alerted navy officers at Cairo, Illinois, that Morgan was steaming down the river toward Paducah.[12]

In another parallel to today's special forces, Morgan used what is now called IPB—intelligence preparation of the battlefield. He sent out detachments to demonstrate against enemy forces, confusing them as to his direction and intent. He was one of the first in military history to tap into enemy telegraph lines and intercept messages and insert imitative communications deceptions (ICD). In *The Secret War for the Union: The Untold Story of Military Intelligence in the Civil War*, Edwin C. Fishel describes Union military intelligence in the Eastern theater from the Battle of First Bull Run through the Battle of Gettysburg. Fishel found interceptions of enemy flag messages, but only one brief tap of a telegraph line in an incident that yielded no useful information. On the other hand, the *London Times* declared Morgan's wiretapping the first significant innovation in the war. Morgan's operator was "like the wolf in Red Riding Hood," or like a pantomime clown performing mischief while minding the shop of an unsuspecting tradesman, the newspaper chuckled.[13]

Morgan had one of his men tap his first Union telegraph line on about May 5, 1862, on the perimeter of Murfreesboro, Tennessee. The unidentified Rebel operator, pretending to be the Federal operator in Murfreesboro, sent a message to Nashville reporting that Morgan had captured Shelbyville and was about to take Murfreesboro. Two months later, for the First Kentucky Raid, Morgan had recruited George A. Ellsworth as his personal telegraph operator. Ellsworth was a muscular, sleepy-eyed man from Canada, a tramp operator working in Houston, Texas, when the war began. He enjoyed drinking and playing practical jokes and seemed most unlikely for success in anything. But along a railroad track, behind enemy lines, he would have a man climb a telegraph pole, fasten wires to the Union line, and attach his pocket instrument. Sitting on a cross tie, with Morgan standing beside him dictating, Ellsworth worked his intelligence magic. Operator William R. Plum, in his history of the Union military telegraph, stated that Ellsworth made Morgan "the special enemy of the Federal telegraph." Ellsworth earned the nickname "Lightning" when on his first tap for Morgan the enemy operator became suspicious and asked "Who are you, and what's your office?" He answered "O.K., Lightning," meaning "Go ahead, a thunderstorm is interfering."[14]

After the war Ellsworth worked for a time in Cincinnati, where he met and became friends with another tramp operator, Thomas Edison. Ellsworth suggested an idea of making the telegraph secure from interception, and later Edison used the suggestion to invent the quadruplex, a system of transmitting four separate messages on the same wire. "Lightning" shot to death a man from Sharpsburg, Kentucky, in a street fight over whether Ellsworth owed him $1.00 for a bottle of whiskey. He was arrested and jailed in Lexington, where Morgan's family placed a carpet and stove in his cell and attended to his daily needs. Eventually released, he resumed wire pounding and died over thirty years after the war, on duty with his finger on the key in a small railroad shack near Antonio, Louisiana.[15] During Morgan's raids, Ellsworth seemed to be everywhere on the wires. Union operators suspected each other of being Ellsworth. During Morgan's advance into Kentucky on the Great Raid, General Burnside made so many inquiries about Gen. Henry Judah, who was slow starting in pursuit, that the post commander in Munfordville, Col. Charles D. Pennebaker, suspected Burnside of being Ellsworth. "Has not Morgan swung a thief on the wires?" Pennebaker asked. "Too many inquiries for General Judah."[16] A few days later in Osgood, Indiana, Ellsworth captured operator Frank Crawford and used Crawford's call letter to send messages to Burnside. "I soon gave Gen. Burnside an idea where Morgan was—*not*," he recalled. Crawford sat beside Ellsworth occasionally laughing heartily at the ruse.[17] Finally catching on, Burnside resorted to closing his messages with: "Answer in cipher."[18]

During the same raid, on July 2, 1863, a company of the 8th Michigan Cavalry led by Capt. Sam Wells conducted a scout from Camp Nelson in Jessamine County and, preparing to return to camp, stopped in the telegraph office in Danville to report. General Samuel D. Sturgis at Camp Nelson refused to believe that it was really Wells on the line. "I know Capt. Wells," he wired, "but it may be that he is captured and compelled to send reports to suit the enemy." Sturgis required his operator to ask the Danville operator for a sign that it was truly him. Danville replied: "I loaned you ten dollars three years ago, and you have never paid me. Now do you know me?" This convinced the general and he ordered Wells to report the next morning.[19]

On a raid in Gallatin, Tennessee, on August 12, 1862, Ellsworth bedeviled the Nashville operator nearly all day, and when at the end of the raid, he asked one more time who was on the wire, Morgan gave Ellsworth permission to identify himself. "I am Ellsworth," he tapped, and immediately came the response: "You damn wild Canadian, what are you doing there?" Ellsworth answered that he came over for the day to dispatch trains for the L&N Railroad.[20] He deserves credit for using electronic deception to lure three trains into Morgan ambushes, for obtaining valuable intelligence on enemy dispositions on several occasions, and in at least one instance for the unusual accomplishment of cancelling an enemy movement by electronic deception. At Midway, Kentucky, on the First Kentucky Raid, Ellsworth posed as the Union operator and learned that in Lexington Gen. William T. Ward had ordered a force in Frankfort to attack Morgan. Ellsworth informed Morgan, who instructed Ellsworth to deceive Ward by telling him that the raiders had just left Midway and were advancing on Frankfort. Ward assumed the fake dispatch was genuine and ordered the force withdrawn to Frankfort to defend the state capital.[21]

Usually, at the end of a raid, Morgan would dictate teasing messages to his Union opponents. One warned George Prentice, editor of the *Louisville Journal*, that Morgan's Cherokee Indians were coming for his scalp, and another accused the mayor of Union-occupied Nashville of infidelity. From Somerset, Kentucky, at the close of the First Kentucky Raid, Morgan greeted General Boyle: "Good morning, Jerry. This telegraph is a great institution. You should destroy it, as it keeps me too well posted. My friend, Ellsworth, has all your dispatches since the 10th of July on file. Do you wish copies?"[22]

Ellsworth helped make Morgan the nemesis of the L&N as well as the Union telegraph. The L&N became Morgan's target for the first of the five raids into Kentucky, the Cave City Raid. With a squadron of 325 men Morgan set out from Gen. Pierre G. T. Beauregard's camp in Corinth, Mississippi, where the Confederate army had withdrawn after the Battle of Shiloh. The raiders advanced to Lebanon, Tennessee, and on the rainy night of May 5, 1862, Morgan slept in the hotel with his men guarding the town. Early the next morning a Union cavalry force under Gen. Ebenezer Dumont surprised and scattered the Rebels in what is known as the "Lebanon Races," a rout that cost Morgan six men dead and 100 captured. He gathered his men and recruited local militia, finally moving into Kentucky with 150 men. At Cave City, in the area of Mammoth Cave on May 11, 1862, they captured and burned a train of four passenger cars and 45 freight cars. They exploded the locomotive by filling the firebox and sending it out of control down the track toward Nashville. Then, a passenger train from Louisville arrived and they took $6,000 cash from the express agent and made prisoners of two officers and a few enlisted men. There were many women passengers on board, mostly Union officers' wives bound for Nashville, with large trunks bearing the tall hats that were then in fashion. Upon the request of the women Morgan allowed the train to return to Louisville, baggage and ladies intact. This made headlines in the South and first established Morgan's reputation as a romantic cavalier who treated women with respect.[23]

At this time early in the war the L&N was short on rolling stock, and Morgan's efforts were taking their toll. Combined with an earlier raid in Tennessee, he had now destroyed two engines, fifty-four freight cars and four passenger cars. The railroad's president, James Guthrie, complained that Morgan had cost the company more than it had profited in four years of carrying the mail. The Union government transferred several freight cars and locomotives from other railroads to the L&N to relieve the shortage. Yet, it was only the beginning. On June 30, 1863, Guthrie reported that in the previous twelve months the road had been open only seven months and twelve days.[24]

Some of Gen. John Hunt Morgan's men in Allegheny Prison, Pittsburgh, Pennsylvania after the Indiana-Ohio Raid in 1863. Shell jackets, tall cavalry boots and broad-brimmed hats of every description marked the men of Morgan's Division. *University of Kentucky Special Collections*

Morgan soon learned that the Cave City Raid made him an even greater hero. Leaving his men in Chattanooga, he traveled to Confederate headquarters in Corinth to request permission to organize a regiment. Along the circuitous route through Atlanta, Montgomery and Mobile, crowds gathered at the stations to see him. "Hurrah for Morgan!" wrote an editor in Atlanta. "Our people had rather get a sight of him than Queen Victoria. Again we say, Hurrah for Morgan." In Opelika, Alabama, a small boy walked down the aisle selling cigars. Morgan took one and reached for his pocketbook. "I don't charge you anything," the boy said. "Why?" Morgan asked. "Oh, you are Colonel Morgan who has been fighting for us, and you are welcome to anything I have." In Okolona, Mississippi, Kate Cumming, a hospital administrator, joined the crowd. When introduced she complimented him and he "blushed like a school boy." She said that she hoped to hear a great deal about him in the future, and he answered that he only wanted to hear of himself twenty years from now. The train started off, the crowd cheered, and she noticed that "he looked abashed and blushed again." Meanwhile, in Charleston, South Carolina, Mrs. Bee, the widow of Gen. Barnard E. Bee, mortally wounded at First Bull Run, sent Morgan her husband's pistols—she selected him as the leader worthy of the honor.[25]

Beauregard authorized the 2nd Kentucky Cavalry, and Morgan launched the First Kentucky Raid with the regiment, plus a squadron of Texas Rangers, a regiment of Georgia partisan rangers and two companies of Tennessee partisans—a brigade of 867 mounted men. The mission was to recruit men, obtain horses, and inspire "revolutionary fermentation." Well informed, Morgan only demonstrated against the strong garrisons in Frankfort and Lexington, but chose to attack the 350 Union soldiers and home guards in Cynthiana, having them outnumbered over two to one. The Union men had a strong defensive position in houses on the opposite bank of the Licking River near the covered bridge on the Leesburg Pike, and Cincinnati fireman Capt. William H. Glass had a 12-pound brass cannon in the street at the courthouse about a block from the bridge. The Federals bravely withstood three dismounted attacks, but retreated and surrendered when Morgan ordered a mounted assault across the bridge. Morgan suffered eight dead and 35 wounded, and the Federals counted about 17 of their force killed 35 wounded.[26]

To Morgan's chagrin, only 300 Kentuckians joined the raiders. Morgan confused curiosity to see him and his men with support of the cause, and sent exaggerated estimates of sympathy that misled the Confederate high command into assuming that the people of Kentucky were ready to rise in support of an invading Rebel army. General Braxton Bragg's invasion failed, and Morgan's next independent raid into Kentucky came at Christmas, 1862. The objective was to destroy the two large L&N trestles five miles north of Elizabethtown. He had the largest force that he ever commanded, a division of 3,900 men with seven cannon, but he lacked the advantage of surprise. Union newspapers in Nashville, enemy army headquarters, reported the raid before it began, and Morgan's friend Gen. William J. Hardee warned that he would probably fail.[27]

Morgan bypassed the well-defended Green River bridge at Munfordville and struck the L&N early on the morning of December 26, at Upton depot, twelve miles to the north. At the same time a detachment captured the stockade and burned the bridge at Bacon Creek between Upton and Munfordville. These attacks assured that Union pursuers coming north on the L&N would have to leave the cars once they reached Munfordville.[28]

The raiders moved steadily up the track toward Elizabethtown, burning cross ties and telegraph poles and twisting rails. When Morgan arrived in sight of Elizabethtown on the morning of December 27, one of his scouts handed him an envelope. A penciled message was scrawled on the back from Union Lt. Col. Harry S. Smith, the town's commander. Morgan could hardly believe what he read: "Sir: I demand an unconditional surrender of all your forces. I have you surrounded, and will compel you to surrender." Basil Duke later reflected that it was "the most sublimely audacious" missive imaginable from a Union officer, "who, as a class, rarely trusted to audacity or bluff."[29]

Indeed, it would be difficult to imagine anyone in a more vulnerable position than Smith that morning. He had no artillery and was outnumbered almost six to one, having with him only 652 men of the 91st Illinois Infantry. Smith and his men had just arrived from the lower trestle north of Elizabethtown. He had positioned his troops on the Southern edge of town on the Nashville Pike in an unfinished stockade and behind the railroad embankment, which ran perpendicular to the pike. It was the best that he could do and would have been adequate against a roughly equal force of small arms, but Morgan had seven cannon, and rising above Smith's men on the Union right was the cemetery, on a hill 40 and 60 feet in elevation and only 650 yards distant. Just beyond were other hills 80 and 95 feet above Smith's position and still within range of the Rebel guns. Morgan took this high ground and answered Smith that the situation was actually reversed, and the Union force should surrender. Smith, however, replied that it was "the business of an United States officer to fight, and not to surrender."[30]

By now, Morgan had dismounted a regiment on each side of the Nashville pike, with mounted men in reserve and on both flanks. He personally positioned and supervised the fire of four cannon on the hill above the cemetery. Duke placed a ten-pound Parrott rifle in the pike, and Morgan ordered the guns to commence firing. After several rounds, Smith withdrew from the stockade and the railroad embankment, retreating to several brick buildings in town. Morgan moved two of his cannon closer, down into the cemetery, and Duke advanced one of the mountain howitzers, called a "bull pup" for its barking sound, onto the abandoned railroad embankment. Smith had a United States flag on his headquarters building and the Rebel artillerymen aimed at the flag. The guns were so close that it was almost impossible to miss. From the edge of the cemetery to Smith's headquarters was less than 650 yards, and the bull pup was less than 330 yards from Smith's headquarters.[31]

Morgan intended to avoid a frontal assault, but one company, without authority and with more courage than sense, charged into town on foot. The Illinois men, realizing that they outnumbered the force, ran from the buildings and counterattacked, driving the Confederates back out of town and chasing the cannoneers from Duke's bull pup. The officer in command of the small piece, Lieutenant C. C. Corbett, refused to move and sat defiantly on top of the carriage, with bullets bouncing off, left and right. The Union men withdrew and Corbett and his men resumed firing, regularly arching shot into the enemy buildings like a fire engine pumping water.[32]

The shelling continued for about thirty minutes; the citizens of Louisville heard the booming over forty miles away. Many of the solid shots perforated the walls of buildings and went all the way through the structures, coming out on the other side. Nearly every building on the square was struck including the Masonic Hall, the Baptist Church and the Catholic Church. A shot embedded in the brick wall of a three-story building where it became a tourist attraction. Later the building burned but someone saved the ball, and when a new building was erected the bricklayers reinstalled the ball in the new brick wall; it lodges there still, a monument to the fighting spirit of Smith and his men. One shot crashed through the room occupied by Smith and his staff, killing one man and driving a splinter into Smith's face. At that point, he decided that his men had fought cannon with small arms long enough and surrendered.[33]

The next morning, December 28, Morgan easily captured the forces north of town and burned the trestles. That night the raiders camped a few miles eastward, on the southwestern bank of the swollen and swiftly running Rolling Fork River, at the lower ford one mile downstream from the Bardstown Road. Perceiving no danger, the following morning Morgan crossed the river with the main column at the lower ford, which was more shallow than the one on the road, and proceeded toward Bardstown. He left behind in a brick house near the lower ford a court martial in session that included the *corps d'elite* of his command: both brigade commanders, Duke and Col. William Campbell Preston Breckinridge, and regimental commanders Col. Leroy S. Cluke, Lt. Cols. Robert G. Stoner and John B. Hutchinson. These officers were trying Lt. Col. J. M. Huffman, who as commander of the 7th Kentucky Cavalry had allegedly violated the lenient terms Morgan had granted to the Union prisoners captured in the Bacon Creek stockade. The court was protected by a rear guard of 300 men, who were also holding the ford for the 8th Kentucky Cavalry Regiment, which Morgan sent with two cannon to capture the stockade and burn the Rolling Fork bridge on the main stem of the L&N about 30 miles south of Louisville. Colonel Cluke commanded the 8th Kentucky, but since he was a member of the court, the regiment was led by Maj. Robert S. Bullock.[34]

At about 11:00 a.m., the court acquitted Huffman and adjourned. They were leaving the house when they heard an artillery shell explode a mile or two in the rear, toward Elizabethtown, where Morgan had posted videttes. Duke and the other officers realized that the shell was a greeting from Union General Rosecrans in Nashville.[35]

With advance intelligence of this raid, Rosecrans regarded it as the ideal time to capture Morgan. On December 14, eight days before the raid began and twelve days before Morgan intersected the L&N, Rosecrans alerted all troops in the stockades from Louisville to Nashville to procure fresh water and wood for a siege. He took time from his preparations to attack Braxton Bragg's army at Stone's River, December 31, 1862 – January 2, 1863, to devise a hammer-and-anvil plan to destroy Morgan's men. For the hammer Rosecrans selected Col. John Marshall Harlan and his brigade of 2,300 infantry, with a battery of artillery. Harlan was to take the L&N from Gallatin into Kentucky and pursue and drive Morgan from the railroad and back onto the anvil in southern Kentucky. The anvil would consist of 8,300 men. Some 3,300 were already in Kentucky, concentrated in Lebanon under Col. William A. Hoskins, and Gen. Joseph J. Reynolds's infantry division of 5,000 at Glasgow. Colonel Edward H. Hobson's small cavalry unit joined Harlan's force at Munfordville, and there were a few cavalry at Lebanon and 600 in Glasgow, but Rosecrans was largely chasing Morgan with an infantry force of about 11,000 men. "We will catch and kill those rascals yet," he promised. But one reason he would fail was suggested in the question of Gen. Speed Fry in Gallatin. Fry asked: "Would it not be best to send cavalry in pursuit of Morgan?"[36]

Colonel John Marshall Harlan was a twenty-nine-year-old lawyer and judge from Frankfort, Kentucky, six feet two inches tall, two hundred pounds, with red hair. He was handsome and commanding, with a powerful voice. In Kentucky politics he had been "the young giant" of the Know-Nothing Party. As colonel of the 10th Kentucky Infantry, Harlan arrived at Shiloh just after the battle, and he and his men were ordered to camp on the damp ground on the hillside near Pittsburg Landing. The men requisitioned hay from supply and made beds, but at 2:00 a.m. it rained, and they awoke, drenched and shivering. Nearby in the river there was a large steamboat, brilliantly lighted and empty except for a few officers and enlisted guards. Harlan called his men into line, marched down to the boat, and asked permission to take his men to the lower deck where they could dry their clothes around the boilers. The guard refused, explaining that this was Grant's headquarters boat and he could not admit anyone. Harlan ordered his best captain to lead his company, bayonets fixed, onto the gangway, and if the guard did not give way, throw him into the river. The guard stepped back and Harlan and his men slept the rest of the night warm and dry in the boiler room.[37]

Harlan's pursuit of Morgan turned him into a Union hero, and his promotion to brigadier general was pending when he resigned from the Union army. He claimed the reason was his father's death, but it may have been because he could not accept Lincoln's Emancipation Proclamation. When he recruited his regiment, he said that he would fight to restore the Union, but he owned slaves and declared that if the war became a struggle against slavery he would desert to the South. After leaving the army he openly opposed Lincoln's re-election and opposed emancipation and equal rights for blacks until 1868, when he turned completely and supported Grant for president and became an advocate of equality the rest of his life. President Rutherford B. Hayes appointed him to the Supreme Court and he became the Great Dissenter, a lone voice on the Court against Jim Crow segregation, a champion of black people who provided constitutional arguments used in the next generation to overturn segregation.[38]

Harlan loaded his brigade on three trains in Gallatin, but two engine breakdowns delayed him thirty-six hours. When he reached Munfordville and united with Hobson's 600 men, one-half of them mounted, he left the cars and marched north all day and all night and on the morning of December 29, the day of the court martial at Rolling Fork, he arrived in Elizabethtown. Learning that Morgan's men were on the river eight miles northwest toward Bardstown, he set out immediately in that direction.[39]

It was Harlan's artillery shell Basil Duke heard that morning near Elizabethtown. Duke rushed to form a defensive line to hold the fords until Bullock and the two cannon returned. He sent a courier with an order to Bullock to cancel his mission and come immediately, and another courier to inform Morgan. There was a meadow between the house and the river, with woods on both sides, and about 300 yards from the bank and parallel to the river the ground made a sudden depression,

General Basil Wilson Duke. Born in Scott County, Kentucky, Duke was the brother-in-law of Gen. John Hunt Morgan. Duke commanded the 2nd Kentucky (Confederate) Cavalry and eventually led Morgan's Cavalry Division after the death of Morgan. *University of Kentucky Special Collections*

forming a natural breastwork. Behind this terrace Duke formed his dismounted men. He instructed them to keep moving around and showing themselves at different points, dropping out of sight and appearing again, to make their numbers appear greater than they were. He had skirmishers on the left and right circling in and out of the woods, and officers in view in the rear, riding back and forth shouting orders to imaginary regiments.[40]

When Harlan came over the Muldraugh Ridge, about 260 feet in elevation above the meadow two miles away on the left of the road, he could see Duke's battle line and horses standing in the rear near the ford. "From a high hill I saw quite distinctly a very large body of cavalry formed in line of battle near the river," Harlan later reported. "Their officers were riding along their line, apparently preparing to give us battle. Knowing that Morgan had a larger force than I had, I proceeded cautiously, and yet as expeditiously as the nature of the ground and the circumstances admitted." Rather than attacking a force he outnumbered over nine to one, Harlan delayed over one hour, carefully positioning a section of artillery on a hill that rose 170 feet above the meadow on the Union right, with the other section in the meadow on the left, behind the infantry line. Finally with the infantry in two lines on the field and Hobson's cavalry mounted on the right rear, Harlan ordered the artillery to open fire.[41]

Just as the shells began falling, Bullock arrived and his 500 men dismounted and joined Duke's line on the Confederate right. Harlan still outnumbered the Rebels by over three to one. Duke made a show of racing the two cannon across the field in full view, sending them to safety across the river at the ford on the Bardstown Road. He avoided using the guns to save them from capture and to avoid turning a rear guard action into a general skirmish. Harlan and his officers were amazed at such self-confidence—the Rebels must be in great number behind that terrace, they thought, for they are not using their artillery.[42] In fact, Duke wanted to retreat now that Bullock had arrived, but the Union artillery on the hill on Duke's left was directing its fire at the ford and the Confederate horses standing near the ford. Shells were bursting in the water and on the bank with such frequency that it was impossible to cross. It was the most accurate artillery fire Duke had seen in the war.

Ten horses were killed within a space of twenty square feet. Unable to withdraw, Duke watched as Harlan's infantry line moved forward across the meadow, bayonets glistening in the sunshine, with Hobson's cavalry ready to pounce, and he confessed that his blood ran cold. A courier arrived with orders from Morgan to withdraw. "In common with quite a number of others," Duke recalled, "I devoutly wished I could."[43]

The blue lines moved forward to within one hundred yards of Duke's men and the Confederates sent up a defiant yell and commenced firing. The Union line held and withdrew, in perfect order. It did not recoil; it simply withdrew. Harlan's official report stated: "Every circumstance on the occasion indicated to my command that the enemy were disposed to give us battle in force, yet nowhere, along the whole line, was there to be observed any, even the slightest, faltering by either officers or men." Harlan's brigade had caught up with Morgan's rear guard, marched to within rifle range, and gone on the defensive. Duke never understood it. After the war he wrote that Harlan's force "if handled vigorously and skillfully, if its march had even been steadily kept up, would have, in spite of every effort we could have made, swept us into the turbid river at our backs."[44]

Now Duke seized the initiative and ordered a demonstration on the Union center to divert attention from a frontal assault on the Union artillery position on the hill that was firing so accurately on the ford. The Rebels charged up the hill, killing one Union soldier, wounding three, two of them mortally, and silencing the guns for about fifteen minutes. The Confederates had two men wounded including their leader, Capt. Virgil M. Pendleton.[45]

But just as Pendleton's charge began, a Union shell exploded killing two horses and striking Duke in the head with a piece of shrapnel, knocking him unconscious to the ground. Quirk's scouts gathered him up and placed him on Quirk's horse, which carried him across the river. Quirk obtained a carriage, filled it with bedding, and the vehicle served as Duke's ambulance for the remainder of the raid. Breckinridge took charge and withdrew safely with the entire Confederate force.[46]

This was Duke's second wound (the first was at Shiloh). Thirty-eight years later, in the autumn of 1901, Union veterans from the Army of the Cumberland held a reunion in Louisville and invited Duke to attend. Veterans were present who had been on the other side during both of Duke's wounds. By now he was sixty-three years old, had a great career as chief counsel of the L&N Railroad behind him, and was one of the South's most distinguished personalities. Colonel Andrew Cowan, toastmaster, introduced Duke with the following: "We greeted you in the morning, saluted you with a good-night, and now are happy to meet you again." Duke replied, in part: "Mr. Toastmaster, Ladies and Gentlemen, and Comrades (I hope I may say) of the Army of the Cumberland—The toast which you have given me reminds me very forcibly of our past relations. . . . You used to greet me in the morning . . . with a warmth of welcome with which I could have well dispensed . . . in all candor, I used to think your conduct sometimes abrupt, if not altogether rude." There was much merriment, and he said: "I am glad to know that you have learned to correct it—I prefer the present welcome."[47]

When news of the Rolling Fork action reached Louisville, reporters grasping for anything that looked like a victory over Morgan hailed Harlan as the man of the hour. The *Louisville Journal* declared that the "grand skirmish" of Harlan's "gallant brigade" saved Louisville, the Rolling Fork trestle, and the Shepherdsville trestle over Salt River. The *New York Times* gave Harlan credit for an attack of one and one-half hours that resulted in the "Defeat of the Guerrillas under John Morgan."[48]

Rosecrans learned the futility of chasing Morgan with infantry and ordered the organization of new mounted infantry units. When Morgan entered Kentucky again the next summer, instead of only 300 mounted men, Hobson was able to pursue with 2,500—a force equal in size and stamina to Morgan's.[49]

The trestles were Morgan's most strategic target in Kentucky; their destruction closed the L&N for five weeks and silenced for the moment the rumors that his recent marriage had depleted his fighting spirit. The raid began only eight days after his wedding to his second wife, the beautiful and intelligent Southern belle, Martha Ready of Murfreesboro. His friends warned that the marriage would ruin his career, and he determined to prove them wrong. On December 23, the second day of the expedition, he wrote "Mattie" that he hoped to return within six days, "& then my *precious one*.I shall try & get back to you as fast as possible

& then my pretty one nothing shall induce me to again leave you this winter. How anxiously I am looking forward to the moment when I shall again clasp you to a heart that beats for you alone. *Do not forget me* my *own Darling & you may rest* assured that my whole thoughts are of you. Farewell my pretty wife, my command is leaving I must be off."[50]

Four days later on December 27, in Elizabethtown, he went for a stroll with Belle McDowell, a young woman from Louisville. "You ought not to have married," Belle said. "For there are a thousand hearts that beat at the sound of your name." He replied: "I wish that I had a thousand hearts, and I would give them all to my wife."[51] Reunited after the raid, he kept his promise to not leave Mattie again that winter; while they honeymooned, the morale and cohesion of his command declined.

When summer came he made the spectacular raid into Indiana and Ohio and was captured and incarcerated in the Ohio State Penitentiary in Columbus. The Southern people celebrated nevertheless and many were almost beside themselves when he escaped on November 27, 1863. Returned to duty in command of men that he had not recruited, in the summer of 1864 Morgan raided from southwestern Virginia into Kentucky on what would be his Last Kentucky Raid. Discipline broke down and some of the men robbed the Farmer's Bank of Kentucky in Mount Sterling and kept the money.

Morgan was killed in Greeneville, Tennessee, on September 4, 1864, having been suspended, with a court of inquiry on the robbery scheduled for September 10. Public opinion in the South had turned against guerrilla warfare and the Confederate Congress had repealed the Partisan Ranger Act. Still, Morgan was mourned throughout the South. Kate Cumming wrote in her diary: "Alas! How fleeting is every thing in this world; it seems but yesterday that he took for his bride one of Tennessee's fairest daughters. She is now bereft of her all, and, like the bride of Glenullen,

Shall await,
Like a love-lighted watch-fire, all night at the gate;
A steed comes at morning, no rider is there;
But its bridle is red with the sign of despair.[52]

* * *

Morgan's Cavalry

First Kentucky Raid, July 1862

John Hunt Morgan's Brigade
Col. John Hunt Morgan

2nd Kentucky Cavalry Regiment
Lt. Col. Basil W. Duke

Texas Cavalry Battalion
Maj. Richard M. Gano
2 companies, Texas cavalry
2 companies, Tennessee Partisan Rangers

1st Regiment Georgia Partisan Rangers
Col. A. A. Hunt
Lt. Col. F. M. Nix

O.R. 16(1):766-767, 771; Penn, *Civil War in Cynthiana*, 179.

Christmas Raid, December 1862 - January 1863

Morgan's Cavalry Division
Brig. Gen. John Hunt Morgan

1st Brigade
Col. Basil W. Duke

2nd Kentucky Cavalry
Lt. Col. John B. Hutchinson

7th Kentucky Cavalry
Lt. Col. J.M. Huffman

8th Kentucky Cavalry
Col. Leroy S. Cluke

Artillery Battery
Capt. Baylor Palmer

2nd Brigade
Col. William C.P. Breckinridge

9th Kentucky Cavalry
Lt. Col. Robert G. Stoner

10th Regiment Kentucky Partisan Rangers
Col. Adam R. Johnson

11th Kentucky Cavalry
Col. D.W. Chenault

14th Tennessee Cavalry
Col. James Bennett

Artillery Battery
Lt. C.C. Corbett

Duke, *History of Morgan's Cavalry*, 324-325.

Great Indiana and Ohio Raid, June - July 1863

Morgan's Cavalry Division
Brig. Gen. John Hunt Morgan

1st Brigade
Col. Basil W. Duke

2nd Kentucky Cavalry
Maj. T.B. Webber
5th Kentucky Cavalry
Col. D.H. Smith
6th Kentucky Cavalry
Col. J.W. Grigsby
9th Tennessee Cavalry
Col. W.W. Ward

2nd Brigade
Col. Adam R. Johnson

7th Kentucky Cavalry
Lt. Col. J.M. Huffman
8th Kentucky Cavalry
Col. Roy S. Cluke
10th Kentucky Cavalry
Maj. W.G. Owen
11th Kentucky Cavalry
Lt. Col. J. Tucker
14th Kentucky Cavalry
Col. Richard C. Morgan

Artillery
Kentucky Battery
Capt. E. P. Byrne

Lester V. Horwitz, *The Longest Raid of the Civil War* (Cincinnati, OH, 1999), 8.

Last Kentucky Raid, June, 1864

Morgan's Cavalry Division
Brig. Gen. John Hunt Morgan

First Brigade
Col. Henry L. Giltner

4th Kentucky Cavalry
Col. Tandy Pryor
10th Kentucky Cavalry Battalion
Lt. Col. Edwin Trimble
1st Kentucky Mounted Rifles Battalion
Major Holliday
2nd Kentucky Mounted Rifles Battalion
Col. Tom Johnson
10th Kentucky Mounted Rifles Battalion
Maj. Tom Chenoweth
6th Confederate Battalion
Lt. Col. George Jessee

Second Brigade
Col. D. Howard Smith

1st Battalion Cavalry
Col. Bowles
2nd Battalion Cavalry
Capt. Kirkpatrick
3rd Battalion Cavalry
Maj. Cassell

Third Brigade
Col. Robert Martin

1st Battalion
Lt. Col. Robert Alston
2nd Battalion
Major George Diamond

Penn, *Cynthiana in the Civil War*, 181.

NOTES

1. James A. Ramage, *Rebel Raider: The Life of General John Hunt Morgan* (Lexington, Ky., 1986), 40, 45; undated article in the *Atlanta Commonwealth*, reprinted in *Richmond Enquirer*, April 1, 1862. The author is grateful to Sharon Taylor, Dr. Macel Wheeler and Steven L. Wright for their assistance with the research for this essay.

2. Basil W. Duke, *A History of Morgan's Cavalry* (1867; reprint, Millwood, New York, 1981), 328.

3. Printed broadside, Aug. 22, 1862, copy in possession of the author.

4. Ramage, *Rebel Raider*, 98-102.

5. *Ibid.*, 145.

6. *Ibid.*, 109, 137; India W. P. Logan, ed., *Kelion Franklin Peddicord* (New York, N.Y., 1908), 49, 56-7.

7. Ramage, *Rebel Raider*, 93.

8. John E. Kleber, ed., *The Kentucky Encyclopedia* (Lexington, Ky., 1992), 109; Robert E. McDowell, *City of Conflict: Louisville in the Civil War, 1861-1865* (Louisville, Ky., 1962), 67.

9. *The War of the Rebellion: A Compilation of the Official Records of the Union and Confederate Armies*, 128 vols., (Washington, D.C., 1880-1901) (hereinafter cited as *O.R.*) (all references are to Series I), 16(1):735-8.

10. Erastus Winters, *Serving Uncle Sam in the Fiftieth Ohio* (East Walnut Hills, 1905), 43.

11. *O.R.,* 23(1):704-5.

12. *Ibid.*, 710.

13. R. F. Riccardelli, review of *Rebel Raider* by James A. Ramage, *Military Intelligence* (October-December 1995), 56; Edwin C. Fishel, *The Secret War for the Union: The Untold Story of Military Intelligence in the Civil War* (Boston, Mass., 1996), 4-5; *London Times,* Sept. 12, 1862.

14. Ramage, *Rebel Raider*, 84, 97; William R. Plum, *The Military Telegraph during the Civil War in the United States*, 2 vols. (1882; reprint, New York, N.Y., 1974), 1:193; John A. Wyeth, *With Sabre and Scalpel: The Autobiography of a Soldier and Surgeon* (New York, N.Y., 1914), 182-3.

15. Matthew Josephson, *Edison: A Biography* (New York, N.Y., 1959), 54; *Cincinnati Gazette*, Feb. 20, 1867; *Hammond Times*, Dec. 4, 1960; Henrietta Morgan to Martha Morgan, Feb. 19, no year, John Hunt Morgan Papers, Southern Historical Collection, University of North Carolina, Chapel Hill (hereinafter cited as JHMP-SHC). Ellsworth died November 29, 1899.

16. *O.R.*, 23 (1):703.

17. *Richmond Dispatch*, Aug. 25, 1863.

18. *O.R.*, 23(1):711, 718.

19. Grover S. Wormer, *The Morgan Raid of 1863: Memoirs of General G. S. Wormer* (Detroit, Mich., 1897), 6-7.

20. Plum, *Military Telegraph*, 1:276-7; *New Orleans Times-Democrat*, June 11, 1882.

21. Ramage, *Rebel Raider*, 96.

22. *New Orleans Times-Democrat*, June 11, 1882; Duke, *History of Morgan's Cavalry*, 214; Plum, *Telegraph*, 1:200.

23. Ramage, *Rebel Raider*, 84-8.

24. *Ibid.*, 87; Maury Klein, *History of the Louisville & Nashville Railroad* (New York, N.Y., 1972), 31, 36; Ramage, *Rebel Raider*, 87.

25. Ramage, *Rebel Raider*, 87-9; Kate Cumming, *A Journal of Hospital Life in the Confederate Army of Tennessee* (Louisville, Ky., 1866), 28.

26. William A. Penn, *Rattling Spurs and Broad-Brimmed Hats: The Civil War in Cynthiana and Harrison County, Kentucky* (Midway, Ky., 1995), 69-89; Ramage, *Rebel Raider*, 91, 93, 97-9. Penn's excellent scholarly book includes new maps and heretofore unpublished details.

27. Ramage, *Rebel Raider*, 102, 106, 137, 139.

28. *O.R.*, 20(1):155.

29. *Ibid.*, 156; Duke, *History of Morgan's Cavalry*, 332.

30. *Louisville Journal*, Dec. 29, 31, 1862; Ramage, *Rebel Raider*, 139; Duke, *History of Morgan's Cavalry*, 333; Contour map, Elizabethtown Quadrangle, U.S. Department of the Interior Geological Survey, 1991.

31. Duke, *History of Morgan's Cavalry*, 333-4; Contour map, Elizabethtown Quadrangle.

32. Duke, *History of Morgan's Cavalry*, 334.

33. *Cincinnati Enquirer,* Dec. 31, 1862; *Louisville Journal,* Dec. 31, 1862; *Covington Kentucky Post,* Feb. 27, 1991.

34. Duke, *History of Morgan's Cavalry*, 335-6.

35. *Ibid.*, 336.

36. Ramage, *Rebel Raider*, 140-1; *O.R.*, 20 (2):238.

37. Loren P. Beth, *John Marshall Harlan: The Last Whig Justice* (Lexington, Ky., 1992), 57-8, 279 n.2; Louis Hartz, "John M. Harlan in Kentucky, 1855-1877: The Story of His Pre-Court Political Career," *Filson Club History Quarterly,* 14 (1940), 17, 19.

38. Hartz, "John M. Harlan," 25; *Kentucky Encyclopedia*, 407-8; Beth, *John Marshall Harlan.*

39. Ramage, *Rebel Raider*, 142; *O.R.*, 20 (1):137-8.

40. Duke, *History of Morgan's Cavalry*, 336-7; Contour map, Lebanon Junction Quadrangle, U.S. Department of the Interior Geological Survey, 1991.

41. *O.R.*, 20 (1):139; Duke, *History of Morgan's Cavalry*, 337; Contour map, Lebanon Junction Quadrangle.

42. Duke, *History of Morgan's Cavalry*, 338.

43. *Ibid.*

44. *Ibid.*, 337, 339; *O.R.*, 20 (1):140.

45. Duke, *History of Morgan's Cavalry*, 339; *O.R.*, 20 (1):139, 157.

46. Duke, *History of Morgan's Cavalry*, 339; Ramage, *Rebel Raider*, 142. Some of the Confederates used a third ford on the right, discovered upon the withdrawal. Duke, *History of Morgan's Cavalry*, 339.

47. *Society of the Army of the Cumberland, Thirtieth Reunion, Louisville, Kentucky, October 8, 9, 1901* (Cincinnati, Ohio, 1902), 126-7.

48. *Louisville Journal*, Jan. 5, 1863; *New York Times*, Dec. 31, 1862.

49. Ramage, *Rebel Raider*, 145, 167. For an excellent, comprehensive study of Hobson's life see Steven L. Wright, "Edward H. Hobson," *Green County Review* (Spring 1992), 35-45.

50. John Hunt Morgan to Martha Morgan, Dec. 23, 1862, JHMP-SHC.

51. *Louisville Courier-Journal*, Sept, 27, 1936.

52. Cumming, *Journal*, 149.

Kent Masterson Brown

A Tribute to the Orphan Brigade of Kentucky

No Kentucky commands which fought in the Civil War, save for Gen. John Hunt Morgan's cavalry, were more well-known and well-respected than those which formed the First Kentucky Brigade, or, as it was affectionately known, the Orphan Brigade.

The brigade was composed of the 2nd, 4th, 6th and 9th Kentucky Infantry regiments, Cobb's, Byrne's and Graves's batteries of artillery and, at times, the 3rd Kentucky Infantry and the 5th Kentucky Infantry. The Orphans also had an Alabama and Tennessee connection. At Shiloh in April 1862, they were brigaded with the 4th Alabama Battalion, 31st Alabama Infantry, and Crews's Tennessee Battalion. From Shiloh to Chattanooga, they fought alongside the 41st Alabama Infantry. The Orphans campaigned over more territory (eight states), suffered higher casualties, and lost more brigade commanders than any other comparable unit in the war. And as if those trials were not enough, after February 1862, the brigade was never able to return to Kentucky to fight for its native state; instead, it fought the entire war far from home.

The officers and enlisted men of the famed Orphan Brigade, like all people, can fit into no certain mold. Although the brigade was composed of men of ordinary everyday looks and means, they became idolized by the people of the South, and the Commonwealth of Kentucky in particular, during and long after the war. A November 1864 circular prophesied: "However this war may terminate, if a man can truthfully claim to have been a worthy member of the Kentucky Brigade he will have a kind of title of nobility."[1] Indeed, no greater tribute was ever paid to a fighting unit than the *Mobile Advertiser and Register* which

Private John Hampton Short

Private Short, seen here in a hitherto unpublished ambrotype, served in Company E, 3rd Kentucky (Confederate) Infantry (Col. Lloyd Tilghman's) at the outbreak of the war. Short, holding a model 1816 flintlock musket and wearing a coarse jean jacket, presents the appearance of a typical member of the Orphan Brigade in 1861 and early 1862.

Editor's Collection

---

commented about the fighting at Nashville, Tennessee in December, 1864. "Troops should have been placed at [a certain defensive position outside of Nashville]," it read, "a point of which not the slightest doubt existed. Had the Kentucky Brigade been there, all would have been safe."[2]

The officers and men of the six hard-fighting Kentucky infantry regiments and the three Kentucky artillery companies that composed the Orphan Brigade—the 2nd, 3rd, 4th, 5th, 6th and 9th Kentucky Infantry Regiments and Capts. Robert Cobb's, Edward P. Byrne's and Rice E. Graves's artillery batteries—came from virtually every walk of life: mechanic, carpenter, blacksmith, professional man, politician, merchant and farmer. They hailed from thirty-three of Kentucky's now one hundred twenty counties, and from every region of the old Commonwealth; from as far east in the mountains as Johnson, Morgan and Breathitt Counties, to as far west as Graves and Trigg Counties. They came from counties along the Tennessee border—Logan, Simpson, and Allen—and they came from counties along the Ohio River—Union, Henderson, and Daviess. They poured into the ranks from the great belt of counties in central Kentucky—from Hardin, Nelson, Mercer, Boyle, Shelby, Anderson, Franklin, Fayette, Harrison,

Scott, Woodford, Jessamine, and Bourbon, and from a host of others. There were town boys, but, more often than not, those who served in the Orphan Brigade were yeoman farmers; rugged, independent, self-reliant. Mostly, the members of the brigade came from regions of Kentucky (and areas of particular counties in the state) where the people identified, economically and politically, with the lower Southland. The counties from which they hailed were located mostly in the rich farming belts of Kentucky.[3]

The diaries and letters left by the Orphans reveal a set of deeply religious men. Many were firm Southern Baptists, although their commanders were, in large measure, Presbyterians and Episcopalians. The soldiers in the Orphan Brigade were the bravest-of-the-brave—and in some instances they were skulkers.

Almost always without adequate clothing and most of the time ravenously hungry and ill-equipped, those Kentuckians fought across the Western Theater in the hard-luck and usually poorly led Army of Tennessee. Despite exhibitions of grand bravery on a number of battlefields, the army suffered devastating blows from an enemy of overwhelming numbers sent into the field by a nation that had an industrial capacity second-to-none on earth, and with a government that focused and unleashed, for its time, almost unlimited political, economic, and military might. Yet, the hungry, ill-clad and often defeated Orphans retained their remarkable fighting ability throughout the war. According to one account, they would "stick to [the fighting] as long as they [could] find a foe to shoot at!"[4] The record of the Orphans, wrote one distinguished American scholar, is a record of heroism in war that "has never been surpassed."[5] General Joseph E. Johnston, who could truly size up the soldiers in both major theaters of war, remarked once that "the Orphan Brigade was the finest body of men and soldiers I ever saw in any army anywhere."[6]

The Orphans and their "Cause" were ultimately defeated in the most costly war the American people have ever known. They and their fellow Confederates are the only American soldiers to experience not only total defeat in war, but the loss of their very way of life; the economic, political and social institutions they most revered. The Orphans who survived the trials of war returned home economically destitute only to find that, in every sense of the word, they would have to live in an "occupied" Kentucky. They suffered an equally cruel setback after their final surrender at Washington, Georgia, in 1865. The history of their role in the war and their "Cause," written by the war's victors, would not look upon either with sympathy.

With the election of Abraham Lincoln to the presidency in November 1860, the long and bitter sectional struggle between Northern and Southern states reached a climax. From the very birth of the Republic the two sections had tangled over issues which vitally affected their separate social structures and economies. The strongest influence upon Southerners generally, and upon those who fought in the Orphan Brigade particularly, was the "frontier." It was thus no accident that the Orphan Brigade was often referred to by soldiers in the Army of Tennessee as the "Blood of Boone."[7] Independence and self-sufficiency were virtues and political rallying cries to those born on the "frontier." Consequently, limited government, individual rights, republicanism in the eighteenth century sense of the term, and State's Rights were dominant themes in many Kentuckians' political lexicons.[8]

In all sections of the South, and particularly in Kentucky, the overwhelming number of farms were small, subsistence operations. Kentucky and the South generally was the home of the yeoman farmer. It was a poor region. In fact, the typical soldier in the famed Orphan Brigade was lucky to have owned a decent pair of shoes before, during, or after the Civil War.[9]

In spite of the long presence of slavery in the South (over 250 years) and in parts of Kentucky (nearly ninety years), the typical yeoman farmer in the South and Kentucky—and, consequently, the typical member of the Orphan Brigade—did not own any slaves at all. This was not the case among some of the commanders of the Orphan Brigade, nearly all of whom were from slave-owning families and had married into prominent slave-owning Kentucky families. General William Preston, for instance, married the daughter of Gov. Robert Wickliffe, while Gen. Benjamin Hardin Helm married the daughter of Robert Todd. Both Preston and Helm were slave-owners and their wives were from families that owned large numbers of slaves.[10]

The Southerners and Kentuckians of 1860 did not introduce slavery into their region. Most believed that the institution of slavery was, and ought to be, doomed, but they also firmly maintained that gradual emancipation of the nearly four million slaves in the South would be best for the slave and white population. Gradual emancipation, to them, was a concern only of the states where slavery existed, not of the Federal government. The very order of society, they thought, was at stake in the issue. Such was the public position taken before the Civil War by such eminent Kentuckians as Henry Clay, John J. Crittenden and John C. Breckinridge.[11]

By 1861, it became apparent to Southerners, including many Kentuckians, that they were fighting a losing battle over national policy. Fears of the region being impoverished by Northern industrial pressures and worries of it being torn asunder by the abolition of slavery were real concerns then. Southerners and many Kentuckians in 1860 felt the national government was hostile to them and to their region. The two regions had been on a collision course for years. Few roads or rail lines connected the North with the lower South; social intercourse between the two regions hardly existed. Their economic, ethnic, social and cultural differences were vast; their rivalry deep and bitter.[12]

But because the Ohio River, Kentucky's northern border, was also the southern boundary of Ohio, Indiana, and Illinois, Kentucky unlike her sister Southern states had always looked north as well as south for its economic well-being. Over the years, many members of Kentucky families had migrated north to those states. Thus marks the great difference between Kentucky and the states of the lower South. The Blue Grass State was economically and socially tied to its Ohio River neighbors. Those who became members of the Orphan Brigade recognized that doing so meant cutting off one of Kentucky's strongest economic and social lifelines.[13]

Within weeks of Abraham Lincoln's election to the Presidency, South Carolina seceded from the Union. By April 1, 1861, every state in the lower South save Virginia, Arkansas, North Carolina, and Tennessee had passed ordinances of secession. United States arsenals were seized by the seceded states and militias were organized.

The stalemate over the occupation of Fort Sumter by a United States garrison in Charleston Harbor (commanded by Kentuckian Maj. Robert H. Anderson) erupted in the bombardment of that bastion on April 12, 1861. After the fort's surrender the Lincoln Administration issued a call for 75,000 troops to "suppress the rebellion." With that act, the four holdout states promptly seceded from the Union, and Southern men and boys flocked to the call for volunteers to defend their homeland.[14]

Though terribly conflicted, Kentucky—through its governor, Southern-sympathizing Beriah Magoffin—ultimately declared its "neutrality" on May 20, 1861. Many of its citizens were not in accord with that act. Because no official recruiting could be conducted in "neutral" Kentucky, those who sympathized with the plight of the seceded states flocked to camps in Tennessee to cast their lots with the South. The most prominent of these camps, not surprisingly, was named "Camp Boone," near Clarksville, Tennessee. There and at nearby Camp Burnett, West Point-trained Gen. Simon Bolivar Buckner, the commander of the pro-Southern Kentucky State Guard, assembled most of his elite force and its officer core. These men included Capt. Philip Lightfoot Lee of Bullitt County; Capt. Joseph P. Nuckols of Barren County; Capt. Thomas W. Thompson of Jefferson County; Maj. Thomas H. Hunt of Fayette County; Capt. John W. Caldwell of Logan County; and Maj. Thomas Bell Monroe, Jr., of Franklin and Fayette Counties, to name a few. They formed the nucleus around which the Orphan Brigade was organized.

At Camp Boone, Col. Roger W. Hanson's 2nd Kentucky Infantry was organized, along with Col. Lloyd Tilghman's (and subsequently Col. Benjamin Anderson's) 3rd Kentucky Infantry. Captain Robert H. Cobb's Kentucky Battery and Capt. Rice E. Graves's Kentucky Battery were also formed there.[15] All of these units moved north to Bowling Green, Kentucky with General Buckner's command, where they were joined by Col. Robert P. Trabue's 4th Kentucky Infantry (organized at Camp Burnett), Col. Joseph H. Lewis's 6th Kentucky Infantry (organized mostly at Bowling Green and Cave City), Col. Thomas H. Hunt's 9th Kentucky Infantry (organized at Bowling Green), and Capt. Edward P. Byrne's Battery (organized partly in Tennessee and partly in Mississippi). The 5th Kentucky Infantry was organized at Prestonsburg in eastern Kentucky, and would fight there during the first two years of war and then at Chickamauga. It would eventually join the Orphan Brigade on November 5, 1863 at Chattanooga, Tennessee.[16]

Unlike so many of their fellow Confederates, Kentuckians who cast their lots with the South did so without their native state joining them. Kentucky not only did not approve of secession, but evolved to become a "Union" state in every way. Kentucky overwhelmingly sent a pro-Union delegation to Congress after the June 20, 1861, elections. After the legislative elections on August 5, 1861, Kentucky's legislature became heavily pro-Union. The new legislature went so far as to make joining or supporting the Confederate Army a felony. Union recruiting was begun in the state at Camp Dick Robinson in Garrard County after the legislative elections in August 1861 , and a pro-Union Home Guard was raised and financed by the state legislature. Kentucky eventually declared itself for the Union. By the end of the war, the state had raised fifty-five Union infantry regiments and numerous infantry and Home Guard battalions, seventeen Union cavalry regiments, and five batteries of Union artillery from every geographic region of the Commonwealth, including the rich lands of the Bluegrass. Ultimately, Kentucky provided nearly 80,000 of its sons to the Union war effort—three times the number who served in the Confederate armies.[17]

Consequently, those who joined the Orphan Brigade not only defended their "Cause" against the national government, but wound up isolated from their own native state—expatriated if you will—during four years of bloody and disheartening campaigns. Truly, those who served in the Orphan Brigade gave up everything they possessed to fight for the Confederacy: family, home, state, and national identity. Moreover, they were forced to fight the entire war far from the borders of their beloved Commonwealth, which is one reason why they were known as "Orphans."

Cruelly, many of the enlisted men and virtually all of the officers of the Orphan Brigade were indicted for treason by Union-controlled local circuit courts in their home towns in Kentucky. Such indictments in areas like Breathitt County in the eastern Kentucky mountains precipitated feuds among families that lasted for generations. With Kentucky occupied by Union troops early in the war, prominent officers

General John Cabell Breckinridge, a native of Fayette County, Kentucky, rose to become vice president of the United States before the war. He became closely identified with the Orphan Brigade, which fought as part of his division at Shiloh, Vicksburg, Baton Rouge, Stone's River, Chickamauga and Chattanooga. *Library of Congress*

---

in the brigade learned of the confiscation of their lands and personal property by local courts and the harassment of their wives and children by provost marshals, not to mention warrants outstanding for their arrest.[18]

Nevertheless, the Orphans were led by some of Kentucky's most noted men. General Buckner was one of Kentucky's most prominent soldiers, and his presence as the Orphans' first commander was a source of much pride among the rank-and-file. Early in the war, the Orphans came under the command of the magnetic Kentuckian Gen. John Cabell Breckinridge. A lawyer from Lexington, Kentucky, Breckinridge was the grandson of Thomas Jefferson's Attorney General, a Congressman from Henry Clay's "Ashland" district, the former Vice President of the United States under President James Buchanan, and a United States Senator.

Breckinridge was not the only personality of national importance who would lead the Orphans. His cousin, Gen. William Preston of Louisville, was a descendant of Kentucky's earliest Virginia pioneer settlers, a prominent lawyer, and President James Buchanan's minister to Spain. He was also the one-time brother-in-law of Kentuckian Gen. Albert Sidney Johnston, who would die in Preston's arms at the Battle of Shiloh. Preston would lead the Orphans at Vicksburg and would be closely identified with the brigade throughout much of the war.

General Benjamin Hardin Helm, a lawyer and the son of two-time Governor of Kentucky, John Helm of Hardin and Nelson counties, was the grandson of John Hardin, a United States Senator from Kentucky and one of young Capt. Abraham Lincoln's commanders in the Black Hawk War in 1832. Ben Helm was also married to Emily Todd, half-sister to Mary Todd Lincoln, the wife of President Lincoln. Helm would lead the brigade twice and die in its heroic attacks at Chickamauga.[19]

Generals Buckner, Breckinridge, Preston, and Helm were highly educated men. Centre College, Transylvania Law School, Harvard Law School, Yale College, Princeton College, and the United States Military Academy were the *alma maters* these four men attended. Their backgrounds are particularly remarkable when one recognizes that few Kentuckians at that time had any formal education at all.[20]

Not all of the Orphan brigade commanders were highly educated. Generals Roger Weightman Hanson of Winchester, Kentucky and Joseph H. Lewis of Glasgow, Kentucky were mostly self-educated lawyers prior to the war. Colonel Robert Trabue, a native of Columbia,

Kentucky and the grandson of Daniel Trabue, one of the foremost Virginia pioneers to enter Kentucky, was also a largely self-taught lawyer.[21]

Of all these commanders, it was John C. Breckinridge, "Old Breck," whom the Orphans idolized. As veteran E. Porter Thompson wrote years after the war, "The history of the Kentucky Brigade is necessarily in a great measure the military history of General Breckinridge."[22]

In the beginning of the war, the location of the Confederate northern line of defense convinced the Orphans that the conflict would be fought over their native state. This northern boundary, commanded by Gen. Albert Sidney Johnston, was thinly drawn across southern Kentucky from Columbus on the Mississippi River, to Bowling Green, to Kentucky's southeastern foothills near Cumberland Gap. The Orphans' hopes, however, were quickly dashed.

In January 1862, the 2nd, 3rd, 4th, 6th and 9th Kentucky Infantry regiments and Cobb's, Graves's, and Byrne's artillery batteries were part of General Buckner's forces at Bowling Green, Kentucky. On January 19, Johnston's right flank was crushed at the Battle of Mill Springs, in Pulaski County, Kentucky and the Confederacy's northern frontier began to collapse. It was the last time the Orphans saw their native state during the entire war. Almost immediately, General Johnston sent the 2nd Kentucky Infantry and Graves's Battery to Fort Donelson on the Cumberland River below the Kentucky border.[23]

Early 1862 generated a host of bitter Orphan memories. The beastly winter's fight at Fort Donelson resulted in General Buckner's capitulation of that bastion on February 16, 1862. Colonel Roger Hanson's 2nd Kentucky and Capt. Rice E. Graves's Kentucky battery were among those units surrendered. The pain of Donelson was followed by the heartrending retreat out of Kentucky, through Nashville, Tennessee to Corinth, Mississippi of the 3rd, 4th, 6th and 9th Kentucky Infantry regiments and Byrne's and Cobb's batteries. During those terrible months the Confederacy's northern frontier in the West steadily gave way in the face of an advancing Union juggernaut. The Union Army of the Ohio entered Nashville in February, while Grant's Army of the Tennessee ascended the Tennessee River nearly all the way to the northern border of Alabama by April.[24]

Colonel Robert Trabue. Born in Adair County, Kentucky and a prewar lawyer in his hometown of Columbia, Trabue served as commander of the Orphan Brigade at Shiloh and after the death of Gen. Roger W. Hanson at Stone's River. Trabue died of a "violent illness" in Richmond, Virginia in 1863. E. Porter Thompson, *The Orphan Brigade*

And then the Battle of Shiloh was fought along the Tennessee River, two, bloody April days in 1862. It was there that the Orphan Brigade was born in fire and steel; and it was there it freely bled. Commanded by Col. Robert Trabue, the Orphan Brigade was 2,400 men strong and part of Gen. John C. Breckinridge's Reserve Division. It entered the maelstrom near Shiloh Church on Sunday, April 6, against Gen. Ulysses S. Grant's five Union divisions. As the brigade moved onto the battlefield and observed Capt. John Hunt Morgan and his squadron of Kentucky cavalry along the road, the men cheered and sang:

Cheer, boys, cheer; we'll march away to battle;
Cheer, boys, cheer, for our sweethearts and our wives;
Cheer, boys, cheer; we'll nobly do our duty,
And give to Kentucky our arms, our hearts, our lives.[25]

Riding up to Gen. William J. Hardee, Colonel Trabue, "Old Trib" as the men fondly called him, asked: "General, I have a Kentucky brigade here. What shall I do with it?"

"Put it in where the fight is the thickest, sir!" was Hardee's response.[26]

Having detached the 3rd Kentucky and the two battalions from Alabama and Tennessee and now left to his own discretion, Trabue prepared to advance his command—the 4th, 6th and 9th Kentucky Infantry regiments and the 31st Alabama Infantry (with Morgan's Kentucky squadron of cavalry abreast) supported by Cobb's and Byrne's batteries—across the fields toward the Tennessee River. The 4th Kentucky held the left, the 6th Kentucky the center, and the 9th Kentucky the right, with the 31st Alabama Infantry in reserve. Trabue ordered the men to fix bayonets and then called for the brigade to advance. Serving as a volunteer aide to Trabue was George W. Johnson of Scott County, Kentucky. Johnson had been the Confederate governor of Kentucky until the Confederate army withdrew from the state. He was now the governor-in-exile. Johnson's horse was shot down early in the advance, but he picked up a musket and joined Capt. Benjamin Monroe's Company E, 4th Kentucky Infantry, as a foot soldier.[27]

The Orphans slammed into Gen. Benjamin Prentiss's hastily-assembled Union lines along a sunken farm lane in an area covered with scrub trees and underbrush known to the soldiers as the "Hornet's Nest." As the fighting intensified, Breckinridge, fearing the brigade was being prematurely withdrawn, led the Kentuckians himself. A shell exploded nearby. "Never mind this, boys!" yelled Breckinridge. "Press on!" "Charge them!" he cried. Every member of "Old Breck's" staff fell in the melee from wounds or the loss of mounts. The Orphans were cut down in great numbers, but they drove ahead in the storm of gunfire until General Prentiss surrendered his depleted and worn-out Union forces.[28]

On the first day at Shiloh the brigade lost 75 killed and 350 wounded. Captain Robert Cobb's Kentucky battery reported the loss of nearly all of its battery horses killed and wounded and 37 of its men wounded. The Confederates had surprised, beaten and driven the enemy on April 6, but luck and victory eluded them. Colonel William Preston sent word to his cousin, "Old Breck," of the fatal wounding of Gen. Albert Sidney Johnston before mid-afternoon. There were such bright hopes that morning. With Johnston's death, the fortunes of the Confederate army faded as the fighting subsided.[29]

The next morning, General Grant's army, reinforced the previous night by Gen. Don Carlos Buell's Army of the Ohio, which had arrived from Nashville, counterattacked. The Confederate front slowly gave way as the brutal fighting intensified up and down the lines. By the end of the second day the Orphan Brigade had been decimated. The ground it had gained on April 6 had been lost. The 3rd Kentucky suffered the loss of 174 men, including every one of its regimental officers. The 4th Kentucky lost over half of its number, including the noble Gov. George W. Johnson, who fell on the field after bullets struck him in the right thigh and abdomen. Found by triumphant Union soldiers more than twenty-four hours after the fighting ended, and aided by no less a figure than Union Gen. Alexander McDowell McCook, Johnson died aboard the Union hospital ship *Hannibal* on the Tennessee River. His remains were returned to Georgetown for burial through the assistance of Union Gen. James S. Jackson and Col. John Marshall Harlan, both noted Kentuckians.[30]

The second day at Shiloh had pitted Kentuckians against one another. "Old Joe" Lewis's 6th Kentucky had spent part of the day fighting against the 9th Kentucky (Union) Infantry. Not far down the line, Col. John C. Wickliffe, commander of the Confederate 7th Kentucky and cousin to Colonel Preston's wife, was mortally wounded. His own brother, Capt. John D. Wickliffe of the 2nd Kentucky (Union) Cavalry regiment, returned the desperately wounded colonel to his

The graves of the Monroe brothers in the Frankfort, Kentucky, cemetery. Both Maj. Thomas B. Monroe (whose grave is on right) and his brother, Capt. Benjamin Monroe, were mortally wounded at the Battle of Shiloh while serving in the 4th Kentucky (Confederate) Infantry, Orphan Brigade. Governor George W. Johnson died at Shiloh while serving as a private in Captain Monroe's Company E, 4th Kentucky Infantry. *Editor's Collection*

---

comrades under a flag-of-truce! "Whenever Kentucky met Kentucky, it was horrible," wrote Colonel Preston.[31]

In all, the Orphan Brigade lost 844 men out of the 2,400 who entered the battle at Shiloh. The loss of officers was horrendous. Casualties included Maj. Joseph P. Nuckols and Capt. Thomas W. Thompson of the 4th Kentucky, both severely wounded; Maj. Thomas B. Monroe and his brother, Capt. Benjamin J. Monroe, both mortally wounded; Lt. Col. Benjamin Anderson of the 3rd Kentucky, wounded; Lt. Col. Martin Cofer of the 6th Kentucky, severely wounded; and Col. John W. Caldwell, Lt. Col. Robert A. Johnson, and Maj. Benjamin Desha of the 9th Kentucky, seriously wounded. The shattered remains of Maj. Thomas B. Monroe were buried by his men beneath a giant oak tree not far from Shiloh Church. On the tree was inscribed: "T. B. Monroe,

C.S.A., Killed April 7, 1862." Such was the last resting place of the former Mayor of Lexington, Kentucky.[32]

A note recorded by an Orphan after Shiloh describing the sad plight of the Southern Kentuckians in that action would be a melancholy refrain throughout the war:

> Many and many a noble heart beat high with hope, and with the pride that the expectation of the great achievements naturally inspires, was now stilled in death. These, our slain, lay in soldiers graves, scattered promiscuously, and with no mark even so much as to name them, and say to the future generations that such and such a one sleeps here. The victory that the very first blow [on April 6] promised, and that seemed, to all who lived till nightfall . . . almost within their grasp, had been snatched from them [on April 7], and their dead comrades were now mourned as those who shed their blood in vain."[33]

From Shiloh back to Corinth and on to Vicksburg, briefly under the command of Gen. William Preston, the Orphans marched. Farther south, the brigade entered the bloody fighting near Baton Rouge, Louisiana on August 2, 1862, where Gen. Benjamin Hardin Helm, the brigade's new commander, was wounded. Killed at Baton Rouge was General Helm's aide, Lt. Alexander Todd, half-brother to Mary Todd Lincoln. As the Orphans fought their way farther from Kentucky, they watched the Confederacy's western front continue to crumble. After Baton Rouge the Orphans bid farewell to the heroic 3rd Kentucky, which returned to Vicksburg.[34]

From Baton Rouge the Orphans marched on dusty roads north all the way to Knoxville, Tennessee under a new commander. General Roger W. Hanson, who had just been released from Fort Warren prison after his capture at Fort Donelson, was leading his new brigade to join Gen. John C. Breckinridge's Division. All had high hopes of returning to their "Old Kentucky Home." The war had moved into Kentucky with Gens. Braxton Bragg's and Edmund Kirby Smith's invasion of the Orphans' native state in the summer and fall of 1862. The reunion with Kentucky soil was not to be, however. Instead, Bragg's army withdrew from Kentucky in mid-October after the bloody but inconclusive fighting at Perryville on October 8, and the Orphans marched to join General

General William Preston. Born near Louisville, Kentucky, Preston was minister to Spain under President Buchanan. He briefly commanded the Orphan Brigade at Vicksburg during the summer of 1862, and was closely identified with the brigade from Stone's River to Chickamauga. *Library of Congress*

Bragg's Army of Tennessee as it returned to Murfreesboro, Tennessee. The Orphans never stepped foot on their native soil.[35]

In the bitter cold days before and after the 1863 New Year outside of Murfreesboro, the Orphans were called upon to sacrifice themselves again in the fighting along Stone's River. Only slightly engaged against Gen. William Rosecrans's Union Army of the Cumberland near what was called the "Round Forest" on December 31, 1862, Breckinridge's Division and the Orphans were repositioned on the far right flank of Bragg's army.[36]

On January 2, 1863, General Bragg summoned General Breckinridge to his headquarters at noon and directed him to advance his Kentuckians against fellow Kentuckian Gen. Thomas L. Crittenden's Union Twenty-First Corps, which was massed on the Union left in front of a bluff overlooking Stone's River. Citing reports from skirmishers that the ground over which the advance was to proceed was dominated by Union artillery, Breckinridge objected, claiming such an attack would be suicide. The irascible Bragg retorted, "Sir, my information is different. I have given the order to attack the enemy in your front and I expect it to be obeyed." The officers of the brigade, including Colonel Trabue and General Hanson, also denounced the order. General William Preston, who was commanding another one of the five brigades in Breckinridge's Division, consoled his cousin. They all knew in advance what the result would be. Forever after the Orphans believed the poor reception Kentucky had given Bragg's invading army in 1862 triggered the commanding general's dislike for them and their native state; the suicidal attack order at Murfreesboro was Bragg's revenge.[37]

One soldier described the day of January 2 as "gloomy and cloudy." It was cold and "peculiarly dreary," wrote another. Before noon it began to rain and drizzle. The Orphans were directed to hold the left flank of the five-brigade assault column. They would have to pass in front of the Union guns on their left without any protection at all. "Old Joe" Lewis's 6th Kentucky Infantry was deployed on the extreme left of the brigade, with "Old Trib's" 4th Kentucky on the right, and the 2nd Kentucky in the center. To the right of the 4th Kentucky was the 41st Alabama. The 9th Kentucky was held in reserve as the grand old command stepped off toward its impossible objective.[38]

General Roger Weightman Hanson was born in Clark County, Kentucky, and practiced law before the war in Lexington. Hanson was mortally wounded while leading the Orphan Brigade at Stone's River. His brother, Charles Hanson, commanded the 20th Kentucky (Union) Infantry. *Library of Congress*

"Up, my men, and charge!" shouted General Breckinridge at about 4:00 p.m. that dreary and cold afternoon. "Charge bayonets! Double-quick, forward, march!" yelled General Hanson. The drums rolled. Advancing beneath their blue Hardee battle flags adorned with silver discs and hand-painted battle honors, and under a hail of gunfire, the Kentuckians negotiated a swollen pond before crossing the undulating fields alongside the shallow and frozen Stone's River. As they advanced, the Orphans delivered volleys of rifle-fire at General Crittenden's blue columns, which included the 8th, 9th, 11th, 21st, and 23rd Kentucky (Union) Infantry regiments. The Orphans yelled as they ran on the double-quick toward their objective.[39]

The ferocious fire and powerful advance forced the steady withdrawal of the Union skirmish and infantry lines, which unmasked Capt. John Mendenhall's massed Union artillery batteries—fifty-eight guns in all—on top of the bluff to the left of the Orphans. In a moment, the frozen and desolate landscape exploded in the faces of the Orphans. Among the first to fall was Gen. Roger Weightman Hanson. "Old Flintlock" was struck below the left knee by a burning iron fuse from a spherical case shot which had exploded nearby. Admitting his wound was serious, Hanson remarked to Gen. Leonidas Polk as he was being carried to the rear that it was "glorious to die for one's country." Hanson, who suffered for two days before dying in great agony on January 4, was eventually buried in Lexington, Kentucky. The brigade was truly earning its nickname.[40]

The Orphans continued their advance in the face of the punishing artillery fire until pandemonium reigned along the river. The Kentuckians fell by the score. Incoming shells exploded within their ranks, blowing ten or more men to the ground at one time. Colonel Lewis, who assumed command of the brigade after Hanson fell, tried to rally the men forward, to no avail. They were being slaughtered. "The artillery bellowed forth such thunders that the men were stunned and could not distinguish sounds," recalled E. Porter Thompson. "There were falling timbers, crashing arms, the whirring of missiles of every description, the bursting of the dreadful shell, the groans of the wounded, the shouts of the officers, mingled in one horrid din that beggars description." The color-bearer of the 4th Kentucky, Sgt. Robert

Lindsay, was badly wounded in the chest. Somehow he held the colors upright, refusing any assistance although he was bleeding profusely from his mouth and nose. Faint from loss of blood, Lindsay finally handed the colors to a nearby private, who was instantly killed. Finally, Pvt. Joseph Nichols carried the colors off the field. Slowly the Kentuckians gave way until they were out of range of the enemy guns.[41]

In just forty-two minutes the Orphans lost 431 of their 1,197 men, over one-third of their command. So deadly was the enemy gunfire that in the 4th Kentucky alone, seven commissioned officers were killed and six, including Lt. Col. Joseph P. Nuckols, were wounded. Never had so many men fallen in so short a period of time. The 2nd Kentucky lost 108 of its 422 men. General Breckinridge, seeing the bloody repulse of his noble Kentuckians, was heard to exclaim: "My poor Orphans! My poor Orphans!" The men had never seen him so visibly moved. The brigade had won its nickname.[42]

In 1912 Lot D. Young, formerly a lieutenant in the 4th Kentucky, visited the site of the attack at Murfreesboro while attending a Confederate Memorial Day celebration. Upon hearing the singing of "My Old Kentucky Home" by a children's choir, and remembering those who had fallen there (including his dear friend Capt. William P. Bramblett of Frankfort, Kentucky, whose last, parting glance before receiving a mortal wound Young was unable to erase from his memory), the aging soldier tightly hugged a nearby tree and wept out loud, unashamed of his display of emotion.[43]

From the ice, cold and death at Murfreesboro, the Orphan Brigade marched to Tullahoma, Tennessee. From Tullahoma, the Kentuckians moved south to join Gen. Joseph E. Johnston's Confederate force forming in Mississippi to relieve Gen. John C. Pemberton's army bottled up in the trenches surrounding Vicksburg. The Orphans did not arrive in time. On July 4, 1863 Vicksburg was surrendered (along with the old 3rd Kentucky Infantry) by General Pemberton and the western frontier of the Confederacy vanished altogether. Thereafter, the Orphans were transferred all the way back to General Bragg's Army of Tennessee, which was facing Gen. William Rosecrans's growing Union Army of the Cumberland (the same army the Kentuckians had fought at

General Benjamin Hardin Helm, a native of Hardin County, Kentucky, and a lawyer before the Civil War, married Emily Todd, half-sister of Mary Todd Lincoln. Helm commanded the Orphan Brigade at Baton Rouge, where he was wounded, and at Chickamauga, where he was mortally wounded. *Library of Congress*

Murfreesboro). With Rosecrans threatening Chattanooga and north Georgia, Bragg needed the Orphans.[44]

At the Battle of Chickamauga the Orphans were sent into the iron and lead hail of battle again. Beloved Gen. Benjamin Hardin Helm, back from his convalescence after his wound at Baton Rouge, led the brigade into action near Chickamauga Creek. At about 10:00 a.m. on the frosty morning of September 20, 1863 the Orphans suffered terrible losses advancing against the Union log embattlements in the dense north Georgia thickets. Divided into two separate assault columns because of the configuration of the enemy breastworks, the Orphan Brigade struck the extreme left wing of the Union army, held by Gen. George H. Thomas's Fourteenth Corps. The Kentuckians comprised the left flank of Breckinridge's attacking column. Unfortunately, supporting Confederate brigades were too far behind them, and the Orphans entered the fighting with their left flank entirely exposed. The hard-charging soldiers in Lewis's 6th and 4th Kentucky regiments, along with the 41st Alabama, drove General Thomas's Union troops (which included the 15th Kentucky) nearly one-half mile to the Lafayette Road. The gallant attack by the right wing of the brigade captured a section of Bridges's Illinois Light Artillery, but the left wing, comprised of the 2nd and 9th Kentucky regiments along with three companies of Alabamians, all personally led by General Helm, became bogged down in a nightmarish slugfest before the enemy breastworks.[45]

General Helm assaulted the enemy position with his command three separate times trying to break through. His fearless blows were not enough to crack the Union lines. Exposed to enfilading fire, Helm's attack finally faltered. By the time the fighting ended the command suffered losses of nearly fifty-two percent. Helm was straddling his mount in front of the 2nd Kentucky when a rifle ball in his right side tumbled him from his horse. Carried from the battlefield, his last words uttered at a field hospital were "victory, victory." He was dead in a few hours. President Abraham Lincoln, when told of the death of General Helm, wept with grief. "I feel like David of old when he was told of the death of Absolom," Lincoln remarked to Illinois Senator David Davis. The Orphans were orphans again.[46]

The losses were horrendous. The 2nd Kentucky went into the fighting at Chickamauga with 282 men and left 146 on the field, including its colonel, James W. Hewitt, who was killed at the head of his regiment along with three of his company commanders. The 9th Kentucky lost 102 men out of 230 taken into battle, including the

General Joseph H. Lewis. A native of Barren County, Kentucky, and a prewar lawyer in Glasgow, Lewis served as commander of the Orphan Brigade after the death of Gen. Benjamin H. Helm at Chickamauga. After the war Lewis became Chief Justice of Kentucky. E. Porter Thompson, *The Orphan Brigade*

---

desperately wounded Col. John W. Caldwell. The 4th Kentucky not only lost heavily in officers and men, but suffered the final loss of its brave colonel, Joseph P. Nuckols, to a disabling wound. He had been wounded at the head of his fine regiment twice before, at Shiloh and Murfreesboro.[47]

The death of Ben Helm thrust Gen. Joseph H. Lewis into command of the brigade once again—its sixth commander since the war began. From the shallow victory of the Army of Tennessee at Chickamauga, Lewis marched his Orphan Brigade to heights overlooking Chattanooga. There, on Missionary Ridge, the Orphans received into their brigade the 5th Kentucky Infantry, and also bid farewell to the hard-fighting 41st Alabama. On a cold November 25, 1863, the Orphans were forced to abandon Missionary Ridge in the face of tenacious assaults by the Army of the Cumberland and its new commander, Gen. Ulysses S. Grant. Lost at Chattanooga were the favored guns of Captain Cobb's Kentucky Battery, two of them adoringly nicknamed by the Orphans for the wives of their favored commanders: "Lady Breckinridge" and "Lady Buckner."[48]

From Dalton, Georgia, to Jonesboro and the bitter evacuation of Atlanta in the face of Gen. William T. Sherman's three well-fed and well-equipped armies, the Orphans earned a place for themselves in the annals of war that beggars description. From May through September 1864, the Orphans suffered unparalleled losses. Some 1,512 Orphans were present for duty in May 1864 at Dalton, Georgia; only 513 reported present for duty on September 6. By that date, the entire 2nd Kentucky numbered only 69 officers and men; the 6th Kentucky only 74; the 4th Kentucky, 156. Only three years before those regiments counted almost 600 officers and men each. The entire brigade—five Kentucky infantry regiments—numbered only enough to form a battalion on September 6, 1864.[49]

In the 120 days from Dalton through the final hours before Atlanta, the Orphans suffered the almost unbelievable losses of 123 percent. During this period the Orphan Brigade recorded 1,860 cases of death and wounds—23 percent more than there were men in those five peerless regiments. How do we account for such numbers? Men were wounded, returned to the brigade, and wounded again (and again) or killed. Less than fifty men were reported to have passed through the campaign without a wound. The rolls record the desertion of only ten men during this 120-day campaign. The Battles of Dalton, Resaca, Pine Mountain, Kennesaw Mountain, Intrenchment Creek, and Jonesboro are written in red with Kentucky blood.[50]

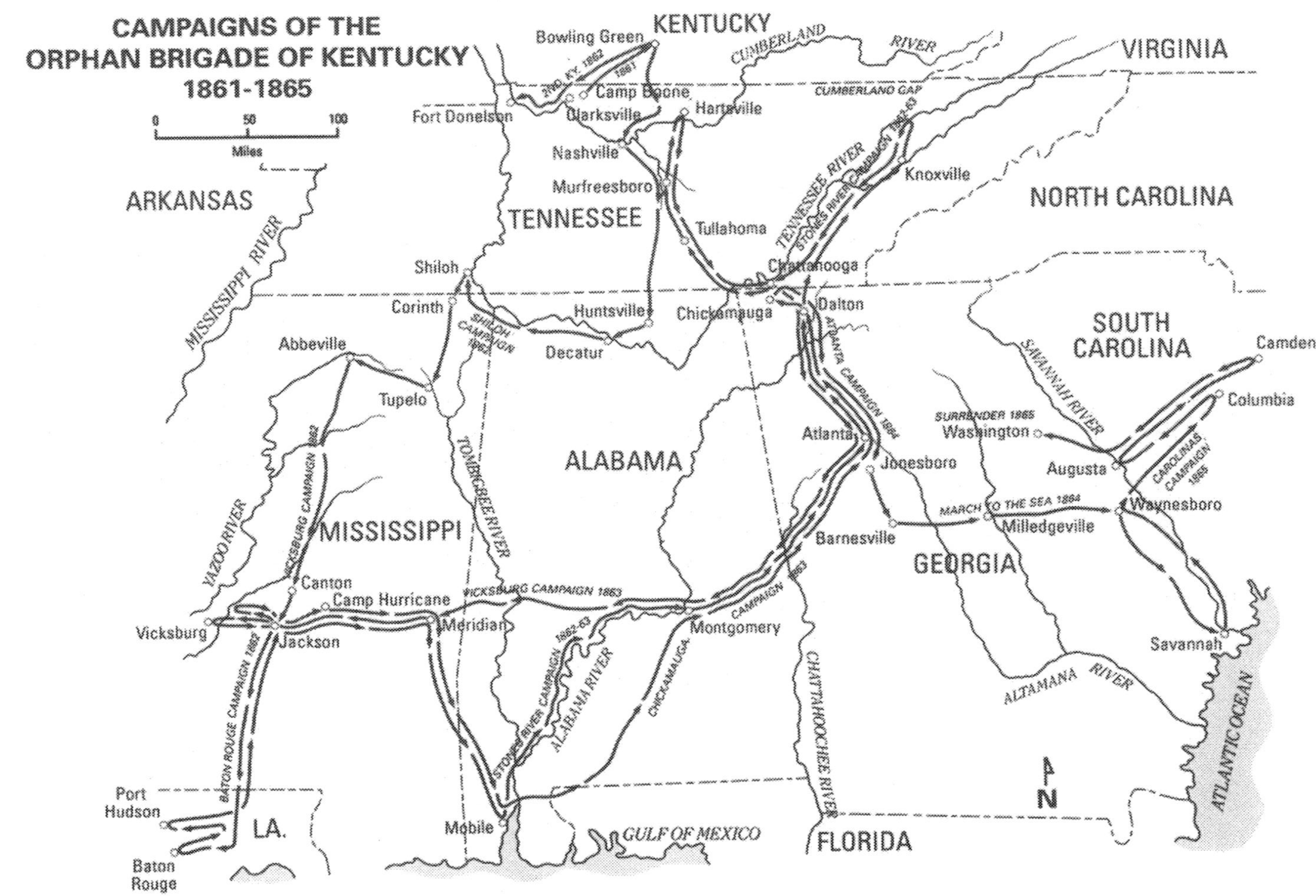
CAMPAIGNS OF THE
ORPHAN BRIGADE OF KENTUCKY
1861-1865
0
50
100
Miles
ARKANSAS
MISSISSIPPI RIVER
KENTUCKY
Bowling Green
2ND. KY. 1862
1861
Camp Boone
Fort Donelson
Clarksville
Hartsville
CUMBERLAND
RIVER
CUMBERLAND GAP
VIRGINIA
Nashville
Murfreesboro
TENNESSEE
Tullahoma
TENNESSEE RIVER
STONES RIVER CAMPAIGN 1862-63
Knoxville
NORTH CAROLINA
Shiloh
Corinth
SHILOH CAMPAIGN 1862
Huntsville
Decatur
Chickamauga
Chattanooga
Dalton
ATLANTA CAMPAIGN 1864
SOUTH CAROLINA
Camden
Columbia
SAVANNAH RIVER
Abbeville
Tupelo
VICKSBURG CAMPAIGN 1862
ALABAMA
Atlanta
SURRENDER 1865
Washington
Augusta
Jonesboro
CAROLINAS CAMPAIGN 1865
YAZOO RIVER
MISSISSIPPI
TOMBIGBEE RIVER
MARCH TO THE SEA 1864
Milledgeville
Waynesboro
Barnesville
GEORGIA
Canton
Camp Hurricane
VICKSBURG CAMPAIGN 1863
Vicksburg
Jackson
Meridian
Montgomery
CAMPAIGN 1863
Savannah
ALABAMA RIVER
CHICKAMAUGA
ALTAMANA
RIVER
BATON ROUGE CAMPAIGN 1862
CHATTAHOOCHEE RIVER
ATLANTIC OCEAN
N
Port Hudson
LA.
Baton Rouge
Mobile
GULF OF MEXICO
FLORIDA

"A search into the history of warlike exploits," wrote historian Nathaniel S. Shaler,

> has failed to show me any endurance to the worst trials of war surpassing this. The men of this campaign were at each stage of their retreat going farther from their firesides. It is easy for men to bear great trials under circumstances of victory. Soldiers of ordinary goodness will stand several defeats; but to endure the despair which such adverse conditions bring for a hundred days demands a moral and physical patience which, so far as I have learned, has never been excelled in any other army.[51]

In early 1862, the Orphan Brigade numbered nearly 4,000 officers and men. By the fall of 1864 the brigade could count barely 500, many of them convalescents and new recruits. With the war winding down, the Kentuckians were mounted and fought General Sherman's advance into the Carolinas, only to be forced to surrender in early May 1865 at Washington, Georgia.[52]

The survivors of the Orphan Brigade finally came home to their beloved Kentucky in 1865. Many were disabled by wounds and exposure. Most of them were penniless. Some managed to find meaningful work. Others were wholly unable to care for themselves and sank into poverty. "Soldiers' homes," like the one at Pee Wee Valley, Kentucky, sheltered some of the once-sturdy Orphans.

Many of the former brigade's officers and enlisted men were under indictment for treason when they returned home from the war. It was not until December 1865 that the state legislature removed that onerous impediment. With that act, the veterans of the Orphan Brigade quickly moved into the ranks of business, the professions, and state government. Indeed, in the years after the war Orphan Brigade veterans dominated Kentucky politics, a circumstance that gave birth to the old saying in Kentucky that "the State never seceded until the war was over." Simon Bolivar Buckner became governor in 1887. Joseph "Old Joe" Lewis was elected to the state legislature, and then served three terms in Congress. In 1880, he became a member of the Kentucky Court of Appeals and, in 1881, Chief Justice of Kentucky, taking the place of the recently deceased former Orphan, Col. Martin Cofer. Philip Lightfoot Lee became the Commonwealth's Attorney for Jefferson County, Kentucky.

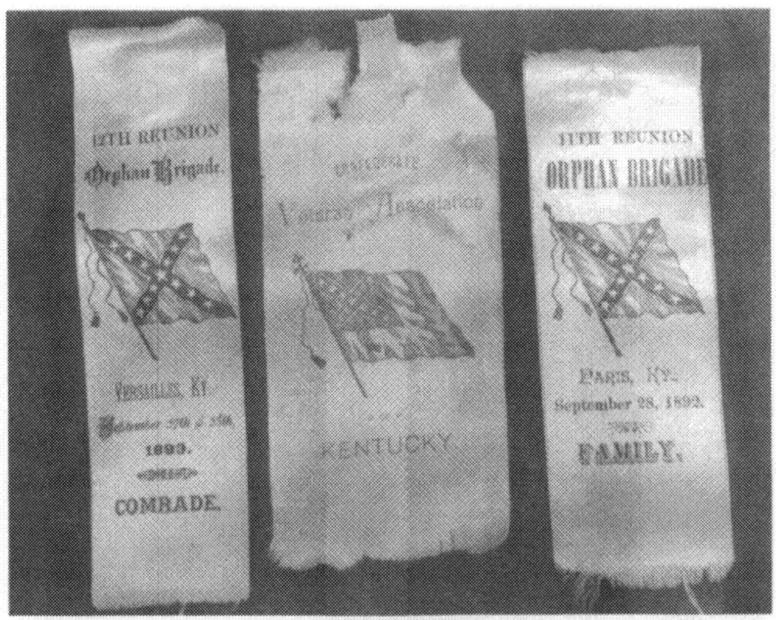

Ribbons worn by the veterans of the Orphan Brigade and their families at the 11th reunion of the brigade held at Paris, Kentucky (September 28, 1892), and the 12th reunion at Versailles, Kentucky (September 27 and 28, 1893). *Editor's Collection*

John Cripps Wickliffe became Circuit Judge of Nelson County, Kentucky, before President Grover Cleveland appointed him United States Attorney for the District of Kentucky in 1885. The twice wounded John W. Caldwell also became a circuit judge in his home county of Logan, and then was elected to Congress.[53]

The Orphan Brigade veterans, to the last, formed a close fraternity. In 1882 they began holding annual reunions. The first was at the Blue Lick Springs Hotel in Robertson County. That was followed by reunions in Lexington in 1883, Elizabethtown in 1884, Glasgow in 1885, Cynthiana in 1886, Bardstown in 1887, Frankfort in 1888, Louisville in 1889, Lawrenceburg in 1890, Owensboro in 1891, Paris in 1892, Versailles in 1893, Russellville in 1894, Bowling Green in 1895 and finally Nashville, Tennessee in 1896.[54]

In the end, the Orphans left behind a magnificent legacy, one never to be repeated in Kentucky. They went to war to fight for what they

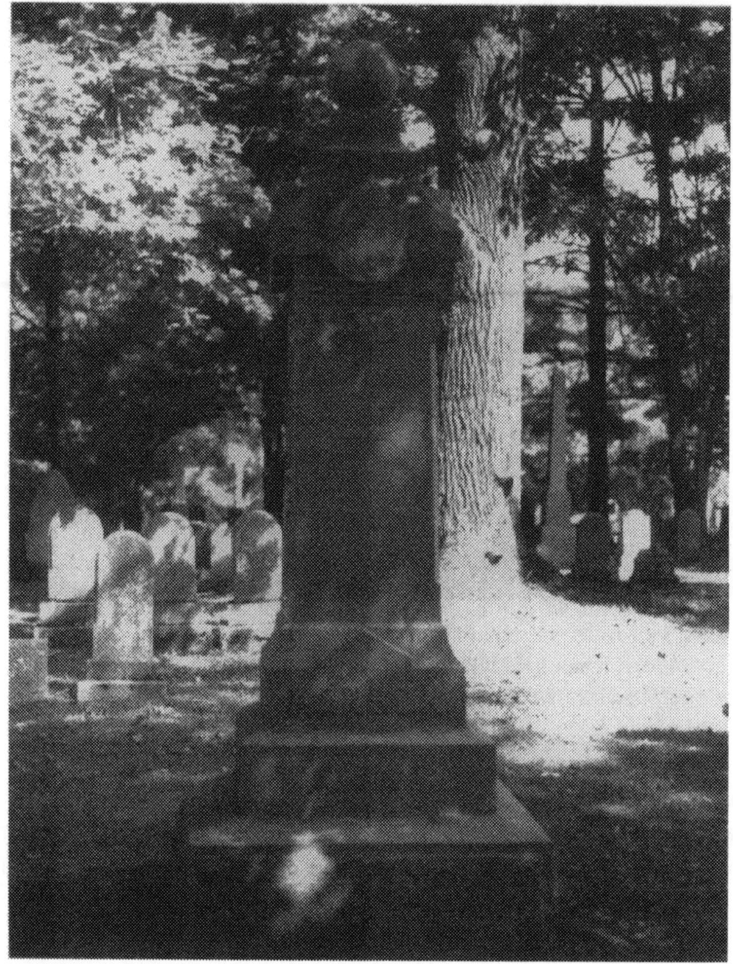

Monument to Gen. Roger Weightman Hanson and his wife, Virginia Hanson, known as "The Mother of the Orphan Brigade," erected by the veterans of the Orphan Brigade in the Lexington Cemetery, Lexington, Kentucky. *Editor's Collection*

---

believed was principle. In doing so, they gave up everything. They lost more commanders and suffered more casualties than any comparable command. And though they believed they fought "for" their beloved Kentucky, their state not only did not support them, but aligned itself with their enemy. In the end they were defeated in war, but not in heart.

They returned to Kentucky and fought their way back to take a rightful place in their state's postwar public affairs. In every way those old Orphans became the idols of Kentuckians.

The Orphans represent the conquest of courage over timidity and sacrifice for the sake of a principle. The cry of General Breckinridge, "My poor Orphans!" "My poor Orphans!" along the cold, wintery fields near Murfreesboro was not in vain. The Orphans' memory lives on. As the Orphans' poet, a Union soldier, wrote:

In the earth that springs where the heroes sleep,
And in love new born where the stricken weep.
That legion hath marched past the setting sun;
Beaten? Nay, victors; the realms they have won
Are the hearts of men who forever shall hear
The throb of their far-off drums.[55]

* * *

The Orphan Brigade

SHILOH
April 6-7, 1862

First Brigade, Breckinridge's Reserve Corps
Col. Robert P. Trabue

4th Alabama Battalion
Maj. J. M. Clifton

Crews' Tennessee Battalion
Lt. Col. J. M. Crews

31st Alabama
Lt. Col. Galbraith

3rd Kentucky
Lt. Col. Benjamin Anderson (w)

4th Kentucky
Lt. Col. A.R. Hynes (w)

6th Kentucky

Col. Joseph H. Lewis

5th or 9th Kentucky
Col. Thomas H. Hunt

Cobb's Kentucky Battery
Capt. Robert Cobb

Byrne's Kentucky Battery
Capt. Edward P. Byrne

Morgan's Cavalry Squadron
Capt. John Hunt Morgan

STONE'S RIVER
December 31, 1862 and January 2, 1863

Fourth Brigade, First Division (Breckinridge's), Hardee's Corps
Brig. Gen. Roger W. Hanson (k)
Col. Robert P. Trabue

41st Alabama
Col. H. Talbird
Lt. Col. M.L. Stansel (w)

2nd Kentucky
Maj. James W. Hewitt (w),
Capt. James W. Moss

4th Kentucky
Col. Robert P. Trabue,
Capt. T. W. Thompson

6th Kentucky
Col. Joseph H. Lewis

5th or 9th Kentucky
Col. Thomas H. Hunt

Cobb's Kentucky Battery
Capt. Robert Cobb

CHICKAMAUGA

September 19-20, 1863

Helm's Brigade, Breckinridge's Division, Hill's Corps
Brig. Gen. Benjamin Hardin Helm (mw), Col. Joseph H. Lewis

41st Alabama
Col. M.L. Stansel

2nd Kentucky
Col. J.W. Hewitt (k)
Lt. Col. James W. Moss
4th Kentucky
Col. Joseph P. Nuckols, Jr. (w)

6th Kentucky
Col. Joseph H. Lewis
Lt. Col. Martin H. Cofer

5th or 9th Kentucky
Col. J. W. Caldwell (w)
Lt. Col. J. C. Wickliffe

CHATTANOOGA to ATLANTA

November 25, 1863 to September 6, 1864

Lewis's Brigade, Breckinridge's Division
Brig. Gen. Joseph H. Lewis

2nd Kentucky
Col. James W. Moss
Lt. Col. Philip L. Lee
Capt. Joel Higgins

4th Kentucky
Lt. Col. T. W. Thompson

5th Kentucky
Lt. Col. H. Hawkins

6th Kentucky
Maj. G. W. Moxson
Col. Martin H. Cofer, Capt. Richard P. Finn

9th Kentucky
Col. J. W. Caldwell

John Hunt Morgan's Dismounted Men

NOTES

1. Ed Porter Thompson, *History of the Orphan Brigade* (Louisville, Ky., 1898), 21.

2. *Ibid.*, 24.

3. Commonwealth of Kentucky, *Report of the Adjutant General of the State of Kentucky, Confederate Kentucky Volunteers War, 1861-1865*, 2 vols. (Frankfort, Ky., 1915), 1:36-331, 410-462, 470-479.

4. Thompson, *History of the Orphan Brigade*, 24.

5. *Ibid.*, 29.

6. *Ibid.*, 24.

7. Glenn Tucker, *Chickamauga: Bloody Battle in the West* (Indianapolis, Ind., 1961), 238; Thomas D. Clark, *A History of Kentucky* (Lexington, Ky., 1960), 60-76.

8. Clark, *A History of Kentucky*, 104-109; Thompson, *History of the Orphan Brigade*, 32-33, 34-35.

9. U.S. Civil War Centennial Comm'n., *The United States on the Eve of the Civil War* (Washington, D.C., 1961), 61-73.

10. Thompson, *History of the Orphan Brigade*, 364, 381; Clark, *A History of Kentucky*, 195 (Robert Wickliffe was the largest slaveowner in Fayette County); R. Gerald McMurtry, *Ben Hardin Helm, "Rebel" Brother-in-Law of Abraham Lincoln, With a Biographical Sketch of His Wife and an Account of the Todd Family* (Chicago, Ill., 1943), 1-19 (Robert Todd owned forty slaves).

11. Clark, *A History of Kentucky*, 191-193, 201-211; Robert V. Remini, *Henry Clay: Statesman for the Union* (New York, N.Y., 1991), 26-27, 439-440, 483ff, 507-509, 525-526, 617-619, 693-694, 740ff (Clay abhorred slavery, but he was a slaveowner); Albert D. Kirwan, *John J. Crittenden: The Struggle for the Union* (Lexington, Ky., 1962), 344-347 (Crittenden abhorred slavery, but owned nine slaves); William C. Davis, *Breckinridge: Statesman, Soldier, Symbol* (Baton Rouge, La., 1974), 46-47, 102-103, 238-239 (Breckinridge argued a most vigorous state's rights position on emancipation).

12. Thompson, *History of the Orphan Brigade*, 30-39.

13. Clark, *History of Kentucky*, 155-172.

14. Charles P. Roland, *The Confederacy* (Chicago, Ill., 1960), 31-33; Clement Eaton, *A History of the Southern Confederacy* (New York, N.Y., 1954), 27-29; Thompson, *History of the Orphan Brigade*, 41-42.

15. R. M. Kelly, "Holding Kentucky for the Union," Robert Underwood Johnson and Clarence Clough Buel, eds., *Battles and Leaders of the Civil War*, 4 vols. (New York, N.Y., 1888; reprint ed., New York, N.Y., 1956), 1:373-378; Thompson, *History of the Orphan Brigade*, 43-46; Commonwealth of Kentucky, *Report of the Adjutant General, Confederate Kentucky Volunteers*, 1:36-193, 286-331, 410-459, 462-463, 470-481.

16. Commonwealth of Kentucky, *Report of the Adjutant General, Confederate Kentucky Volunteers*, 1:84, 142-143, 192, 280-287, 330-331, 458-459, 462-463, 476-479; Thompson, *History of the Orphan Brigade*, 44-57. Colonel Hunt's 9th

Kentucky Infantry was actually organized as the 5th Kentucky, but due to a bureaucratic mishap, another regiment being raised in Prestonsburg, Kentucky was also named the 5th Kentucky. Consequently, the 9th Kentucky fought through the first two years of the war as the "5th Kentucky" or the "5th or 9th Kentucky." When the officially-designated 5th Kentucky joined the Orphan Brigade in November, 1863, Col. Hunt's 5th Kentucky changed its designation to the 9th Kentucky. For reasons of clarity and simplicity, Hunt's regiment is referred to throughout this manuscript as the 9th Kentucky.

17. Kelly, "Holding Kentucky for the Union," 373-381; Thomas Speed, *The Union Cause in Kentucky* (New York, N.Y., 1907), 40-56, 122-139, 306-345.

18. William Preston to Margaret Preston, April 25, 1862; Indictment for Treason against William Preston, Fayette Circuit Court, Jan. 12, 1862, William Preston Papers, Special Collections, University of Kentucky Library (hereinafter cited Preston Papers (UK)).

19. Arndt M. Stickles, *Simon Bolivar Buckner: Borderland Knight* (Chapel Hill, 1940), 92-123; Davis, *Breckinridge*, 41-268, 293-362; McMurtry, *Ben Hardin Helm*, 1-24; Thompson, *History of the Orphan Brigade*, 353-375, 380-387.

20. Thompson, *History of the Orphan Brigade*, 353-375, 380-387.

21. *Ibid.*, 375-380, 387-395, 403-407.

22. *Ibid.*, 358.

23. Stanley F. Horn, *The Army of Tennessee* (Norman, Okla., 1959), 66-81; Thompson, *History of the Orphan Brigade*, 62-81.

24. Thompson, *History of the Orphan Brigade*, 62-81.

25. L. D. Young, *Reminiscences of a Soldier of the Orphan Brigade* (Louisville, Ky., not dated), 27-28.

26. Larry J. Daniel, *Shiloh: The Battle that Changed the Civil War* (New York, N.Y., 1997), 189.

27. *War of the Rebellion: A Compilation of the Official Records of the Union and Confederate Armies*, 128 vols. (Washington, D.C., 1880-1901) (hereinafter cited as *O.R.*) (all citations are to Series I), 10 (1):613-615; Trabue had previously detached the 3rd Kentucky and the 4th Alabama Battalion and Crews's Tennessee Battalion. Thompson, *History of the Orphan Brigade*, 516-522.

28. William C. Davis, *The Orphan Brigade: The Kentucky Confederates Who Couldn't Go Home* (New York, N.Y., 1980), 87-90; Davis, *Breckinridge*, 305-308.

29. *O.R.*, 10 (1):616-617; Davis, *Breckinridge*, 307.

30. *O.R.*, 10 (1):616-617, 621; Commonwealth of Kentucky, *Report of the Adjutant General, Confederate Kentucky Volunteers*, 1:143, 192; Thompson, *History of the Orphan Brigade*, 520; Ky. Div., U.C.V., *Constitution and Bylaws and Membership* (Lexington, Ky., 1895), 44; Wiley Sword, *Shiloh: Bloody April* (New York, N.Y., 1974), 399.

31. Davis, *The Orphan Brigade*, 95; William Preston to Margaret Preston, April 25, 1862, Preston Papers (UK); Commonwealth of Kentucky, *Report of the Adjutant*

General of the State of Kentucky (Union), 2 vols. (Frankfort, Ky., 1867), 1:48-49, Capt. John D. Wickliffe commanded Company A, 2nd Kentucky Cavalry.

32. *O.R.*, 10 (1):615-621; Daniel, *Shiloh*, 277. The remains of Maj. Thomas B. Monroe and Capt. Benjamin J. Monroe, who died on October 4, 1862, were eventually reinterred side-by-side in the family plot in the Frankfort, Kentucky cemetery.

33. *Ibid.*; Thompson, *History of the Orphan Brigade*, 90-91, 95; Daniel, *Shiloh*, 277.

34. Thompson, *History of the Orphan Brigade*, 108-134, 996; McMurtry, *Ben Hardin Helm*, 33-34. Lt. Todd's brother, Samuel Todd, had been killed at Shiloh while serving with the Louisiana Crescent Regiment. Andrew B. Booth, *Records of Louisiana Confederate Soldiers and Louisiana Confederate Commands*, 3 vols. (Spartanburg, S.C., 1984), 1:841.

35. Thompson, *History of the Orphan Brigade*, 145-153.

36. *Ibid.*, 168-175; Peter Cozzens, *No Better Place to Die: The Battle of Stones River* (Urbana, Ill., 1990), 177-178.

37. *O.R.*, 20 (1):785; Davis, *Breckinridge*, 340-342; Cozzens, *No Better Place to Die*, 179.

38. *O.R.*, 20 (1):833; A.D. Kirwan, ed., *Johnny Green of the Orphan Brigade: The Journal of a Confederate Soldier* (Lexington, Ky., 1956), 67; Thompson, *History of the Orphan Brigade*, 177-179; Cozzens, *No Better Place to Die*, 183-186.

39. *O.R.*, 20 (1):826-827, 833; Thompson, *History of the Orphan Brigade*, 179; David, *The Orphan Brigade*, 156; Cozzens, *No Better Place to Die*, 180-192; Young, *Reminiscences of a Soldier of the Orphan Brigade*, 49-51.

40. *O.R.*, 20 (1):827, 833; Davis, *The Orphan Brigade*, 157; Young, *Reminiscences of a Soldier in the Orphan Brigade*, 54-57; Cozzens, *No Better Place to Die*, 186.

41. Gervis D. Grainger, *Four Years With the Boys in Gray* (Franklin, Ky., 1902), 14-15; Thompson, *History of the Orphan Brigade*, 196.

42. *O.R.*, 20 (1):827-829; Thompson, *History of the Orphan Brigade*, 182; Davis, *The Orphan Brigade*, 159-160; Davis, *Breckinridge*, 347.

43. Young, *Reminiscences of a Soldier in the Orphan Brigade*, 51-59.

44. Thompson, *History of the Orphan Brigade*, 204-209.

45. *O.R.*, 30 (2):203-205, 207-216; William C. Davis, *Diary of a Confederate Soldier: John S. Jackman of the Orphan Brigade* (Columbia, S.C., 1990), 87-89; Peter Cozzens, *This Terrible Sound: The Battle of Chickamauga* (Urbana, Ill., 1992), 320-325; Tucker, *Chickamauga*, 238-240.

46. *O.R.*, 30 (2):207-216; Cozzens, *This Terrible Sound*, 323-324; Tucker, *Chickamauga*, 238-240; McMurtry, *Ben Hardin Helm*, 49; Davis, *The Orphan Brigade*, 182-191.

47. *O.R.*, 30 (2):205-206, 208-210, 214, 216.

48. Thompson, *History of the Orphan Brigade*, 229-231.

49. Nathaniel S. Shaler, "Nature and Man in America, Third Paper," *Scribner's Magazine*, 8 (November, 1890), 654; Davis, *The Orphan Brigade*, 236; *O.R.*, 38 (1):171, 645, 655, 674, 38 (3):696.

50. *Ibid.*

51. Shaler, "Nature and Man in America," 654.

52. Thompson, *History of the Orphan Brigade*, 280-286.

53. *Ibid.*, 357, 395, 428, 438, 450; Davis, *The Orphan Brigade*, 261-263.

54. Thompson, *History of the Orphan Brigade*, 340-350.

55. Young, *Reminiscences of a Soldier of the Orphan Brigade*, 4. The verse is from the poem, "The Orphan Brigade," by Nathaniel S. Shaler.

The Contributors

John Y. Simon, one of the nation's leading Civil War historians, is the editor of the more than twenty-volume *Papers of Ulysses S. Grant* at Southern Illinois University, Carbondale, Illinois, and the author of numerous scholarly articles and book reviews on the Civil War.

Charles P. Roland is the emeritus professor of history at the University of Kentucky, Lexington, Kentucky. He is the author of a history of the Civil War entitled *An American Iliad: The Story of the Civil War*, the highly-acclaimed *Albert Sidney Johnston: Soldier of Three Republics*, and *Reflections on Lee*. He is a member of the Perryville Battlefield Commission.

Ron Nicholas is a businessman in Middleboro, Kentucky. He has served as the Director and Chief of Interpretation of the Mill Springs Battlefield for the Mill Springs Battlefield Association.

Lowell H. Harrison is the emeritus professor of history at Western Kentucky University, Bowling Green, Kentucky. He is the author of numerous books on Kentucky history, including the *Civil War in Kentucky*, the standard text on the subject. He is currently working on a history of the establishment of the Confederate Government in Kentucky. Lowell served as a member of the Perryville Battlefield Commission.

Dean Warren Lambert is a professor of history at Berea College, Berea, Kentucky. He is the author of a long-awaited book on the Battle of Richmond, Kentucky, entitled *When the Ripe Pears Fell: The Battle of Richmond, Kentucky*.

Kenneth Noe is professor of history at the State University of West Georgia, Carrollton, Georgia. He is the author of *Southwest Virginia's Railroad: Modernization and the Sectional Crisis*, and is the editor of *A Southern Boy in Blue: The Memoir of Marcus Woodcock, 9th Kentucky Infantry, U.S.A.* Ken is completing a new book on the Battle of Perryville.

Wiley Sword is a businessman in Bloomfield Hills, Michigan. He is the author of many best-selling books on the Western Theater of the Civil War, including *Shiloh: Bloody April*, *Embrace an Angry Wind*, and *Mountains Touched With Fire*.

James A. Ramage is Regents Professor of History at Northern Kentucky University, Highland Heights, Kentucky. He is the author of *Rebel Raider: The Life of General John Hunt Morgan*. His new book, *The Gray Ghost*, a biography of Col. John Singleton Mosby, was released in the fall of 1999.

Kent Masterson Brown is a lawyer and historian who lives in Lexington, Kentucky. He was the creator and first editor of *The Civil War: The Magazine of the Civil War Society*, and is the author of *Cushing of Gettysburg: The Story of a Union Artillery Commander*, as well as numerous scholarly articles and book reviews on the Civil War. Kent was Chairman of the Perryville Battlefield Commission and Chairman of the Gettysburg National Military Park Advisory Commission. He is completing a new book on Lee's retreat from Gettysburg.

Index

Abbott, Maj. Augustus H., 157, 168
Adams, Gen. Daniel W., 192, 212, *Adams's Brigade*, 192, 194, 197-198, 200
Alabama & Florida Railroad, 142
Alabama Troops: *1st Cavalry*, 213, *3rd Cavalry*, 213, *4th Infantry Battalion*, 271, 299, *16th Infantry*, 58, 68, 71, 75, 213, *28th Infantry*, 161, 169, *31st Infantry*, 271, 282, 299, *33rd Infantry*, 213, *41st Infantry*, 271, 287, 292, 294, 300-301, *45th Infantry*, 212
Alexander, Col. John W. S., 209
Allen, Maj. A.C., 211
Allen, Col. Thomas G., 205
Allen, Col. William W., 213
Alston, Col. Robert A., 97, 268
American Colonization Society, 4
Anderson, Col. Benjamin, 276, 284, 299
Anderson, Gen. James P., 183, 194, 200, 212
Anderson, Lt. Col. Nicholas L., 206
Anderson, Gen Robert A., 6, 31, 48, *photo*, 7
Antietam, Maryland, battle of, 66, 177
Arkansas Troops: *1st Dismounted Rifes*, 133, *1st Infantry*, 212, *2nd Dismounted Rifes*, 133, *2nd Infantry*, 212, *4th Infantry Battalion*, 133, *5th Infantry*, 181, 212, *6th Infantry*, 212, *7th Infantry*, 180-181, 212, *8th Infantry*, 213, *13th Infantry*, 120, 213, *13th and 15th Consolidated Infantry*, 133, *15th Infantry*, 120, 213, 225, 227, *30th Infantry*, 133, *31st Sharpshooters*, 132, *Humphrey's Battery*, 132
Armies: *Army of Kentucky*, 109, 125, 143; *Army of Tennessee*, 234-236, 274, 287, 290, 294; *Army of the Cumberland*, 72, 262-263, 287, 290; *Army of the Mississippi* (CSA), 108, 142-143, 146, 149, 160-161, 163, 179, 202, 211; *Army of the Mississippi* (USA), iv, 93; *Army of the Ohio*, iv, 18, 90, 105, 139, 142-143, 146, 250, 161, 163, 168, 176, 179, 204, 249, 280, 283; *Army of the Tennessee*, 280
Atlanta & West Point Railroad, 142
Atlanta Commonwealth, 243
Austin, Maj. J.E., 212
Baird, Capt. John F., 131
Baker, Gen. Edward D., 1
Baker, James, 69
Ball's Bluff, Virginia, battle of, 1
Banks, Lt. G.T., 148
Barbourville, Kentucky, 69, 94, 106, 108, 112, 114-115
Bardstown, Kentucky, 95, 167, 259
Barnes, Col. Sidney M., 207
Barnett, Capt. Charles M., 210
Barr, Jr., Maj. James, 169
Barret, Capt. Overton W., 212
Barrett, Capt. Wallace W., 210
Bartleson, Col. Frederick A., 207
Battle, Col. Joel A., 59, 75
Beatty, Col. John, 192, 205-206
Beauregard, Gen. Pierre G.T., 19, 37, 40-41, 43, 89, 90, 142, 252, *photo*, 38
Bee, Gen. Barnard E., 254
Beech Grove, Kentucky, vi, 53-54, 57-58, 68-69, 71
Bell, John, 4
Belmont, Missouri, 10, 12, 16-17, 34
Benjamin, Judah P., 87-88
Bennett, Col. James, 266
Bennett, Lt. Col. John E., 209
Big Hill, Kentucky, 108, 111-115, 117
Binford, Lt. James R., 59-60, 64
Bingham, Lt. Col. George B., 205
Bishop, Capt. Judson, 56, 68
Bishop, Col. W. H., 154, 169
Blackburn, Dr. Luke P., 85
Blake, Col John W., 208
Blake, Col. William H., 206
Bledsoe, Capt. W.S., 75
Board, Col. Buckner, 205
Bottom, Henry P., 176, *photo*, v, *photo of house*, 193
Bowles, Col., 268
Bowling Green, Kentucky, 1, 23, 27, 30-31, 37, 39, 84, 86-87, 89, 93-94, 138, 143, 145, 148, 247, 280
Boyle, Gen. Jeremiah T., 54, 108, 145, 171, 247, 249, 252
Boyle, Lt. Col. John, 210
Bracht, Maj. Frederick G., 132
Bradford, Sgt. Samuel, 149
Bradley, Capt. Cullen, 208
Bragg, Gen. Braxton, iv, v, 31, 43, 103, 134, 142-143, 211, 285, 287, 290-291, *Cleburne, 234, corruption of plans*, 185, *council of war at Perryville*, 202, *criticized for*

Perryville, 203, *failed invasion,* 255, *march into Middle Tennessee,* 176, *move against Nashville, plan,* 93, *Munfordville, battle of,* 145-146, 151, 160, 163-167, *not strong enough to challange Buell,* 94-96, *offensive fighting concepts,* 236, *Perryville, battle of,* 175-181, 189, 200-204, 230, *Richmond, battle of,* 104-106, 108, 130, *retreat from Perryville,* 202, *Shiloh,* 227, *Stone's River,* 258, *photo,* 141
Bramblett, Capt. William P., 290
Branner, Lt. Col. B. M., 75
Bratton, Lt. Col. H. L. W., 211
Breckinridge, Gen. John C., i, 4, 80, 82-83, 85, 90-91, 94, 275, 279-282, 285, 287, 289-290, 299-301, *photo,* 278
Breckinridge, Col. William C.P., 257, 262, 266
Bridges's (Illinois) Light Artillery, 292
Brooks, Lt. Col. Lewis, 205
Brown, Gen. John C., 185, 197, 212
Brown, Kent Masterson, 308, *A Tribute to the Orphan Brigade of Kentucky,* 271, *Munfordville: The Campaign and Battle Along Kentucky's Strategic Axis, 137*
Browning, Orville, 79
Buchanan, James, 4, 279, 286
Buckner Kentucky Guards, 169
Buckner, Gen. Simon B., i, 6, 8, 27, 39-40, 82, 86, 94, 140, 161, 163-167, 170, 183, 192, 212, 276, 279, 296, *photo,* 162
Buell, Gen. Don C., iv, 18, 31, 39, 43, 48, 53, 94-95, 105, 108, 112, 114, 130, 137, 139, 142, 160-161, 163, 166-167, 176, 179-181, 198, 203-204, 247, 283, *photo,* 177
Buell, Col. George P., 207
Buford, Lt. Col. John W., ii, 211
Bullard, Lt. Col. James G., 155, 169
Bullock, Maj. Robert S., 257, 259, 261
Bunn, Lt. Col. Henry C., 133
Burke, Lt. Col. Joseph W., 205
Burkes, Col. J.C., 132
Burnam, John Q., 85
Burnett, Henry C., 83, 85
Burnett, Theodore L., 85
Burnside, Gen. Ambrose E., 249, 251
Bush, Capt. Asahel K., 196, 205
Byrd, Col. Robert K., 74
Byrne's (Kentucky) Battery, 271-272, 276, 280, 300
Byrne, Capt. Edward P., 267, 272, 276
Caldwell, Col. John W., 276, 284, 293, 297, 301
Caldwell, Col. William W., 209, 213
Calhoun, John C., 80
Calvert's (Arkansas) Battery, 213
Cameron, Simon, 48
Camp Andrew Johnson, 49
Camp Barnett, 276
Camp Boone, 80, 276
Camp Dick Robinson, vii, 50-51, 110, 277
Camp Nelson, vii, 251
Campbell, Lt. Col. Archibald P., 210
Canby, Lt. Samuel, 206
Carey, Lt. Col. O. H. P., 206
Carlile, Lt. Col. J. B., 207
Carlin, Col. William P., 200, 209
Carnes's (Tennessee) Battery, 196
Carnes, Capt. W.W., 211
Carpenter, Capt. Stephen J., 209
Carroll, Gen. William H., 58, 66, 72, 75, *Carroll's Brigade,* 68
Carter, Col. J.P.T., 74
Carter, Col. John C., 211
Carter, Gen. Samuel P., 74
Casey, Col. Thomas S., 206
Cassell, Maj., 268
Cave City Raid, 252, 254
Cave City, Kentucky, 138, 148-149, 151, 252
Central Alabama Railroad, 138
Chalmers, Gen. James R., 148-149, 151-155, 157, 159-161, 169, *photo,* 148
Chandler, Lt. Col. William P., 209
Chapin, Col. Alfred R., 204
Chaplin River, 185
Chapman, Col. Charles W., 208
Chattanooga, Tennessee, 93-94, 105, 254
Cheatham, Gen. Benjamin F., 183-187, 194, 204, 211, *photo,* 186, *Cheatham's Division,* 189, 197
Chenault, Col. D.W., 266
Chenoweth, Maj. Tom, 267
Chester, Col. John, 211
Chickamauga, battle of, 236, 291, 294, 301
Chiles, Lt. Col. John C., 111, 131
Choate, Lt. Col. William A., 208
Church, Capt. Josiah W., 209
Churchill, Gen. Thomas J., 105, 119, 132, *Churchill's Division,* 106, 114-116, 126
Cincinnati, Ohio, 112, 249-250, 254

Index

Cinninnati Commercial, 68
Clark, C. H., 187
Clark, Maj. J.W., 132
Clarksville & Louisville Railroad, 138
Clay's Ferry, 113
Clay, Cassius M., 85, 111-112
Clay, Henry, 4, 275
Cleburne, Gen. Patrick R., 105, 115, 117, 118-120, 130, 133, 135, 200, 213, 221, 223-225, 227, 229-239, *photo,* 222, *Cleburne's Brigade and Division,* 106, 114, 116-117, 122, 143, 197-198
Cleveland, Grover, 297
Clifton, Maj. J. M., 299
Cluke, Col. Leroy S., 257, 265, 267
Cobb's (KY) Battery, 271-272, 280, 294
Cobb, Capt. Robert H., 272, 276, 283, 300
Cochran, Lt. Col. Thomas B., 206
Cockerill, Capt Daniel T., 206
Cofer, Lt. Col. Martin, 284, 296, 301
Coleman, Kitty, 97
Columbia, Kentucky, 54
Columbus, Kentucky, ii, 1, 9-10, 12-17, 25, 30, 34, 41, 47, 79, 280
Committee of Sixty, 85
Conaway, Lt. George W., 161, 168
Confederate Troops (Military Units): 3rd Infantry, 213, *5th Infantry,* 213, *6th Cavalry,* 213, 267
Confiscation Act, 16
Connecticut Troops: *11th Infantry,* 166
Connell, Col. John M., 53, 208
Connelly, Thomas, 177
Constitutional Union party, 4
Cooper, James L., 66
Cooper, Gen. Samuel, 95
Corbett, Lt. C. C., 256, 266
Corinth, Mississippi, iv, 19, 41, 93, 142-143, 247, 252, 254
Corps (USA), *XIV,* 292, *XXI,* 287
Cowan, Col. Andrew, 263
Cowen, Lt. Col. D. D. T., 210
Cox, Capt. Jerome B., 208
Crab Orchard, Kentucky, 53, 113
Cram, Lt. Col. George H., 207
Crawford, Col. Martin J., 213
Crawford, Frank, 251
Crew's (Tennessee) Battalion, 271, 299
Crittenden Compromise, 4
Crittenden, Gen. George B., i, ii, 34, 50, 54, 56, 58, 60, 63-64, 68-69, 71-72, 75, 89, *photo,* 55
Crittenden, John J., 4-5, 55, 275
Crittenden, Gen. Thomas L., i, 181, 198, 202, 206, 287, 289, *photo,* 182
Croxton, Col. John T., 208
Cruft, Gen. Charles, 113, 117, 122, 124-125, 128, 131, 206, *Cruft's Brigade,* 115, 121
Cubberly, Maj. George, 153
Cumberland Gap, 25, 27-28, 36, 47-48, 93, 105-106, 111, 143
Cumberland River, ii, 1, 25, 36, 39-40, 54-57, 89, 112, 137-138, 145
Cumming, Kate, 254, 264
Cummings, Col. D. H., 59, 63, 75
Cummins, Lt. Col. John E., 207
Cynthiana, Kentucky, 112, 254
Dagenfield, Maj. Chriss M., 207
Danville, Kentucky, 51, 111, 179, 203
Darden, Capt. P., 213
Davis, Garrett, 6
Davis, Jefferson, i, 1, 106, 155, *admission of Kentucky as a state,* 87, *concession to use slaves,* 239, *condemns Cleburne,* 235, *critical importance of Kentucky,* 47, *defense of Kentucky,* 236, *did not understand soldiers,* 237, *friend of A.S. Johnston,* 25, *funds to support Kentucky,* 88, *Johnston request for troops,* 34, *Johnston's concerns,* 31, *Kentucky neutrality,* 6, 85-86, *Kentucky plans,* 3, 23, *Kentucky policy,* 17, *reassurance from Magoffin,* 9, *response to Harris,*12, *Richard Hawes,* 93, 97, *started the war,*4, *urged to support Kentucky invasion,* 94, *victory message from,* 166, *photo,* 24
Davis, Gen. Jefferson C., 110, 176
de Arnaud, Charles, 13
Decatur, Alabama, 137
Departments: *Number Two*, 25, 265; *East Tennessee*, 93, 143; *Kentucky*, 145; *Ohio*, 48, 51, 109, 137
Desha, Maj. Benjamin, 284
Diamond, Maj. George, 268
District of Southeast Missouri, 13
Dixon, Senator Archibald, 5
Dixon, Lt. Joseph, 30
Dobson, Capt. George, 155
Doctor's Creek, 176, 189, 192, 225

Donelson, Gen. Daniel S., 185, 187, 189, 197, 211, *Donelson's Brigade,* 196
Donnell, Lt. Col. D. M., 211
Douglas's (Texas) Artillery, 117-118
Douglas, Capt. James P., 108, 133
Dowd, Col. William F., 212
Drury, Capt. Lucius H., 207
Duke, Gen. Basil, i, 167, 232, 243, 256-257, 259, 261-263, 265
Dumont, Gen. Ebenezer, 96, 252
Dunham, Lt. Col. Cyrus L., 151-152, 157, 160, 161, 164, 168
Earp, Col. C.R., 132
East Tennessee & Georgia Railroad, 138
East Tennessee & Virginia Railroad, 138
Ector, Col. Matthew D., 132
Edgefield, Tennessee, 39
Edison, Thomas, 250
Elizabethtown, Kentucky, 138, 255-256, 258-259, 264
Ellsworth, George A., 250-252
Emerson, Col. Frank, 146, 153, 164, 168
Enyart, Lt. Col. David A., 206
Este, Lt. Col. George P., 208
Estep, Lt. George, 207
Featherston, Col. L., 212
Ferguson, Col. John, 207
Field, Charles W., i
Field, Col. H. R., 211
Finn, Capt. Richard P., 301
Fisk, Col. S. W., 212
Fitzgerald, Col. Edward, 133
Florida Troops: *1st Cavalry,* 132, *1st Infantry,* 212, *3rd Infantry,* 212, *Marion Light Artillery,* 108, 133
Flanagin, Col. Harris, 133
Floyd, John B., 39-40
Foote, Andrew H., Flag Officer, 36, 40
Footman, Capt., 132
Fort Craig, vi
Fort Donelson, Tennessee, ii, 1, 18-19, 28, 37, 39-41, 72, 89, 139, 163, 280, 285
Fort Heiman, 36
Fort Henry, Tennessee, ii, 1, 19, 28, 30, 36-37, 72, 89, 137, 139
Fort Sumter, 3, 5-6, 8, 276
Fort Warren Prison, 163, 285
Frankfort, Kentucky, 86, 95-96, 179, 252, 254, 258
Franklin, Kentucky, 138
Franklin, Tennessee, battle of, 237, 239
Frazer, Col. John W., 161, 169
Freedman's Bureau Act, 98
Fremont, Gen. John C., 10, 12-14, 16-17, 20
French, Sgt. William, 155
Frierson, Lt. Col. W., 211
Frizell, Col. Joseph W., 204
Fry, Gen. Speed S., i-ii, 60-62, 64, 74, 180, 208, 258, *photo,* 61
Fulton, Col. John S., 213
Fyffe, Col. James P., 207
Gainsboro, Tennessee, 71
Galbraith, Lt. Col., 299
Gallatin, Tennessee, 138, 251, 258-259
Gano, Maj. Richard M., 265
Garnett, Capt., 132, 169
Garrard, Col. Theophilis T., 131, 205
Garrity, Lt., 153-154, 169
Gay, Capt. Ebenezer, 210
George, Col. James, 208
Georgia Troops: *1st Cavalry,* 132, 169, *1st Infantry,* 108, *1st Partisan Rangers,* 265, *2nd Cavalry,* 213, *3rd Cavalry,* 213, *41st Infantry,* 211
Gibson, Col. R. L., 212
Gilbert, Gen. Charles C., 151, 164, 180-181, 194, 198, 200, 202, 208
Gillespie, Col. D. A., 212
Gilmer, Maj. Daniel H., 209
Gilmer, Jeremy, Col., 30
Giltner, Col. Henry L., 267
Glasgow, Kentucky, 94, 143, 146, 258, 279
Glass, Capt. William H., 254
Gober, Col. D. C., 212
Gooding, Col. Michael, 198, 202, 209
Gorman, Lt. Col. George W., 207
Grant, Gen. Ulysses S., ii, iv, 10, 14, 16, 19, 29, 39, 90, 138, 245, 259, 294, *assumes command at Cape Girardeau,* 13, *attack on Belmont,* 16-17, 34, *attacks Fort Donelson,* 40, *attacks Fort Henry,* 36, *Shiloh,* 41, 90, 281, *sieze Paducah,*25, *photo,* 11
Graves, Capt. Rice E., 271-272, 276, 280
Green River Bridge, 142-143, 145-148, 160, 166-167, 255
Green River, Kentucky, 89, 139-140, 142, 147, 154, 157, 161, 163, 166, 249
Greenville, Tennessee, 98
Greenwood, Capt. Charles, 74
Greusel, Col. Nicholas, 199, 210

Index

Grigsby, Col. Louis B., 208
Grigsby, Col. J. W., 266
Grose, Col. William, 206
Guthrie, James, 253
Hafendorfer, Kenneth, 198
Hagan, Col. James, 213
Hale, Lt. Luther F., 131
Hall, Col. Albert S., 205
Halleck, Gen. Henry W., 16, 19, 108, 137-138, 142, 247, *photo,* 17
Hambright, Col. Henry A., 205
Hamilton, Col. Orville S., 207
Hannibal (hospital ship), 90, 283
Hanson, Col. Charles S., 206, 288
Hanson, Gen. Roger W., 276, 279-281, 285, 287, 289, 300, *photo,* 288
Hardee, Gen. William J., 28, 37, 89, 161, 163, 179, 185, 189, 194, 197, 200, 212, 255, 282, 289, 300
Harker, Col. Charles G., 207
Harlan, Col. John M., 74, 259, 261-263, 258, 283
Harmon, Col. Oscar F., 210
Harper, Col. Robert W., 133
Harrington, Lt., 60
Harris, Isham, 8, 12, 27, 30, 36
Harris, Col. Leonard A., 189, 194, 197-198, 204
Harris, Capt. Samuel J., 187, 206
Harrison, Lowell H., 307
Harrodsburg, Kentucky, 179, 181, 202-203
Hascall, Gen. Milo S., 207
Hatch, George, 247
Hathaway, Col. Gilbert, 207
Hattaway, Herman, 179,
Hawes, Richard, 85, 90-91, 93-98, 179, *photo,* 92
Hawkins, Lt. Col. H., 301
Hawkins, Col. Joseph G., 207
Hawkins, Col. Pierce B., 207
Hayes, Lt. Col. William H., 208
Hayes, Rutherford B., 259
Hazen, Col. William B., 206
Heg, Col. Hans C., 209
Helm, Gen. Benjamin H., i, 274, 279, 285, 291-294, 301, *photo,* 291
Hescock, Capt. Henry, 194, 210
Heth, Gen. Henry, 106, 132
Hewitt, Col. James W., 292, 300-301
Higgins, Capt. Joel, 301
Hill, Col. Benjamin J., 106, 120, 122, 124, 133,
Hill's Brigade, 117-119, 121, 126
Hines, Col. Cyrus C., 208
Hobson, Col. Edward H., 258, 261-262
Hodgenville, Kentucky, 167
Holliday, Maj., 267
Hollinsworth, Lt. Col. E. W., 207
Hood, Gen. John B., i, 236
Hopkins, Maj. Enos, 205
Hoppe, Capt. Walter, 210
Horse Cave, 138, 151
Hoskins, Col. William A., 74, 208, 258
Hotchkiss, Capt. William A., 209
Houck, Col. Leonidas, 131
Huffman, Lt. Col. J. M., 257, 265, 267
Hughs, Col. John M., 213
Hughs, Lt. Col. T. R., 133
Humphrey's (Arkansas) Battery, 132
Humphrey, Col. George, 205
Humphreys's (Arkansas) Battery, 121
Humphreys, Capt. John T., 106, 132
Hunt, Col. A. A., 265
Hunt, Col. Thomas H., 276, 300, 302-303
Hunter, Col. Morton C., 208
Hunton, Lt. Col. K. A., 74
Hutchinson, Lt. Col. John B., 171, 257, 265
Hynes, Lt. Col. A. R., 299
Illinois Troops: *21st Infantry,* 209, *24th Infantry,* 205, *25th Infantry,* 209, *35th Infantry,* 209, *36th Infantry,* 209, 210, *38th Infantry,* 209, *44th Infantry,* 210, *59th Infantry,* 209, *73rd Infantry,* 210, *74th Infantry,* 209, *75th Infantry,* 209, *80th Infantry,* 205, *84th Infantry,* 206, *85th Infantry,* 210, *86th Infantry,* 210, *88th Infantry,* 210, *91st Infantry,* 255, *100th Infantry,* 207, *110th Infantry,* 206, *123rd Infantry,* 187, 205, *125th Infantry,* 210, *Bridges's Artillery,* 292
Indiana Troops: *4th Artillery,* 196, 205, *5th Artillery,* 189, 204, *7th Artillery,* 207, *8th Artillery,* 207, *9th Infantry,* 206, *10th Artillery,* 208, *10th Infantry,* 57, 59, 60, 64, 66, 74, 180, 208, *12th Infantry,* 109, 113, 122, 131, *13th Artillery,* 146, 168, *15th Infantry,* 147, 208, *16th Infantry,* 112-113, 119-121, 131, *17th Infantry,* 145-146, 168, 207, *19th Artillery,* 187, 206, *22nd Infantry,* 209, *31st Infantry,* 206, *32nd Infantry,* 140, *35th Infantry,* 207, *36th Infantry,* 206, *38th*

Infantry, 204, *40th Infantry,* 208, *42nd Infantry,* 205, *44th Infantry,* 207, *photo,* 18, *50th Infantry,* 151, 161, 168, *51st Infantry,* 207, *55th Infantry,* 112-113, 118-120, 131, *57th Infantry,* 208, *58th Infantry,* 207, *60th Infantry,* 161, 164, 168, *66th Infantry,* 109, 113, 122, 131, *67th Infantry,* 146, 157, 164, 168, *68th Infantry,* 161, 164, 168, *69th Infantry,* 111, 113, 118-121, 131, *71st Infantry,* 112-113, 118, 120-121, 126, 131, *73rd Infantry,* 207, *74th Infantry,* 146, 168, 208, *78th Infantry,* 151, 161, 169, *79th Infantry,* 207, *80th Infantry,* 205, *81st Infantry,* 209, *82nd Infantry,* 208, *86th Infantry,* 207, *87th Infantry,* 208, *88th Infantry,* 205, *89th Infantry,* 146-147, 153, 164, 168, *Indiana Legion Home Guards,* *249*

Innes, Col. William P., 208

Irons, Col. David D., 210

Jackson, Governor Claiborne F., 1

Jackson, Lt. Col. J. P., 206

Jackson, James S., 131, 134, 185, 187, 196, 205, 283, *photo,* 188

Jackson, Capt. Thomas K., 30

Jacob, Col. Richard T., 131

James, Lt. Col. Thomas C., 210

Jaquess, Col. James F., 210

Jessee, Lt. Col. George, 267

Johnson, Col. Adam R., 266

Johnson, Gen. Bushrod R., 192, 194, 197, 213, 225, *photo,* 224, *Johnson's Brigade,* 192, 194, 227, 232

Johnson, Gen. George W., 30, 80, 82-84, 86, 89-90, 93, 282-284, *photo,* 81

Johnson, Lt. Col. Robert A., 284

Johnson, Col. Tom, 267

Johnston, Gen. Albert S., i-ii, iv, 1, 19, 25, 27, 34, 82, 88, 90, 138-139, 163, *anticipated moves,* 36, *"arrogant display of power,"* 31, *bold strategy needed,* 8, *Bowling Green,* 28, *concerned about Zollicoffer,* 54, *death of,* 142, *defensive line,* 137, 140, *demonstrates strategic vision,* 41, *Fort Henry,* 37, *given task to defend Kentucky,* 47, *judgment of policy,* 33, *Kentucky border,* 280, *lack of manpower,* 32, *most serious mistake,* 39, *notified of success at Fort Donelson,* 40, *relied on Zollicoffer,* 48, *request for troops,* 34, *Shiloh,* 279, 283, *sooth relations with Kentucky,* 27, *status of Fort Henry and Donelson,* 30, *urged not to withdraw from Kentucky,* 37, *violated policy,* 32, *Zollicoffer's strategy,* 51, *photo,* iii, 265

Johnston, Col. J. Stoddard, 100, 183, 189, 202

Johnston, Gen. Joseph E., 236, 273, 290

Jones, Archer, 179

Jones, Col. James G., [illegible]05

Jones, Col. Thomas M[illegible] 185, 189, 212

Jones, Col. W. P., 211

Jones, Lt. Col. Frederick C., 206

Joseph, Lt. Col. Charles, 208

Judah, Gen. Henry, 25[illegible]

Kammerling, Maj. Gustav, 66, 74

Kansas Troops, *8th Infantry Battalion,* 209

Keeble, Lt. Col. R. H., 213

Keith, Lt. Col. Squire [illegible]., 209

Kell, Lt. Col. John, 20[illegible]

Kelly, Col. John H., 2[illegible]3

Kelsoe, Maj. George W., 211

Kenny Jr., Capt. Dennis, 74

Kentucky Brigade, 90, 271, 280

Kentucky Buckner Guards, 108

Kentucky General Assembly, 80, 243

Kentucky River, 111-112, 114-116, 128, 130

Kentucky Resolution of 1798, 80

Kentucky Resolution of 1799, 80

Kentucky State Guard[illegible] 163, 276

Kentucky Troops, *Confederate: 1st Cavalry,* 211, 213, *2nd Cavalry,* 132, 169, 254, 265-266, *2nd Infantry,* 271-272, 276, 280, 287, 290, 292, 294, 300-301, *2nd Mounted Rifles Battalion,* 26[illegible], *3rd Infantry,* 271-272, 276, 280, 282-285, 290, 299, *4th Cavalry,* 267, *4th Infantry,* 271-272, 276, 280, 282-284, 287, 289-[illegible]90, 292-294, 299-301, *5th Cavalry,* 266, *5th or 9th Infantry,* 300-301, *5th Infantry,* 271-272, 294, 303, *6th Cavalry,* 266, *6th Infantry,* 271-272, 276, 280, 282-284, [illegible]87, 292, 294, 299-301, *7th Cavalry,* 257, [illegible]65, 267, *7th Infantry,* 283, *8th Infantry,* 257, 265, 267, *9th Cavalry,* 266, *9th Infantry,* 271-272, 276, 280, 282, 284, 28[illegible], 292, 302-303, *10th Cavalry,* 267, *10th Mounted Rifles Battalion,* 267, *10th Partisan Rangers,* 266, *11th Cavalry,* 26[illegible]-267, *14th Cavalry,* 266-267, *Buckner Guards,* 132, 169,

Index

Byrne's Battery, 271, 282, 300, *Cobb's Battery*, 271, 280, 300, *Graves's Battery*, 271, 280

Kentucky Troops *(USA)*: *1st Artillery*, 196, 205, *1st Cavalry*, 57-60, 74, *1st Infantry*, 206, *2nd Cavalry*, 171, 205-206, 283, *2nd Infantry*, 206, *3rd Infantry*, 207, *4th Infantry*, 57, 60-64, 66, 74, 108, *6th Cavalry*, 131, *6th Infantry*, 113, 115, 206, *7th Cavalry*, 109, 111-112, 117, 131, 171, *7th Infantry*, 113, 115, 205, *8th Infantry*, 207, 289, *9th Cavalry*, 131, 210, *9th Infantry*, 207, 283, 289, *10th Infantry*, 74, 208, 258, *11th Infantry*, 207, 289, *12th Infantry*, 64, 66, 74, 208, *13th Infantry*, 207, *15th Infantry*, 192, 205, 292, *18th Infantry*, 111, 113, 122, 132, *19th Infantry*, 71, *20th Infantry*, 206, 288, *21st Infantry*, 207, 289, *23rd Infantry*, 206, 289, *24th Infantry*, 208, *26th Infantry*, 207, *27th Infantry*, 206, *28th Infantry*, 161, 168, *32nd Infantry*, 205, *33rd Infantry*, 146-147, 168, 171, *34th Infantry*, 168, 171

Kentucky, Morgan's First Raid, 247, 50-252, 254, 265

Kentucky, Morgan's Second Raid, 265

Kentucky, Morgan's Third Raid, 266

Kentucky, Morgan's Last Raid, 264

Kerr, Lt. Col. James B., 209

Ketchum's (Alabama) Battery, 149, 169

Key, John M., 170

King, Col. Edward A., 161, 164

Kingsbury, Col. Henry W., 166

Kingston, Kentucky, 111, 115-117, 130

Kirkpatrick, Capt., 268

Kise, Col. WIlliam C., 59, 74, 208

Knetler, Col. Frederick, 207

Knight, Maj. John, 211

Know-Nothing Party, 258

Knoxville, Tennessee, 25, 48, 93, 105, 143

Konkle, Capt. Andrew, 161, 164, 169

Korff, Lt. Col. Harman J., 113, 120, 131

Laiboldt, Lt. Col. Bernard, 181, 210

Lambert, D. Warren, 307, *The Decisive Battle of Richmond*, 103

Lancaster, Kentucky, 109 111, 114, 116, 125

Lane, Col. John Q., 208

Lanphere, Lt. Edwin O., 131

Larrabee, Col. Charles H., 210

Laughlin, Maj. James, 208

Lebanon, Kentucky, 53, 56, 112, 249, 258

Lee, Lt. Col. Philip L., 276, 296, 301

Lee, Gen. Robert E., 103, 235

Lewis, Abner D., 170

Lewis, Col. Joseph H., 276, 279, 283, 287, 289, 292, 294, 296, 300-301, *photo*, 293

Lexington Rifles Volunteer Infantry, 243

Lexington, Kentucky, 94-95, 109, 112-114, 116, 129, 250, 254, *photo*, 129

Liddell, Gen. St. John, 34, 180-181, 202, 212

Lincoln, Abraham, i, 3, 5, 85, *Black Hawk War*, 279, *call for volunteers*, 4-5, 276 *Columbus move*, 12, *confers with Buckner*, 8, *critical importance of Kentucky*, 47, *death of Helm*, 292, *disenchantment with Buell*, 179, *election*, 274-275, *Emancipation Proclamation*, 259, *importance of Kentucky*, 79, *Kentucky neutrality*, 6, *Kentucky plans*, 19, *letter from Fremont*, 20, *Magoffin's protest*, 9, *maintaining loyalty*, 19, *McClellan to command*, 1, *message to Congress*, 8, *Morgan's First Raid*, 247, *opposes Confiscation Act*, 16, *quote about God and Kentucky*, 23, *re-election*, 259, *thanks Thomas for Mill Springs*, 72, *urges action in East Tennessee*, 137, *wants a campaign in East Tennessee*, 53, *photo*, 2, *"Lincoln, Grant and Kentucky in 1861,"* by John Y. Simon, 1

Lincoln, Mary Todd, i, 279, 285, 291

Lindsay, Sgt. Robert, 290

Link, Col. William H., 109, 111-113, 131

Lister, Lt. Col. Frederick W., 208

Lock, Maj. Frederick J., 204

London Times, 250

London, Kentucky, 53, 114

Loomis, Capt. Cyrus O., 205

Louisiana Troops: *1st Cavalry*, 132, 169, *1st Infantry*, 108, 149, *13th Infantry*, 212, *14th Battlion Sharpshooters*, 212, *16th Infantry*, 212, *20th Infantry*, 212, *25th Infantry*, 212

Louisville & Nashville Railroad, iv, 6, 53, 138-140, 142-143, 145-149, 151-152, 160-161, 164, 166-168, 247, 251-253, 255, 257-258, 263

Louisville Journal, 252, 263

Louisville, Kentucky, iv, 31, 130, 139, 161, 167, 176, 247, 257, 263

Love, Lt. Col. S. P., 207

Lucas, Col. Thomas J., 112-113, 131
Lumsden, Capt. Charles L., 189, 192, 212
Lyon, Nathaniel, 1
Lythgoe, Col. A.J., 161, 169
Lytle, Col. William H., 192, 194, 197-198, 205, 227
Machen, Willis B., 87
Mackall, Lt. Col. W.W., 30
Magevney, Jr., Lt. Col. Michael, 133
Magoffin, Governor Beriah, 4-6, 8-9, 12, 80, 83, 86, 276
Mahan, Lt. Col. John R., 112, 131
Malone, Thomas, 187
Manchester, Kentucky, 114
Maney, Gen. George E., 187, 189, 196, 211, *Maney's Brigade,* 187, 197
Manigault, Col. Arthur M., 161
Manson, Col. Mahlon D., 59, 61, 63, 74, 113-117, 119-122, 124-125, 128-129, 130-131
Maple, Lt. Thomas S., 204
Marion (Florida) Light Artillery, 108, 133
Marks, Col. A. S., 213
Marshall, Gen. Humphrey, 85, 91, 94-95, 97
Martin, Lt. Col. John A., 209
Martin, Capt. John M., 108, 133, 135
Martin, Col. Robert, 268
Mason, James M., 3
Mason, Lt. Tyler A., 168
Matthews, Col. Stanley, 207
Mauff, Capt. August, 205
Maxwell, Col. Cicero, 207
McClain, Lt. Col. Richard W., 207
McClellan, Gen. George B., 1, 8
McClellan, Lt. Col. George R., 75
McClelland, Lt. Col. James S., 209
McClung, Capt. Hugh L.W., 54, 75, *McClung's Battery,* 58, 68
McCook, Gen. Alexander M., 90, 140, 181, 183, 185, 188, 192, 194, 198, 200, 202, 204, 283
McCook, Col. Daniel, 180, 210
McCook, Col. Robert L., 74
McCray, Col. Thomas H., 106, 119-122, 124, 126, 128, 132
McDaniel, Col. Charles A., 211
McDonough, James L., 177, 194
McDowell, Belle, 264
McKee, Robert, 85
McMillen, Col. William L., 121-122, 132
McMurray, Col. Libscomb P., 133
McNair, Col. Evander, 106, 126, 128, 132-133
Memphis & Charleston Railroad, iv, 30, 41, 105, 138, 142
Memphis & Ohio Railroad, 138
Mendenhall, Capt. John, 206, 289
Metcalfe, Col. Leonidas K., 109, 111-112, 115, 117, 131
Michigan Troops: *1st Artillery,* 205, *1st Artillery*, Battery F, 112, 131, *1st Artillery, Battery G,* 131, *1st Engineers & Mechanics,* 74, 205, 208, *2nd Cavalry, 210, 4th Artillery,* 209, *8th Infantry,* 251, *13th Infantry,* 207, *21st Infantry,* 210, *photo,* 199
Military department #2, 82
Mill Springs National Cemetery, 63
Mill Springs, battle of, ii, vi, 19, 34, 49, 52-54, 57-59, 61, 68, 89, 280, *Mill Springs: The First Battle for Kentucky,* 47
Miller, Capt. Silas, 210
Miller, Lt. Col. T.C.H., 75
Miller, Col. William, 212
Milliken, Col. Minor, 209
Minnesota Troops: *2nd Artillery,* 209, *2nd Infantry*, 56, 64-66, 68, 74, 208
Mississippi River, ii, 1, 6, 280
Mississippi Troops: *7th Infantry,* 149, 154, 159, 169, *9th Infantry,* 149, 153-154, 159, 169, *photo,* 150, *10th Infantry,* 149, 153-155, 157, 159, 169, *15th Battalion Sharpshooters,* 169, 213, *15th Infantry,* 58-60, 63, 66, 75, *24th Infantry,* 212, *27th Infantry,* 212, *29th Infantry,* 149, 153-154, 159-160, 169, *30th Infantry,* 212, *37th Infantry,* 212, *41st Infantry,* 212, *44th Infantry,* 149, 151, 154-155, 159, 169, *45th Infantry,* 213, *Ketchum's Battery,* 149, 169, *Richards Sharpshooters,* 153-154
Missionary Ridge, battle of, 221, 236, 294
Missouri Troops: *1st Artillery, Battery G,* 194, 210, 212, *2nd Infantry,* 210, *15th Infantry,* 210
Mitchell, Gen. Robert B., 200, 209
Mobile & Great Northern Railroad, 142
Mobile & Ohio Railroad, iv, 41, 43, 142
Mobile Advertising and Register, 271
Monroe, Capt. Benjamin J., 90, 104, 282, 284
Monroe, Col. James, 205
Monroe, Jr., Maj. Thomas B., 276, 284, 304
Montgomery & West Point Railroad, 142

Index

Monticello, Kentucky, 111
Moore, Lt. Col. James, 154-155, 169
Moore, Lt. Col. Oscar F., 204
Moore, Col. Robert S., 210
Moore, T. H., 58
Moore, Col. W. L., 211
Morgan, Gen. George W., 106, 112, 131
Morgan, Henrietta, 269
Morgan, Maj. J. B., 160
Morgan, Gen. John Hunt, i, ii, v, 89, 93, 97-98, 100, 105-106, 108, 111, 132, 147, 169, 243, 245, 247, 249-259, 261-265, 267, 271, 282, 300-301, *photo,* 244, 246
Morgan, Col. Richard C., 267
Morgan, Lt. Col. William E., 133
Morrison, Col. James J., 132, 169
Morrison, Maj. Thomas G., 131
Morton, Oliver P., 151
Moss, Capt. James W., 300-301
Moxson, Maj. G.W., 301
Mt. Vernon, Kentucky, 113-114
Mullen, Col. Bernard F., 207
Munday, Lt. Col. Reuben J., 113, 115, 131
Munfordville, Kentucky, vi, 94, 251, 255, 259
Munfordville, Kentucky, battle of, iv, 138-140, 142-143, 146-147, 149, 151-152, 155, 157, 160-161, 163, 167, *Munfordville: The Campaign and Battle Along Kentucky's Strategic Axis,* 137
Murfreesboro, Tennessee, battle of, 204, 250, 287, 290-291
Murray, Col. Charles D., 146, 164, 168
Murray, Col. J.P., 75
Muscle Shoals, 137
Mygatt, Lt. Col. George S., 206
Nashville & Chattanooga Railroad, 138
Nashville, Tennessee, iv, 37, 39-41, 48, 138, 140, 168, 203, 252, 255, 258, 272, 280, 283, *photo,* 39
Nelson, Capt., 132
Nelson, Gen. William, ii, 6, 8, 109, 112-114, 116, 122, 124-126, 128-129, 131, 143, 176, *photo,* 110
New Albany Daily Ledger, 203
New Orleans Picayune, 89
New York Times, 263
New Madrid, Missouri, 10, 13
Nicholas, Ron, 307, *Mill Springs: The First Battle for Kentucky*, 47
Nichols, Pvt. Joseph, 290
Nix, Lt. Col. F. M., 265
Nixon, Lt. Col. James O., 132-133, 169
Nobel Ellis (steamer), 54, 69
Noe, Kenneth W., 307, *Grand Havoc: The Climactic Battle of Perryville*, 177
Nuckols, Capt. Joseph P., 276, 284, 290, 293
Oakes, Lt. Col. James, 204
Oglesby, Richard J., 13
Ohio River, 137, 249
Ohio State Penitentiary, 264
Ohio Troops: *1st Artillery,* 57, 64, 69, *1st Artillery*, Battery B, 74, 206, *1st Artillery, Battery C,* 209, *1st Artillery, Battery D,* 161, 164, 169, *1st Artillery, Battery F,* 206, *1st Cavalry,* 208-209, *2nd Infantry,* 204, *3rd Infantry,* 192, 205, *6th Artillery,* 208, *6th Infantry,* 206, *9th Artillery,* 74, *9th Infantry,* 64-65, 74, 208, *10th Infantry,* 192, 205, *13th Infantry,* 207, *14th Infantry,* 74, 208, *17th Infantry,* 53, 75, 208, *19th Infantry,* 207, *24th Infantry,* 206, *26th Infantry,* 207, *31st Infantry,* 75, 208, *35th Infantry,* 208, *38th Infantry,* 53, 74-75, 208, *41st* Infantry, 206, *50th Infantry,* 205, *51st Infantry,* 207, *52nd Infantry,* 210, *59th Infantry,* 207, *64th Infantry,* 207, *65th Infantry,* 208, *94th Infantry,* 204, *95th Infantry,* 109, 113, 121-122, 124, 132, *97th Infantry,* 208, *98th Infantry,* 206, *99th Infantry,* 207, *101st Infantry,* 209, *105th Infantry,* 189, 205, *121st Infantry,* 206
Orphan Brigade, i, ii, 245, 271-274, 277-279, 281, 283-284, 286, 289-290, 292-294, 296-297, 303
Osborn, Lt. Col. John, 206
Owen, Col. Richard, 161, 164
Owen, Maj. W.G., 267
Paddock, Lt. Byron D., 112
Paducah, Kentucky, 13-14, 16, 21, 25
Palmer's Battery, 212
Palmer, Capt. Baylor, 265
Parker, Samuel, 65
Parson's Battery, 205, 216
Parson, Lt. Charles C., 187, 189, 196, 205
Partisan Ranger Act, 264
Peace Convention in Frankfort, 86
Pell, Lt. Col. James A., 213
Pemberton, Gen. John C., 290
Pendleton, Capt. Virgil M., 262
Pennebaker, Col. Charles D., 206, 251

Pennsylvania Troops: *7th Cavalry,* 204, *9th Cavalry,* 131, 210, *79th Infantry,* 205, *93rd Infantry,* 281
Perryville Battlefield State Historic Site, 216
Perryville, Kentucky, vi, 18, 167, 176, 180-181, 183
Perryville, Kentucky, battle of, iv, v, 71, 96, 177, 223, 225, 229-230, 234-236, 239, 285
Pettus, John J., 32
Peyton Jr., Lt. Bailie, 68, 70
Pillow, Gen. Gideon J., 9-10, 12, 14, 17, 21, 39-40
Pillsbury, Josiah, 85
Pinney, Capt. Oscar F., 209
Plum, William R., 250
Polk, Gen. Leonidas, ii, 10, 12-13, 20, 25, 28, 34, 36, 41, 47, 163, 179, 181, 183, 185, 202, 211, 289, *photo,* 29
Polk, Col. Lucius E., 120, 133
Poorman, Col. Christian, 206
Pope, Col. Curran, 205
Porter, Col. George C., 211
Powell, Col. Samuel, 75, 194, 212, *Powell's Brigade*, 194, 200
Prentice, George, 252
Prentiss, Gen. Banjamin M., 13, 282-283
Preston, Gen. William, i, 83, 85, 274, 279, 284-285, 287, 303, *photo,* 286
Price, Col. S. Woodson, 207
Provisional Government of Kentucky, 84
Pryor, Col. Tandy, 267
Quirk, Tom, 245, 262
Raccoon Springs, 114
Ramage, James A., 308, *General John Hunt Morgan and His Great Raids Into Kentucky*, 243
Ready, Martha, 263-264
Reed, Col. Hugh B., 207
Reichard, Col. August, 212
Reid, Col. William P., 206
Reynolds, Col. Daniel H., 133
Reynolds, Gen. Joseph J., 258
Reynolds, Thomas C., 30
Rice, Maj. Horace, 75
Richmond Dispatch, 95
Richmond, Kentucky, 11, 106, 113-115, 117-118, 124-126, 169
Richmond, Kentucky, battle of, iv, 110, 176, 197, 221, 223, 225, 233-235, 239
Ringgold Gap, battle of, 221, 237
Rogersville, Kentucky, 116-117, 119, 122
Roland, Charles P., 307, *The Confederate Defense of Kentucky*, 23
Rolling Fork Creek, 257, 259
Rolling Fork, engagement at, 263
Rosecrans, Gen. William S., 203, 245, 258, 287, 290-291
Ross, Col. Isaac N., 206
Ross, Maj. Jesse A., 133
Rousseau, Gen. Lovell H., ii, 196, 198, 200, 204, *photo,* 184, *Rousseau's Division,* 183, 189
Rowlett's Station, engagement at, 140, 153, 160-161
Russellville Convention, 84, 86, 93
Russellville, Kentucky, 83, 88
Rutledge's Artillery, 58, 63,
Rutledge, Capt. A. M., 60, 75
Salt River Bridge, 147
San Jacinto, USS, 3
Sanders, Capt. T.C., 75
Savage, Col. John H., 185, 211
Schoepf, Gen. Albin, 51, 53-54, 56-58, 68, 71, 75, 198, 208, *Schoepf's Division,* 202
Scott, Col. John, 108, 111-112, 115-117, 126, 128, 132, 151-152, 157, 159, 169
Scott, Lt Col. William T., 207
Scribner, Col. Benjamin F., 204
Sedgwick, Col. Thomas D., 206
Semple, Capt. Henry C., 197, 213
Shaler, Nathaniel S., 296
Shepherdsville, Kentucky, 138, 147
Sherer, Capt. Samuel B., 209
Sheridan, Gen. Philip H., 180-181, 194, 199-200, 210
Sherman, Col. Francis T., 210
Sherman, Gen. William T., 31, 48, 221, 294, 296
Shiloh, Tennessee, battle of, 18, 41, 71-72, 90, 128, 142, 146, 149, 171, 227, 230, 237, 247, 252, 262, 279, 281, 283-285, 293, 299
Short, Pvt. John H., *photo,* 272
Shryock, Col. Kline G., 208
Sill, Gen. Joshua, 96
Simms, W. E., 85
Simon, John, 307, *Lincoln, Grant, and Kentucky in 1861*, 1
Simonson, Capt. Peter, 189, 204
Slidell, John, 3
Slocomb, Capt. Cuthbert H., 192, 212

Index

Smith, Maj. Albert J., 30
Smith, Lt. Frank G., 209
Smith, Col. D. Howard, 266, 268
Smith, Gen. E. Kirby, iv, 93-96, 103, 106, 108-112, 114-115, 119, 126, 128, 130, 132, 134, 143, 151, 167, 176, 179-180, 202, 223-224, 285 *photo,* 103
Smith, Lt. Col. Harry S., 255-257
Smith, Lt. Col. Joseph A., 133, 213
Smith, Col. Preston, 106, 133, 118-122, 143
Smith, Col. Robert A., vi, 154-155, 157, 159, 169
Smith, Gen. William S., 206
Somerset, Kentucky, 53, 111
South Carolina Troops: *19th Infantry,* 161, 169
Southwick, Capt. Daniel K., 209
Sparta, Tennessee, 94
Speed, James, 6, 16
Speed, Joshua, 6
Standart, Capt. William E., 206
Stanford, Capt. T.J., 211
Stansel, Lt. Col. M. L., 300-301
Stanton, Edwin M., 171, 247
Stanton, Col. S. S., 59, 75
Starkweather, Col. John C., 194, 196-197, 205
Starnes, Col. James W., 132, 169
Steedman, Gen. James B., 74, 202, 208
Stem, Col. Leander, 209
Stevens, Col. Ambrose A., 210
Stevens, Lt. Alanson J., 207
Stevenson, Gen. Carter L., 106, 132
Stewart, Gen. Alexander P., 187, 189, 196-197, 211
Stone's River, battle of, 230, 234, 236, 245, 258, 287, 289, 300
Stone, Capt. David, 196, 205
Stoner, Lt. Col. Robert G., 257, 266
Strahl, Col. O.F., 211
Streight, Col. Abel D., 207
Strickland, Lt. Col. Silas A., 205
Strickland, Capt. Watt E., 154
Strout, Lt. Tenbroeck, 68
Sturgis, Gen. Samuel D., 251
Swallow, Capt. George R., 207
Sweet, Col. Benjamin J., 205
Swett's (Mississippi) Battery, 213
Sword, Wiley, 308, *General Patrick R. Cleburne: Earning His Spurs as a Field Commander in Kentucky, 1862*, 221
Talbird, Col. H., 300
Tansil, Col. E. E., 211
Tate, Samuel, 30
Taylor, Col. Jonah R., 205
Tennessee River, ii, iv, 1, 13, 28, 36-37, 41, 89, 90, 137, 280, 282
Tennessee Troops, (Confederate): *1st Infantry,* 187, 196, 211, *2nd Cavalry,* 53, *2nd Infantry,* 213, *3rd Infantry,* 132, 169, *4th Cavalry,* 75, 211, *5th Infantry,* 211, *6th Infantry,* 211, *8th Infantry,* 196, 211, *9th Cavalry,* 97, *9th Infantry,* 211, *12th and 47th Consolidated Infantry,* 133, *13th Infantry,* 121, 133, *15th Infantry,* 211, *16th Infantry,* 185, 187, 211, 216, *17th Infantry,* 58, 68, 75, 213, *photo of flag,* 232, *19th Infantry,* 58-60, 62-63, 75, *20th Infantry,* 58-60, 63-64, 66, 68, 75, *23rd Infantry,* 213, *24th Infantry,* 211, *25th Infantry,* 58-59, 63, 75, 192, 211, 213, *28th Infantry,* 58, 75, *29th Infantry,* 58, 63, 75, 212, *31st Infantry,* 211, *33rd Infantry,* 211, *35th Infantry,* 133, *37th Infantry,* 192, 213, *44th Infantry,* 192, 213, *48th Infantry,* 133, *51st Infantry,* 196, 211, *154th Infantry,* 119-120, 133, *Crew's Artillery Battalion,* 271, 299, *Independent Cavalry,* 75, *Partisan Rangers,* 265, *Rutledge's Tennessee Light Artillery,* 58, 60, 7
Tennessee Troops, (Union): *1st Infantry,* 64, 66, 74, *2nd Infantry,* 64, 66, 74, *3rd Infantry,* 111, 131, 205
Terrill, Gen. William R., 185, 187-189, 196, 205, *Terrill's Brigade,* 185, 194, 196
Texas Troops: *1st Artillery,* 133, *8th Cavalry,* 142, 211, *10th Cavalry, (Dismounted),* 132, *11th Cavalry, (Dismounted),* 132, *14th Cavalry, (Dismounted),* 132, *15th Cavalry, (Dismounted),* 132
Thomas, Gen. George H., 34, 53-54, 61, 63, 74, 204, *decides to attack at Mill Springs,* 56, *did not pursue after Mill Springs,* 68, *Mill Springs,* 51, 57-58, 63, 65-66, 71, *Murfreesboro,* 292, *post Mill Springs,* 69, *refusal to take command from Buell,* 179, *thanks from Lincoln,* 72, *Zollicoffer's remains,* 70, *photo,* 50
Thompson, E. Porter, 280, 289
Thompson, Maj. John C., 155, 169
Thompson, Lt. Col. Thomas W., 276, 284,

300-301
Tilghman, Gen. Lloyd, 14, 36, 272, 276
Timberlake, Lt. Col. John, 209
Todd, Lt. Alexander, 285
Topping, Lt. Col. Melville D., 112, 131
Townsend, Maj. Frederick, 209
Trabue, Col. Robert P., 90, 276, 279-282, 287, 299-300, *photo,* 281
Trent, HMS, 3
Trimble, Lt. Col. Edwin, 267
True American, 85
Tucker, Lt. Col. J., 267
Tupelo, Mississippi, iv, 43, 105, 142
Turnbull, Col. Charles, 133
Turner's (Mississippi) Battery, 196
Turner, Lt. William B., 196, 211
Tyler, Col. R.C., 211
United States Troops: *4th Artillery, Battery H*, 206, *4th Artillery, Battery I,* 209, *4th Artillery, Battery M,* 206 *18th Infantry,* 146, 168, 209
Van Cleve, Gen. Horatio P., 64, 74, 206
Van Derver, Col. Ferdinand, 208
Van Dorn, Gen. Earl, 27
Vaughan, Col. Alfred J., 121-122, 133, *Vaughan's Brigade,* 124, 126, 128
Venable, Col. C. D., 211
Virginia & Tennessee Railroad, 138
von Zinken, Col. Leon, 212
Waagner, Col. Gustav, 10, 12
Wagner, Col. George D., 208
Walker, Lt. Col. Francis M., 75
Walker, Capt. J.M., 155, 169
Walker, Leroy P., 12
Walker, Col. Moses B., 208
Wallace, Gen. Lew, 109, 111-112
Walthall, Col. E. C., 59-60, 75, 153, 169
Ward, Col. W. W., 266
Ward, Gen. William T., 252
Warner, Col. William A., 113, 132
Washington Artillery, 192, 212
Washington, Georgia, 274, 296
Waters, Col. Louis H., 206
Watkins, Sam, 177, 187, 196-197
Watson, Lt. Henry, 146, 169
Weaver, Col. James A., 132
Webber, Maj. T. B., 266
Weber, Maj. John, 210
Webster, Col. George P., 188, 197, 205, *Webster's Brigade,* 187, 200
Wells, Maj. Samuel T., 169, 251
West, A.R., Capt., 52
West, Capt. O.F., 169
Western & Atlantic Railroad, 142
Wetmore, Capt. Henry S., 74
Whaley, Maj. C. A., 213
Wharton, Col. John A., 183, 185, 211
Wheeler, Col. James, 183, 202, 213, 249
Whig party, 4, 91
Whitaker, Col. Walter C., 206
White, Capt. Frank, 147
White, Col. Moses, 213
White, R. J., 122
White, Col. Thomas W., 153, 169
Wickliffe, Capt. John D., 283
Wickliffe, Col. John C., 283, 297, 301
Wickliffe, Robert, 274
Wildcat Mountain, battle of, 51
Wilder, Col. John T., 145-148, 151-154, 157, 159-160, 163-166, 168, 171, *photo,* 145
Wilkes, Capt. Charles, Capt., 3
Williams, Col. Edward C., 131
Willich, Col. August, 140
Wilson's Creek, battle of, 1
Wilson, Capt. Cyrus J., 168
Winters, Maj. Joshua C., 209
Wisconsin Troops: *1st Infantry,* 205, *3th Artillery*, 207, *5th Artillery,* 209, *8th Artillery,* 209, *10th Infantry,* 204, *15th Infantry,* 209, *21st Infantry,* 196, *24th Infantry,* 210
Withers, Gen. Jones, 148, 161, 180
Wolford, Col. Frank, 74
Wood, Lt. Col. Gustavus A., 208
Wood, Gen. S. A. M., 185, 200, 202, 213
Wood, Gen. Thomas J., ii, 163, 207
Wood, Col. William B., 71, 75
Worden, Lt. Col. Frederick W., 207
Worsham, W. J., 58
Wright, Gen. Horatio G., 109, 114, 130, *photo,* 109
Wyncoop, Maj. John E., 204
Yates, Richard, 247
Young, Lt. Lot D., 290
Young, Lt. Col. William H., 208
Zollicoffer, Gen. Felix, 28, 34, 48-49, 51-55, 58-59, 61-64, 70, 72, 75, *photo*, 49

www.ingramcontent.com/pod-product-compliance
Ingram Content Group UK Ltd.
Pitfield, Milton Keynes, MK11 3LW, UK
UKHW041038180625
459791UK00003B/8